The FALL
and RISE of
FRENCH
SEA POWER

Titles in the Series

Studies in Naval History and Sea Power

Christopher M. Bell and James C. Bradford, editors

Studies in Naval History and Sea Power advances our understanding of sea power and its role in global security by publishing significant new scholarship on navies and naval affairs. The series presents specialists in naval history, as well as students of sea power, with works that cover the role of the world's naval powers, from the ancient world to the navies and coast guards of today. The works in Studies in Naval History and Sea Power examine all aspects of navies and conflict at sea, including naval operations, strategy, and tactics, as well as the intersections of sea power and diplomacy, navies and technology, sea services and civilian societies, and the financing and administration of seagoing military forces.

The FALL
and RISE of
FRENCH
SEA POWER

France's Quest for an
Independent Naval
Policy, 1940–1963

HUGUES CANUEL

Naval Institute Press
Annapolis, Maryland

Naval Institute Press
291 Wood Road
Annapolis, MD 21402

Library of Congress Cataloging-in-Publication Data

Names: Canuel, Hugues, date, author.
Title: The fall and rise of French sea power : France's quest for an independent naval policy, 1940–1963 / Hugues Canuel.
Other titles: France's quest for an independent naval policy, 1940–1963
Description: Annapolis, Maryland : Naval Institute Press, 2021. | Series: Studies in naval history and sea power | Includes bibliographical references and index.
Identifiers: LCCN 2020044351 (print) | LCCN 2020044352 (ebook) | ISBN 9781682476161 (hardcover) | ISBN 9781682476307 (pdf) | ISBN 9781682476307 (epub)
Subjects: LCSH: France. Marine—History—20th century. | Sea-power—France—History—20th century. | France—History, Naval.
Classification: LCC VA503 .C33 2021 (print) | LCC VA503 (ebook) | DDC 359/.03094409045—dc23
LC record available at https://lccn.loc.gov/2020044351
LC ebook record available at https://lccn.loc.gov/2020044352

♾ Print editions meet the requirements of ANSI/NISO z39.48-1992 (Permanence of Paper).
Printed in the United States of America.

29 28 27 26 25 24 23 22 21   9 8 7 6 5 4 3 2 1
First printing

Map by Chris Robinson.

CONTENTS

TABLES

ACKNOWLEDGMENTS

The number of people who assisted me through the research and drafting of my previous PhD thesis and turning it into this book form are too numerous to mention all by names. Please accept my apologies in advance for any omission.

I am pleased to acknowledge the incomparable support provided by the staff of several institutions who tolerated with admirable patience the burden of guiding me through this endeavor, my first attempt at professional archival research. First and foremost, those in France: the Archives de l'Assemblée nationale in Paris, the Archives nationales in Pierrefitte-sur-Seine, the Service historique de la défense in Vincennes and its affiliated section in Cherbourg, the Échelon de Cherbourg. I also traveled to repositories outside of France in order to obtain contemporary views and perspectives from supporters and detractors of the French effort at pursuing an independent naval policy within a strategy of alliance: the NATO Archives Service in Brussels, Belgium; the National Archives in Kew, Great Britain; the U.S. National Archives and Records Administration in College Park, Maryland; and the Dwight D. Eisenhower Presidential Library in Abilene, Kansas.

I must also express my sincere appreciation to the librarians of the Department of National Defence, who provided me with essential assistance when I was working from homeport as I struggled through the Royal Military College doctoral program in war studies while a serving officer in the Royal Canadian Navy. I often needed to access the holdings of academic institutions in Canada and from around the world. The staff of the Information Resource Centre at the Canadian Forces College in Toronto, Ontario, as well as that of the National Defence Headquarters Library in Ottawa, Ontario, provided invaluable support in allowing me to pursue my research and check the archives remotely.

I would like to offer my gratitude to my supervising professor, Dr. Chris Madsen, from the Department of Defence Studies at the Canadian Forces College. His valued perspective, outstanding advice, and timely encouragement throughout this lengthy and occasionally frustrating endeavor played a key role in ensuring its completion. I have been extremely lucky to have a supervisor who cared so much about my work and responded to my numerous queries promptly, providing much-needed wisdom and order to my scattered thoughts. All glaring mistakes, silly misinterpretations, foolish assumptions, and erroneous conclusions that remain in the text are mine alone.

Last, it gives me great pleasure to acknowledge the role played by Christopher Bell, professor in the Department of History at Dalhousie University in Halifax, Canada, who facilitated my introduction to the Naval Institute Press—and to all individuals from that prestigious publishing house involved in the publication of my book. Their wise and patient counsel during this long process proved essential in guiding this first-time author to success through the course of the past year.

ABBREVIATIONS

AA	antiair
AFHQ	Allied Force Headquarters
AMP	additional military production
ASW	antisubmarine warfare
CCS	Combined Chiefs of Staff
CDN	Comité de Défense nationale (National Defense Committee)
CEA	Commissariat à l'énergie atomique (Atomic Energy Commission)
CFLN	Comité français de Libération nationale (French Committee of National Liberation)
CSM	Conseil supérieur de la Marine (Superior Council of the Navy)
DE	Destroyer Escort
FF	French franc
FFI	Forces françaises de l'intérieur (Free French Forces of the Interior)
FFL	Forces françaises libres (Free French Forces)
FMA	Forces maritimes d'Afrique (Africa Maritime Forces)
FNFL	Forces navales françaises libres (Free French Naval Forces)
FNGB	Forces navales de Grande-Bretagne (Naval Forces in Great Britain)
FOST	Force océanique stratégique (Oceanic Strategic Force)

JRC	Joint Rearmament Committee
LCM	landing craft, mechanized
LCVP	landing craft, vehicle and personnel
LSD	landing ship, dock
LSIL	landing ship, infantry large
LSSL	landing ship, support large
LSV	landing ship, vehicle
MAAG	Military Assistance Advisory Group
MAC(A)	Munitions Assignments Committee (Air)
MAC(G)	Munitions Assignments Committee (Ground)
MAC(N)	Munitions Assignments Committee (Navy)
MDAP	Mutual Defense Assistance Program
MTB	motor torpedo boats
NATO	North Atlantic Treaty Organization
OSP	offshore procurement
PC	patrol craft
RAF	Royal Air Force
RN	Royal Navy
SACEUR	Supreme Allied Commander Europe
SACLANT	Supreme Allied Commander Atlantic
SHAEF	Supreme Headquarters Allied Expeditionary Force
SLBM	submarine-launched ballistic missile
SSBN	subsurface ballistic nuclear (submarine)
USN	U.S. Navy

INTRODUCTION

Five hundred reporters sat in tight rows in a crowded room at the Élysée Palace on Monday, 14 January 1963. French president Charles de Gaulle had called for a press conference that day in his official residence in Paris. The tall patrician walked from behind dark drapes in the front of the room to a table on a raised stage and sat alone, facing two microphones and the throng of journalists from France and around the world. The event came after a tumultuous year. At home, le Général—as supporters and detractors alike still referred to the former acting army brigadier—had launched an aggressive program of economic reforms the previous spring. On 28 October he had won a referendum proposing an amendment to the constitution of the Fifth Republic to have the president elected by direct popular vote rather than by an electoral college subject to the influence of the political parties he claimed to despise. Voters endorsed his proposal by a wide margin, in part as a result of the sympathy that still endured following a shocking assassination attempt on 22 August. At the Petit-Clamart, on the outskirts of Paris, a dozen men wielding machine guns had ambushed the presidential Citroën carrying the president, his wife, and their son-in-law, but the driver had succeeded driving through the poorly coordinated gunfire, all passengers unscathed. The perpetrators were disgruntled over the General's agreement to grant Algeria its full independence in the summer of 1962, after eight years of bloody rebellion.

The end of the Algerian War of Independence meant that France was at peace for the first time in a quarter century, from the outbreak of World War II in 1939 to the conclusion of successive insurgencies that had ripped the colonial empire apart after 1945. Guns had fallen silent across the Communauté française—the Fifth Republic's shrinking association of overseas territories—but tensions and conflicts continued on the international scene, rising to a climax during the Cuban missile crisis. Although uninvolved in the diplomatic and military maneuvering during those October days that brought the United States and the Soviet Union to the nuclear brink, de Gaulle stood resolutely at the side of his ally. He publicly supported U.S. president John F. Kennedy when the latter claimed the right to oppose a Communist military buildup in the Western Hemisphere, and de Gaulle reiterated in private that France would fight if the Warsaw Pact moved against West Berlin in retaliation for the naval blockade of Cuba.[1]

But such commitment to the United States in time of crisis did not reflect the General's larger approach to the strategy of alliance adopted by his Fourth Republic's predecessors. He had grown weary of the North Atlantic Treaty Organization (NATO). He recognized the importance of the 1949 pact in committing the United States, Great Britain, and Canada to the defense of continental Western Europe, but he deemed the integrated organization overly subservient to les Anglo-Saxons, who repeatedly refused to recognize France's rightful place of influence—or at least his definition of it. On 4 July 1962 the Kennedy administration sought to reinvigorate Atlanticism through a grandiose "Declaration of Interdependence, that we will be prepared to discuss with a united Europe."[2] On 14 January 1963 de Gaulle abruptly declined the offer, seeking to resurrect France's grandeur by leading a strong continental Europe instead.

As was his wont, de Gaulle did not begin the press conference with prepared remarks but simply opened the floor to questions.[3] For more than one hour, while answering seemingly random queries, he actually laid out an ambitious program of wide-ranging political, diplomatic, and military initiatives to reaffirm his country's standing in the world. British prime minister Harold Macmillan had sought to join the six nations that formed the European Economic Community through the Treaty of Rome on 25 March 1957. France did not say no at first, but negotiations over the British application had dragged on for the past two years. That day, in a calm but determined tone, de Gaulle announced that France would veto Great Britain's request, denouncing its membership as a Trojan horse for U.S. influence threatening to infiltrate and eventually dominate the affairs of Europe. In the same breath he praised the ongoing Franco-German reconciliation and pronounced in favor of ever closer cooperation between the two continental powers. This statement set the stage for the signing of the Élysée Treaty with West Germany the following week, on 22 January.[4]

De Gaulle also announced his refusal to join the NATO Multilateral Force, proposed by Kennedy to provide the European allies a greater role in the formulation and execution of the alliance's nuclear strategy. Under that concept, multinational crews would sail in ships and submarines armed with American missiles, but U.S. personnel would control the arming of the warheads. Just the previous month, at the Nassau Conference of 19–22 December 1962, Prime Minister Macmillan had abandoned the ambition of maintaining a purely national deterrent, agreeing instead to acquire Polaris missiles from the United States to equip Royal Navy submarines, which would patrol as elements of the Multilateral Force, although not with multinational crews.[5] Kennedy immediately extended a similar offer to France, but de Gaulle used the press conference to inflict a dramatic snub on the American design. Not only did de Gaulle decline to participate in the Multilateral Force, he also reiterated his intent to continue assembling the constituent parts of an independent and credible nuclear deterrent, built and controlled by France alone.

Le Général declared that the future *force de frappe* (strike force) would develop into a triad similar in nature, though not in scale, to those of the United States and the Soviet Union. Mirage IV long-range aircraft were already in production, capable of unleashing atomic devastation on the enemy with gravity bombs delivered at supersonic speed. As well, studies were under way to develop a land-based, nuclear-tipped ballistic missile. But the press conference witnessed the first public commitment by the French president to the addition of a sea-based component to the national deterrent with the construction of nuclear-powered, ballistic missile–carrying submarines.

Although mentioned in a rather casual manner, this development constituted a momentous decision on the part of the French leader. His announcement launched a herculean effort to design and build a force that would eventually include six *Le Redoutable*–class vessels, each carrying sixteen missiles tipped with a boosted fission warhead of 450 kilotons. They would sail out of their own complex on the Île Longue, across the bay from the Brest naval base on the Atlantic coast, enough in numbers to keep up to three submarines deployed at sea simultaneously. Dispatched to different locations, they would patrol silently and provide a nearly invulnerable first- and second-strike capability.

The lead vessel, *Le Redoutable*, only undertook her first deterrence patrol in 1972, and the last submarine of the class, *L'Inflexible*, did not enter service until 1985. Nevertheless, the 1963 decision launched the closing chapter of an unprecedented renewal for the Marine nationale. Within two decades of nearly losing the entire fleet during World War II, France had rebuilt her navy, having acquired or being actively engaged in the construction of every one of the instruments required of a credible blue-water navy.[6] These included aircraft carriers (*Clémenceau* and *Foch*), a converted helicopter carrier (*Arromanches*), two antiaircraft cruisers (*Colbert* and *De Grasse*), and a helicopter-carrying training cruiser (*Jeanne d'Arc*) as well as numerous destroyers, amphibious vessels, and conventional submarines. By 1963, as in 1939 (see table I.1), the French navy was not without defects, but it had resumed its status as the first navy in continental Europe and its sailors, naval aviators, *fusiliers-marins* (naval infantry), and *commandos marine* (special forces) were confident of their ability to make a potent contribution to the defense of France and its allies within the context of the Cold War.

The turnaround was dramatic as World War II had left France a devastated country. Although sitting at the side of the victors in 1945 as the leader of the Gouvernement provisoire de la République française (Provisional government of the French Republic), Charles de Gaulle faced a bewildering array of conflicting tasks and competing priorities: rebuilding civilian infrastructure and ending political divisions at home, keeping Germany down in Europe, and regaining control of the colonial empire abroad. These challenges required immediate action in order to resume the country's position as a leading power

Table I.1: French Naval Strength, 1 September 1939

Category[a]	Number of Hulls per Category	Combined Tonnage	Remarks
Dreadnought battleships	5: *Courbet, Paris, Bretagne, Provence, Lorraine*	112,750	Entered service: *Courbet,* 1913; *Paris,* 1914; *Bretagne,* 1915; *Provence,* 1915; *Lorraine,* 1916
Fast battleships	2: *Richelieu, Jean Bart*	70,000	Not yet in service but completing fitting out in Brest (*Richelieu*) and Saint-Nazaire (*Jean Bart*)
Light battleships	2: *Dunkerque, Strasbourg*	60,000	Also referred to as battle cruisers or pocket battleships; entered service: *Dunkerque,* 1938; *Strasbourg,*1939
Aircraft carrier	1: *Béarn*	22,500	Entered service 1928
Seaplane carrier	1: *Commandant Teste*	10,160	Entered service 1932
Heavy cruisers	19	157,000	Mostly "treaty cruisers" built under the Washington Treaty regime
Light cruisers	8	21,500	Most classified as *contre-torpilleurs* (destroyers) but reclassified as light cruisers in later years
Destroyers	24	57,600	Modern, mostly built during interwar period
Torpedo boats	39	45,000	Wide range of capabilities, some going as far back as World War I
Submarines	80[b]	73,000	Wide range of capabilities, some going as far back as World War I
Corvettes/ patrol boats	53	42,900	Wide range of capabilities, some going as far back as World War I
Gunboats	7	1,800	All based in China and Indochina
Misc. auxiliaries[c]	47	70,920	
Totals	**288**	**745,130**	

Notes

[a] Civilian ships armed for the hostilities but that continued to be crewed by merchant seamen (from ocean liners to trawlers and large pleasure craft) are not included.

[b] Figures for submarines under Combined Tonnage indicate submerged displacement.

[c] Miscellaneous auxiliaries refer to minesweepers, repair ships, tenders, tankers, and so on. Tugs and other small craft dedicated to harbor duties are not included.

on the Continent and as a nation of influence overseas.[7] Such concerns were only compounded by the dawn of the Cold War as his Fourth Republic successors sought greater security through the Atlantic Alliance but could not avoid dependency on the Anglo-American powers in the face of the Communist threat in Europe as well as insurgencies in Asia and Africa.

In this context, the French army and air force faced challenging but clear-cut missions in the aftermath of the nominal peace: maintain occupation forces in Germany, prepare to wage conventional warfare to stop a Soviet thrust into Europe, and conduct counterinsurgency operations in rebellious colonies. At the time the issue for French soldiers and aviators did not seem to be how to fight but determining whether France could afford to provide the means to discharge these tasks simultaneously. Prospects for the French navy appeared much more uncertain. Of the three services, the Marine nationale had fared worst through the years of German occupation and fratricidal infighting between forces loyal to the collaborationist regime in Vichy and those wishing to resist at the side of the Allies under the leadership of Charles de Gaulle. Finding refuge in Great Britain in June 1940, he immediately set about building up the Free French movement—the Forces françaises libres—which included a small navy, the Forces navales françaises libres (Free French Naval Forces). The General and his naval commanders effectively mixed soothing diplomacy and aggressive brinkmanship in order to rally French crews dispersed around the world as well as secure a commitment from the British to refurbish existing vessels and transfer new units to the Free French Naval Forces. Following the Anglo-American landings in North Africa in November 1942, the Franklin Roosevelt administration committed to rearm those French forces that rallied to the Allied cause, including the former Vichy navy. The Marine nationale formally reunited in August 1943, and France could again boast the fourth-largest fleet in the world in the immediate aftermath of the war.[8] But those numbers also implied grave drawbacks, as became obvious in the following years.

By then the French navy included a bewildering array of ships, submarines, and aircraft of various origins, ranging from outdated French prewar designs to emergency U.S. and British wartime production and, after 1945, disparate

German and Italian transfers. The challenge of supplying the right munitions and spare parts, and of maintaining vessels using different engineering plants and technologies, was compounded by the devastation inflicted on naval bases and commercial shipyards in metropolitan France and the colonies. Planning deployments and fleet maneuvering also proved a challenge for senior officers trained during the interwar period in the spirit of the *bataille d'escadre*—fleet action—when the battle line was still divided in squadrons of ships of common speed and armament following tactics of a bygone era. Few admirals of the postwar navy had been exposed to the operations of task forces combining the eclectic strengths of aircraft carriers, battleships, cruisers, and destroyers into one whole capable of discharging a range of missions, as developed by the Americans in the Pacific and carried over to shape naval doctrine during the Cold War.

Worse, observers on both sides of the Atlantic would soon question the relevance of sea power altogether, especially for a continental state facing the renewed threat of land invasion—this time by Soviet troops massed across the Iron Curtain—a recurring theme in France's long history of attempts at building a navy of the first rank. One could easily apply to the French context of the early Cold War this dispirited quote uttered in 1871 by the minister for the navy, retired admiral Louis Pothuau, appointed soon after the catastrophic defeat at the hands of Prussia: "I am going to be obliged to reduce our unfortunate budget. All our efforts must be concentrated on land. Indeed, what good will a navy be to us now?"[9] The dawn of the atomic age only compounded doubts as air-power enthusiasts grew confident that nuclear weapons would finally allow the strategic bomber to deliver victory from the air. The offensive would be short and decisive, eliminating the need for a long campaign of attrition warfare by mass armies on land as well as the clash of fleets at sea to secure lines of communication and blockade the enemy coast.

Such discourses could have been expected to attract the attention of politicians in France, confronted as they were with the quandary of maintaining adequate land and air forces in Europe and overseas without undermining the process of reconstruction in the *métropole*.[10] And yet few French political and military leaders actively challenged the requirement to develop and maintain naval forces in the wake of World War II. The pace, scope, and priority of naval rearmament may have been controversial, but no figure of note dared asking "what good will a navy be to us now?"—be it under the wartime provisional government, during the controversial years of the Fourth Republic's chronic instability, or following de Gaulle's return to power and the inauguration of the Fifth Republic. Subject to one exception—the short-lived 1948 strategy of "Defense of the Rhine" seeking to focus investments on a powerful *corps aéroterrestre* (a joint army–air force corps) to defend the Rhine—one can actually distinguish a remarkable continuity in the naval policy pursued from one regime to the other.

This study of the rejuvenation of French sea power, from the 1940 armistice to the decision to go nuclear in 1963, will reflect this singularity of purpose through the dramatic period that shaped France, in times of war and peace. Some authors, especially those mesmerized by the Gaullist narrative, have argued that the Marine nationale of that period amounted to little more than another French attempt at creating a "prestige fleet" reminiscent of previous episodes of vainglorious ambitions. France's allies—more particularly, the United States and Great Britain—grew concerned that such plans were misplaced and prevented Paris from fully meeting its alliance commitments. A fundamental dissonance permeated relations between French and Anglo-American naval planners throughout the period in question. The former refused to confine themselves to the same subordinate duties of coastal defense and convoy escort that the latter sought to assign to the continental navies while retaining blue-water missions for themselves.

Washington and London claimed to pursue efficiency through special-ization among nations, with the U.S. Navy and the Royal Navy handling maritime strike missions and maintaining the security of transoceanic lines of communications while the continental powers should take care of their coasts and local sea lanes. But where the Anglo-Americans talked of specialization in support of the greater good, French admirals only saw collusion to deny France's rightful status as a naval power with worldwide interests. In their view, the defense of these interests necessitated the acquisition of the instru-ments befitting a blue-water navy, including carrier aviation in the immediate postwar years and, eventually, nuclear-powered submarines and ballistic missilery. Such ambitions would quickly be perceived in other capitals as detrimental to alliance effectiveness, if not outright destabilizing in the atomic age, particularly as development, production, and control of such strategic assets would occur outside of the Allied framework. Thus, once the Western powers set upon restoring the North Atlantic compact to confront the Soviet juggernaut at the dawn of the Cold War, France faced the renewed challenge of formulating an independent naval policy within a strategy of alliance. This study demonstrates that French politicians and admirals succeeded in that endeavor, even if they often had to accept, in the words of one postwar commander, "a forced compromise, the least bad possible."[11]

Rather than a reckless and misguided quest for vain grandeur at sea, the renaissance of French sea power was in fact framed within a naval policy and a military strategy closely adapted to the needs of a continental state with worldwide interests, from the desperate days of the armistice to the early Cold War era. During the hostilities, unlike their counterparts in the forlorn Vichy navy, French admirals in London and later in Algiers successfully leveraged the assistance of the Allies to rebuild while negotiating a tightrope that allowed their naval forces to make a marked contribution to the Allied cause and, simultaneously, preserve the national interest as envisioned by their political leaders. Following a short period of uncertainty in 1946–47, France resumed a policy of alliance in the face of the Soviet threat in Europe while confronting fervent nationalist forces overseas. Marine nationale planners built upon the lessons from the war to develop a unique approach to again leverage Allied support in acquiring the means to defend French home waters (smaller escorts, minesweepers, coastal patrol craft) while focusing national resources for building the instruments required to act overseas (aircraft carriers, fast escorts, and long-range submarines) without undermining national reconstruction. Such perspective contradicts the standard narrative of the irrelevance of French sea power during the war years, seemingly compounded after 1945 by floundering Fourth Republic officials whose ineptitude was only salvaged by the return to power of the decisive and inspiring de Gaulle in 1958.

This study aims to fill a distinct void by challenging such narrative in three distinct ways. First, it seeks to overcome the limitations imposed by the traditional chronicle built around overly simplistic periods. These markers often impede discerning important elements of continuity in France that shaped naval and military affairs as well as domestic politics and foreign relations. French historiography of the mid-twentieth century revolves around three outwardly monolithic blocks: the war years of 1939–45, the short-lived Fourth Republic of 1946–58, and the era of de Gaulle thereafter.[12] While one may seize upon these markers when initially grappling with the complexities of France's history through these troubled decades, one must also beware of the limitations that result from framing the scope of research along set milestones. This concern is of particular relevance when studying the fall and rise of French sea power from World War II to the Cold War. As the Vichy navy quickly faltered in the wake of the Armistice, the U.K.-based Free French Naval Forces had already embarked upon a path of renewal. The postwar naval rearmament was really initiated during the war years—namely, after the 1942 North African landings when American financial and material support kicked in. The mechanisms to distribute Allied assistance under NATO in the 1950s largely reflected processes and practices elaborated by the wartime Combined Chiefs of Staff. De Gaulle's decision to go nuclear in 1963 would not have been possible without earlier research efforts and financial investments made by the reputedly feckless leaders of the Fourth Republic.

Second, in addition to breaking down such epochal markers, this inquiry seeks to bestride the divide of policy and strategy that affects historical studies of French sea power. Most writings related to the evolution of the Marine nationale from the 1940s to the 1960s tend to focus on specific and largely tactical or technical elements—carrier aviation, cruisers and destroyers, submarines and nuclear deterrence—or narrate operational histories in theaters such as Indochina and Algeria.[13] Although the postwar years are also covered in several larger chronological narratives of the history of the French navy, most writers have paid less attention to the forging of naval strategy during these years, looking instead at the evolution of naval policy and the budgetary debates that affected the growth of the fleet and shore infrastructures during the Cold War.[14] The importance of such discussions cannot be neglected and will indeed feature extensively here, but this work also regularly draws the attention of the reader back to the issues of strategy. One must not only be concerned with the types and numbers of seagoing platforms and maritime aircraft French planners sought to acquire. Fleet mix requirements were, first and foremost, generated as a result of extensive reflection on the fundamentals of strategy as it evolved at the dawn of the atomic age from a French perspective.

A third element reappears throughout these pages, the actual command arrangements and mechanisms established between France and successive allies to coordinate operations and provision of Allied assistance in times of war and peace. As put succinctly by Canadian author Sean Maloney, the "problems of coordinating one nation's naval, air, and land forces with those of other nations had never been addressed satisfactorily before World War II."[15] Most works concerned with these issues and their evolution from the war years to that of the Cold War remain primarily focused on the dominating factor of the Anglo-American relations that shaped such issues, from the establishment of the Combined Chiefs of Staff in 1942 to the command architecture implemented in support of NATO in the early 1950s.[16] Given the smaller forces France contributed to these large coalitions, the relative neglect of the French factor in shaping alliance arrangements is largely understandable but regrettable. Several Franco-British and Franco-American initiatives during the war years and in the early NATO era constituted important precedents that eventually shaped alliance relationships and processes through the following decades, if not to this day.

Such an approach to the historiography of the period also underscores what this study is not. It is not a general history of the Forces navales françaises libres, the Vichy navy, and the reunited Marine nationale through the years 1940–63. It does not include a detailed narrative of the operations conducted during World War II and postwar insurgencies. Those can be found elsewhere.[17] Brief discussions of ongoing deployments, technological innovations, and the evolutions of tactics reoccur throughout the text in order to provide context and demonstrate the evolving strengths and flaws of the Marine nationale as the instrument shaped by a naval policy formulated within a strategy of alliance. References to previous works discussing tactical and technological matters more extensively appear where appropriate.

The reader may also question the sparse discussions of the merchant navy. It is recognized that this component forms one of the essential foundations of sea power, and France dedicated much importance to its fleet of ocean liners, bulk carriers, oil tankers, and fishing vessels of all types in the modern era. The world wars showed the importance of building and controlling the fleet that ferried troops and supplies from the colonies and Allied countries whenever *la mère-patrie* (the motherland) faced the threat of invasion across its land borders in Europe. The need to rebuild a large merchant navy in the postwar era constituted an important concern for French political and naval leaders. Indeed, demands for that particular effort came into direct competition with the reconstruction effort at home as well as rejuvenating the fighting fleet. This study cannot address renewal of the merchant navy in a more fulsome manner given space restrictions, but the element of competition in priorities and over resources is addressed in the text when warranted.[18]

Such shortcomings are regrettable but unavoidable in seeking to determine the essential elements of the renaissance of French sea power from the desperate days of the armistice to the early Cold War era, especially for a continental nation determined to uphold worldwide interests at the dawn of the nuclear age. A recent study of the challenges facing the naval historian in presenting an all-inclusive portrait of any given period outlined the challenge well: "As a historian of the late-seventeenth-century English navy put it in 1953, 'If national history may be compared to a cake, then naval history is not a layer but a slice of that cake.' In other words, naval history cannot be understood unless the multiple contexts (social, economic, technological, cultural, political and diplomatic) in which navies are constructed and put to sea are also understood. To this must be added that if naval conflict and sea power are to be understood, then multiple national contexts and navies have also to be understood."[19]

The two decades covered in this book provide but the speck of a glimpse in the long and tortuous history of the French nation. And yet all of the dimensions mentioned above appear at some point or the other in this work seemingly focused on the narrow topic of the tribulations of the Marine nationale through these years. All of them needed consideration and discussion in order to provide the reader with the background necessary to assess the competing interpretations that confronted the author seeking to assemble a coherent narrative of France's quest for an independent naval policy within a strategy of alliance at this critical juncture of history—a quest that began under the darkest of clouds as the French navy suffered an ostensibly treasonous blow at the hands of its closest ally within weeks of the humiliating armistices concluded with Germany and Italy in June 1940, the start point for this study.

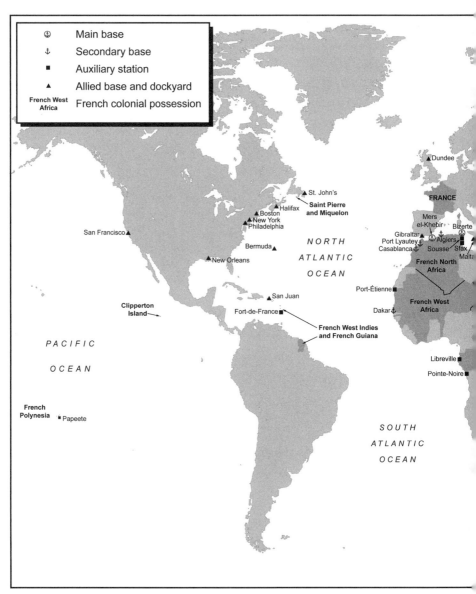

Twentieth-Century French Colonial Empire and Naval Installations

Chris Robinson

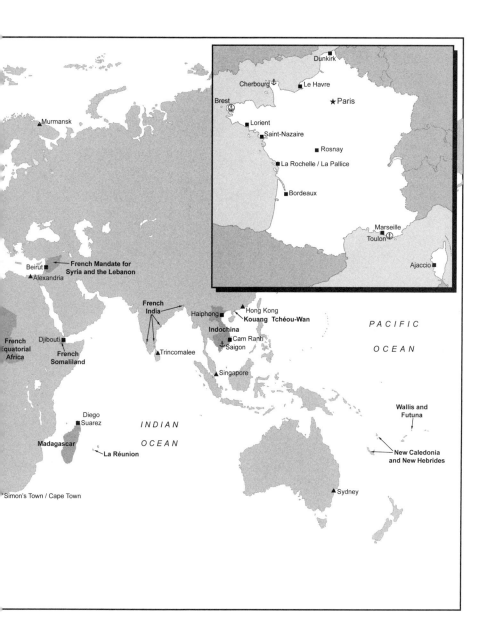

Murmansk

Cherbourg
Dunkirk
Le Havre
Brest
★ Paris
Lorient
Saint-Nazaire
Rosnay
La Rochelle / La Pallice
Bordeaux
Marseille
Toulon
Ajaccio

Beirut ■ French Mandate for
Syria and the Lebanon
▲ Alexandria

French
India

Haiphong ■
Hong Kong
Kouang Tchéou-Wan

Indochina
Cam Ranh
Saigon

PACIFIC

OCEAN

French
Equatorial
Africa
Djibouti ■
French
Somaliland

▲ Trincomalee

▲ Singapore

Wallis and
Futuna

Diego
Suarez

INDIAN

Madagascar
OCEAN
La Réunion

New Caledonia
and New Hebrides

Simon's Town / Cape Town

▲ Sydney

CHAPTER 1

SETTING THE PRECEDENT

Building Up a Free French Fleet

Alone figure looked despondent while walking along the quiet streets of London in the early morning hours of Thursday, 4 July 1940. Dressed in the standard French naval uniform but sporting a small *croix de Lorraine* on his right breast, Vice Admiral Émile Muselier entered St. Stephen's House, the austere headquarters of the Forces françaises libres (FFL), and reported to his leader, Charles de Gaulle. They were meeting in the aftermath of Operation Catapult, launched by the British the previous day. The fate of the French fleet had become a pressing concern for Great Britain as France fell under the blows of the German blitzkrieg. Convinced of the immediate need to prevent the Axis powers taking control of the vessels of the Marine nationale, British prime minister Winston Churchill had ordered the seizure, neutralization, or destruction of all elements of the French navy that were within reach.[1]

British troops boarded more than one hundred surface warships, submarines, and merchant navy vessels that had found refuge in Great Britain and its dominions, taking control by surprise and interning the sailors in camps ashore. Other ships were disarmed with skeleton crews remaining on board (Force X in Alexandria, Egypt) or left damaged in colonial ports without adequate repair facilities (battleships *Richelieu* in Dakar, Senegal, and *Jean Bart* in Casablanca, Morocco).[2] Nowhere was the blow more brutal, though, than in Mers el-Kébir, on the outskirts of Oran in Algeria. Following unsuccessful negotiations between local commanders, the Royal Navy (RN) inflicted a devastating gun and aerial assault that destroyed or severely damaged most ships in port, including the battleships *Bretagne* and *Dunkerque*, and killed or wounded nearly two thousand French sailors and officers.[3]

One ally had turned on another without warning at the moment of France's greatest distress following the debilitating armistices signed with Germany and Italy less than two weeks earlier. The grizzled seaman sat down in the office of the younger acting army brigadier, lamenting the fate of the fleet—including the beloved *Bretagne* that Muselier had commanded ten years earlier.[4] Both men commiserated together, then contemplated an abrupt departure from London for a colony beyond Vichy's reach, such as Saint-Pierre and Miquelon in North America or Pondicherry in India. They even broached the possibility of retiring to Canada as private citizens.[5] Their despondence did not last, however, and the discussion concluded with a renewed commitment to the Free French movement and a continued alliance with Great Britain. Realpolitik prevailed over emotions for de Gaulle. In the words of a biographer: "To have denounced the British would have brought him no dividend. On the other hand, to express understanding at what had been done could bring only gratitude from the government on which he depended. It was the first of a number of wartime decisions in which, while never abandoning his vision, the General would draw tactical advantage from adversity."[6]

De Gaulle instructed Vice Admiral Muselier to continue building up the movement's fledgling navy. The challenge of that single task was considerable. On that day, most French sailors outside of France's metropolitan and colonial ports found themselves corralled in British detention camps and their vessels impounded by the Royal Navy. Their captors soon offered to facilitate the return to France of those who wished to follow famed marshal Philippe Pétain into proclaimed neutrality rather than rallying the unknown de Gaulle. As for those who wished to fight the Axis, senior British commanders instructed that they be provided with the option of joining the king's armed forces rather than the FFL, although Prime Minister Winston Churchill also committed his country to supporting de Gaulle's movement. This awkward stance on the part of their "host" in the critical months that followed Operation Catapult drove de Gaulle and Muselier to maintain a guarded attitude in their dealings with

British authorities. They had to balance implied dependency on a reluctant ally and proclaimed autonomy for the FFL. Such modus operandi came to define Anglo–Free French military relations at first, and those with the United States later in the war.

The Free French forces are remembered today through the feats of soldiers who gallantly resisted German general Erwin Rommel's tanks at Bir Hakeim in 1942 and followed Free French general Philippe Leclerc in his race to Paris in 1944.[7] Less well understood is the earlier contribution made by sailors sporting the *croix de Lorraine*, the symbol adopted in early July 1940 by the Free French movement.[8] They provided a forlorn de Gaulle with the initial means to rally political support within the French colonial empire and make a small but early military contribution to the Allied cause. This chapter discusses that endeavor. De Gaulle and Muselier focused their first efforts through the summer of 1940 on securing recognition and increased support from the British authorities in the wake of Operation Catapult. The fledgling fleet slowly grew in size and effectiveness, achieving notable successes in the two years that led to the Anglo-American landings in French North Africa and the invasion of France's Free Zone by the Germans. Thereafter, the United States assumed an overriding role in the rebuilding of a newly reconciled French navy. This new relationship, though, grew out of the Anglo–Free French precedents set earlier. De Gaulle's concerns with the recognition and autonomy of his movement informed his approach to naval matters during this darkest time in the history of modern France, a necessary start point for this study.

The Quest for Recognition and Autonomy

De Gaulle quickly bounced back after Mers el-Kébir. As he recalled later: "In spite of the pain and anger . . . , I considered that the saving of France ranked above everything, even above the fate of her ships, and that our duty was to go on with the fight."[9] His legitimacy remained an issue, however. No prominent figure from the political class, nor from the ranks of the diplomatic and civil services, joined the French National Committee de Gaulle proposed to assemble in London.[10] The British cabinet formally acknowledged him on 28 June as "leader of all Free Frenchmen, wherever they may be, who rally to him in support of the allied cause."[11] And yet Great Britain did not grant the movement diplomatic recognition as a government-in-exile, unlike national leaders who had sought refuge in the British Isles, such as those from Belgium and the Netherlands.[12] London in fact continued to recognize the Vichy regime until Pétain broke off diplomatic relations on 8 July 1940 as a result of Operation Catapult.[13] Thereafter, Whitehall pursued a rather ambiguous approach by keeping ties with the collaborationist regime until 1942 through a Canadian representative.[14] Neutral powers—most critically, the United States—also maintained diplomatic representation in Vichy, thus recognizing Pétain and the ostensibly lawful transfer of power that had occurred in France on 10 July 1940.

On that fateful day, a quorum of French senators and deputies sat for an extraordinary parliamentary session in the small southern town of Vichy, in the *zone libre*, the free zone left unoccupied by the German and Italian invaders. The assembled politicians ratified the terms of the two armistices and agreed to make the unelected Marshal Philippe Pétain head of state, cumulating both executive and legislative powers, thus "voting the Third Republic out of existence."[15] For de Gaulle, that regime had accepted defeat before the war was lost and sacrificed the French people while they were still fighting, therefore relinquishing the authority to represent the citizenry and rule the country.[16] In order to restore the nation and reestablish France as a great power after the hostilities, he considered it essential that the French people continue fighting and that organized French military forces make a significant contribution to the liberation of the homeland. It was clear to de Gaulle that this campaign could not be left to the Allies alone, however benevolent they appeared, if France wished to stand alongside the victors at the war's end. De Gaulle wanted his movement to make a contribution to the eventual defeat of the Axis and much more. Le Général sought to achieve a "transfer of sovereignty" from the vanquished regime in Vichy, and this momentous ambition necessitated legitimacy, internally among his people and externally among foreign leaders, none more so than Churchill.

The British prime minister certainly needed a French ally to keep that country's fleet and its colonies out of Axis hands. This position stood in contrast to that of several members of his government as well as key figures in diplomatic and military circles. The unprecedented situation resulting from the presence of a militant de Gaulle in Great Britain and an ostensibly legitimate regime in Vichy left British leaders facing a conundrum many were reluctant to resolve.[17] Active and forceful interventions on the part of Churchill would often be required that summer, whenever Free French leaders went knocking on closed doors around London, seeking support in standing up their fledgling forces. The prime minister sent a blunt message to the services' chiefs of staff on 12 July 1940:

> It is the settled policy of His Majesty's Government to make good strong French contingents for land, sea and air service . . . and to have them as representatives of a France which is continuing the war. It is the duty of the Chiefs of Staff to carry this policy out cordially and effectively . . . Mere questions of administrative inconvenience must not be allowed to stand in the way of this policy of the State. . . . I hope I may receive assurances that this policy is being whole-heartedly pursued.[18]

Tensions between the Free French and London, as well as within the British establishment itself, became particularly apparent when de Gaulle sought to assemble effective military forces in the aftermath of Operation Catapult and the bloody legacy of Mers el-Kébir. This complex environment greatly complicated the task he assigned to his naval commander that summer, a seasoned sailor but largely devoid of experience in the formulation of higher naval policy and negotiations with foreign powers.

Muselier in July

Acting Brigadier General Charles de Gaulle appointed retired Vice Admiral Émile Muselier as commander of the Forces navales françaises libres, or Free French Naval Forces (FNFL), and the Forces aériennes françaises libres (Free French Air Force) on 1 July 1940.[19] Muselier would prove both an asset and a liability for de Gaulle. The first officer of the general rank from any of the three services to respond to de Gaulle's call, he was the only flag officer, out of the fifty or so then serving in the Marine nationale, to join the Free French until the North African landings in November 1942.[20] However, tensions in the command relationship between the senior sailor and the much more junior army officer, younger in age by eight years, arose immediately and were never quite resolved. De Gaulle was but a colonel at the start of the war and had been made acting brigadier in late May 1940, a fact that clearly grated on Muselier.[21] Although a competent sailor and effective organizer, Muselier's reputation in naval circles was controversial. Graduating from the École navale in 1901 as a classmate of Admiral François Darlan, head of the Marine nationale since 1937 already, Muselier had made rear admiral in 1931, a fairly good pace in those years, but he was not promoted again until October 1939.[22] Even then, promotion only occurred as a result of the wartime requirement to elevate the rank for the position he had held since the previous year—commander of the Marseille Defense Sector, a low-profile appointment—and this only to be "retired" within weeks by *ministre de la Marine* (navy minister) César Campinchi, under pressure from the local business community after Muselier publicly mouthed accusations of war profiteering against prominent citizens.

Muselier never forgave Darlan and the navy's senior leadership for sacrificing him in the face of political pressure. An alliance with the Free French thus made sense, but de Gaulle did not know the retired vice admiral. When advised that Muselier wished to meet with him, he resorted to seeking counsel from Admiral Arandal, the French naval attaché in London, even though the latter had already declined to rally the Free French movement and would soon choose repatriation to Vichy France. De Gaulle recollected the telephone conversation in a 1946 confidence to his aide Claude Guy:

> "I [de Gaulle] must know if he [Muselier] is a man of honor." Before answering me, Admiral Arandal paused to reflect. I must actually say that he paused for a very long time (said the General, smiling). Eventually he answered: "Admiral Muselier, you see, is a swashbuckler. But he is a swashbuckler who would never violate his honor. If you take him, you will in turn admire and abhor in him all the qualities and all the faults of a swashbuckler." The General then concluded: "I had to consider myself forewarned. Nevertheless, he was a vice-admiral and a vice-admiral, at that point when the number of those joining me had been negligible, had to be considered. This is why I took him."[23]

Recruitment at all rank levels was a pressing challenge for the embryonic Free French navy, even though plenty of Marine nationale vessels had evacuated the Atlantic ports ahead of the fast-moving columns of German tanks in June 1940. They sought refuge in Great Britain with 11,500 crew members on board. Another 10,000 shore-based sailors and army personnel, and 2,500 civilians had also scrambled on board as the ships and submarines slipped their moorings. A few hundred fishermen and 2,500 merchant sailors came with their boats, while 200 aviators flew aircraft directly to England and Gibraltar. Some 4,500 injured personnel evacuated from Dunkirk were still in British hospitals, and the bulk of the 6,000-strong alpine division that had participated in the Norway campaign was back in England after an ill-starred attempt at setting up a redoubt in Britany before the Germans broke through to the Channel and the Bay of Biscay. In total, nearly 35,000 French military personnel and civilians could be found on British territory in the aftermath of the armistice. And yet barely 400 ratings and a dozen officers had pledged allegiance to the Free French navy by the end of June, while 20,000 of their countrymen had chosen evacuation in a convoy of twelve ocean liners and cargo ships bound for Morocco. Another 10,000 would leave until the departure of the last repatriation ship on 26 November 1940.[24] Why such a small uptake?

De Gaulle was partly to blame. His haughty manners, perceived self-aggrandizement, and cruel attacks on the personal character of Marshal Pétain—as much a revered figure in French military ranks as among the civilian populace at that early stage—badly undermined the few visits he made to camps accommodating his fellow French in England.[25] The reputation of Vice Admiral Muselier within the Marine nationale did not help either, but British authorities also played a part in these inauspicious beginnings.[26] By the time of the armistice, disquieted by the presence in their rear of thousands of French military personnel and civilians of doubtful allegiance as the country was preparing to repulse a German invasion, most British authorities came to favor repatriation unless Frenchmen formally rallied to the Union Jack. Memoirs by early adherents of la France libre abound with examples of British representatives undermining Free French recruitment through offers to join Great Britain's armed forces, with higher rates of pay and promises of British citizenship after the hostilities. More immediate measures, such as relocating

FFL recruits to camps where the living conditions were clearly worse, also harmed this effort.[27]

In addition to the difficulties facing de Gaulle and Muselier in attracting sailors to the movement was that of wresting control over French vessels detained in British ports in the wake of Operation Catapult. The Royal Navy wished to make up for its losses by sailing many of these ships under the White Ensign, either with British crews or those of other European navies that had found refuge in Great Britain.[28] Even a supporter of de Gaulle such as Churchill could at once sound generous toward the leader of *la France libre* and appear ruthless in the requirement to use ships of the Marine nationale for British purposes. He stated in a note to the Admiralty: "I think it important that de Gaulle should have one or two or even three ships, even perhaps a battleship, where the Frenchmen predominate and which fly the French flag. . . . These ships may be of use in parleying with French Colonies and in getting into French harbors on one pretext or the other. . . . [As for the others], by all means take at once and commission under the White Ensign all French vessels that are of immediate practical use to us."[29]

Churchill released this instruction on 5 July, immediately after Mers el-Kébir and the same day that Vice Admiral Muselier met the British First Sea Lord, Admiral Dudley Pound, to propose a comprehensive "navy-to-navy" agreement to delineate relations between the Royal Navy and the FNFL.[30] The meeting did not start well. When Muselier expressed his intent to take command of all French warships and merchantmen in the British Isles, Pound replied that the cabinet had already endorsed a decision for British crews to take over an initial allotment of twelve vessels. For the Royal Navy, this arrangement was necessary to ensure that the crews not be treated as "rebels" in opposition to the Vichy regime. Muselier retorted that the Pétain government was not legitimate, but the Second Sea Lord, Admiral Charles Little, stated rather dismissively that world opinion would likely disagree with the leader of the FNFL. And Pound reiterated the promise that any French sailors wishing to join the Royal Navy would be taken in.

Notwithstanding these differences and several hours of testy exchanges, an initial—and fundamental—quid pro quo was reached. FNFL crews would be allowed to take back those French ships they could crew as long as they accepted to operate under the orders of British fleet commanders at sea. To Muselier's chagrin, Pound's superiors never formally accepted this bilateral military agreement. That may have been for the best. The Free French naval commander had not consulted with the de Gaulle on this matter, nor Pound with Churchill. The admirals concluded a deal in the absence of higher political direction, and the terms obtained by Muselier presented the potential to make the FNFL a naval foreign legion rather than a fleet serving Free French interests. Meanwhile, de Gaulle, during a 12 July meeting with Vice Admiral Gerald Dickens, RN liaison officer to the Allied navies, agreed that French units could be "lent" to other navies, another important precedent.[31] Remarkably, the General proffered this commitment without even consulting his naval commander. Although ill omen for their already fraught relations, these discussions provided the basis necessary to build up a viable Free French fleet pending the conclusion of a larger political entente.

On the very day de Gaulle met with Dickens, FNFL sailors boarded the battleship *Courbet* in Portsmouth. Muselier formed the first contingent of *fusiliers-marins* the next day. In the following weeks, Free French crews resumed control of submarines *Rubis* and *Narval*; armed trawlers *Président Houduce*, *Le Vaillant*, and *Viking*; and smaller utility vessels and some cargo ships. Most of the crew of *aviso colonial* (colonial sloop) *Savorgnan de Brazza* elected to join the Free French, and they were allowed to return to the ship as a group later that month.[32] Conscious that the hostilities would endure and concerned that half of the FNFL recruits had no naval experience, an embarked *école navale* (naval school) was stood up in *Courbet*. Arrangements were soon made for officer candidates to attend the wartime three-month midshipman course at the Royal Naval College in Dartmouth. FNFL detachments were also assigned to RN trade schools for French ratings to train in the rapidly evolving techniques of antisubmarine and antiair warfare as well as study communications, engineering, and other disciplines.[33]

This seeming goodwill could not mask the Admiralty's continued ambition to leverage French ships for its own purposes, but it turned out that the Royal Navy could do little with those stranded in the British Isles. RN authorities quickly realized that the issues caused by different technical specifications, equipment standards, ammunition calibers and by the absence of drawing left behind in France created debilitating delays in those yards assigned to maintain or upgrade the foreign vessels.[34] It also became clear that the best units of the Marine nationale had been evacuated to North Africa, leaving but second-class material in English ports. Battleships *Courbet* and *Paris* had first seen service before the Great War while many of the light destroyers and sloops designed to operate in the Mediterranean possessed neither the autonomy nor seakeeping capabilities necessary for long transatlantic escort missions. Also telling, all French submarines were deemed technically and materially unsuitable for service under the White Ensign. By the end of 1940, the Royal Navy had largely given up on the concept of arming French ships itself and accepted that FNFL sailors were the best source of manpower to return French units to service. This turnaround was but one more small victory for Muselier as de Gaulle set about formalizing the Anglo–Free French relationship at the political level.

De Gaulle in August

While Muselier failed to secure a formal navy-to-navy agreement on 5 July 1940, de Gaulle tried to obtain a higher-level accord with Prime Minister Churchill. French law professor Pierre Cassin had followed the French government to Bordeaux in the weeks leading up to the armistice, but he later escaped France on board a British freighter. Reporting to de Gaulle's headquarters on 29 June, he was immediately tasked to draft a proposal that would give concrete shape to the declaration of the previous day when the British cabinet had acknowledged "the leader of all Free Frenchmen."[35] Negotiations then unfolded acrimoniously over the course of the following month. Operation Catapult contributed to the alacrity, but repeated demands by the French negotiator for Great Britain to commit to controversial issues, such as the full restoration of France's colonies after the war or the exercise by de Gaulle of some form of control over those French citizens recruited into the British armed forces, also delayed the negotiations.[36] Nevertheless, compromises on both sides led to an accord through an exchange of letters between de Gaulle and Churchill on 7 August 1940.

Although an important step, the agreement still revealed the continued uneasiness of the Anglo–Free French relationship. The text carefully avoided any terms couching it as a formal treaty or a form of diplomatic recognition, merely labeling it "a memorandum which . . . will constitute an accord between us concerning the organization, employment and conditions of service of the [Free French] forces."[37] Churchill agreed that "His Majesty's Government is resolved, once Allied armies have won victory, to ensure the integral restoration of the independence and greatness of France."[38] By doing so he avoided specific reference to the future status of France's colonies, a prime concern for de Gaulle. Strikingly, Churchill only referred to the episode in one curt and noncommittal sentence in his 1949 memoirs: "On August 7, I signed a military agreement with [de Gaulle] which dealt with practical needs."[39] This stands in sharp contrast to negotiator Cassin celebrating the text as the "fundamental charter of the Free French movement."[40] De Gaulle also commemorated the event in later years in rousing terms:

> The August 7th agreement had a considerable importance for Free France, not only because it got us out of immediate material difficulties, but also because the British authorities, having now an official basis for their relations with us, no longer hesitated to make things easier for us. Above all, the whole world knew that a new beginning of Franco-British solidarity had been made in spite of everything. The consequences soon made themselves felt in certain territories of the Empire and among French residents abroad. But in addition, other States, when they saw Great Britain proceeding to a beginning of recognition, took some steps in the same direction.[41]

Beyond its political ramifications, the accord laid in practical terms fundamental principles of military support and coordination between Great Britain and the Free French movement. The parties mutually agreed that the FFL would preserve a French character in terms of flags, discipline, and the administration of personnel, thus avoiding the perception of an amalgamation in the armed forces of another country. Great Britain accepted that de Gaulle's forces exercised priority of assignment for all French equipment found in territories under British control—from ships and aircraft to ammunition, stores and supplies—as long as these forces could crew and effectively use such equipment. Churchill also committed to furnishing additional items when necessary to bring French units up to par with their UK equivalent.

As a quid pro quo, de Gaulle accepted that Great Britain and other Allied powers could avail themselves of unused French equipment—including ships, submarines, and aircraft—on a temporary basis, as such items would remain French property to be returned to France after the war. De Gaulle further agreed that, while he retained national command over all Free French forces, these would be placed under British control when taking part in a given campaign—which would be the case for most operations involving the FFL for the foreseeable future. Lastly, Great Britain consented to fund all FFL expenses subject to having those sums reimbursed after the war. The agreement represented major concessions from both sides that underpinned a practical and effective wartime working arrangement. They would fight together against a common enemy instead of each other.

Although the text of the accord did not provide a detailed plan to implement its wide-ranging clauses, the framework was unprecedented.[42] It managed the support and employment of the seemingly autonomous military forces of a smaller ally within the bounds of the strategy and control of a larger one, long a matter best avoided in the conduct of war at sea. Up to that point, coordinating the movements and support of ships from different countries involved in a single coalition, whether at the tactical level within one combined fleet or strategically over wider theaters of operations, had proven most difficult. Franco-British naval staff talks in the months preceding the conflict sought to lay the foundations for closer cooperation between the two fleets. But again, these had defaulted to geographical separation as the best means to coordinate the movements of forces at sea, or, rather, to avoid interference between them. Allied commanders were invited to "cooperate" when operating in the same vicinity rather than having one formally placed under the other.[43] The problem was particularly genuine in the narrow waters of the Mediterranean.[44]

France's dispatch of Force X to Alexandria in the spring of 1940 to supplement Admiral Andrew Cunningham's depleted forces conformed to this fleet operating concept of "autonomy and collaboration" rather than command and control. Promoted to vice admiral on 19 June, in part to match Cunningham's rank, René-Émile Godfroy's instructions had been to operate as an independent commander but in "cooperation" with his British host.[45]

Godfroy rapidly came to believe that effective operations in these waters could only be conducted under a single naval commander. He elected to informally subordinate his command to that of Cunningham: "[Success] required mutual understanding and close collaboration between British and French naval forces. Such cooperation, to deliver best effects, could only result from unity of command. . . . Thus, when we first met, I did not hesitate to tell Cunningham that I would follow his orders in the execution of operations as long as he included me in their planning beforehand, subject to Force X remaining first and foremost dedicated to whatever tasks may be received in the future from the French naval command."[46]

Although couched in rather guarded terms, this gentlemen's agreement proved effective in the weeks prior to the armistice and played a role in the peaceful resolution of the standoff between Force X and the Royal Navy on 4 July.[47] The result stood in stark contrast to the brutal blow inflicted at Mers el-Kébir the previous day. Nevertheless, the arrangement remained a local initiative, unsanctioned by higher authorities, and it did not address the range of issues facing any naval force hosted in a foreign station while isolated from its home port—from provisioning to maintenance, taking on fuel and ammunition, and disciplining sailors ashore on leave. Although these matters are rarely addressed in narratives dealing with fighting fleets in wartime, they exercise a tremendous impact on the operational status of ships as well as the effectiveness and morale of their crews. The Churchill–de Gaulle agreement of 7 August 1940 was mostly silent on specifics as well, but this unique framework shaped the precedents that followed as the small naval force flying the *croix de Lorraine* flag grew slowly but did not hesitate to step eagerly into the fight at sea.

A Fledging Free French Fleet in Action

While de Gaulle avoided on 7 August 1940 the prospect of the Free French movement becoming a foreign legion fighting under the British flag, the constant struggle for personnel and resources continued. Barely one thousand French volunteers joined the FNFL ranks while seven hundred enlisted in the Royal Navy that summer. Only three sloops (*Savorgnan de Brazza, Commandant Duboc,* and *Commandant Dominé*), three armed trawlers (*Président*

Houduce, *Le Vaillant*, and *Viking*), and four submarines (*Rubis*, *Minerve*, *Junon*, and *Narval*) could be made available for service at sea in August. The force grew slowly through the fall months as more qualified personnel became available to crew French vessels, including two modern destroyers (*Le Triomphant* and *Léopard*), the world's largest submarine (*Surcouf*), and one torpedo boat (*La Melpomène*).[48] By the end of the year, 3,300 sailors sported the *croix de Lorraine* on their breast, although less than half of those were veterans of the Marine nationale.[49] One thousand or so had transferred from the merchant navy while the rest were civilians or former army personnel who had joined without experience of life at sea. They would require months of training before joining formed ship companies ready to deploy into combat.

To alleviate inherent difficulties of maintenance and training with mixed equipment and standards, Muselier and Pound agreed in April 1941 that FNFL crews could take over new warships under construction in British shipyards instead of recommissioning existing French vessels. This important step started with six Fairmile wooden motor launches and six Flower-class corvettes acquired through the course of that year.[50] Such newfound largesse on the part of the Royal Navy was facilitated by the enactment in the United States of the Lend-Lease Act on 11 March 1941. Roosevelt did not extend Lend-Lease to *la France libre* as he still considered Vichy the more viable and legitimate French regime at that point, but the Royal Navy now had access to a bounty of new vessels in North America. They required manning by experienced personnel from Great Britain, leaving more British ships available for employment by Allied crews while efforts to bring older Marine nationale units into service were virtually abandoned.

Three more corvettes were added in 1942 as well as six Fairmile motor launches.[51] Later that year, the Fairmiles were returned to the Royal Navy and their crews used to man eight seventy-foot Vosper motor torpedo boats (MTBs), forming the 23rd MTB flotilla. This initiative carried much significance as a mark of increased respect by the RN leadership for the professional competence of the Free French to handle more complex offensive operations, often at night. By then the motor launches and other FNFL craft had been actively engaged in coastal escort and patrol duties as well as cross-Channel incursions, such as the daring raids against Saint-Nazaire. The MTB flotilla was based on the Dart

River, moored next to French sloop *Belfort*, taken over by the Royal Navy as part of HMS *Cicala*, the coastal forces establishment at Kingswear, opposite Dartmouth. The Free French MTBs carried out their first offensive operations in March 1943. A similar sign of professional trust was the handover of the Hunt-class destroyer HMS *Haldon* on 15 December 1942. Although only just over one thousand tons and small by destroyer standards, she was a modern Type III evolution of the original escort destroyer design, having been laid down in January 1941. Rechristened *La Combattante*, she would go on to serve as the flagship of the Free French fleet as battleship *Courbet* was disarmed in March 1941, another sign of renewed focus on operations rather than prestige.

The sum of these transfers, combined with those French units already refurbished, made for a small but effective force. But the fleet also suffered severe losses as it deployed ships and submarines during the most challenging years of the war at sea. U-boats were poised to cut off Great Britain's Atlantic lifelines while German surface forces and aircraft actively challenged the Royal Navy and the Royal Air Force in the Channel and the littoral waters of the British Isles. FNFL forces needed to make an immediate contribution to the fight even as its sailors, aviators and *fusiliers-marins* were still familiarizing themselves with new equipment and updated tactics to defeat the formidable Axis opponents. And yet one of the first such actions at sea saw *croix de Lorraine* sailors fighting fellow French off the coast of Senegal to rally that colony and, it was hoped, the whole of French Western Africa, whose leaders had pledged allegiance to Pétain.[52] The race was on between Vichy and *la France libre* to secure the loyalty of the French empire.

Both de Gaulle and Churchill believed that an early show of force by Free French ships backed up by the Royal Navy would suffice to bring isolated Pétain loyalists over to the Allied camp. The scheme backfired dramatically.[53] Dismissive of the rebellious de Gaulle, local leaders perceived Operation Menace as "perfidious Albion" seeking to invade the colony, the FNFL flotilla acting as nothing more than a fig leaf. A violent confrontation ensued during the three-day Battle of Dakar (23–25 September 1940) when several Vichy navy units sortied to confront their opponents, with support provided by shore batteries and the battleship *Richelieu* firing from her alongside berth. They succeeded in inflicting significant damage on the British force. The submarine

Bévéziers torpedoed the battleship *Resolution*, which withdrew from the scene and remained out of action for nearly a year to undergo repairs in an American shipyard. Shore batteries also inflicted damage on battleship *Barham* and two cruisers. The Vichy camp suffered heavily too, with submarines *Persée* and *Ajax* sunk, destroyer *L'Audacieux* set ablaze and beached. Battleship *Barham* struck *Richelieu* twice while faulty rounds damaged three of the four barrels in one of the latter's two main turrets.[54] On balance, though, the outcome was an unmitigated success for the Pétain camp. The Anglo–Free French force withdrew sullenly while the Vichy government boasted that its forces could and would defend the colonies against any invaders, be they British, Germans, or Gaullists.

This resistance demonstrated unexpected resolution on the Vichy side and constituted a grievous political defeat for de Gaulle, badly undermining his ability to rally other colonies and affecting the little credibility he held in neutral countries like the United States.[55] Nevertheless, FNFL units had performed well, integrating smoothly with the larger British fleet, a good omen for future operations. Two months later, the sloops *Savorgnan de Brazza*, *Commandant Dominé*, and *Commandant Duboc* participated in the taking of Gabon, the only French Equatorial Africa colony that refused to rally *la France libre*.[56] This campaign, the first rallying obtained through the force of arms, was largely an army affair as a column led by Colonel Philippe Leclerc marched on Libreville to take the capital from its less protected inland side.

Still, the presence outside the harbor of Free French ships and, further offshore, of a small group of RN cruisers and destroyers caused the Vichy submarine *Poncelet* and the sloop *Bougainville* to sortie against overwhelming odds. The *Poncelet* closed in on the British force but was forced to the surface by the sloop *Milford*. The captain, Lieutenant Bertrand de Saussine, first evacuated the crew to lifeboats, then reentered his submersible and scuttled her at the cost of his own life. Two days later, *Savorgnan de Brazza* disabled her sister ship, *Bougainville*, with withering gun and small arms fire, the first clash that saw an FNFL ship engage another ship flying the tricolor and kill French sailors.[57] By then, both sides had shed French blood, and more fratricidal actions would follow while the Free French navy went about taking the fight to the Axis as well.

Submarines went back into action in the fall of 1940. The Malta-based *Narval* patrolled the central Mediterranean while *Rubis* deployed out of Scotland to roam the North Sea and lay minefields off the coast of Norway. The latter was joined by the *Minerve* in January 1941 and the *Junon* in December, all praised for their performance by the Admiralty and contributing to increased coverage of the FFL in the British media.[58] Small surface ships, based closer to the Channel, undertook the escort of coastal convoys, and *Chasseur 41* recorded the first FNFL victory against an Axis target at sea by shooting down a German aircraft in April 1941. Other submarine chasers and torpedo boats participated in cross-Channel incursions, such as the raid on the radar installation at Bruneval in February 1942, the attack against the Saint-Nazaire dry dock the following month, and the ill-fated landing at Dieppe in August of that same year. While committed to these operations in the European littoral, Muselier also understood the importance of taking on the main threat to the Allied effort at the time, the U-boats.

The destroyer *Léopard* commenced convoy escort work in Great Britain's Western Approaches in November 1940 and claimed a first U-boat kill for the Free French on 29 June 1942, having joined the RN ships *Sprey* and *Pelican* in the destruction of *U-136* west of Madeira.[59] Several of the British-built corvettes acquired by the FNFL in 1941 saw service with the Newfoundland-based Mid-Ocean Escort Force starting that summer. Three others were dispatched to operate out of South African ports, and some saw service on the Arctic run to Murmansk starting in 1942. Despite their dedicated service through the most challenging years of the Battle of the Atlantic, French corvettes would not be able to claim a first U-boat kill until 7 February 1943, a seemingly poor performance not unlike that of other corvette fleets struggling to defeat German wolf pack tactics. Convoy escort was grinding and frustrating work, offering few rewards in the face of ongoing danger in a hostile environment. Nevertheless, the presence of these gritty ships and their hardened crews deployed from Murmansk to South Africa and patrolling relentlessly across the breath of the North Atlantic earned them growing respect from the Allied navies.[60] De Gaulle could only rejoice at the fawning media coverage they received, especially in England and the United States.

Political missions in support of de Gaulle's effort to rally French colonies also continued. After the dramatic affairs of Dakar and Libreville, the colonial sloop *Savorgnan the Brazza* sailed to the Indian Ocean and participated in the blockade of Djibouti, still loyal to Vichy, for most of 1941–42.[61] Destroyer *Le Triomphant*, torpedo boat *Chevreuil*, and the armed merchant cruiser *Cap des Palmes* arrived separately in the Pacific through the fall of 1941 to patrol France's possessions in Micronesia and escort convoys out of Australia and New Zealand, showing flexibility in combining national missions and Allied interests.[62] Meanwhile, Vice Admiral Muselier personally led a naval force to rally Saint-Pierre and Miquelon, two small islands off the Newfoundland coast, which took place without a fight on Christmas Eve.[63] A year later, in November 1942, destroyer *Léopard* moved into the Indian Ocean to take the island of La Réunion. As the ship approached the main harbor, two Vichy soldiers and one Free French officer lost their lives during a gun duel between the vessel and a shore battery.[64] Cut off from the *métropole* and short of supplies, the local governor accepted to turn his office over to a representative of de Gaulle without further resistance. This action turned out to be the last deadly confrontation between the two French camps as the British had already taken Madagascar without FFL involvement earlier in the year, and Djibouti finally abandoned its allegiance to Vichy in the weeks that followed the Anglo-American landings in North Africa.[65]

De Gaulle's small navy was quite stretched by then, as shown in tables 1.1 and 1.2. Through 1940 and 1941, Muselier's fleet took on increasing national commitments while continuing to discharge its Allied tasks in European waters and in the North Atlantic. Rallying colonies not only entailed responsibility for their political affairs and public administration but charge for their defense as well. The legitimacy and credibility of *la France libre* necessitated that the FFL allocate sufficient forces to show their capacity to exercise sovereignty locally while the British (and later the Americans) had little appetite to deploy their own assets in locations too remote to be of significance in the war against the Axis powers. *Commandant Duboc*, *Président Houduce*, *Viking*, and other craft remained after 1940 to patrol the shores of French Equatorial Africa as well as escort small convoys transiting through these waters. Others rotated through Free French possessions in the Indian and Pacific Oceans for the remainder of the war. More (such as *Commandant Dominé* and another armed merchant cruiser, the *Reine des Flots*) commenced sailing out of Beirut in the Eastern Mediterranean after the seizure of Lebanon and Syria by a British-led force, augmented by Gaullist troops but without the involvement of FNFL ships, in the summer of 1941.[66]

But a navy is more than its ships and submarines, as Muselier and his staff knew well. That fall also witnessed the birth of Free French naval aviation with the stand-up in October 1941 of a combined navy–air force fighter formation, the Groupe de chasse Île de France, designated 340 (Free French) Squadron and assigned to the Royal Air Force Fighter Command.[67] Veterans from French naval aviation (formally the Aéronautique navale, most often shortened to the Aéronavale) had rallied to Free France since the armistice but were employed with the Royal Air Force as individual augmentees. *Île de France* was the first squadron formed as an integral Free French unit to include pilots and ground crews from the FNFL. Its Spitfires commenced conducting defensive patrols over southern England before moving on to offensive sweeps in northern France and antishipping missions in the Channel and the Bay of Biscay. After joining the hostilities, the United States accepted to train Free French naval aircrews on the Consolidated PBY Catalina amphibious patrol aircraft for antisubmarine missions, starting in July 1942. Other pilots embarked in HMS *Indomitable* that December to gain expertise in carrier operations as FNFL leaders developed the ambition to create a well-rounded naval air service.[68]

Retaking colonies and mounting offensive operations against the Axis also necessitated land forces, an object of special attention on the part of Muselier ever since the summer of 1940. Although always short of personnel to crew Free French ships, Muselier continued to press for larger numbers of naval troops to exercise some influence during operations on land and defend colonial outposts. The first battalion of *fusiliers-marins* embarked in September 1940 for Operation Menace off Dakar and then landed in Libreville to garrison the Gabon capital in November. Transported to Palestine the following spring, the battalion took part in the drive to Damascus, Syria, in June 1941. Converting to the air defense role, its gunners fought in North

Table 1.1: Free French Units of French Origin, 12 July 1940–31 December 1942

Category[a]	Vessel Name	Tonnage[c]	Remarks
Dreadnought	~~Courbet~~[b]	~~22,550~~	Seized Op Catapult, transferred to FNFL 12 July 1940. Floating barrack/AA battery (five kills) in Portsmouth, disarmed 31 March 1941
Destroyers	Le Triomphant	2,570	Seized Op Catapult, transferred to FNFL 28 August 1940
	Léopard	2,160	Seized Op Catapult, transferred to FNFL 31 August 1940
Torpedo boats	~~La Melpomène~~[b]	~~610~~	Seized Op Catapult, transferred to FNFL 31 August 1940. Transferred back to the RN 15 October 1942 and placed into reserve
Submarines	~~Surcouf~~[b]	~~4,000~~	Seized Op Catapult, transferred to FNFL 15 September 1940. Lost in collision with U.S. cargo ship in the Caribbean 18–19 April 1942
	~~Narval~~[b]	~~1,440~~	Rallied Malta 26 June 1940. Sunk by Italian mine off Tunisia 19 December 1940
	Minerve	800	Seized Op Catapult, transferred to FNFL 15 August 1940
	Junon	800	Seized Op Catapult, transferred to FNFL 21 July 1940
	Rubis	925	Seized Op Catapult but returned to her French crew on the same day as they had already rallied to de Gaulle
Sloops / Avisos	Savorgnan de Brazza	1,960	Seized Op Catapult, transferred to FNFL 17 July 1940
	Chevreuil	630	Seized Op Catapult, transferred to FNFL 3 September 1940
	Commandant Duboc	630	Seized Op Catapult, transferred to FNFL August 1940
	La Moqueuse	630	Seized Op Catapult, transferred to FNFL 10 August 1940
	Commandant Dominé	630	Seized Op Catapult, transferred to FNFL 26 July 1940
Misc. auxiliaries[d]	Président Houduce (Armed trawler)	1,179	Rallied Gibraltar 17 June 1940, never seized
	Reine des Flots (Armed trawler)	608	Seized Op Catapult, transferred to FNFL June 1941
	~~Viking~~[b] (Armed trawler)	~~1,159~~	Seized Op Catapult, transferred to FNFL 31 July 1940. Torpedoed by German submarine off Lebanon 16 April 1942
	Cap des Palmes (Armed merchant)	3,082	Seized by the FNFL in Gabon 9 November 1940
	~~Chasseur 8~~[b] (Submarine chaser)	~~114~~	Seized Op Catapult, transferred to FNFL 21 April 1941. Sunk off Plymouth by German aircraft 13 July 1942
	Chasseur 10	114	Seized Op Catapult, transferred to FNFL 22 October 1940

(continued)

Table 1.1 (continued)

Category[a]	Vessel Name	Tonnage[c]	Remarks
	Chasseur 11	114	Seized Op Catapult, transferred to FNFL 5 February 1941
	Chasseur 12	114	Seized Op Catapult, transferred to FNFL 1 May 1941
	Chasseur 13	114	Seized Op Catapult, transferred to FNFL 16 December 1942
	Chasseur 14	114	Seized Op Catapult, transferred to FNFL 19 December 1942
Misc. auxiliaries[d]	Chasseur 15	114	Seized Op Catapult, transferred to FNFL 6 February 1941
(continued)	Chasseur 41	114	Seized Op Catapult, transferred to FNFL 9 September 1940
	Chasseur 42	114	Seized Op Catapult, transferred to FNFL 16 September 1940
	Chasseur 43	114	Seized Op Catapult, transferred to FNFL 9 September 1940
	V.T.B. 11	28	Seized Op Catapult, transferred to FNFL June 1942
	V.T.B. 12	28	Seized Op Catapult, transferred to FNFL June 1942
Total in service on 31 December 1942	24 ships and submarines	17,686	2.4% of the total tonnage of the 1939 French fleet

Notes
[a] Categories do not include naval units used purely as barrack ships or dedicated to alongside training.
[b] Figures stricken through indicate vessels no longer part of the fleet on 30 December 1942 due to losses, disarmament, etc.
[c] Tonnage figures for submarines indicate submerged displacement.
[d] The Miscellaneous auxiliaries category does not include tugs and other small craft dedicated to harbor duties.

Africa throughout the following year, from Bir Hakeim to El Alamein and Tripoli, and then took part in the liberation of Tunisia in 1943.[69] A second battalion was raised in the fall of 1940 and later undertook garrison duty in Gabon and then Syria while Muselier ordered a third to form a commando unit based on the British model. After arduous training in the hills of Scotland, troops of the 1er Bataillon de fusiliers-marins commandos (1st Battalion of Naval Commandos) took part in several raids on the French coasts from mid-1942 on, starting with Dieppe on 19 August.[70]

In total, these operations at sea, in the air, and on land brought great credit to the FNFL, notwithstanding some significant costs. The small utility vessel *Poulmic* struck a mine outside Portsmouth in the fall of 1940, taking eleven of her eighteen crew to their watery grave, the first unit lost under Muselier's command.[71] The Malta-based submarine *Narval* also struck a mine, but off the coast of Tunisia in December 1940, with the death of all fifty sailors on board.[72] Although 1941 provided reprieve with no ship or submarine

Table 1.2: Free French Units of British Origin, 12 July 1940–31 December 1942

Category[a]	Vessel Name	Tonnage[c]	Remarks
Destroyer	La Combattante	1,500	RN Hunt-class destroyer, transferred to FNFL 15 December 1942
Corvettes (Flower-class)	~~Mimosa~~[b]	~~950~~	Transferred to FNFL 5 May 1941, torpedoed 9 June 1942
	~~Alysse~~[b]	~~950~~	Transferred to FNFL 10 June 1941, torpedoed 10 February 1942
	Lobélia	950	Transferred to FNFL 16 July 1941
	Aconit	950	Transferred to FNFL 23 July 1941
	Renoncule	950	Transferred to FNFL 28 July 1941
	Commandant Detroyat	950	Transferred to FNFL 16 September 1941
	Commandant Drogou	950	Transferred to FNFL 26 January 1942
	Commandant d'Estienne d'Orves	950	Transferred to FNFL 23 May 1942
	Roselys	950	Transferred to FNFL 12 September 1942
12 X Fairmile B motor launches	~~ML 123, 182, 192, 205, 245, 246, 247, 262, 267, 268, 269, 303~~[b]	85	First one transferred to FNFL in July 1941 and last one returned to RN in August 1942
Vosper 70-foot motor torpedo boats (Provided in replacement of the Fairmile MLs)	M.T.B. 94	47	Transferred to FNFL 24 October 1942
	M.T.B. 98	47	Transferred to FNFL 24 October 1942
	M.T.B. 90	47	Transferred to FNFL 11 November 1942
	M.T.B. 91	47	Transferred to FNFL 17 November 1942
	M.T.B. 96	47	Transferred to FNFL 24 November 1942
	M.T.B. 227	47	Transferred to FNFL 2 December 1942
	M.T.B. 239	47	Transferred to FNFL 7 December 1942
	M.T.B. 92	47	Transferred to FNFL 24 December 1942
Total in service on 30 December 1942	**16 ships**	**8,526**	**32% of the total FNFL tonnage**

Notes
[a] Categories do not include naval units used purely as barrack ships or dedicated to alongside training.
[b] Figures stricken through indicate vessels no longer part of the fleet on 30 December 1942 due to losses, disarmament, etc.
[c] Tonnage figures for submarines indicate submerged displacement.

sunk, the following year proved particularly grim, with the loss in April 1942 of the submarine *Surcouf* and her complement of 130 in the Caribbean, in circumstances that remain controversial today. *Alysse* and *Mimosa* were the first British-built corvettes to be lost, falling victims to German torpedoes in the North Atlantic, in February and June 1942, respectively. A U-boat sank the armed trawler *Viking* off Lebanon in April, and the Luftwaffe sank the small *Chasseur 8* in the Channel in July. To this must be added losses among the flying personnel operating out of English and Egyptian airfields as well as the *fusiliers-marins* fighting on the front lines of the Middle East.

The overall number of Free French naval personnel killed and missing rose to 567 by the summer of 1943, when the FNFL were formally amalgamated with the former Vichy navy.[73] Few as these numbers may have seemed when gauged against the cataclysmic scale of World War II, they showed the commitment of Muselier's fledgling navy to the Allied cause, especially during the forlorn years of 1940 and 1941, when Great Britain and its dominions stood nearly alone against the Axis. They also suggest that despite its limited size—5,700 sailors, *fusiliers-marins*, and aviators by the end of December 1942; 40 ships, small craft and submarines for a total of 26,212 tons, or 3.5 percent of the September 1939 French tonnage—the FNFL had met the goals assigned by de Gaulle in the summer of 1940. Free French ships and submarines were making a direct contribution to the overall Allied war effort, paying an important cost in blood and equipment while demonstrating a growing effectiveness under British operational control. Of particular importance, Muselier's units were the first Gaullist assets to actively join the fight against the Axis in the immediate aftermath of the 7 August 1940 agreement, when de Gaulle was most anxious to build up his legitimacy among the Allies. Admittedly, de Gaulle also used his flotilla for narrower ends in national terms.

These affairs did not always conform to British wishes, such as seizing remote French colonies that would contribute to the expansion of *la France libre* but not necessarily in accordance with Allied priorities. The Saint-Pierre and Miquelon episode showed this tendency. De Gaulle ordered Muselier in December 1941 to rally the islands' population, but the timing of this *coup de main* proved problematic for London, coming as it did within weeks of Pearl Harbor. Just days earlier, the Roosevelt administration had reaffirmed its commitment to the principle of "mutual nonintervention" with Vichy forces based in the Western Hemisphere. Even though an active belligerent by then, Washington still recognized the Pétain regime over that of de Gaulle. Muselier's arrival in the small fishing village of Saint-Pierre on Christmas Eve triggered a serious crisis between the United States, Free France, and Great Britain.[74] U.S. leaders apportioned as much blame to the British prime minister as to de Gaulle for such aggressive move in its sphere of interest, just as Churchill was in Washington for the first of the wartime Anglo-American conferences.

Short of inter-Allied politics, dissensions also appeared between Vice Admiral Muselier and his British colleagues over purely naval matters. The former sometimes promoted the rearmament of what the latter would call "prestige units," such as the battleship *Courbet* and the submarine *Surcouf*, both requiring large crews and material resources that the small fleet could ill afford. Emotional and too often public outbursts by the FNFL commander over the allocation of new hulls, dockyard repair time, supplies, shore accommodations, and other logistical issues often plagued relations between the two admiralties despite a growing consensus over operational matters. Nevertheless, Muselier did succeed in maintaining an effective—if tense—working relationship with the sea lords.[75]

Muselier proved especially astute in assigning British transfers to Allied tasks in the Atlantic and the Mediterranean (coastal defense and raiding enemy shores by the MTBs, convoy escort by the corvettes) while dispatching French units of lesser interest to the Royal Navy for those missions more narrowly focused on the national objectives demanded by de Gaulle. Thus, the provision of British-built units to the Free French constituted a valuable return on the investment for Great Britain, as it needed to deploy every operational warship that could put to sea during this period. Muselier and his officers appreciated the serviceability and range of such new vessels, which were much better than older French construction of doubtful operational readiness. This seeming *bonne entente* between naval leaders, however, could not alleviate the growing personal tensions that permeated relations between de Gaulle and Muselier through these years, leading to a dramatic divorce in the spring of 1942.

Exit Muselier

Discord among the two Free French leaders was always more about politics than military matters, eventually reaching a breaking point between the older leftist radical and the younger but imperious conservative. Muselier's aggravation with de Gaulle took root in the very first days of his appointment as commander of the Free French navy and never really went away. Muselier expressed great annoyance that de Gaulle did not support his attempt to obtain a navy-to-navy agreement with the First Sea Lord on 5 July 1940 while refusing him the opportunity to shape the higher-level accord of 7 August.[76] These negotiations remained the purview of a very narrow circle of de Gaulle advisers, to whom Muselier clearly did not belong, despite his seniority in rank. Indeed, the grizzled admiral was never formally appointed as a deputy to de Gaulle. The latter created, instead, the Délégation d'état-major (Staff Group) within FFL headquarters.

This "staff within a staff" reported directly to the Free French leader, even when de Gaulle was away from London for extended periods of time. On such occasions, Muselier acted in the capacity of *commandant supérieur des forces militaires en Grande-Bretagne* (senior commander of military forces in Great Britain) but the Délégation d'état-major continued to issue political and military directives without consulting him, a source of great frustration for the vice admiral. Contrary to Muselier, who dedicated a whole chapter of his memoirs to this matter, de Gaulle only mentioned it briefly when discussing preparations for his departure for the Dakar expedition in late August 1940: "I left our forces in course of formation under the orders of Muselier, an embryo administration under the direction of Antoine, and, in the person of Dewavrin, an element of liaison and direct information."[77] The wording implied parity between Vice Admiral Muselier, army major Aristide Antoine and army captain André Dewavrin, a situation that the much more senior flag officer could hardly accept.[78] This situation was but one symptom of the larger difference of views between the two men.

They never actually agreed on the fundamental nature of the Free French movement, a matter where the sailor manifested a grievous political naiveté when compared with the shrewd instincts of the soldier. Muselier envisioned a Free French movement that was purely apolitical, a military legion fighting alongside the Allies until a legitimate government could be restored in a liberated France.[79] De Gaulle, for his part, was convinced of the inherently political nature of the FFL, of the requirement to immediately institute the organs of an independent state within the framework of the larger military alliance, based on the three pillars of government, territory, and armed forces. Hence, de Gaulle created in October 1940 the Conseil de défense de l'Empire—the Empire Defense Council, an executive body to manage governmental affairs—in addition to the military headquarters structure proposed by Muselier on 10 July.[80] Hence, de Gaulle urgently sought to rally the colonies, even at the risk of shedding French blood in Dakar and earning American censure over Saint-Pierre and Miquelon. Muselier actively militated against all of these initiatives in their planning stage only to be maneuvered into reluctant endorsement by the more politically agile de Gaulle.

Combined with this dissonance over the nature of the movement was the approach to leading it. Once he had accepted a political role as commissioner on the Conseil de défense de l'Empire, Muselier argued for collegial decision making. He sought to curb a domineering de Gaulle by constraining him as "first among equals," an endeavor that the general easily checked with the support of other commissioners.[81] Muselier led another attempt to isolate de Gaulle in the weeks leading up to the replacement of the Conseil de défense de l'Empire with a more evolved Comité national français (French National Committee) in September 1941.[82] The general again easily neutralized the admiral's play by leveraging alliances within the Free French senior leadership. De Gaulle also enlisted the help of British foreign secretary Anthony Eden and First Lord of the Admiralty Albert Alexander to convince Muselier to join the new committee as commissioner for the FNFL and the merchant navy without further remonstrance.

The latter reluctantly agreed but, thereafter, dedicated himself to more or less openly contain what he referred to as de Gaulle's "dream of absolute power."[83] The accusation shows the gulf between a republican of the Left inspired by the cabinet practices he was then observing in Great Britain—which allowed ministers to challenge Churchill on key decisions—and the conservative general who blamed the bickering of Third Republic politicians for the fall of France.[84] The conflict erupted at a meeting of the French National Committee on 3 March 1942 as a result of the accumulated slights perceived by Muselier. Having just returned from Saint-Pierre and Miquelon, where he had had some time to reflect upon his position within the Free French movement, he resigned from his political post as commissioner but proclaimed his intention to retain his military appointment as commander of the navy.

Three months of confused discussions and veiled threats between the two men followed, with various intermediaries, including British naval and political authorities, seeking to avoid a public rift between their Free French allies.

It was to no avail, and de Gaulle won the confrontation. First placing Muselier on extended leave, he appointed Philippe Auboyneau to the French National Committee as commissioner for the navy on 5 March 1941. De Gaulle then put Muselier on a reserve status of sorts, "withdrawn from active service but available for operations." The latter refused to accept this decision and turned down an appointment to a new post, inspector general of the Free French Forces, fearing—rightly—that it would be a purely honorific appointment without actual powers. Muselier then recklessly went so far as hinting of his ability to bring the FNFL into open dissidence, still fighting on the side of the Allies but no longer taking orders from de Gaulle. This intrigue proved too much, even for Muselier's remaining supporters within the Free French movement and in British circles. De Gaulle brought the confrontation to a close by fully retiring the vice admiral on 30 June 1942.[85] In his postwar memoirs, de Gaulle dismissively questioned Muselier's judgment: "The Admiral had a kind of double personality. As a sailor he gave proof of capacities which deserved high consideration and to which the organisation of our small naval forces was largely due. But he was periodically possessed by a sort of fidgets, which impelled him to intrigue. . . . A few days later this admiral, who had done much for our Navy, notified me that his collaboration with Free France was finished. I was sorry for his sake."[86]

In this statement, the leader of *la France libre* simultaneously denounced the clumsy politician and praised the accomplished sailor. Indeed, Muselier had played a critical role in the earliest years of the nascent Free French movement, largely implementing his vision in terms of putting to sea the most effective means in the most efficient way. The sheer will he showed, in the dark days that followed the Armistice and Operation Catapult, in assembling a small but capable fleet proved essential to de Gaulle's rise during the war years and the eventual rebuilding of France's sea power. Muselier's chosen replacement as commander of the FNFL demonstrated that clearly by pursuing remarkably similar policies afterwards.

Philippe Auboyneau first saw service at sea during the last year of the Great War and continued to serve with distinction until June 1940, when he found himself stranded in Alexandria with Force X. Within a month, he organized his escape from the battleship *Lorraine* and rallied to de Gaulle in London.[87] Though a mere *capitaine de frégate* (commander), Auboyneau was one of the most senior officers to join the FNFL that summer, and he took command of *Le Triomphant*, the first French destroyer brought back into service that fall. Promoted to *capitaine de vaisseau* (captain) in 1941, he assumed responsibility for all FNFL forces then operating in the Pacific until his urgent recall to Great Britain in the wake of Muselier's resignation, which also entailed his promotion to the rank of *contre-amiral* (rear admiral). Politically savvy and attuned to the requirement for compromise with allies—be they French or British—Auboyneau proved much more effective in dealing with the imperious de Gaulle and the reluctant sea lords, but he also retained Muselier's single-minded focus on the development Free French sea power.

Although they came to despise each other, de Gaulle and Muselier proved capable of adopting an approach that balanced implied dependency and proclaimed autonomy for their forces. This effort can hardly be called a fulsome naval policy but served the FFL well. Muselier found himself forced to take on older French and British vessels and, in due course, new constructions at a rate dictated as much by the vagaries of FNFL recruitment and RN dockyard availability as by that of a comprehensive rearmament plan. Six practices came to shape naval matters within the Anglo–Free French relationship: (1) refurbishing former French ships for use by Free French crews; (2) transferring existing and new British warships for manning by French sailors; (3) upgrading FNFL units as war fighting at sea evolved; (4) training French sailors in British establishments and seagoing units; (5) sustaining logistical and financial support by the British to the French; and (6) employing French assets under British operational control while they remained under French national command. De Gaulle and Muselier also understood the value of committing their best vessels to alliance tasks and assigning older French units to national tasks such as rallying isolated colonies. All of these practices left a legacy of enduring precedents.

In that sense, as equivocal as it may have been, the assistance of Great Britain to de Gaulle's navy at the dawn of the Free French movement proved critical to the rise of *la France libre*. But it also shaped relations between France and its allies for the remainder of the war and beyond, as discussed throughout the following chapters. More immediately, the Royal Navy continued dedicating appreciable resources to fostering the FNFL into a small but effective organization while the Vichy navy carried on its path of atrophy. The November 1942 Anglo-American landings in French North Africa would inflict even more losses on that hollowed shell, culminating in the Toulon scuttling three weeks later that seemingly plunged the remnants of the Marine nationale into oblivion. It remained to be seen whether the precedents set under the Anglo–Free French framework could revert this fate as a new actor, the United States, burst onto the scene.

CHAPTER 2

LAYING THE FOUNDATIONS FOR REARMAMENT

"The Americans Have Landed!"

A trouser-less U.S. Army major general Mark W. Clark stood wet and shivering on an isolated Algerian beach late in the evening of Thursday, 22 October 1942. He and a small team of American staff officers and British commandos had just returned to the landing located next to the small fishing village of Cherchell, ninety kilometers west of Algiers. They had battled heavy surf when trying to leave in fragile two-man collapsible canoes known as "folbots." Clark's uniform pants and a belt of heavy gold coins were missing as he had packed them at the bottom of his small craft, expecting a rough ride but underestimating the force of the waves crashing onto the beach in the middle of the night. The group's precipitated attempt had followed a hurried escape from the nearby house where they were meeting in secrecy with Vichy officers and diplomat Robert D. Murphy, U.S. minister to French North Africa.

The daylong discussions broke when an informer phoned in that the police were about to raid the house, suspicious of the activities taking place there. After hiding in the basement wine cellar while the French authorities searched upstairs, the Anglo-American team rushed down to the beach and failed in their first attempt to row out to sea. They then waited for the weather to abate and eventually crossed the surf and reembarked in the Royal Navy submarine *Seraph*, which had surreptitiously landed them in the same location the previous night. Operation Flagpole ended with the usually sharply dressed American general wearing the rough cloth of peasant's pants lent him by one of the French conspirators. The submarine left the Algerian coast undetected, setting course for Gibraltar as the Anglo-American party rejoiced, feeling their mission was a success.

Clark was deputy to Lieutenant General Dwight D. Eisenhower, supreme commander of the Allied Expeditionary Force, who was responsible for the planning and execution of Operation Torch, the Anglo-American landings in French Morocco and Algeria. Clark's main interlocutor at Cherchell, Brigadier Charles Mast, had assured him that Vichy forces in North Africa would first put up a token resistance and then quickly defect to the Allied cause. Famed general Henri Giraud, once clandestinely exfiltrated from southern France, would stand ready to take command of the operation and rally the French military and the civilian population. Clark remained guarded in his replies, if not disingenuous. He prevaricated on the role of Giraud (whom the Allies did not envision taking command of Anglo-American troops), the timing of the assault (by then set to take place in just over a fortnight while Mast believed it would only occur months later), and the size of the invasion force (Clark suggested half a million troops, a far cry from the 107,000 who landed on 8 November).[1] But he also relayed a clear and potentially massive commitment to France on behalf of the United States.

General George C. Marshall, chief of staff of the U.S. Army, communicated significant strategic guidance to Eisenhower and Clark in the days leading up to Operation Flagpole. On behalf of his political master, President Franklin D. Roosevelt, Marshall directed that the American emissary "should state . . . the U.S. will furnish equipment for French Forces which will operate against the Axis."[2] This matter-of-fact but momentous pledge—given that nearly 300,000 European and indigenous Vichy troops were garrisoned in French North and West Africa—clenched the deal, allowing Eisenhower's deputy to transmit this succinct report once safely back in Gibraltar: "Discussion followed general lines previously anticipated. Giraud will be contacted by Mast with favorable decision expected by Tuesday. All questions settled satisfactorily except time of assumption of supreme command by French. Valuable intelligence data obtained which will be disseminated to commanders. Our plan of operations appears to be sound."[3]

Another line in that same report would prove much more problematic, however: "Initial resistance by French navy and coastal defenses indicated by naval information which also indicates that this resistance will fall off rapidly as our forces land." As Eisenhower's armada approached the shores of Morocco and Algeria at dawn on 8 November 1942, the Vichy navy did resist, but such opposition did not cease until the Anglo-Americans had inflicted grievous losses on the naval forces based in North Africa, the last such violent confrontation between French and Allied forces during World War II. In Algiers, two shore batteries manned by sailors continued firing throughout the first day, only knocked out of action by gun and aerial bombardment in the late afternoon. Two submarines, the *Caïman* and the *Marsouin*, immediately sailed out but were soon detected by British units and heavily depth-charged until they broke off to escape to Toulon, in metropolitan France. Meanwhile, fighting to the west took on an even more violent turn.

A large force of Vichy ships and submarines left Mers el-Kébir and Oran that morning, only to be quickly overwhelmed by a torrent of gunfire and aerial assault, leaving the sloop *La Surprise* as well as destroyers *Tramontane* and *Tornade* sunk while *Typhon* was badly mauled but able to return to port later that day. Submarines *Argonaute* and *Actéon* were soon lost with all hands, and another (*Fresnel*) eventually escaped the heavy barrage of depth charges, setting off for Toulon. On 9 November the local naval commander, Rear Admiral André Rioult, ordered another sortie, only to see the heavy destroyer *Épervier* set ablaze and beached while *Typhon* once again turned back to find refuge in port under heavy fire. Following the loss of 347 sailors in two days, Rioult admitted defeat that evening and ordered the scuttling of his remaining units in port, resulting in the sinking of *Typhon*, four submarines, and seven small patrol boats.

The heaviest fighting took place off Morocco, where the Vichy fleet was second in size only to the one based in Toulon. Landings north and south of Casablanca were accompanied by a heavy bombardment of the naval base and the adjacent airfield by an American force composed of the battleship *Massachusetts*, the heavy cruisers *Augusta*, *Brooklyn*, and *Tuscaloosa* as well as the aircraft carrier *Ranger*, the smaller escort carrier *Suwannee*, and several destroyers. Vichy coastal batteries had fired first but ineffectively, and

U.S. Navy return fire quickly disabled those guns as well as a French heavy destroyer, two smaller ones, three submarines, and three merchant ships in the port of Casablanca. Vice Admiral François-Félix Michelier, commander of all naval forces in Morocco, ordered Rear Admiral Gervais de Lafond to take his 2nd Light Cruiser Squadron to sea for a gallant but doomed sortie that led to the loss of the cruiser *Primauguet* as well as the destroyers *Albatros*, *Fougueux*, *Milan*, and *Boulonnais*. Heavily damaged, destroyers *Frondeur* and *Brestois* made it back into port but capsized later that night despite ongoing damage control efforts, leaving *Alcyon* the only ship from the group still in fighting trim.

The next day witnessed renewed resistance ashore by mixed units of soldiers, sailors, and air personnel thrown together overnight to block the advance onto Casablanca led by Major General George S. Patton. The mercurial cavalry officer called for a final gun and aerial assault on the port on 10 November. The Americans focused the attack on the battleship *Jean Bart*, immobilized at her berth with one turret of four 15-inch guns still capable of engaging ships at sea. She soon settled on the shallow bottom, upright but with her upper decks ripped open by two 1,000-pound bombs dropped by aircraft from the *Ranger*. Seven other warships and five submarines were also quickly disabled during this last demonstration of overwhelming force. By the time the guns fell silent across French North Africa, on 11 November 1942, the Vichy navy accounted for the bulk of the nearly 1,500 French who lost their lives standing up for Pétain against the Anglo-American assault. Another 2,000 were wounded, while the Allied losses stood at 500 dead and 700 injured.[4] At least this episode did not result in another occurrence of fratricidal infighting as the Forces françaises libres did not participate in Torch.

Charles de Gaulle did not even know of the assault. By the fall of 1942, the likelihood of a landing in North Africa was obvious to friends and foes alike. Nevertheless, secrecy about the exact timing of the operation worried the Allies, and FFL headquarters suffered from a bad reputation regarding its ability to guard sensitive information. Planners in Washington and London were also concerned with the prospect of serious disturbances—if not outright civil war—breaking out if troops sporting the *croix de Lorraine* paraded as victors in the streets of Algiers and Casablanca in the aftermath of the landings.[5] British prime minister Winston Churchill had the disagreeable duty to meet with the shocked Free French leader after the landings to explain why he had been kept in the dark.[6] Churchill had indicated to Roosevelt that he wished to inform de Gaulle the day before the landings as a gesture of courtesy, and he proposed to offer him the trusteeship of Madagascar as a compensation for the exclusion of *la France libre* from North Africa. On 5 November Roosevelt curtly refused that de Gaulle be informed in advance and disagreed with the Madagascar proposition. He only accepted that Churchill tell him the Americans were behind the decision to exclude his movement from the operation.

Such exclusion demonstrated the complexities that continued to bedevil the Anglo–Free French relationship in 1942 and foreshadowed difficulties ahead as the United States joined the fight. The Roosevelt administration abandoned its recognition of the Pétain regime but continued to ignore de Gaulle. The Americans espoused a "third way" to facilitate the mobilization of French forces in support of the Allied war effort. General Henri Giraud was eventually promoted to take on that role. This domineering vision would fail over the long term, but the herculean effort to rearm France's combatants who joined the Allied camp eventually succeeded despite continued personal mistrust, conflicting strategic priorities, and clashing ambitions among American, British, and French political and military leaders. These factors all came to the fore during the dramatic weeks that followed the landings. To understand this intricate outcome, however, one must first recall the complexities that evolved from the reticent approach adopted by a neutral America confronted with a divided France in the wake of the Armistice.

Early Franco-U.S. Relations

The fall of France in June 1940 left the Americans facing a geopolitical conundrum similar to that of Great Britain but different in its circumstances. Both liberal democracies relied on the use of the seas to access worldwide markets for their prosperity and link their overseas territories. Both Churchill and Roosevelt viewed the dominance of continental Europe by Germany and the expansion of Imperial Japan in the Pacific as fundamental threats to their national interest.[7] Both perceived each other as mutually supportive.

Churchill recognized that "the U.S. held the key to Britain's survival," and Roosevelt believed that "America was obliged to make every effort to prevent Great Britain's defeat."[8] But the United States was not at war that summer and did not face the threat of immediate invasion that Great Britain did. On the one hand, Prime Minister Churchill wanted France to continue fighting because he needed an ally to keep those forces outside of occupied France actively engaged in the hostilities at his side. Churchill's support to Charles de Gaulle and *la France libre* was calculated. Roosevelt, on the other hand, merely needed to keep French colonies and the fleet out of Germany's grasp for the time being. The American president would not tolerate an assembly of forces that could overwhelm the British Isles before he had time to convince the American people to abandon its isolationism. His endorsement of a neutral France sought to prevent active collaboration with the Axis and dissuade France from joining hostilities on Germany's side against Great Britain.

If anything, Roosevelt believed the United States needed to support the Pétain regime in order to reinforce the Old Marshal's will to face down future demands on the part of the Axis.[9] Vichy's brittle control over France's colonial empire came to the fore in the very first months of the new government as Japan sought to make inroads in northern Indochina to support immediate operations in China and, potentially, a future advance into Southeast Asia.[10] Throughout the summer of 1940, Japanese authorities increased pressure on the French colony, by then cut off from metropolitan France with negligible forces of its own: 12,000 European troops and another 30,000 ill-trained indigenous forces, sixty airplanes, the light cruiser *Lamotte-Picquet*, two smaller sloops, and a few more antiquated gunboats. In August, the local governor, Vice Admiral Jean Decoux, made a first concession by formally acknowledging Japan's "preeminent position in the Far East" and in September agreed to the stationing of Japanese forces in the Tonkin (the northernmost of the Indochina provinces, abutting the border with China).[11] In exchange for these concessions, Decoux obtained the recognition by Japan of Vichy's nominal sovereignty over Indochina, but these events greatly alarmed American military planners and President Roosevelt himself.

Whether in the Pacific or closer to Europe, the potential for Axis powers to take control of French overseas possessions could tip the overall strategic balance, offsetting the United States' ability to support Great Britain, if not threatening the security of continental America itself. Much was made during the fall of 1940 of the potential for Dakar as a launch point for German long-range bombers capable of reaching the eastern seaboard via airfields in South American countries friendly to the Axis. The West African colony, as well as French territories in the Caribbean, could serve as bases for Kriegsmarine surface raiders and submarines.[12] As disturbing were indications that the Vichy regime could turn away from neutrality to active collaboration with Germany at any moment.

On 24 October 1940 a photograph of Pétain shaking hands with Adolf Hitler in the Montoire-sur-le-Loire train station (two hundred kilometers southwest of Paris) circulated around the world and was perceived as symbolic of the rising influence of Vichy foreign affairs minister Pierre Laval. The meeting took place during the führer's return from his visit to the caudillo of Spain, Francisco Franco. Laval, who openly promoted the integration of an independent France into a German-dominated European order, had actively lobbied both Pétain and German authorities to arrange the brief stop in Montoire.[13] Roosevelt outlined his thoughts on the matter in a letter addressed to retired Admiral William D. Leahy on 17 November 1940, calling on him to take up the appointment of U.S. ambassador to Vichy:

> We are confronting an increasingly serious situation in France because of the possibility that one element of the present French government may persuade Marshal Pétain to enter into agreements with Germany which will facilitate the efforts of the Axis powers against Great Britain. There is even the possibility that France may actually engage in a war against Great Britain and in particular, that the French Fleet may be utilized under the control of Germany. We need in France at this time an Ambassador who can gain the confidence of Marshal Pétain, who at the present moment is the one powerful element of the French Government who is standing firm against selling out to Germany.[14]

This missive highlighted that Roosevelt shared with Churchill a deep concern with the fate of Pétain's navy, especially its larger, heavier units. The British air raid against Italian warships in the port of Taranto had taken place just a week earlier (11–12 November 1940), but Pearl Harbor and the major aircraft carrier engagements of the Pacific war had yet to occur, seemingly leaving the large "gun carrier" as queen of the battle at sea.[15] Thus, even after the attack against Mers el-Kébir by the Royal Navy, the Vichy fleet could still be perceived as a strong opponent, or at least capable of tipping the scales against Great Britain's naval supremacy in European waters were its largest ships to join forces with the Kriegsmarine and Italy's Regia marina. Admittedly, its units were dispersed and their readiness difficult to assess.

The British knew they had inflicted some damage on the battleship *Richelieu* in Dakar during Operation Catapult, and the fact that her sister ship *Jean Bart* had found refuge in Casablanca before completing her fitting out and sea trials was well known. Nevertheless, neither British nor American authorities could clearly gauge the ability of the French to progress repairs on these ships in 1940 from such remote locations. They were also aware that Toulon still hosted the Forces de haute mer—the High Sea Forces—which included the battleships *Provence* and *Dunkerque* (both damaged at Mers el-Kébir but transferred to Toulon for repairs) and *Strasbourg* (which had escaped Mers el-Kébir unscathed). As late as in the days leading up to Operation Torch, Churchill could still be heard stating dramatically: "If I could meet Darlan, much as I hate him, I would cheerfully crawl on my hands and knees for a mile if by doing so I could get him to bring that fleet of his into the circle of Allied forces."[16]

British and American naval planners could not dismiss the possibility of these capital ships—and their powerful escorts of heavy cruisers and destroyers—eventually resuming wartime readiness and breaking out of their respective ports to meet in the Atlantic or the Mediterranean. Reflective of this apprehension was the "Dudley North Affair" in the fall of 1940, when the British Admiralty relieved the flag officer commanding North Atlantic Station, Admiral Dudley North, for failing to intercept a Vichy squadron (Force Y—cruisers *Montcalm*, *Georges Leygues*, and *Gloire*; destroyers *Le Malin*, *Le Fantasque*, and *L'Audacieux*) that transited unchallenged from Toulon to the Atlantic through the Strait of Gibraltar in September.[17] The Roosevelt administration, in November 1940, went as far as offering to purchase the battleships *Richelieu* and *Jean Bart* from Pétain.[18] The old *maréchal* demurred, replying that such an initiative would violate the terms of the armistice, but he reiterated his guarantee to the American president that French ships would never be used offensively against the British. In contrast to this focus on Vichy's fleet, Roosevelt's indifference to the Free French movement continued.

De Gaulle's failure at Dakar in September 1940, the imperial ambitions he seemed to hold through the relentless pursuit of the allegiance of French colonies, and his ostentatious behavior as the seemingly self-selected savior of France contributed to undermining the leader of *la France libre* in the eyes of key American leaders, such as the president and Secretary of State Cordell Hull.[19] Inept Free French representation in the United States only compounded the issue when compared with the experienced and professional Vichy officials established in France's embassy in Washington. On the one hand, a disparate league of autonomous groups—collaborating loosely under the banner of "France Forever"—dedicated tremendous energy to a vigorous media campaign which eventually turned American public opinion in favor of the seemingly valiant and tenacious Free French movement.[20] On the other hand, a similarly loose approach allowed a wide range of figures to lobby administration officials from the summer of 1940 into 1941, badly undermining the FFL's claim of forming a credible and legitimate movement representing the united will of the French people. As surmised by Undersecretary of State Sumner Welles when the British ambassador in Washington made a case on the General's behalf in July 1941: "I told the ambassador that I would be glad to consider the views advanced by [de Gaulle] but that at first glance it seemed to me that it would be difficult for the United States to maintain diplomatic relations with Vichy and, what was far more important, cooperative relations with the authorities in North Africa if anything in the nature of official recognition were to be given by this government to the Free French Committee."[21]

But faith in Pétain also eroded through the course of 1941. The Paris Protocols agreed to in May by Vichy and German representatives opened the door to active military cooperation such as the use of French airfields in the Levant. For many this agreement constituted the tipping point that saw the regime go from seemingly neutral to actively collaborationist.[22] As well, Germany obtained transit rights along the Rhône for Kriegsmarine shallow-draft patrol boats and minesweepers to move through the free zone into the Mediterranean. Tunisian ports and railways were used to transport German supplies to Rommel's Afrika Korps, while the latter also gained from the direct transfer of French guns, ammunition, and trucks from Algeria to be used against the British Eighth Army in Egypt.[23] The trend was confirmed in April 1942 with the return of Pierre Laval to head the Vichy government, putting an end to any hope the Roosevelt administration may have had in the Old Marshal and his regime.[24]

Military necessity also contributed to the beginning of a slow rapprochement between the United States and Free France. As Axis forces nearly closed the Mediterranean route to Allied shipping through 1941, the most expedient path to deliver Lend-Lease material from America to the beleaguered British in Egypt was through French Equatorial Africa, controlled by de Gaulle forces. A military commission from the United States was established in Libreville in August, and airfields set up with American aid from Gabon to Chad to allow ferrying aircraft disembarked in Free French ports. Hostilities in the Pacific then brought France's sleepy Micronesian possessions to the forefront in early 1942. New Caledonia and Polynesia, already rallied to de Gaulle, assumed a prominent role, placed as they were at the outer edge of the Japanese advance and along the vital lines of communications between North America and Australia. American consuls established themselves in the islands to oversee distribution of economic assistance in the form of loans, food, and supplies for civilian use.

Military strategists included the use of Free French territories as part of plans to roll back the Axis, both in the Pacific and in Africa.[25] Even before Pearl Harbor, President Roosevelt announced a dramatic policy shift when he stated on 11 November 1941: "I hereby find the defense of any French territory under the control of the French Volunteer Force (Free French) is vital to the defense of the United States."[26] And yet such recognition remained purely military in its nature, whereas the politics of legitimacy continued to shape American diplomacy. In that same statement, Roosevelt indicated that assistance to the Free French would continue to be disbursed "by way of re-transfer from His Majesty's Government in the United Kingdom or their Allies." As Secretary of State Cordell Hull reiterated in his postwar memoirs: "We would give them material assistance wherever necessary in their effort to combat the Axis. We would keep in touch with them through our consular representatives. But we would not recognize them as a Government."[27]

In other words, neither economic assistance nor military cooperation meant political recognition. President Roosevelt rejected on 10 April 1942 another request to negotiate a formal Lend-Lease agreement with Free France.[28] Meanwhile, the Roosevelt administration continued to lose faith in Pétain. Even William Leahy, a forceful supporter of *le maréchal* at the beginning of his ambassadorship in Vichy, became skeptical of Pétain's ability to contain, let alone refuse, German demands over the long run. He reported to Roosevelt in November 1941:

> While the great inarticulate and leaderless mass of the French people remain hopeful of a British victory and continue to hope that America will rescue them from their present predicament without their doing anything for themselves, the Government of France today, headed by a feeble, frightened old man surrounded by self-seeking conspirators is altogether controlled by a group which, probably for its own safety, is devoted to the Axis philosophy. . . . It seems necessary to reluctantly relinquish what was perhaps always a faint hope that it might be possible for me through personal relations and pertinent advice to give some semblance of backbone to a jellyfish.[29]

Caught between Pétain in Vichy and de Gaulle in London, the Roosevelt administration set about looking for a "Third Man" in 1942, one who could rally North Africa against the Axis and oversee the considerable military buildup that would ensue. The benefactor of such Allied largesse would likely find himself in a position to take a leading role in the liberation of metropolitan France and dominate the country's politics after the war, at least until conditions were right for the French people "to express their desires unswayed by any form of coercion," as wished by Roosevelt.[30] Suitable candidates were few in the lead-up to the landings in Algeria and Morocco. The race for undisputed recognition that ensued greatly complicated American efforts to rearm the French in the months following that first clandestine meeting in Cherchell on 22 October 1942.

The Unexpected Third Man

The confidence of the Americans in the ability of General Henri Giraud to rally French North Africa appeared well founded at the time. Born in modest circumstances in Paris in 1879, graduating from Saint-Cyr in 1900, Giraud had served on repeated occasions in a variety of North African posts and made a name for himself during the Great War.[31] Although badly wounded and captured in late August 1914, he had escaped two months later from the German hospital where he was still recovering from his wounds and returned to combat duties on the Western Front. He served with distinction for the remainder of the war and rose quickly through the ranks thereafter. A general at the beginning of World War II, Giraud was ordered to rally the shattered 9th Army in May 1940, but German troops captured him just days after he took command. Escaping again in April 1942, he found refuge in the *zone libre* and swore allegiance to Marshal Pétain.[32] However, he refused to take a post in the collaborationist government of Premier Laval while denouncing the Free French as dissidents. Thus, he presented a unique blend of independence vis-à-vis Vichy and London, providing him the credibility to persuade French troops and civilians in North Africa to join hands across France's political divide under his leadership.

The ability of Giraud as Roosevelt's chosen Third Man turned out to be moot in the immediate aftermath of the Allied landings with the presence in Algiers of an unexpected challenger: *amiral de la flotte* (fleet admiral, a unique five-star appointment) François Darlan, commander in chief of Vichy's armed forces and official dauphin to Pétain. He remains to this day one of the most enigmatic and controversial French figures of World War II.[33] Born to a low-level republican politician in 1881, he graduated from the École navale in 1902, a classmate of his Free French opponent, Vice Admiral Émile Muselier. He saw active service at sea until the Great War, then spent the bulk of that conflict on land, commanding heavy naval gun batteries deployed on the Western Front. The interwar period witnessed his meteoric rise as he regularly returned to Paris between sea duties, serving in a series of high-profile positions at naval headquarters and in the offices of successive navy ministers. Darlan actively shaped the modernization of the fleet through these years and made useful connections with politicians of both the Left and the Right through the short-lived cabinets of the Third Republic. He eventually rose to the post of chief of the General Naval Staff, effectively commander in chief of the Marine nationale, on 1 January 1937.

Darlan was still in that post when Pétain brought him into his first cabinet as minister for the navy and the merchant fleet on 16 June 1940, while allowing him to retain his operational role as commander in chief. Initially opposed to a cease-fire and negotiations with the Germans, Darlan quickly rallied to support the armistice and assumed a growing influence in Vichy circles until Pétain appointed him head of government in February 1941. From there on, the admiral clearly espoused the marshal's reactionary program of *révolution nationale* and actively promoted collaborationist policies, as when he led the delegation that negotiated the dubious Paris Protocols of May 1941.[34] Darlan used his authority to place sailors in key positions throughout Vichy's military structure and civil administration, leveraging the loyalty of serving naval officers, vast numbers of whom had been made redundant in the wake of Operation Catapult and the immobilization of the fleet. They in turn actively promoted and implemented the policies of the Vichy regime, leading one historian to quip "that while two-thirds of [the] country was in the hands of the enemy, the rest was occupied by the Navy."[35]

In part under German pressure and as a result of Vichy internal politics, Pétain recalled Pierre Laval to the post of premier in April 1942, letting go of Darlan. This move led some American observers such as Admiral Leahy and the diplomat Robert Murphy to envisage the fleet admiral as a potential interlocutor instead of the weakened marshal.[36] Nevertheless, Pétain retained Darlan as his designated successor as head of state and even made the sailor commander in chief of all Vichy armed forces—navy, army, and air force—on that same occasion.[37] This continued and very public affiliation with the discredited Vichy regime seemingly disqualified Darlan as a credible alternative in the weeks leading up to Operation Torch. And yet an unexpected twist of fate put Pétain's favorite subordinate back in contention to lead French North Africa to the Allied side on the very morning of the landings.

Admiral Darlan had been in and out of Algeria for the preceding three weeks. He performed an inspection tour of French North and West Africa and then attended to his son Alain, hospitalized in Algiers for a sudden attack of life-threatening poliomyelitis in mid-October.[38] Although the Allies were aware of his movements, the presence of Darlan in Africa did not raise undue alarm since French conspirators were meant to arrest the highest-ranking military and civilian authorities in Algeria and Morocco on the morning of the landings. They failed to do so, however, and the commander in chief maintained his ability to communicate by telephone with subordinates across North Africa and with Vichy, via a submarine cable, as Allied troops landed ashore. Forty-eight hours of frantic negotiations ensued between French leaders in North Africa, U.S. diplomats in Algiers and Casablanca, Anglo-American generals and admirals on and off the beaches of Morocco and Algeria, and Eisenhower and his staff in Gibraltar as well as Pétain himself and his closest advisers in Vichy.

Darlan prevaricated at first and refused to issue instructions for French forces to either resist or lay down their arms. Local authorities reacted on their own while he alerted Vichy to the invasion and sought guidance from Pétain. Darlan then relented and ordered a cease-fire limited to the Algiers region in the evening of 8 November, but stout resistance continued the next day off Oran and Casablanca, even as Giraud and Clark finally set foot in Algeria. Meanwhile, German troops started pouring into Tunisia. They quickly took the French protectorate when the local commander, Admiral Jean-Pierre Esteva, surrendered his forces without a fight as instructed by Pétain in an attempt to mitigate Hitler's reaction to Operation Torch.[39] Darlan eventually agreed to the terms of a cease-fire put forward by Clark for the whole of French North Africa late on 10 November. Fighting ceased in Morocco the next day, following the hopeless defense put up by the Vichy navy off Oran and Casablanca as recounted earlier. To everyone's surprise, Roosevelt's Third Man turned out to be Darlan himself.

Protracted negotiations facilitated by General Clark led on 13 November to an agreement between the French factions.[40] Darlan took the title of high commissioner for French Africa, responsible for coordinating all political, civil, and military affairs, while Giraud assumed the role of military commander in chief under Darlan. Controversially, most Vichy figures—civilian administrators and military leaders—remained in place while those French conspirators who had sought to facilitate the Allied landings found themselves isolated from power. As for de Gaulle, he remained alone in London.[41] And yet the bullets of a French assassin removed the admiral a mere six weeks later, ensuring that the name Darlan remains shrouded in controversy to this day. In the words of French historian François Kersaudy, "Few assassinations have been denounced with so much indignation in public and yet welcomed with so much relief in private."[42]

In the afternoon of 24 December 1942 a young civilian, Fernand Bonnier de la Chapelle, simply walked into Darlan's headquarters and waited for the admiral to return from lunch. Upon his arrival, de la Chappelle drew out a pistol and shot Darlan at point-blank range. Sentinels immediately seized the shooter, and a military court condemned the accused to death the next day. A firing squad executed the sentence in the morning of 26 December, while his victim was buried with full military honors later that afternoon. The assassin never divulged his motives or sponsors, beyond a hatred of Darlan and what the Vichy admiral stood for. The balance of evidence available today supports the theory that the plot was initiated by yet another faction that had arrived surreptitiously in Algiers in the wake of the Anglo-American landings: monarchists hoping to restore the claimant to the French throne, Henri d'Orléans, Count of Paris, then in exile in Spanish Morocco.[43] But no such consensus existed at the time, as put succinctly by Kersaudy: "Roosevelt suspects de Gaulle, Churchill accuses the Germans, Giraud thinks the Gaullists are behind it, the OSS [Office of Strategic Services, the wartime predecessor of the CIA] believes the monarchists did it, and de Gaulle sways between the Giraud camp and the Americans as the likely organisers."[44]

Regardless of these mutual suspicions, all were seized with the pressing requirement to agree on a successor to unite the former Vichy territories in Africa while working closely with the Allies to rebuild the new Armée d'Afrique, as the French army based in Africa was known. The Imperial Council, a committee formed by Darlan on 2 December to assist him in managing French North African affairs, assembled immediately after the admiral's funeral on 26 December.[45] Following a lengthy debate, conscious that the Allies would not accept another figure too closely affiliated with Pétain, the participants agreed to make Giraud "High Commissioner in

French Africa and Command-in-Chief of the French Army, Navy and Air Force."[46] Thus, Roosevelt's quest for a Third Man had come full circle, with his pick finally in charge. The solution left many issues unresolved: what of the former Vichy officials that remained in position of authority across North Africa, what of those colonies that had yet to rally to Giraud, what of de Gaulle and the Free French movement? Nevertheless, Giraud appeared poised to lead French Africa into the fight on the Allied side. As importantly, he would be the man to oversee implementation of the rearmament blueprint proposed by the French conspirators at Cherchell and endorsed by Clark on behalf of the Allies, the Mast Plan.

Grandiose visions of American arms and military equipment flowing across the Atlantic to assist France in her struggle against Germany had long predated the discussions at Cherchell. In the immediate wake of the Munich crisis of September 1938, French negotiators convinced the Roosevelt administration to facilitate the purchase of two hundred Curtiss P-36 fighters and Glenn Martin bombers from American manufacturers, an order increased to one thousand units just months later. Acquisition of U.S. matériel continued right up to the fall of France.[47] Symbolically, the French aircraft carrier *Béarn*, ferrying one hundred American planes destined for France, found herself mid-Atlantic in the days leading up to the armistice, in company with the training cruiser *Jeanne d'Arc*. Darlan instructed both ships to find refuge in Martinique and wait for further instructions.[48] There they remained for the next three years, having disembarked the crated aircraft, which slowly rotted away in the Caribbean sun.

Meanwhile, some Vichy officers set about formulating rearmament plans based on support by the United States. They sincerely believed that the Roosevelt administration would come to France's succor at some future point, and U.S. officials, while remaining uncommitted, did not dissuade them as the planning effort coalesced around the Algiers conspirators.[49] Successive iterations resulted in the Mast Plan presented to General Clark at Cherchell. The document stated that, within a month of the Allied landings, French authorities could muster enough trained personnel to form a battle force (*corps de bataille*) of eight mechanized infantry divisions and two armored divisions. However, these units would require urgent rearmament with modern

American equipment to augment their firepower and mobility.[50] In a letter to General Giraud dated 2 November 1942 (trying to rally him to the Allied side), Murphy confirmed that the Roosevelt administration would extend "the Lend-Lease Act to the requisitions for material from the United States intended to give the French Army the means to participate in the common struggle."[51] Brigadier Mast and his staff then refined the plan to include additional logistics, artillery, and air assets (fighter-bombers and transport) to make the *corps de bataille* a more flexible and autonomous formation, although entirely focused on land operations.

Such "army centricity" in the days leading up to the Allied landings was to be expected given the composition of the dissident group behind the Mast Plan, with only one naval officer present at Cherchell. The Vichy navy was still viewed as a potent force at that time, and few expected the fleet's destruction through the course of the following month, first by the Allies off the shores of North Africa and then at the hands of French sailors in the final suicidal act of 27 November 1942 in Toulon. On that fateful day, German troops that had crossed into France's free zone in response to the North African landings pounced on Vichy's last metropolitan base not yet occupied by Axis forces, intent on seizing the French ships and submarines intact. Taken by surprise and incapable of repulsing the Wehrmacht assault from landward, French crews failed to raise steam in time to escape to sea. Local commanders ordered the immediate scuttling of all vessels at their berth. Some 248,800 tons of capital ships, escorts, auxiliaries, and submarines went down, more than ninety vessels making up a third of the naval strength held by France at the beginning of the war.[52] French sea power had reached its nadir in spectacular fashion.

This drama dealt a terrible blow to Darlan. Persuaded ever since the armistice that the fleet, *his* fleet, would follow him wherever his allegiance took him, he did not expect that the oath sworn to Pétain would prevail in the minds of his fellow Vichy admirals, in Toulon, and among other French flotillas isolated overseas.[53] The few torpedo craft and gunboats left in Indochina would have made little difference, admittedly, neutralized as they were under the close surveillance of Japanese forces that had moved south in the summer of 1941.[54] However, the refusal by Admiral Georges Robert and forces based in the Martinique to abandon Vichy, combined with a similar reaction by Vice Admiral René-Émile Godfroy's Force X in Alexandria, came as unexpected rebuffs to Darlan.[55] Also indicative of Darlan's limited influence, French West Africa only rallied as a result of the vigorous action of its civilian administrator, Governor General Pierre Boisson. He confronted the local military commanders who wished to remain loyal to Vichy. Boisson eventually prevailed and accepted on 22 November an accord negotiated directly with the Allies, after having extracted some important concessions from them.[56]

Regardless of how that rallying came about, French West Africa did provide Darlan with a strong naval force and extended his control to the naval base at Dakar, strategically positioned at the narrowest part of the Atlantic between Africa and South America. Although the battleship *Richelieu* could not be considered operational in view of the damages sustained at the hands of the British in 1940, ships of the former Force Y (cruisers *Montcalm*, *Georges Leygues*, and *Gloire*, and destroyer *Le Fantasque*) were available for immediate employment, despite their rudimentary radar and sonar equipment and their outdated antiair armament.[57] Such support would play an important role at this critical juncture of the war at sea, with 1942 proving an abysmal year for the Allies at sea—overstretched from the Atlantic to the Pacific and facing down the Italians in the Mediterranean. Churchill and the Admiralty had pressed for the urgent return to sea of those Marine nationale vessels that had found refuge in Great Britain in the summer of 1940, whether under the *croix de Lorraine* or the White Ensign. Rapidly bringing Darlan's fleet into the fight at the side of the Allies would prove as pressing in 1943, a goal that French and Anglo-American officials set about achieving immediately after Operation Torch.

From Darlan in Algiers to Giraud in Casablanca

The accord of 13 November had signified Allied recognition of Darlan as the French North African leader but provided precious few details on the practicalities of the "deal," including the process to integrate his forces in the fight against the Axis and execution of the Mast rearmament plan. Clark and Darlan immediately set about negotiating a more formal understanding reached on 22 November.[58] The preamble presented an ambitious commitment on the part of the signatories: "French forces will aid and support the forces of the United States and their allies to expel from the soil of Africa the common enemy, to liberate France and to restore integrally the French Empire."[59] This pledge appeared more generous than that between Churchill and de Gaulle on 7 August 1940. The British prime minister had avoided any specific reference to France's colonies, using vaguer terms in defining his commitment to "ensure the integral restoration of the independence and greatness of France."[60] Regarding naval forces, Darlan adroitly managed to maintain control of "his" fleet. Article IX may have stated that "all port facilities, harbor and naval installations . . . [were to] be placed intact at the disposal of the Commanding General, United States Army," but Article VII proposed a much more accommodating approach in the employment and support of French ships by the Allies: "French warships shall operate in close *cooperation* with the Commanding General, United States Army . . . for the accomplishment of the purpose set forth in the preamble hereof. Such warships will continue to fly the French flag and be placed under French command . . . and *will be provided with fuel and all necessary supplies* to enable them to become effective fighting units"[61] [Emphasis added].

In that sense, the agreement went further in committing the Allies to supporting Darlan's navy than Giraud's army, and British assistance to the Free French as there was no mention of operating under Allied control or the requirement to reimburse costs of supplies after the war. The Mast Plan did not appear in the text, nor did any of the clauses allude to supply or rearmament of land and air forces found in French North Africa. The matter of repairing or modernizing ships and submarines was also missing from the agreement, but it provided a solid enough base for former Vichy units to commence making a contribution to the fight. As commented approvingly by the British Admiralty, "there would be advantage both from a practical and a morale point of view in giving the French such operational employment as is possible in the circumstances."[62]

Within weeks, cruisers *Georges Leygues*, *Gloire*, and *Montcalm* rotated out of Dakar and Casablanca to replace Royal Navy and U.S. Navy units conducting anti-raider patrols in the Atlantic narrows between West Africa and

South America.[63] Sloops *Gazelle* and *Commandant Bory* joined the destroyer *Tempête* to form an escort group dedicated to fast American transatlantic convoys, while smaller vessels undertook the escort of French merchantmen too slow to transit at those speeds.[64] Other ships discharged the myriad of coastal defense duties along the shores of West and North Africa that the overstretched Anglo-American navies did not wish to take on.[65] French officers also joined Allied naval headquarters in Algeria, Morocco, and Gibraltar. In a manner similar to that of the Free French in England, they assisted in coordinating the integration into the Anglo-American scheme of operations of ships, submarines, and shore-based naval aviation assets that had survived the onslaught of Operation Torch.[66]

Darlan's fleet was just slightly ahead of the Free French navy in number hulls, with forty-five ships and submarines against de Gaulle's forty. It cut a more impressive figure in terms of tonnage, with 135,000 tons compared to a mere 26,000 for the Forces naval françaises libres. The difference lay in the makeup of these forces as Darlan's command included battleships and cruisers while de Gaulle's largest vessel remained the destroyer *La Combattante*. But the poor technical readiness of units isolated in Africa for three years, as well as the want of modern sensors and armament, undermined their fighting value. As concerning was the impracticality of rehabilitating the fleet using the meager national resources and infrastructure in the region, as reported later by a French historian:

> There were no technical services as the administration had always been centralized in the metropole. . . . There was a near total absence of technicians and, above all, no industrial infrastructure in North Africa. This meant no spare parts, no dry dock, very few munitions and torpedoes. . . . While the navy wished to assume its place in the liberation of France and play its part in regaining control of the Empire, it did not even have enough munitions to fight for more than a few months, nor the means to fabricate more. In other words, the French could not rearm by themselves. American aid was the only solution.[67]

By late December 1942 the situation appeared clear to those officers going briskly about their business in the French Africa admiralty newly established

Table 2.1: French Naval Strength in West and North Africa, 31 December 1942

Category	Vessel(s) Name	Combined Tonnage[a]	Remarks
Fast battleships	Richelieu, Jean Bart	70,000	Richelieu damaged in Dakar but main armament still operational Jean Bart out of action in Casablanca
Cruisers	Gloire, Georges Leygues, Montcalm	23,070	Gloire operational in Casablanca Georges Leygues and Montcalm operational in Dakar
Light cruisers, large destroyers reclassified as light cruisers by the Allies	Le Fantasque, Le Malin	4,900	Le Fantasque operational in Dakar Le Malin damaged in Casablanca
Destroyers	Simoun, Tempête, L'Alcyon	4,500	Simoun damaged in Casablanca Tempête and L'Alcyon operational in Casablanca
Colonial sloops (Avisos colonials)	Dumont d'Urville	2,000	Operational in Conakry (Guinea)
Minesweeping sloops (Avisos-dragueurs de mines)	Gazelle, Commandant Bory, Commandant Delage, La Boudeuse, La Gracieuse	3,150	La Boudeuse operational in Algiers Commandant Delage, La Gracieuse operational in Casablanca Gazelle, Commandant Bory operational in Dakar
Sloops (1st class) (Avisos de 1ère classe)	Calais	600	Operational in Dakar
Sloops (2nd class) (Avisos de 2e classe)	Tapageuse, Engageante	600	Both operational in Casablanca
Armed trawlers	L'Algéroise, La Sablaise, La Servanaise	1,800	La Servanaise operational in Casablanca L'Algéroise and La Sabalaise in reserve in Casablanca
Submarine chasers	Chasseur 2, Chasseur 3	260	Both operational in Oran
Submarines	Marsouin, Archimède, Argo, Le Glorieux, Le Centaure, Casabianca	9,000	Marsouin, Le Glorieux, Casabianca operational in Oran Archimède, Argo, Le Centaure operational in Dakar
Coastal submarines	Aréthuse, Antiope, Amazone, Atalante, Orphée, La Vestale, La Sultane, Perle	6,400	Aréthuse, Amazone operational in Oran Antiope, Atlante, Orphée operational in Casablanca La Vestale, La Sultane operational in Dakar Perle available but in reserve in Dakar
Submarine tender	Jules Verne	4,350	Operational in Dakar
Misc. auxiliaries[b]	Various	5,000	Various locations
Totals	**45**	**135,630**	**18.2% of the 1939 French fleet**

Notes

[a] Tonnage figures for submarines indicate submerged displacement.
[b] Miscellaneous auxiliaries do not include tugs and other small craft dedicated to harbor duties.

in Casablanca.[68] After a few days of fierce fighting and weeks of complex political maneuvering, their navy had rejoined the side of the Allies. The latter would willingly dedicate tremendous resources to rejuvenating the fleet, in line with the spirit of Cherchell and the agreement of 22 November. Their services would be necessary to redress the balance against the Axis at sea and eventually make an important contribution to the liberation of France. The death of Darlan had been regrettable, but Vice Admiral Michelier—the naval commander in Morocco at the time of the landings—now headed a unified *marine d'Afrique*, willing to serve under Giraud, whose star within Allied circles continued to rise. All that was needed to complete this shining vision was amalgamation of the Free French fleet into a truly reunited Marine nationale, which was bound to follow as the Americans devoted resources to Michelier's forces. They were wrong.

Bitter infighting continued to divide supporters of Giraud and de Gaulle into the next year. Neither man accepted to serve under the other, nor were their partisans willing to rally the opposite camp. Free French troops were fighting at the side of the British in Libya while former Vichy General Alphonse Juin led Giraud's army supporting the American advance into Tunisia. The FNFL, largely based in Great Britain, remained focused on the convoy battles in the North Atlantic and raiding across the Channel while Michelier's ships and submarines conducted coastal defense duties in the Mediterranean and off the shores of Western Africa. De Gaulle continued to vilify Giraud as heading an administration of "Vichyites" while the latter was hard-pressed to find alternate figures of suitable experience to replace them. This very public spat between the two French camps greatly complicated the planning of operations in North Africa as well as the viability of future operations on European soil. Roosevelt and Churchill set about resolving that issue once and for all at the upcoming Casablanca Conference.

Anglo-American political and military leaders met in Morocco to determine the course of strategy following the final defeat of the Axis in North Africa, expected within months. They sought to resolve fundamental differences between British strategists "who advocated a war of opportunity ending with a landing in France as the *coup de grâce* and the Americans who advocated a war of concentration beginning with a collision of forces."[69] Compromise ensued through a hectic round of formal meetings, alcohol-fueled dinners, and late-night arguments from 14 to 24 January 1943 in Anfa, an affluent suburb of Casablanca.[70] Roosevelt ensured that the final communiqué expressed the ultimate goal of the Allies as no less than the unconditional surrender of the Axis powers, but Churchill prevailed in imposing the invasion of Sicily for that summer rather than the direct assault on France sought by American military planners.[71] As for dissensions among the French, Roosevelt envisioned a straightforward solution as he cabled to the British prime minister: "We'll call Giraud the bridegroom, and I'll produce him from Algiers, and you get the bride, de Gaulle, down from London, and we'll have a shotgun wedding."[72]

Despite this bonhomie, Roosevelt's hostility toward de Gaulle continued. He had agreed with Churchill that the two rival generals would co-chair a new French coordinating body. However, Roosevelt insisted that Giraud would hold supreme military command, an important nuance as this regime would be recognized as a military ally but not as a legitimate national government. Gaullists and former Vichy figures would be included in equal numbers as part of the committee's membership. Churchill doubted that de Gaulle would settle for such terms, but he believed that an agreement could be hammered out once the two opponents were brought together. Giraud responded immediately to Roosevelt's invitation to Casablanca. He realized that attending these proceedings would likely reinforce his position and speed up execution of the Mast Plan.[73] De Gaulle firmly declined at first but eventually relented under increasing pressure from the Foreign Office and members of his own Free French committee in London, arriving on 22 January just as the conference concluded.[74]

Countless meetings among staff and more intimate discussions between the two French leaders as well as with Roosevelt and Churchill followed but with little effect in terms of obtaining a formal accord. On the morning of 24 January Giraud agreed to sign a statement proclaiming the formation of a representative French committee under dual control, but de Gaulle refused, vetoing the inclusion of former Vichyites in the membership. The only symbolic display of union between the two generals occurred when they exchanged an awkward handshake for photojournalists assembled outside the Hôtel Anfa as Roosevelt and Churchill set out to reveal to the world the larger discussions that had just taken place in Casablanca.[75] Giraud and de Gaulle also issued a common, if blunt, public statement: "We have met. We have talked. We have registered our entire agreement on the end to be achieved, which is the liberation of France and the triumph of human liberties by the total defeat of the enemy. This end will be attained by the union in the war of all Frenchmen fighting side by side with all their Allies."[76]

Giraud and de Gaulle had stated their agreement on the ultimate end and the need for union but failed to settle on a mechanism to achieve this goal. One small step was taken with the appointment of General Georges Catroux as de Gaulle's representative to Giraud's headquarters in Algiers.[77] Nevertheless, this gesture fell quite short of justifying the optimism manifested by Roosevelt when he cabled Churchill on 5 February: "I take it that your bride and my bridegroom have not yet started throwing the crockery. I trust the marriage will be consummated."[78] As he had feared when first summoned to meet with the Allied leaders, de Gaulle did not fare well in Casablanca. He failed to impress Roosevelt, and he badly strained his relationship with Churchill, returning to London even more isolated, at least in the short term. Giraud had not inspired tremendous confidence on the part of the Anglo-Americans—Roosevelt quipped to his son Elliott after first meeting Giraud, "I'm afraid we're leaning on a very slender reed."[79] But he remained firmly in charge in North Africa. As importantly, he made much headway in securing American support for rearmament of his forces.

While de Gaulle delayed his travel to Casablanca until the very end, Giraud had arrived on 17 January, giving him the opportunity to meet informally with many of the most senior figures making up the American and British delegations. He then attended a formal session of the Combined Chiefs of Staff (CCS) on 19 January, using this opportunity to lay out his plan for rejuvenating his forces. He outlined a more ambitious vision than that conveyed so far in the Mast Plan, increasing the size of the proposed *corps de bataille* from ten to thirteen divisions (three armored and ten motorized infantry divisions) and an air force of no less than fifty fighter squadrons, thirty light bomber squadrons, and additional transport elements for a total of one thousand planes. On the naval side, the request was limited, but Giraud introduced two lines of effort that would shape the rearmament of the Marine nationale in the years to come: "Concerning the navy, we have some good vessels but those are lacking anti-air weaponry and sensors. As well, we need escorts for our convoys. Thus, I ask, on the one hand, for the modernization of the ships we have and, on the other hand, the delivery of a small number of new ships of limited tonnage."[80]

The CCS did not endorse the specifics of the proposal right away, although they agreed with the vision therein. As remarked by General Marshall: "[It is] not a question of whether to equip the French Army, but rather how to do it."[81] Both sides accepted that limitations in Allied shipping would likely impede the timely provision of modern American equipment to French forces in Africa, and the CCS stopped short of issuing a formal recommendation to their political masters for the execution of Giraud's vision. This left the next step unclear, a situation the French general determined to remedy when he met the American president in person for the third and last time that week. Following the handshake with de Gaulle on 24 January, Giraud presented a memorandum to Roosevelt who, after reading it over once, promptly recorded his agreement on the margin of the document.[82] The *memorandum d'Anfa* or the Anfa Plan would thereafter guide the rearmament of France's Armée d'Afrique and shape the future of the country's military forces for the remainder of the war and beyond.

Although they were not at Roosevelt's side when he agreed to the detailed clauses included therein, the CCS did not resist this unexpected fait accompli given that it largely reflected the nature of their own discussions with Giraud. However, nowhere in the Anfa Plan did the question of rearming the French navy appear. Not even Giraud's earlier statement to the CCS about modernizing existing ships and acquiring new ones was cited in the *mémorandum d'Anfa*; at most, the text did not constrict the clauses to the Armée d'Afrique specifically, using the more inclusive term "French forces." This neglect could have worried Vice Admiral Michelier once he learned of the agreement, but it likely did not. He and his staff had already engaged in extensive navy-to-navy discussions with their U.S. Navy counterparts in the spirit of Cherchell and the Darlan Deal, as will be discussed next. French and American sailors had not waited for the Anfa Plan to lay out the framework and processes necessary to undertake a large-scale modernization of existing vessels as well as the transfer of new ships and aircraft to a navy reborn. Nevertheless, Roosevelt's signature provided necessary political legitimacy for French and U.S. admirals to commence turning these ambitious plans into reality.

On the negative side of the ledger, the Casablanca Conference left unresolved many of those issues that had plagued Franco-Allied relations leading up to Operation Torch and continued since. Despite his domineering bravado in bringing de Gaulle and Giraud to shake hands, Roosevelt failed to impose his proposed "third way" to remedy the French divide, and the two generals kept bickering acrimoniously from then on. *La France libre* and Giraud's forces were engaged against the Axis but fighting separate campaigns under different command and support arrangements. For the time being, the former remained aligned with the British while the latter dealt almost exclusively with the Americans. Even more ominous, who sided with whom among *les Français* and which country sought to propel one leader at the expense of the other left deep scars on the French psyche, for the remainder of the hostilities and into the postwar era.

CHAPTER 3

REARMING FOR WAR

Allied Framework, French Rivalry

N ew York City mayor Fiorello Henry La Guardia smiled broadly from a stand erected outside City Hall in Lower Manhattan on Tuesday, 23 February 1943. A large group of senior figures from the United States and several Allied nations accompanied him. An early supporter of the France Forever movement, the ebullient politician had called for a day of celebration, inviting a contingent of seven hundred sailors from battleship *Richelieu* and cruiser *Montcalm* to parade down Broadway Avenue. The ships were recently arrived from Dakar, Senegal, to undertake extensive refits, the former in the Brooklyn Navy Yards and the latter in Philadelphia. *Richelieu*'s arrival in New York Harbor on 11 February proved particularly symbolic, sailing past the Statue of Liberty and then up the East River, passing under the Brooklyn Bridge in broad daylight in full view of cheering New Yorkers. This grand entrance and the day's reception in downtown Manhattan were meant to symbolize the dedicated support of the United States to a reawakened France.

Unexpectedly—or perhaps as should have been expected—the celebration failed to conceal continuing divisions that undermined the country's internal politics. Two contingents of French officials stood at the side of La Guardia, the Giraud camp led by Major General Antoine Béthouart and the Gaullists under civilian representative Adrien Tixier. Called to the podium, Tixier first adopted a conciliatory tone by welcoming the sailors to the Allied side but soon followed with a vitriolic diatribe against those who rallied at the eleventh hour while *la France libre* had been fighting ever since Pétain cravenly agreed to the armistice. Also present on the stand, *Richelieu*'s commanding officer, Captain Marcel Deramond, left his seat visibly irritated and marched off in full view of the public and the press as La Guardia pushed Tixier aside to return a semblance of conviviality to the event.[1]

This awkward moment constituted but one episode in the continued campaign waged by Free French authorities to denigrate the Giraud regime in the United States. Admittedly, the officers of *Richelieu* and *Montcalm* played into their hand by continuing to denounce de Gaulle as leading a movement of renegades and proudly displaying portraits of Pétain in the ships' messes. For them, the Old Marshal, by then under German house arrest in occupied Vichy, still remained the legitimate head of the French state, and they only reluctantly accepted General Henri Giraud as a wartime military leader. Divided loyalties at the top sowed confusion in the minds of lower ranks, a trend that officers from the Forces navales françaises libres sought to exploit. They set up recruiting stations outside the gates of the shipyards where ships of the Forces maritimes d'Afrique (FMA—Africa Maritime Forces) underwent refits. Within weeks, upward of one hundred crew members from the *Richelieu* abandoned the battleship, most going on to serve in smaller destroyers and corvettes under the *croix de Lorraine*.[2] Still, work continued unabated to bring France's largest warship back into the fight.

Richelieu entered the No. 5 Dock at the Brooklyn Navy Yard on 24 February 1943. From that date, three shifts of two thousand workers each took turns on board, twenty-four hours a day, seven days a week, for the next five months. The battleship left North American waters in October after a period of trials and training in Norfolk, Virginia, to arrive on 24 November in Scapa Flow, Scotland (via Boston, the Azores, and Algeria), to take up her first operational assignment with the British Home Fleet.[3] This refit and prompt return to operations was symbolic in many ways, providing a potent display of the collaborative spirit required to initiate and sustain the wartime rearmament of the French forces willing to fight the Axis. But it also exposed the clashing ambitions that would greatly complicate the planning and execution of that effort in the following years. For the Americans, the *Richelieu* modernization was as much a matter of French prestige as that of an effectual contribution to Allied sea power.[4] The continued U-boat threat in the Atlantic and the aircraft carrier battles that had dominated the Pacific war in 1942 simultaneously highlighted the dire requirement for more surface escorts and the decline of the battleship as the queen of the battle at sea.

Giraud's naval commander, Vice Admiral François-Félix Michelier, had insisted in December 1942 that the ship could be made ready for an Atlantic crossing within days. He eventually gained the support of U.S. Navy authorities for the project, especially as *Richelieu* would be accompanied by the cruiser *Montcalm*, that type of ship being of more interest to them. Four American destroyers also escorted the two vessels on their oceanic journey, the first time in the war that French and U.S. vessels operated together as an integrated formation.[5] Their prompt departure in late January 1943 showed that French and American admirals had not wasted the long weeks of political haggling that had followed the North African landings. By then they had already instituted most of the framework and many of the processes that would guide the wartime rearmament of the Marine nationale, regardless of the latter's internal divisions and the heavy demands already placed on Allied shipyards.

Implementing the Framework for Rearmament

Mechanisms to coordinate the production and distribution of armaments among the Allies were already in place when the Anglo-Americans landed on the shores of North Africa. Sitting at the top were the Combined Chiefs of Staff (CCS), a body first proposed at the Arcadia Conference, which took place in Washington over the Christmas and New Year period in 1941–42.[6] The new body, based in Washington, quickly grew in stature, and the Chiefs immediately tackled the immense challenges ahead of them, starting with the division of the world into British and American theaters of war. CCS Directive 50/2 on 24 March 1942 then established "a system of adoption by which the members of the United Nations would look for all of their military supplies either to the United Kingdom or the United States."[7] The distribution of war matériel by each country became the responsibility of two bodies, the Combined Munitions Assignments Board in Washington and its coequal, the London Munitions Assignments Board, which coordinated the allocation of their respective national resources through the CCS.[8]

Each board oversaw subordinate committees looking after their respective areas of responsibility: the Munitions Assignments Committee (Navy), or MAC(N); the Munitions Assignments Committee (Ground), or MAC(G); and the Munitions Assignments Committee (Air), or MAC(A).[9] Demands from Allied governments for war matériel—this term meant to include any type of war productions, from uniforms and munitions to guns and tanks, fighters and bombers, ships and submarines—were relayed to the CCS who passed those down to the appropriate ammunition boards (in Washington or London) to be handled by the relevant ammunition committee (navy, ground, or air). Committee membership on both sides of the Atlantic was a combination of American and British representatives. Disagreements within the committees or at the board level would be resolved by the CCS since they retained "the final authority in the matter of the granting or rejecting of munitions requests from individual members of the United Nations."[10] This framework continued for the remainder of the war.

The directive also considered support to the Free French. Roosevelt still denied diplomatic recognition to the Gaullist movement and refused to negotiate a Lend-Lease agreement with *la France libre*. Instead, de Gaulle had to submit requests for war matériel to the British government for furtherance to the CCS. Although awkward, this arrangement did not prevent the provision of direct American support for specific cases. CCS 50/2 acknowledged the tyranny of geography and instructed that munitions for the Free French forces in the Atlantic, Africa, and the Middle East be provided from British allocations while the United States would support those operating in the Pacific.[11] Obviously absent from the directive at that time was the matter of rearming Vichy forces in French North Africa, but General Eisenhower set about tackling this issue within days of establishing Allied Force Headquarters (AFHQ) in Algiers on 23 November 1942.[12]

Eisenhower faced two critical supply bottlenecks. The lack of working port facilities in French North Africa and the want of Allied shipping imposed severe limitations on the preparation and implementation of operational plans. Although Algiers had come through Operation Torch largely unscathed, Oran and Casablanca had suffered extensive damage as a result of bombardments by the Anglo-Americans and sabotage by the Vichy forces. Other harbors were much smaller in capacity, either closer to Tunisia but within range of

Axis bombers (Bône and Bougie in eastern Algeria) or safer to the west but much farther from the front lines (Rabat in Morocco and Dakar in faraway Senegal). U.S. Navy and U.S. Army contingents quickly rehabilitated the ports and augmented their air defenses, but this added capacity did not alleviate the shortcomings of the North African road and rail infrastructure.[13] As a result, Eisenhower came to prioritize four conflicting requirements to sequence the flow of supply into theater:

1. Matériels for the Anglo-American buildup;
2. Essential food and goods for the civilian population;
3. Vehicles, weapons, and ammunition to replenish those French forces already engaged in combat in Tunisia; and
4. War matériel for the longer-term rearmament of the Armée d'Afrique under the terms of the Mast Plan.[14]

In other words, Eisenhower considered the question of French rearmament a matter for future consideration in terms of its execution. He viewed support to ongoing operations in Tunisia the more pressing requirement. Not surprisingly, Giraud thought otherwise, as fighting in Tunisia was bound to end by the summer of 1943. Not privy to the strategic way ahead adopted by the Anglo-American leaders in Casablanca, the French could only guess that the Allies would undertake another campaign in the Mediterranean, perhaps even an amphibious landing directly on the shores of southern France.[15] The supply of French units currently engaged in combat in Tunisia and building up a powerful *corps de bataille* in the rear needed to take place simultaneously, and it needed to start soonest, in Giraud's view. The Armée d'Afrique had to make an immediate contribution to defeating the Axis in Africa while a new expeditionary force took possession of modern American equipment and trained with it in time to join the next campaign, wherever it might take place.[16] Dissensions over such priorities would test relations between Eisenhower and Giraud, and the latter sought to circumvent the former by dispatching a military mission to Washington to discuss all matters related to rearmament of the Armée d'Afrique directly with the CCS.[17]

Although American authorities reluctantly approved the mission as a gesture of goodwill toward Giraud, the effective requisition channel on behalf of the French remained with AFHQ. Once in Washington, Major General

Béthouart quickly accepted that he could only settle for a liaison function, which the French delegation retained for the remainder of the hostilities.[18] Indeed, as support for the Armée d'Afrique could only be generated at the expense of the Anglo-American buildup in the region (in terms of shipping space and war matériel redirected to the French), the Combined Chiefs agreed that "implementing the rearmament programs subsequently established by decision of the CCS rested with the Allied Commander in Chief in the theatre of operations."[19] AFHQ sent requests with recommendations in order of priority to the CCS, and these, in turn, were forwarded to the Munitions Assignment Board and the relevant MAC for action.[20] In order to handle this coordinating function, Eisenhower set up a dedicated agency within AFHQ. The Joint Rearmament Committee (JRC) met for the first time in Algiers on 23 December 1942.[21] This agency, reporting directly to the Allied Forces chief of staff, Major General Walter Bedell Smith, included nine members (four American, one British, and four French) working under the senior U.S. officer, Colonel William Tudor Gardiner of the U.S. Army Air Forces.[22]

In turn, the French set up the Service central des approvisionnements et matériels américains (Central Service for American Supplies and Matériels) to coordinate the reception and distribution of Allied rearmament goods.[23] Although a positive development from the French perspective, initial deliberations of the JRC also highlighted the divergence in priorities between Eisenhower and Giraud, the former continuing to focus on arming those forces engaged on the Tunisian front at the expense of the latter's *corps expéditionnaire*. By and large, the Combined Chiefs agreed with Eisenhower as briefed to Major General Béthouart when he first called on them on 7 January 1943. Incidentally, the CCS had just reviewed a U.S. Army staff briefing that outlined how the diversion of resources to meet the targets laid out in the Mast Plan would severely impact replenishment of American formations already abroad, disrupt worldwide shipments scheduled for the remainder of the year, and interfere with equipping new divisions under training in the continental United States.[24]

The matter remained unresolved until President Roosevelt endorsed the *mémorandum d'Anfa*, presenting the Combined Chiefs and Eisenhower with a fait accompli. Telling was a discussion between General Marshall and British representatives in Washington after he was made aware of what had transpired between Roosevelt and Giraud: "Present list of equipment required is, [Marshall] says, ridiculous. . . . He is at present investigating what can be done by slowing up equipment of U.S. divisions in [America] to meet reasonable French demands within the very limited shipping possibilities."[25] In contrast to this bitter statement, French and American naval authorities had already launched parallel discussions in Algiers and Casablanca. These exchanges commenced in a much more collaborative atmosphere, at least in the early months.

Framework for Naval Rearmament

Rebuilding Giraud's navy took place within the larger Allied framework, discussed above, with requests handed from his staff to Eisenhower's JRC for initial review and furtherance to the CCS, the Combined Munitions Assignment Board, and MAC(N). Matters concerned with the rejuvenation of the Aéronavale would make their way to MAC(A) when appropriate. MAC(G) handled some demands as well, such as those concerned with coastal artillery and antiaircraft batteries, the shore defense of naval bases being a responsibility of the navy under the French system. But a critical distinction differentiated the context of these discussions from those concerned with building up Giraud's army and air force. Both of the latter involved very large demands on shipping bound for North Africa, in direct competition with the buildup of Anglo-American forces. In contrast, given the lack of suitable facilities in Algeria, Morocco, and French West Africa, planners could only assume that units of the Marine nationale would have to sail in the opposite direction for refitting and modernization in North America. Construction of new ships and submarines for transfer to the French would also take place in Allied yards. Not competing so directly for Africa-bound shipping took much potential for alacrity out of the naval rearmament talks.

Of course, French admirals still made some demands on Allied shipping, such as material for the reconstruction and expansion of African commercial ports and naval bases damaged during Operation Torch. This effort called for large amounts of building material, antiaircraft guns, and ammunition at the expense of supplies badly needed on the Tunisian front lines. Ships and submarines flying the tricolor out of French African ports also exacted pressures on shipping for transport of fuel, munitions, and supplies as well as for transfer of weapon systems and sensors that could be installed locally on smaller vessels based in North and West Africa. Nevertheless, such investment directly contributed to current operations while alleviating the burden on the U.S. Navy and the Royal Navy for coastal defense and local convoy escort duties. In other words, these demands made the FMA an immediate contributor to the Allied cause, and Eisenhower had no hesitation in meeting those, just as he favored supporting General Alphonse Juin's troops then fighting in Tunisia.

More challenging for the JRC staff, however, was assessing the ability of the Allies to meet French demands to refit larger ships and submarines as well as build new units for transfer to Michelier's fleet. The rallying of French West Africa to the Allied cause on 22 November 1942 triggered the CCS to approach the matter of naval rearmament from a more fulsome perspective. As Eisenhower pointed out on 20 November, "inasmuch as West Africa is outside the Torch theatre, I am without authority to participate in the [negotiations]," especially as initial contacts with Governor General Boisson "progressed to the point of discussing such details as to how the *Richelieu* might be taken to the United States for repairs."[26] By the end of the month, the CCS directed Rear Admiral William A. Glassford Jr. to lead a military mission to Dakar to evaluate opportunities and challenges found in that base. They were already aware of the limited means available in the theater of operations as Glassford's instructions included the need to initiate discussions on repair and modernization of French vessels in American shipyards. Within weeks, the CCS instructed Glassford to include French North Africa in his mandate.[27]

In the meantime, Vice Admiral Michelier did not remain idle. Nearly the same day that the CCS dispatched Glassford to Algiers, Giraud's naval commander submitted to the JRC his own proposal for "desired repairs and alterations to French naval ships [found] in North and West African ports."[28] Michelier sought the refit of eight small escort vessels, six destroyers, three cruisers, and the battleship *Richelieu*. These refits would provide all vessels with modern antiaircraft armament, radars, and sonars and with new degaussing systems against the threat of magnetic mines. In addition, the cruisers and *Richelieu* would gain from extensive refurbishment of their aircraft catapults as well as repairs and upgrades to various auxiliary systems. The French also proposed that more than a dozen submarines be fitted with American sonars. This proposal was well received by Eisenhower and his staff: "The French here are ready and willing to start immediately on this general program. I urgently recommend that action be started by taking some escort vessels in hand now and giving the rest active employment while the many technicalities in the refits of the large ships are being settled."[29]

This cable clearly signaled that the matter of French naval rearmament had assumed a momentum of its own by early January 1943, moving from under the shadow of the Mast Plan and the reluctance of the American theater commander to equip the *corps expéditionnaire* as a matter of priority. The trend became even clearer when Eisenhower sent to the CCS another assessment of the French proposal following more extensive discussions with Admiral Glassford and his own naval commander, Admiral Andrew Cunningham (RN). In an extensive cable dated 18 January 1942, Eisenhower outlined an elaborate plan seeking to maximize resources from naval establishments in North America and French Africa in order of priority:

1. Fit new sonars and AA [antiair] batteries on seven ocean escorts using local facilities in Dakar;
2. Provide new sonars to twenty-one trawlers and inshore patrol vessels using local facilities in Dakar and Casablanca;
3. Dispatch *Richelieu*, one cruiser, and two destroyers for overhauls in the United States while other cruisers commenced mid-Atlantic patrols; and
4. The first two of fourteen submarines proceed for refit in the United States, while the remainder provided training support and patrolling in the Atlantic and the Mediterranean prior to their turn for overhaul.[30]

Another task was that of providing basic repairs to four destroyers badly damaged during Operation Torch before they could undertake the trans-Atlantic voyage for more extensive refits in the United States. Eisenhower mentioned additional ships that "can usefully be employed in their present condition with alterations to armament which can be done on the spot," while reiterating the necessity "that supplies already requested for rehabilitation of French naval bases at Dakar, Oran, Algiers and Casablanca be furnished as soon as practicable." The cable then raised the difficult issue of the battleship *Jean Bart*, *Richelieu*'s sister ship, badly damaged in Casablanca. The prognosis was guarded, deferring a final recommendation for at least four months, until the French restored some semblance of a seagoing capability to the ship. Eisenhower completed his missive by recognizing that executing such an aggressive program did not rest entirely with him, especially the allocation of American shipyards to execute this extensive work, thus the requirement for higher guidance on these matters.

Meanwhile, Great Britain, while supportive of French naval rearmament, could only offer minimal support since that country's own shipyards and dockyard facilities—in the United Kingdom and overseas territories—were already running at full capacity.[31] British shipyards did eventually conduct overhauls for smaller French units in Bermuda and lesser work in Gibraltar, but the bulk of refit and modernization work remained to be carried out in American yards.[32] U.S. authorities were willing to take on that commitment by adopting a phased approach using U.S. Navy dockyards for refits while commercial shipyards continued working on new constructions already on order for the United States and other Allies. On 22 January 1942, while still assembled in Casablanca, the CCS endorsed the Glassford proposal: "Upon arrival can take [battleship] *Richelieu* at New York, [destroyers] *Fantasque* and *Terrible* at Boston, [cruiser] *Montcalm*, [submarines] *Archimede*, *Amazone* at Philadelphia. Will arrange for Philadelphia to take additional cruisers, destroyers and submarines when foregoing are completed. It must be understood that heavy workloads, shortage of critical material and time for manufacture must be distributed through extended period. Submarine overhauls will probably be particularly slow."[33]

"Extended period" may not have been as expedient as some French naval officers might have liked, but this cable officially launched the rehabilitation of the FMA, showing that Michelier did not need Giraud to lobby President Roosevelt on his behalf while in Anfa. Campaigning in Washington was another matter. The Amirauté was already considering the next step—namely, calling on additional Allied resources to not only refit and modernize existing units but to obtain outright transfer of new ships to augment the size of the fleet. Eisenhower announced this development to the CCS on 26 January 1943. The task, he said, would likely involve the French naval mission dispatched to Washington in the previous weeks, *la mission Fénard*: "Admiral Michelier has requested the provision from Allied new constructions of 30 corvettes and 6 modern destroyers similar to British J class fitted for minesweeping, also 8 tugs, in addition to proposals for rearmament for existing French ships. . . . I will make clear to him that this is a long-term matter, and that the possibilities of providing any of this requirement must be taken up with the Combined Chiefs of Staffs by Admiral Fénard's mission."[34]

The delegation led by Vice Admiral Raymond-Albert Fénard arrived in Washington on 1 February 1943. The French admiral worked independently of but in close cooperation with Major General Béthouart, who continued looking after French army and aviation issues.[35] Fénard proved a wise choice. A jovial officer, fluent in English, he quickly ingratiated himself with government officials and the Combined Chiefs, including U.S. Navy chief of naval operations, Admiral Ernest J. King, a severe character many foreign officers found difficult to befriend.[36] That positive relationship would prove useful since the American admiral acted as the CCS' executive agent in coordinating the shipborne delivery of matériel overseas once apportioned by the Combined Munitions Assignments Board machinery.[37] King found himself at the center of decision making regarding demands for matériel deliveries to French Africa, the refitting of ships and submarines in American yards, and the transfer of new units to the FMA.

On 1 March 1943 Eisenhower reminded the Combined Chiefs that decisions were required regarding all three in response to the various demands placed by French naval authorities, growing more detailed by the day.[38] He listed the latest request for new surface ships as 12 destroyers, 30 corvettes, and 12 tugs, while the Aéronavale sought to acquire 33 Catalina flying boats, 18 two-seater Seagulls floatplanes, 100 B-25 bombers modified for antisubmarine patrolling, and 110 Curtiss P-40 ground-attack fighters as well as 38 miscellaneous aircraft (in addition to the 20 Supermarine Walrus amphibians the British had already agreed to provide for inshore patrolling). Admiral King amplified Eisenhower's concerns in an April memorandum to the CCS. The document stated in part: "Though various decision [have] been taken by Combined Chiefs of Staff, Admiralty and Navy Department, no overall agreement had been reached in this matter."[39] In order to provide clearer directions to the MABs and better confront growing French ambitions regarding naval rearmament, King proposed to determine "the extent of the rehabilitation program, the procedure to be followed for the issue of materials, and the respective participation of the United States and the United Kingdom in the commitment."[40] He attached a draft policy, which was thorough and met most French expectations regarding direct support to FMA operations, overhauls of its vessels, and repairs to shore infrastructure.

Subject to minor amendments proposed by British authorities, CCS Directive 194/1, Supply Policy for French African Naval Forces and Naval Bases, became official on 17 April 1943.[41] The Amirauté and AFHQ welcomed such commitment by the United States and Great Britain to supporting rehabilitation and supply of existing French forces in Africa. And yet the very first clause—"no ships will be assigned at present to French by either the United States or United Kingdom"—caused consternation in Algiers. Even Eisenhower soon commenced promoting direct transfer of escorts to the French, stating on 3 May 1943 that "existing French escort vessels are unable to meet escort requirements [and there] is a genuine need for French escort vessels of this type in this theatre."[42] This last appeal drew a sharp rebuke from the Combined Chiefs who replied that no escort vessels could be made available before the invasion of Sicily in the summer.[43]

These exchanges clearly defined the form and extent of support the CCS could provide to Giraud's navy in mid-1943. Ships would not be transferred to the French wholesale and existing units were to be refitted and modernized in Allied yards only as space became available. The United States and Great Britain would directly support and supply those ships and submarines operating within their respective areas of responsibility, and they would provide repair and consumables to French bases in Africa. Commanders of the FMA were grateful for such assistance, but they could not fail to notice that these arrangements remained narrowly focused on wartime requirements, exploiting French naval assets and personnel to augment the overall Allied fighting power at sea, not rebuilding a great power navy.

As concerning, Allied support to French naval rearmament remained divided along the fault line that still fractured the Marine nationale and the larger French war effort. The Americans shepherded Giraud's FMA while the British continued looking after the FNFL, although Anglo-American authorities grew convinced of the need for greater coordination between the two camps. As underlined by Admiral Cunningham late in December 1942: "It is evidently a matter of great urgency to get the two naval factions together if we are to start working with French ships out here."[44] And yet concerns over military effectiveness did not supplant political infighting among the French. Although de Gaulle and Giraud had shaken hands in Casablanca, renewed bickering followed, negating any possibility of Auboyneau and Michelier initiating talks toward greater cooperation between their forces. A bitter rivalry continued to permeate the ranks of the divided Marine nationale in 1943, a reflection of the larger national fracture that endured that year.

A Failed Shotgun Wedding

The Machiavellian combinations that led to the eventual removal of Giraud as commander in chief in April 1944 and de Gaulle's rise as the sole leader of the French camp dramatically impacted reunification of the French navy and its rearmament by the Allies. Giraud appeared to gain most from the handshake sponsored by Roosevelt in Casablanca, but de Gaulle proved ruthless in undermining the credibility of the *commandant en chef civil et militaire* thereafter. Much more popular than Giraud in Allied public opinion, the resilient FFL leader also boasted of the allegiance of several resistance networks in metropolitan France. He had already relabeled his movements from *la France libre* to *la France combattante* (Fighting France) in July 1942, claiming to direct the forces of both free and occupied France.[45] His supporters incessantly denounced the retention of former Pétainistes in positions of authority under Giraud, generating much debate in the British and American press. The administration in Algiers also proved slow in repealing the most controversial of the Vichy policies and regulations still in effect across French North Africa, especially anti-Semitic measures and those promoting the tenets of the Old Marshal's *Révolution nationale*.[46] Of greatest assistance to de Gaulle, though, was his opponent's reluctance to tackle political matters in the midst of the military campaign then under way in Tunisia and his focus on the rearmament of the Armée d'Afrique.

Many parties, within French circles and among the Allies, put intense pressure on Giraud and de Gaulle to achieve some level of reconciliation during the spring of 1943. Months of acrimonious negotiations led to a tentative agreement and the Free French leader flew to the Algerian capital on 30 May to conclude these talks. On 3 June de Gaulle's French National Committee and Giraud's African administration joined to become the Comité français de Libération nationale (CFLN—French Committee for National Liberation). Residing in Algiers, the two generals co-presided over the new body, chairing meetings alternatively, with decrees requiring both of their signatures to be valid. Membership was meant to be equal between Gaullists and Giraudists, but a vaguely worded clause left open the possibility of future expansion in numbers. The Allies did not grant diplomatic recognition to the CFLN but largely left it free to oversee France's war effort on the Allied side and exercise sovereign control over French territories not under Axis occupation.

Anglo-American leaders considerably underestimated de Gaulle's ability to outmaneuver Giraud as they kept a relatively hands-off approach to the internal affairs of the committee. Within weeks, the Free French leader expanded the CFLN's membership from seven to fourteen, filling the balance with his supporters and taking control of the proceedings. By late summer many high-ranking officials with past affiliations to the Vichy regime resigned or were forced out of key posts, such as Pierre Boisson in West Africa, Marcel Peyrouton in Algeria, and General Charles Noguès in Morocco. De Gaulle's old ally and nemesis, Vice Admiral Muselier, who joined Giraud in May 1943 to assume the awkward title of "deputy to the commander in chief for maintaining order in the Algiers region," lost that post on 2 July and was "retired" yet again in August as a result of a new decree lowering the retirement age for general and flag officers.[47] This last measure obviously served de Gaulle's purpose in forcing the departure of several senior individuals who had refused to join his movement after the armistice.

Appointed commander of the FMA by Darlan after the Anglo-American landings, Vice Admiral Michelier was also eased out that summer. The decree of 12 August 1943 forced the retirement of vice admirals Jacques Moreau and

André Rioult, who were still in command in Algiers and Oran, as well as the former commander of Force X, Vice Admiral Émile Godfroy, and Rear Admiral Robert-Ernest Leloup, in command of naval forces in the Caribbean. In all, 30 percent of France's generals and admirals left France's nominally reunited armed forces that month or shortly thereafter. Some did freely, but most departed their posts without choice and with great bitterness as France was still at war and the momentous opportunity to participate in the liberation of the *métropole* lay in the near future.[48] As for Giraud, he proved impotent in avoiding the forced retirement of many of his closest allies, a clear sign of his political isolation and an ominous message to those officers who still wondered where their loyalty should lie.

Although he remained copresident of the French Committee, Giraud could not challenge decisions agreed to by the majority of the membership, so he most often ended up rubber-stamping edicts conveying de Gaulle's will, as in the case of the decree of 12 August. Nevertheless, he remained commander in chief of the armed forces, actively overseeing the vigorous effort in rearming the Armée d'Afrique and preparing the deployment of an expeditionary force to Europe. Frustrated at the exclusion of his troops from the invasion of Sicily (July–August 1943) and the initial landings in Italy on 3 September 1943, Giraud seized the opportunity to launch a hastily planned raid two weeks later, landing a small force in Corsica to join the local resistance in expulsing the Axis garrison, which had seized the island in November 1942.[49] The campaign, conducted autonomously by French forces from North Africa without allied support, came to a victorious end on 4 October. This important accomplishment for a rejuvenated Armée d'Afrique, ironically, accelerated the political downfall of its leader.

Giraud had neither formally informed nor sought authorization from the CFLN to liberate Corsica, labeling it a military operation that fell squarely within his right to launch as head of the committee's armed forces. Seizing the opportunity, de Gaulle mounted a campaign to denounce the seeming incompatibility between the post of military commander in chief and the political copresidency held by Giraud.[50] Within weeks de Gaulle managed to prevail over his adversary, obtaining his accord to dissolve the committee and reconstitute it under the same name but as a reformed organization that looked closer to a country's government, including ministries. On 9 November Giraud learned, to his great surprise, of a new decree confirming his duties as commander in chief but excluding him from membership in the committee. De Gaulle had won; Roosevelt's shotgun wedding had proved a delusion. With the copresidency abolished, even forceful Prime Minister Churchill had to admit his inability, and that of the American president, to shape the course of French internal politics by that stage: "I am not at all content with the changes in the French National Committee which leave de Gaulle sole President. The body we recognized was of a totally different character, the essence being the co-presidency of Giraud and de Gaulle. I suggest we maintain an attitude of complete reserve until we can discuss the position together."[51]

As the Gaullist camp steadily shorn Giraud's military post of actual operational responsibilities, the old general eventually gave up and retired in April 1944.[52] His departure left de Gaulle largely in control of the political apparatus outside the *métropole* and in command of all French armed forces rallied to the Allied cause. This concluding act should have marked the final reconciliation of a divided people and its competing military factions. In the latter case, that process had been initiated more than a year earlier but the fusion would prove a challenge, none the more so than in the case of the Marine nationale. In Alexandria, Vice Admiral Godfroy and the senior officers of Force X refused all entreaties from French and British representatives to proceed to North African ports. They also turned down an offer from President Roosevelt to sail directly to the United States for immediate refitting.[53] Godfroy only relented in May 1943 and announced a middle course whereby his vessels would not rally to any one man (i.e., Giraud) but to an organization, the FMA, and sail to a territory free of foreign powers (i.e., Senegal, not Morocco or Algeria) to serve purely French interests.

The squadron eventually made its way to Dakar, and Force X was disbanded on 10 September 1943.[54] Meanwhile, the rallying of the French forces based in the Martinique proved as laborious.[55] Although he had "lost" Saint-Pierre and Miquelon to de Gaulle in December 1941, the French high commissioner for the Western Atlantic, Admiral Georges Robert, maintained a firm grip on the remainder of his domain under the benevolent eye of the United States.

After Torch, however, Washington adopted a harsher tone, asking that Robert sever all ties to Vichy and rally to Giraud or begin direct cooperation with the United States. Guyana (on the South American coast) relented first but rallied to de Gaulle's *France combattante* on 17 March 1943 rather than the Algiers regime. Meanwhile, Robert stayed the course in Martinique, and the Roosevelt administration imposed a military blockade, cutting off supplies to the French possessions until popular pressure forced the high commissioner to turn his post over to a French Committee of National Liberation representative on Bastille Day.[56]

This turn of events left Indochina as the sole overseas domain still loyal to Pétain. Isolated and surrounded by the Japanese, the French colony was virtually cut off from rest of the world.[57] Governor General Jean Decoux had succeeded in limiting Japanese advances to the northern province of Tonkin in September 1940, but renewed pressure from Tokyo forced a new agreement on 29 July 1941, acknowledging a "common responsibility" for the defense of Indochina. Within days Japanese forces occupied naval bases, air fields, and army barracks throughout the southern province of Cochinchina, from where they would spring forward to invade British Malaya as well as sink battleship *Prince of Wales* and battle cruiser *Repulse* in December 1941.[58] Nevertheless, the Vichy administration continued to operate semiautonomously until 9 March 1945, when Japanese troops completed their takeover of Indochina, eliminating the colonial regime and incarcerating all French civil servants, military personnel, and their families. By the end of the conflict, virtually all ships based in Indochina had been wiped out as a result of hostile action by the Japanese, scuttling by French crews, or destruction by the Allies as part of the larger bombing campaign launched across Southeast Asia in the last stage of the war in the Pacific.

But this tragic fate still lay in the future in the summer of 1943 as French admirals remained concerned with the more immediate challenge of resolving the bitter rivalry that kept the FNFL and the FMA apart. The practical advantages of integrating the two forces were obvious in terms of increased efficiencies in conduct of operations, coordination of mutual support and deconfliction of competing demands addressed simultaneously to the Allies. But the matter of which side would come to dominate an integrated navy was still not satisfactorily settled. The issue was not wholly limited to a divided Marine nationale since similar rivalries existed in the army and the air force. Partisans of Giraud boasted of their strength in vastly larger numbers—in the case of the *marine d'Afrique*, 250,000 tons and 45,000 all ranks in contrast to 30,000 tons and 7,000 individuals in the FNFL—while the Gaullists claimed the moral high ground based on their continued opposition to the Axis and their sacrifices in the face of the enemy since the armistice.[59]

Following weeks of acrimonious discussions, members of the French Committee of National Liberation agreed on 31 July 1943 to a compromise: each of the military services would be united under one chief of staff from the Giraud camp, assisted by a Gaullist deputy.[60] On the naval side, the transition presented challenges of its own as the first candidate to replace Michelier as head of the FMA—Vice Admiral Louis Edmond Collinet, commander of naval forces in French West Africa—turned down the post because it did not come with a political appointment to the French Committee of National Liberation.[61] Giraud and de Gaulle eventually turned to Rear Admiral André Lemonnier to take on the role of *chef d'état-major de la marine* (chief of the naval general staff), despite his junior rank in relation to several other Vichy flag officers who were unacceptable to the Gaullists. Rear Admiral Philippe Auboyneau, former commander of the FNFL who was already in North Africa as a sort of Free French liaison to Michelier, remained in place as number two to Lemonnier.

A figure of compromise, Lemonnier came to exercise considerable influence on wartime rearmament and operations of the Marine nationale as well as its postwar struggles, remaining at the helm until August 1950. He had entered the École navale in 1913, ranking first among the applicants and graduating just in time to see service during the Great War, including the Dardanelles campaign and a tour with a naval gun battery on the Macedonian front. Lemonnier demonstrated outstanding skills at sea and rare political instincts ashore during the interwar period. He commanded submarines and surface vessels of all types, passed first of his class at the École de guerre (Staff College), served with the French delegations at the 1930 London and 1932 Geneva naval conferences, and served as naval adviser to France's Senate in 1937–39. The navy's youngest *capitaine de vaisseau* (captain) at the beginning of World War II, he led naval gun batteries that moved into Belgium when Hitler unleashed the blitzkrieg in the Ardennes.

Once in contact with the enemy, Lemonnier coordinated successive but orderly withdrawals under withering fire, in sharp contrast to other French army units fleeing the crumbling front in disarray. Making his way to Toulon that summer, he chose the Pétain side and took command of cruiser *Georges Leygues* just in time to fight the Anglo–Free French forces at Dakar in September 1940. At Darlan's side at the time of Operation Torch, Lemonnier was promoted two weeks later to the rank of *contre-amiral* (rear admiral) to take charge of the merchant navy, a position he would retain until his selection to head the Marine nationale in July 1943.[62] Although records are scant regarding de Gaulle's opinion of the former Vichy admiral at the time, he provided a firm endorsement of Lemonnier in his postwar memoirs: "Absorbed by the technique which is its life and passion, which kept its recent ordeals from deterring it, [our Navy] reconstituted itself while taking an active share in operations. Admiral Lemonnier, appointed in July 1943 as chief of the Navy's general staff, brought to this feat of reorganization remarkable ability and a tenacious will, disguised beneath a misleadingly modest manner."[63]

A modest manner and tenacious will would prove key qualities for a leader seeking to bring together two factions so far apart as the Free French sailors and the FMA. Adopting a conciliating attitude, Lemonnier initially accepted that the two entities would continue to exist in an uncomfortable duality, in terms of both geography and missions. On 3 August 1943 the Forces navales françaises libres were relabeled the Forces navales de Grande-Bretagne (FNGB—Naval Forces in Great Britain). Operating out of the British Isles, they remained focused on convoy duties in the Atlantic and in the Arctic up to Russia's Kola Peninsula as well as coastal raiding in the Channel, the North Sea, and Norway. The FMA, operating out of French West and North Africa, continued looking after coastal defense and local convoy escorts in those regions and in the mid-Atlantic while also seeking to regenerate and operate heavier units (battleships, cruisers, and an aircraft carrier). Lemonnier established a single Amirauté in Algiers, meant to amalgamate the functions exercised previously by Michelet's staff in Casablanca and Auboyneau's headquarters in London. Nevertheless, the FNGB also continued to operate semiautonomously under Rear Admiral Georges Thierry d'Argenlieu, former Free French high commissioner in the Pacific.[64]

D'Argenlieu had been an ardent Gaullist of the first hour, and he proclaimed that his forces would still fly the *croix de Lorraine*, a divisive measure that the conciliatory Lemonnier dared not oppose.[65] Far more important to the latter was rearmament of a fighting fleet and renewed participation in operations at sea. In that effort, Lemonnier and Auboyneau proved an effective pair in Algiers, providing much needed continuity in the wake of Michelier's sudden dismissal. Regardless of the political divide between partisans of Giraud and de Gaulle, leaders of a slowly reuniting Marine nationale set about pursuing the rejuvenation of the wartime fleet and formulating a vision for a powerful postwar navy. The latter quickly brought about a clash of ambitions with the Allies as the CCS simultaneously set about articulating a new approach to France's naval rearmament while the strategic environment dramatically evolved in the fall of 1943.

Framing a New Approach: CCS Directive 358 (Revised)

Throughout the confrontation between Giraud and de Gaulle in Algiers, American authorities maintained their commitment to regenerate the FMA. Vast numbers of engineering and support troops set about rehabilitating infrastructures in French West Africa's most important harbors as well as those across Morocco, Algeria, and Tunisia. Local workers in North Africa fitted smaller ships and older units with new weaponry and sensors under supervision of Allied personnel who also provided training to French sailors unfamiliar with these systems. Deemed most critical by Michelier, Lemonnier, and Auboyneau, however, were the more thorough refits of those modern and larger ships to be completed in North American shipyards in accordance with the Glassford Plan approved by the CCS on 22 January 1943.[66]

Following *Richelieu* and *Montcalm*, the cruisers *Gloire* and *Georges Leygues* were respectively refitted in Brooklyn (July to November) and Philadelphia (July to October).[67] Destroyers *Le Fantasque* and *Le Terrible* arrived in Boston in February 1943, the same navy yard where their sister ship *Le Malin* would start refit in March. Another vessel of that same class, *Le Triomphant*, employed by the Free French in the Pacific since the fall of 1941, arrived in

Boston to commence modernization in April 1944.[68] Submarines *Archimède* and *Amazone* proceeded to Philadelphia in the spring of 1943, followed by *Le Glorieux* in October, the first two spending nearly a year in that American yard. Submarine modernization proved more technically challenging than many expected, hence the lengthy periods spent in America.[69] From Martinique, cruiser *Émile Bertin* set sail in August 1943 for refitting in Philadelphia while *Béarn*, a battleship left unfinished in 1920 and converted into an aircraft carrier in 1928 with a top speed of twenty-one knots—too slow to conduct carrier operations in modern combat—was directed to New Orleans for conversion to the aircraft transport role.[70]

Less ambitious refits took place in smaller allied yards. This work aimed to rehabilitate the basic cruising abilities and armament of older vessels rather than the more extensive modernizations conducted in North American dry docks. The training cruiser *Jeanne d'Arc* left Guadeloupe for a quick overhaul in Puerto Rico before joining the FMA just in time for the liberation of Corsica in September 1943.[71] Gibraltar looked after some French units too small to cross the Atlantic, while shipyards in Australia and South Africa handled Free French corvettes already deployed in those waters. The Royal Naval dockyard in Bermuda accommodated FMA ships in successive groups of two or three throughout 1943 to install British asdic equipment, Oerlikon 20-mm antiaircraft guns, and RDF ("range and direction finder," an early form of radar) Type 271 sets. These vessels varied in type from destroyers to sloops to armed trawlers.[72]

Although the Algiers Amirauté made the best of the assistance offered by the Allies in 1943, French admirals wanted more. They considered that the cruisers and destroyers of the former Force X should also proceed for modernization in North American or Bermuda yards, and a greater number of submarines warranted consideration for refit in 1944.[73] The CCS flatly refused. It was assessed that these older vessels did not warrant so much dedicated Allied yard time, although they halfheartedly agreed that such work could be conducted locally: "[Installing AA equipment] is satisfactory if and when the material becomes available, provided the work can be done by the French in Africa."[74] As for the submarines, refits continued slowly. *La Perle* arrived in Philadelphia in early 1944 for conversion to the mine-laying role, followed successively by *Le Centaure* and *Casabianca* in May and July.[75] *Antiope* would be the last vessel to undertake such a refit in the United States, abbreviated to three months in the last year of the war, from January to March 1945.[76]

The CCS also proved reluctant when faced with repeated requests from Algiers to take *Jean Bart* to the United States. Throughout the first half of 1943, French authorities expended precious resources in Casablanca to make the battleship seaworthy. This work required repairing the worst of the damage inflicted by the Americans during Operation Torch and completing some of the initial work left undone when the ship had escaped Saint-Nazaire in June 1940. In May 1943 U.S. authorities agreed provisionally to take on the *Jean Bart* but stated that they could not complete the vessel to her full specifications, especially in terms of heavier gunnery. The battleship conducted sea trials off Morocco in September while the French Committee of National Liberation sought confirmation that *Jean Bart* could proceed to an American shipyard that same month.[77] The CCS withdrew their earlier agreement in the fall due to higher priorities. Admiral Fénard then proposed an alternate plan to complete the ship as an aircraft carrier, but this was rejected curtly in October 1943: "C.C.S. agreed that *Jean Bart* should be employed as a station ship. . . . No Allied facilities to be expanded on its reconditioning."[78]

The Algiers Admiralty made another plea for *Jean Bart* on 8 December 1943, but "in March 1944 it was informed that the U.S. Navy was unwilling to divert resources to the ship."[79] After the British denied a request to dock the battleship in Gibraltar, the French gave up and satisfied themselves to leave the vessel in Casablanca for the remainder of the war for use as a floating barracks and technical school.[80] Additional appeals from Lemonnier for the transfer of an aircraft carrier, either an existing one or a new construction, from the United States or Great Britain, did not meet with success either.[81] The substance of the debate between the French and the Allies regarding *Jean Bart* in the fall of 1943 was markedly different than that about *Richelieu* in the immediate aftermath of Operation Torch. Arguments were no longer about the intrinsic relevance of the battleship to modern warfare at sea or matters of prestige for a reawakened France. Instead the evolving needs and priorities of the Allies came to the fore. The Glassford Plan of January 1943 acknowledged that American shipyards were already taxed at maximum capacity. But it also underlined the advantages of rapidly refitting existing

Table 3.1: Major Refits of French Vessels in North American Yards, 1943–45
(not including routine overhauls and unforecasted repairs)

Category	Vessel(s)	Location	Remarks
Battleship	Richelieu	New York	February–August 1943
Aircraft carrier	Béarn	New Orleans	Conversion to aircraft transport role September 1943–December 1944
Cruisers	Montcalm	Philadelphia	February–August 1943
	Gloire	New York	July–November 1943
	Georges Leygues	Philadelphia	July–October 1943
	Émile Bertin	Philadelphia	August–November 1943
Heavy destroyers (Reclassified light cruisers on completion of refit)	Le Fantasque	Boston	February–July 1943
	Le Terrible	Boston	February–July 1943
	Le Malin	Boston	March–August 1943
	Le Triomphant	Boston	April 1944–March 1945
Submarines	Archimède	Philadelphia	February 1943–January 1944
	Amazone	Philadelphia	March–December 1943
	Le Glorieux	Philadelphia	October 1943–March 1944
	La Perle	Philadelphia	January–June 1944
	Centaure	Philadelphia	May–December 1944
	Casabianca	Philadelphia	July 1944–March 1945
	Antiope	Philadelphia	January–March 1945
Various	Destroyer Tempête	Bermuda	Spring 1943
	Sloop Commandant Bory	Bermuda	Spring 1943
	Sloop Gazelle	Bermuda	Spring 1943
	Sloop La Gracieuse	Bermuda	Summer 1943
	Sloop Commandant Delage	Bermuda	Summer 1943
	Sloop Annamite	Bermuda	Summer 1943
	Destroyer Simoun	Bermuda	Fall 1943
	Sloop La Boudeuse	Bermuda	Fall 1943
	Trawler Victoria	Bermuda	Fall 1943

French vessels in order to get them into the fight as quickly as possible to assist Allied navies still facing major challenges at the time.

The bulk of German submarines had returned to the North Atlantic, and the Japanese were putting up a stiff fight in the Pacific despite their catastrophic losses at Midway. The Afrika Korps was on the defensive but the Mediterranean remained treacherous for allied ships and submarines in the face of shore-based Axis air power, while the Italian fleet weighed heavily on the minds of Allied naval leaders. However, its surrender without a fight following the capitulation of the Italian government of Marshal Pietro Badoglio on 3 September 1943 capped a succession of dramatic developments that marked a definitive change in the naval balance around the world through the course of that year. Admiral Karl Dönitz withdrew his U-boats from the North Atlantic after the critical battles of April and May. Japan commenced a slow retreat in New Guinea and the Solomons and adopted a defensive stance on the frontiers of India, while American submarines and air power tightened the noose around the Empire's sea lines of communications. Back in the Mediterranean, the liberation of Corsica and the Sicilian landings as well as the neutralization of Axis airfields based in Southern Italy and the Greek islands—not to mention the expulsion of the last of the German troops from North Africa—considerably degraded the enemy's capacity to threaten friendly lines of communications through the Middle Sea.

In this context, French North and West Africa retained their value as useful bases to support Allied operations in the Atlantic and against the "soft underbelly" of Europe, but these territories also went from contributors to consumers of sea power in the fall of 1943. The focus of Allied operations shifted away from the region at the time, but the need to provide resources for coastal defense and local convoy escort duties remained, especially as German submarines fell back on more remote regions such as the African periphery and the Caribbean after evacuating the North Atlantic. The Anglo-American navies wished to extract their forces from these areas in order to concentrate units in Great Britain and the Western Pacific. They encouraged the French to take up such secondary roles in their own waters, but they did not need the Marine nationale to rejuvenate the instruments of a sea power of the first rank such as aircraft carriers, fast battleships, and heavy cruisers. The Allied prevalence in capital ships grew exponentially over those of the Axis navies throughout these months. In other words, the Anglo-Americans "were mainly interested in building up those parts of the French fleet that complemented those of the Allies," not refitting just any vessel that could make its way across the Atlantic to North America or transfer vessels to the French based on priorities formulated by the Algiers Amirauté.[82] This stance would be made even clearer through a new policy promulgated on 4 October 1943.

CCS Directive 358 (Revised), "Policies Regarding French Naval Vessels," sought to "consolidate into one paper all the policies on the subject of French naval vessels."[83] It superseded previous directives generated through the CCS machinery but respected the spirit of standing agreements such as those concluded between Churchill and de Gaulle in August 1940 as well as those entered with French North African authorities since Operation Torch. As put succinctly by an historian of French rearmament, the directive "covered all aspects of administration and operational control, such as overhauling, refitting, assignment and employment; it also proposed a detailed supply policy in connection with repairs and the issue of materiel."[84] The note began by clarifying command and control issues, avoiding the collaborative terms of the initial Clark-Darlan Agreement by using, instead, the clearer construct of the Churchill–de Gaulle framework: "French naval vessels are given initial assignments to operations areas by the Combined Chiefs of Staff. . . . [They] will operate under the operational command of the Allied naval area commander."[85] Matters of discipline and internal administration remained the purview of French authorities while Admiral King, USN, remained as the executive agent of the CCS "in collaboration with the Admiralty through the head of the British Admiralty Delegation, Washington."[86] The text also confirmed the existing mechanisms to handle French demands: "Requests from the French for new ships, proposals for major overhauls of ships and increases in armament in any theatre should be forwarded to the Allied area and theatre commanders who should give their recommendations. . . . [A] copy should be forwarded to the Munitions Assignment Boards, Washington, via the Chief of the French Naval Mission, Washington, with a copy to Munitions Assignment Board, London."[87]

CCS 358 (Revised) reiterated the existing considerations in selecting ships for "reconditioning" and the extent of the work to be done. Only the most modern and capable vessels that could be refitted in the minimum time would benefit from refurbishment of their hull, machinery, gun batteries, fire control, and damage control equipment; the augmentation of their antiaircraft armament as necessary; and the installation of essential radio, sonar, and radar sets. Reconditioning of other vessels would only be conducted "to the extent that it can be accomplished locally."[88] As for assignment of ships from the United States or Great Britain to the Marine nationale, the CCS themselves retained the ultimate authority for such decisions based on three requirements. Allocated vessels had to be (1) reserved for missions assigned to the French navy by the CCS; (2) manned with trained French personnel; and (3) employed under Allied control.[89] Finally, the policy envisioned the Anglo-Americans divesting themselves from the African theater in the long run: "Equipment now in French African ports, and operated by British or United States personnel, will be turned over to qualified French personnel so that the French may eventually take over the defense of their own territory."[90]

The French admiralty initially welcomed CCS 358 (Revised) because it clarified the policies and processes concerned with naval rearmament that had multiplied through the course of the previous year. Also of great interest to them, the directive provided a viable path for the transfer of vessels from Great Britain and the United States to France, although under strict conditions.[91] And CCS 358 (Revised) opened the channel for such transfers, which began within months and continued at a rapid pace throughout the year 1944. The Anglo-Americans turned over nearly 150 ships and submarines to the French, most notably: 6 U.S.-built destroyer escorts, 6 British River-class frigates (to be crewed by the FNGB), 2 British submarines (in addition to *Curie*, transferred to the Free French in May 1943), 1 former Italian submarine captured by the British, 32 patrol craft, 50 submarine chasers, 30 U.S. minesweepers and 10 British ones, 19 British harbor defense motor launches (in addition to the 2 transferred to the Free French in Beirut in February 1943), and 5 U.S. motor launches for use in the Pacific (in addition to the 3 Fairmile launches transferred from Canada to the FNFL in Saint-Pierre and Miquelon in January 1943).

These transfers constituted a considerable commitment for the Anglo-Americans, who also provided aircraft to the Marine nationale. Four shore-based squadrons of the Aéronavale operating in Africa were equipped with

Table 3.2: Combined U.S. and British Transfers to the French Navy, 1943–44
(including all transfers to the FNFL, FNGB, and FMA but not tugs and other small craft)

Category	Vessel(s) French Name	Country of Origin	Remarks
Cannon-class destroyer escorts	Sénégalais, Algérien, Tunisien, Marocain, Hova, Somali	U.S.	New builds transferred to the FMA between January and April 1944 (except for Tunisien, which would be crewed by the FNGB)
River-class frigates	L'Aventure, L'Escarmouche, Tonkinois, Croix de Lorraine, La Surprise, La Découverte	U.K.	All (except L'Aventure) had seen service in the RN before their transfer to the FNGB between October 1943 and October 1944
U-class submarine	Curie	U.K.	New build transferred to the FNGB in May 1943
V-class submarines	Doris, Morse	U.K.	New builds transferred to the FNGB in June 1944 (Doris) and October 1944 (Morse)
Acciaio-class submarine	Narval	Italy / U.K.	Transferred in February 1944
PC451-class patrol craft	Various (32)	U.S.	All existing builds except for the last six, all delivered between June and November 1944
SC497-class submarine chasers	Various (50)	U.S.	Mix of existing and new builds transferred between November 1943 and November 1944
YMS1-class minesweepers	Various (30)	U.S.	Mix of existing and new builds transferred between March and October 1944
105-ft motor minesweepers (MMS)-class	Various (9)	U.K.	Existing builds transferred between March and July 1944
Harbor defense motor launches (HDML)	Various (21)	U.K.	2 to the FNFL in Beirut in February 1943 3 to the FMA in Dakar in August 1943 16 in Algiers in August 1943
Fairmile motor launches	Galantry, Langlade, Colombier	Canada	All existing builds transferred to the FNFL for service in Saint-Pierre and Miquelon in January 1943
U.S. motor launches	VP 61, VP62, VP 63, VP 51, VP 52	U.S.	Existing builds transferred to the FNFL/FNGB in Micronesia (VP 61, 62, 63 in August 1943, and VP 51, 52 in November 1943)

allied airframes by late 1943: two with Sunderland flying boats and Wellington bombers from the Royal Air Force, one with Walruses from the RN's Fleet Air Arm, and one with Catalina flying boats from the United States.[92] Cynics may point to an overabundance of means on the Allied side by 1944, thus greatly facilitating such seemingly generous sacrifices on the part of the

American and British navies. Nevertheless, as underlined by the biographer of the U.S. chief of naval operations, "in retrospect, there had never been enough ships to fight the war. King was forced to juggle ships from one ocean to the other and, in the European theatre, from one front to the other."[93] France was but one of several Allied nations seeking to rebuild their strength at sea in the closing stages of the conflict, and the CCS remained besieged by competing demands for ships, submarines, and aircraft until the surrender of Japan in September 1945.

But the nature of those transfers also highlights that the CCS had relegated the Marine nationale to subsidiary roles by denying requests from the Amirauté for capital ships. Within weeks of the promulgation of Directive 358 (Revised), Lemonnier submitted an updated requisition to the JRC and another one in mid-February 1944, both including requests for transfers over and above those already approved, including an aircraft carrier. These were promptly dismissed: "The CCS had just decided that it would not be beneficial to the war effort to make further assignments of vessels to the French in the near future."[94] Lemonnier lamented in a letter to Fénard in early 1944: "We have ships but we do not have a fleet . . . in the sense that we no longer possess a main battle force [*corps de bataille*] which is the vital backbone of any fleet."[95]

Acquiring the means to assemble an aircraft carrier–centric *corps de bataille* became the focus of Lemonnier's planning for the remainder of the war and beyond. Not only would this capacity allow the Marine nationale to influence Allied strategy in the closing months of the conflict but planning for an uncertain peace weighted heavily on the admiral's mind. France could count on sitting at the victors' side at the end of the hostilities but would likely stand alone in the immediate postwar era. Disquieting signs already showed that the Alliance was unlikely to continue after the surrender of the Axis powers as tensions grew between Washington, London, and Moscow over the shape of the next international order. Devastated economically and divided politically, France would struggle in conciliating the demands for civilian reconstruction at home and developing armed forces suitable for a continental power with worldwide interests.

CHAPTER 4

PLANNING FOR AN UNCERTAIN PEACE

End of an Alliance, Rebuilding Alone

Three years to the day after her entrance in New York Harbor, battleship *Richelieu* made a triumphal arrival in Toulon on Monday, 11 February 1946. The moment was bittersweet, charged with conflicting emotions for the French sailors and the citizenry witnessing the event. Vice Admiral André Lemonnier, chief of the Naval General Staff, was on hand to present the ship with a prized unit commendation, the *Croix de guerre*. The battleship had performed exemplary service in the years since modernization at the Brooklyn Navy Yard, first joining the British Home Fleet bottling up Germany's few remaining capital ships in the fjords of Norway. She then traveled to the Indian Ocean for service with the Royal Navy's Eastern Fleet tasked with blocking Imperial Japanese Navy ships based in Singapore and striking enemy shore positions in Burma and the Dutch East Indies. And, following the surrender of Japan in September 1945, *Richelieu* escorted troopships dispatched to Indochina to regain control over the colony, later providing fire support to French forces ashore during the first skirmishes with Vietnamese guerillas, the then little-known Vietminh.[1]

The crew of *Richelieu* could be proud of those wartime accomplishments. But the hostilities had left the ship's company bitterly divided between those sailors who had remained loyal to Pétain to the very end, those who had joined de Gaulle into dissidence immediately after the armistice, and those who had followed Darlan when he switched allegiance to the Allies. Such tensions also fragmented the larger Marine nationale, the rest of the country's armed forces, and the whole nation. In more practical terms, Toulon itself was symbolic of the challenges ahead. The base and the city stood devastated by German sabotage and Allied bombings suffered during the Liberation while the harbor remained littered with the wrecks of the ships and submarines scuttled in November 1942. Simultaneously rebuilding civilian infrastructures, the fleet, and its bases would necessitate hard choices in the decade ahead by a body politic as divided as the nation itself. Charles de Gaulle resigned on 20 January 1946 as chairman of the Provisional Government of the French Republic, denouncing the resurgence of party politics he blamed for collapse of the Third Republic in 1940. The move ushered in the era of cabinet instability and national crises that would plague the Fourth Republic until its downfall in 1958.

As worrying for Lemonnier, France's largest warship may have distinguished herself in all assigned tasks, but these had taken place in theaters of secondary interest during the last two years of the conflict. By the time *Richelieu* joined the Royal Navy's Home Fleet, the threat to the British Isles had mostly passed with the largest German ships isolated in Norway. Assignment to the Eastern Fleet had confined the battleship to actions on the periphery of Japan's conquests. *Richelieu* did not have the opportunity to contribute to the liberation of metropolitan France and was instead confined to subordinate roles under British command in the Indian Ocean. This deployment was a far cry from Lemonnier's vision of placing the battleship and an aircraft carrier at the center of a new *corps de bataille* capable of autonomous action and shaping Allied strategy. Meanwhile, the Alliance itself was coming to an end. The United States and Great Britain looked forward to terminating the immense commitments made in wartime to rebuild and support the armed forces of their allies, including the Marine nationale. A sense of foreboding hung over the *Richelieu* even as the battleship was secured alongside and her sailors back in their homeland, at long last.

Wrapping Up a War

The Marine nationale as a whole shared *Richelieu*'s ambiguous record of tactical excellence matched by mitigated strategic influence since amalgamation in August 1943. Light cruisers based out of West Africa (*Georges Leygues*, *Gloire*, *Suffren*, *Duquesne*, *Tourville*, *Montcalm*, *Émile Bertin*) continued anti-raider patrols on the Dakar-Recife line until March 1944. A continuation of the first mission assigned to the Forces maritimes d'Afrique (FMA) after Operation Torch, this effort saw the French holding the eastern part of a line anchored at the other end by American cruisers sailing out of Brazilian ports. The force was also augmented by the Italian ships *Luigi di Savoia Duca Degli Abruzzi* and *Emanuele Filiberto Duca d'Aosta*, operating from the British colony of Freetown after November 1943.[2] But the bulk of the effort for the FMA focused on the Mediterranean. Following refit in the United States and reclassification as light cruisers under the Allied nomenclature, heavy *contre-torpilleurs* of the *Le Fantasque* class, joined by lighter destroyers and small sloops based out of Alexandria and Beirut, proved particularly effective in the conduct of offensive sweeps through the Aegean Sea and the Dodecanese islands in 1944 and deep into the Adriatic in 1945. Smaller units continued discharging the mostly monotonous but essential missions of convoy escort and coastal defense. They also carried out the dangerous tasks of minesweeping along the North African coast while rehabilitating severely damaged ports, such as the naval arsenal in Bizerte, Tunisia.[3]

More glamorous was participation in the amphibious operations conducted in the Mediterranean after the summer of 1943. First employed for the Allied landing in Salerno in early September (Operation Avalanche), light cruisers *Le Fantasque* and *Le Terrible* were suddenly recalled to join the French force tasked by Giraud to liberate Corsica, a significant effort in naval terms. In addition to these two ships, Admiral Lemonnier assigned cruisers *Montcalm* and *Jeanne d'Arc*; destroyers *L'Alcyon*, *Le Fortuné*, *Forbin*, *Basque*, and *Tempête*; and submarines *Casabianca*, *Aréthuse*, and *La Perle* as well as two merchant vessels to ferry 5,600 troops and 208 pieces of artillery, tanks, and other vehicles over the course of nineteen days. This move was without Allied support, save for one British landing craft (*LST 79*), which was the only vessel lost during the operation as a result of a strike by a German bomber on 30 September.[4] Thereafter, several of these same units participated in the buildup of Giraud's cherished expeditionary force by ferrying troops from North Africa to Italy to serve under General Alphonse Juin through the winter of 1943–44 and join the assault on the island of Elba on 17–19 June 1944.[5] French involvement in amphibious operations culminated with the landings in southern France.

Operation Dragoon's airborne drops and seaborne landings on the coast of Provence on 15 August 1944 allowed a Franco-American force to seize the ports of Toulon and Marseille before moving up the Rhône river valley to link up with the Allied armies breaking out of Normandy. The Marine nationale played an important role in the landings and the follow-on support of troops ashore. Under his direct command, Lemonnier assembled a fleet of thirty-four vessels of all tonnage, including the battleship *Lorraine*; heavy cruisers *Georges Leygues, Montcalm, Gloire, Émile Bertin, Duguay-Trouin* (and, later, the training cruiser *Jeanne d'Arc*); and light cruisers *Le Terrible, Le Malin,* and *Le Fantasque* as well as eight destroyers and more than a dozen smaller escort vessels.[6] Afterward, French units undertook the routine duties of securing the line of communications between North Africa and the *métropole*, minesweeping along the coast of southern France, and urgently rehabilitating the Provence ports. Several vessels joined American units to form Task Force 86 on 1 September 1944, initially under Rear Admiral Lyal A. Davidson, USN. In October Rear Admiral Philippe Auboyneau took over the newly renamed Flank Force, the first (and only) Allied naval task force placed under French command during the war.[7] The group was formed to continue harassing the remaining German naval forces still operating in the Gulf of Genoa and those of the Italian Social Republic, the rump fascist state formed by Benito Mussolini in September 1943. The heavier ships also bombarded enemy shore positions at the southern end of the Franco-Italian front, operations that continued until the end of the war in Europe.

Less stirring was the record of French submarines in the Mediterranean, even as the Marine nationale sought to concentrate such forces in that theater after the fusion of August 1943. Admittedly, this concentration commenced under disquieting omens when the Free French submarine *Minerve* left Great Britain for Beirut in October but was attacked by a Canadian Liberator aircraft while navigating on the surface south of Plymouth. The submarine survived, but two sailors were killed and several others wounded, and the vessel returned to the British Isles so badly damaged that it spent the rest of the war in reserve.[8] The former FNFL submarine *Junon* proceeded to Algeria in May 1944 but was found in decrepit state, and the FMA authorities placed her in reserve in August.[9] Meanwhile, the submersible minelaying *Rubis*, also scheduled for transfer to the Mediterranean, had to remain in Great Britain as a result of the loss of her replacement, *La Perle*. Allied aircraft misidentified the latter as it crossed the Atlantic following her refit in Philadelphia, sinking her south of Iceland in July 1944, with only one the fifty-eight crew surviving the attack.[10]

As for the FMA, they could still count on fifteen submarines in the wake of Operation Torch, but all were old. Although these units spent extensive periods of time patrolling off the coasts of northern Italy and southern France through 1943 and 1944, they experienced few successes, in part as a result of the decreasing number of Axis ships in those waters but also due to the poor quality of their sensors and torpedoes.[11] Despite these limited results, Allied authorities appreciated the contribution of French submarines in ancillary roles such as landing resistance agents and commandos on occupied coasts and providing targets for ships conducting antisubmarine warfare training, allowing the deployment of more modern British and American submarines to active theaters of war such as the Pacific. Meanwhile, in the Atlantic, Allied commanders also relegated French naval assets to secondary roles.

The former Free French ships and submarines remained busily committed to convoy escort duties and coastal raids. Several units were deployed for Operation Neptune on 6 June 1944 but did not project a strong French presence, scattered as they were among the immense Allied armada that closed in on the beaches of Normandy that day. The cruisers *Montcalm* and *Georges Leygues* provided fire support to American troops at Omaha Beach while *Duquesne* remained alongside but available in Great Britain; destroyer *La Combattante* supported the Canadians at Juno Beach; frigates *L'Aventure*, *La Surprise*, *L'Escarmouche*, and *La Découverte* as well as corvettes *Aconit*, *Renoncule*, *Roselys*, and *Commandant d'Estienne d'Orves* escorted transports in different groups; six motor torpedo boats of the 23rd MTB Flotilla provided security against German craft; and two divisions of minesweepers discharged their duties all along the waterfront.[12] The 1er Bataillon de fusiliers marins commandos (1st Battalion of Marine Commandos, also known as "Commando Kieffer," so named after its commander) counted as the only French unit landed from the sea that day, with less than two hundred troops taking part in the initial assault.[13] The battleship *Courbet*, first flagship of the Free French Naval Forces in 1940, also played an inglorious but important role, towed from Portsmouth to be sunk in front of Arromanches, part of the breakwater set up to protect one of the two artificial harbors, code-named Mulberries.[14]

The two Mulberries were particularly important to the Allied offensive in northwestern Europe. The lack of working ports to supply the offensive against Germany plagued the Allied effort throughout the following year, a situation made worse early on when the Omaha Beach Mulberry was destroyed in a storm on 19 June 1944.[15] Eventually breaking out of the Normandy beachhead that summer, Allied troops pushed the front lines eastward, but German garrisons stayed behind to hold France's Atlantic ports to the death. The capture of Cherbourg, Brest, and Toulon demonstrated that fighting to take such defended ports only left rubble in its wake. The Anglo-Americans left the French to besiege fortified cities such as Lorient, Saint-Nazaire, and La Rochelle while they focused on the advance to Germany.[16] In mid-December 1944 Lemonnier formed the French Naval Task Force to blockade these pockets from the sea and provide gun fire support to the French troops tasked to probe them from landward. Rear Admiral Joseph Rue remained in command of that unique group of French vessels assigned on and off until its disbandment on 28 May 1945.[17]

French sailors also distinguished themselves ashore. Fighting in France through the summer of 1944, the Commando Kieffer was then granted a short period of rest in Great Britain before taking part in the assault on the Dutch island of Walcheren in November. The 2ᵉ Régiment blindé de fusiliers-marins (2nd Armored Regiment of Marines) and the 2ᵉᵐᵉ Compagnie Médicale et Groupe d'Ambulancières de la Marine (the "Marinettes," female nurses and drivers of the 2nd Naval Medical and Ambulance Drivers Company) landed in Normandy on 1 August 1944 with the French army's 2nd Armored Division. From then on, they followed General Philippe Leclerc during his famous advance to Paris and Strasbourg, before crossing the Rhine into Bavaria and seeing the end of the war in Berchtesgaden. The 1ᵉʳ Régiment de fusiliers-marins (1st Naval Infantry Regiment) fought in Italy in 1943 before landing in southern France and moving up the Rhône valley in the fall of 1944. The regiment then joined the forces besieging German garrisons on the Atlantic coast, but the Ardennes offensive forced its return to the main front in December before finishing the war on the Franco-Italian border. The 4ᵉ Régiment de fusiliers-marins was deployed around Lorient while the 1ᵉʳ Régiment de canonniers-marins (1st Regiment of Naval Gunners) operated in the Gironde region after having served in Tunisia and on the Italian front.[18] The third and fifth regiments of *fusiliers-marins* were formed too late to see active service in the war in Europe but many of these troops would later deploy to Indochina.[19]

The fusion of August 1943 and renewed Anglo-American support also allowed French naval aviators to make an increasing contribution to the fight. Four Free French pilots and a group of mechanics had already taken up their assignment with the Royal Navy's Fleet Air Arm 807 Squadron earlier that year. They flew Seafires from the aircraft carrier *Indomitable* during the invasion of Sicily and then transferred to HMS *Battler* for the Salerno landings.[20] Meanwhile, another 260 of de Gaulle's flying personnel and ground crews traveled to the United States to train with the amphibian PBY-5A Catalina, eventually forming the 6ᵉ Flottille d'exploration (6th Patrol Flight) and deploying to Morocco in 1944 to conduct antisubmarine operations over the Atlantic for the remainder of the hostilities.[21] This formation joined those of the FMA already being reequipped in whole or in part with Allied aircraft. Based in Dakar were one patrol squadron of British Sunderlands (and older French Potez-CAMS 141), responsible for the sinking of *U-105* on 2 June 1943, and another flying Wellingtons, which sank *U-403* on 18 August 1943. A fighter squadron flew French Dewoitine, and two smaller sections operated Walrus amphibious biplanes out of bases in Algeria. By the end of the hostilities, eight shore-based Aéronavale squadrons flew fighters, dive-bombers (mainly American Douglas SBD Dauntless) and long-range patrol aircraft procured through Lend-Lease.[22]

French sailors, *fusiliers-marins*, commandos, and aviators served effectively after the fusion of August 1943, but they paid a high price discharging the peripheral tasks assigned to the Marine nationale by the Combined Chiefs of Staff. Symbolic of the unglamorous missions at hand, most of the French vessels sunk thereafter were lost to mines or accidents, as illustrated in table 4.1.

In addition to those losses, a serious mishap involved two French warships on Christmas Day 1944 when the light cruisers *Le Terrible* and *Le Malin*

Table 4.1: French Warships Lost at Sea, August 1943–May 1945
(excluding those lost in Indochina)

Date	Vessel Type and Name	Dead / Total Crew	Remarks
23 November 1943	Trawler-minesweeper *Marie Mad*	24 / 24	Mine strike off Ajaccio, Corsica FMA unit (French build)
21 December 1943	Submarine chaser *Chasseur 5 (Carentan)*	18 / 24	Floundered in a Channel storm FNGB unit (French build returned from the RN to the FNFL on 1 March 1943 and renamed *Carentan*)
29 December 1943 (approximately)	Submarine *Protée*	70 / 70	Mine strike off Marseilles FMA unit (French build formerly with Force X in Alexandria)
9 June 1944	Battleship *Courbet*	0 / 0	FNGB unit (French build scuttled off Normandy as a breakwater for the Mulberries)
8 July 1944	Submarine *La Perle*	54 / 55	Sank by Allied aircraft in mid-Atlantic FMA unit (French build modernized in Philadelphia Navy Yard)
22 October 1944	Minesweeper *D-202*	25 / 30	Mine strike off Marseille FMA unit (ex USS *YMS-77*)
9 January 1945	Submarine chaser *L'Enjoué*	60 / 60	Torpedo strike by *U-870* off Morocco FMA unit (ex USS *PC-482*)
15 February 1945	Submarine chaser *L'Ardent*	0 / 60	Collision with British freighter near Casablanca, Morocco FMA unit (ex USS *PC-473*)
23 February 1945	Destroyer *La Combattante*	68 / 185	Mine strike at the mouth of the Humber river in Great Britain FNGB unit (British Hunt-class destroyer transferred to the FNFL in December 1942)

collided at high speed near Naples, the latter losing her entire bow section, at the cost of seventy sailors between the two ships, sixty-two of them in *Le Malin* alone. Both ships survived, but neither saw active service for the remainder of the hostilities. The last French wartime losses at sea occurred on 17 April 1945, when an Italian motor torpedo boat struck the destroyer *Trombe* in the Gulf of Genoa. Nineteen sailors died as a result of the torpedo hit, and the ship made her way back into port only to be taken out of active service, damaged beyond repair.[23]

Through the course of the entire war, the various elements of the Marine nationale—the pre-armistice fleet, the FNFL, the Vichy Navy, the FMA, the reunified force after August 1943, and the forgotten Indochina flotilla (see table 4.2)—lost 249 warships and submarines (457,000 tons) and another 57,000 tons in auxiliary vessels at the hands of the Axis, Anglo-American forces, infighting among rival French factions, and scuttling by their own sailors. The dead or missing included 8,358 military crews, of whom 361 were officers. One must also recall that these losses do not include those suffered on land by the *fusiliers-marins* and the commandos, and in the air by the Aéronavale, nor the dozens of merchant seamen who continued losing their lives to Axis mines, submarines, and shore-based aircraft until the end of the hostilities. Nearly half of the 1939 merchant fleet vanished, with 1,328,858 tons lost to enemy action and accidents, and more than 1,500 mariners going to a watery grave on the high seas.[24]

These sacrifices had not been for naught. Heavy losses of men, ships, and submarines in the immediate aftermath of the armistice sustained the legitimacy of whichever political regime they pledged allegiance to and among the military powers with whom they aligned. The reunited Marine nationale could boast of a meaningful contribution to the Allied war effort in the last two years of the conflict and the eventual restoration of France as a self-governed and united country. But French admirals did not share the laurels of victory bequeathed onto army generals by popular opinion, and their vessels were relegated to secondary roles subservient to Allied strategy rather than shaping it to suit French interests. And even such mitigated results would have been impossible to achieve were it not for the proactive support of the Anglo-Americans in refurbishing and modernizing existing French units, training its officers and sailors, and transferring new assets to the fleet. As the hostilities came to an end, time had come to bring that essential support to a bittersweet conclusion, leaving much uncertainty in its wake.

Wrapping Up Aid

The Combined Chiefs of Staff decided in February 1944 to complete the delivery of those vessels already assigned for transfer to the French but declined follow-on requests from Lemonnier's staff. Deliveries of larger combatants were completed by the late fall of 1944.[25] In October Great Britain transferred the last two of six British River-class frigates and the last one of three

Table 4.2: Agony of the Indochina Fleet, 1943–45

Date	Vessel Type and Name	Remarks
26 November 1943	Armed trawler *Béryl*	Lost to a mine or torpedo strike by a U.S. submarine near Tuy Hòa
1 January 1944	Submarine *Pégasse*	Stripped of usable parts, abandoned on a riverbank near Saigon
26 February 1944	Survey ship *Astrolabe*	Sunk by U.S. bombers in Da Nang
26 February 1944	Armed trawler *Picanon*	Sunk by U.S. bombers in Da Nang Raised and refurbished, foundered in a typhoon north of Hue on 3 October 1944
30 April 1944	Sloop *Tahure*	Sunk by U.S. submarine while conducting coastal convoy escort near Cam Ranh Bay
12 January 1945	Cruiser *Lamotte-Picquet*	Sunk by U.S. bombers in the Donnai River
12 January 1945	Survey ship *Octant*	Sunk by U.S. bombers in Cam Ranh Bay
9 March 1945	Submarine chaser *Commandant Bourdais*	Scuttled by own crew in Haiphong
9 March 1945	Gunboat *Vigilante*	Scuttled by own crew in Haiphong
9 March 1945	Gunboat *Francis Garnier*	Scuttled by own crew on the Mekong River in Kratié, Cambodia
9 March 1945	Armed trawler *Paul Bert*	Sunk by French gunfire after seizure by Japanese troops in My Tho (near Saigon)
9 March 1945	Gunboat *Mytho*	Sunk by French gunfire after seizure by Japanese troops in My Tho (near Saigon)
9 March 1945	Submarine chaser *Avalanche*	Scuttled by her own crew in My Tho (near Saigon)
10 March 1945	Colonial sloop *Amiral Charner*	Sunk by Japanese bombers in My Tho (near Saigon)
10 March 1945	Gunboat *Tourane*	Scuttled by own crew in the Song Be River (near Da Nang)
10 March 1945	Sloop *Marne*	Scuttled by own crew in Can Tho (near Saigon)
12 March 1945	Survey ship *Lapérouse*	Scuttled by own crew in Can Tho (near Saigon)
12 March 1945	Armed trawler *Capitaine Coulon*	Scuttled by own crew in Can Tho (near Saigon)
Mid-May 1945	Armed buoy tender *Armand Rousseau*	Sunk by U.S. bombers while operated by a Japanese crew near Rach Gia (Gulf of Thailand)

Note
The only ships of the Indochina Fleet that survived the war were the gunboats *Frézouls* and *Crayssac*, which escaped to China after the Japanese coup of 9 March 1945. They sailed back to Haiphong on 15 August 1945, the first French military forces to return to Indochina in the wake of the Japanese surrender.

submarines it provided through the course of the war for crewing by the Free French/FNGB.[26] That same month, U.S. Navy crews delivered to Toulon the last of thirty YMS1-class minesweepers. The last of thirty-two American PC451-class patrol craft and the last of fifty submarine chasers arrived in November. The provision of British minesweepers lagged behind by a few months, with the last of fifteen 105-ft motor minesweeper-class delivered in the early months of 1945, along with six 126-ft motor minesweeper-class during that same timeframe. The completion of major amphibious operations in Europe also led to handing over a motley mix of landing vessels through the winter of 1944–45: thirty U.S. landing craft, vehicle/personnel; eight U.S. landing craft, medium; two U.S. landing craft, tank; twenty-one British landing barges, vehicle; nine British landing barges, oil; and six British landing barges, water. This list does not include transfer by the Allies of the multitude of smaller auxiliaries necessary to support day-to-day operations of a large navy: tugs, net tenders, floating cranes, fire boats, and such.

The Americans also made an important contribution by leaving behind large shore infrastructures that the French navy could eventually leverage in its postwar planning. In addition to rehabilitating the commercial ports in North Africa and the *métropole*—from Casablanca and Oran to Marseilles and Le Havre, among others—they dedicated great efforts to restoring the naval dockyards in Bizerte, Toulon, and Brest. They also created a string of new bases and facilities, as reported by an American historian of the World War II French navy: "Before the end, there were some twenty-one identifiable [U.S.] naval bases of various kinds located in French North Africa, and two in France itself. Many of them were as large as small cities."[27]

Another important legacy for the fledgling Aéronavale was the opening of American flight schools to French candidates, with nearly half of all naval aircrews who obtained qualifications during the years 1942–46 doing so in the United States (193 pilots in total, with another 92 trained in Great Britain, 32 in Canada, and 83 in France).[28] Still, as grateful as French admirals may have been for such support, it remained that the steadfast refusal by the CCS to consider requests for completion of the battleship *Jean Bart* and modernization of additional cruisers (namely the older *Duquesne*, *Tourville*, and *Suffren*), let alone the allocation of a fleet aircraft carrier, grated on Lemonnier and his subordinates.[29]

The old *Béarn* was refitted in New Orleans as an aircraft transport in 1943–44. French naval rearmament plans sought to build on this meek beginning by including an obstinate demand for a large, fast aircraft carrier capable of the full range of combat operations expected of those vessels deployed in powerful task forces in the Pacific. Ships of the American *Essex* class came to dominate that category at 30,000 tons, with nearly one hundred aircraft embarked and sustained speed of more than thirty knots. Smaller units displacing from 10,000 to 15,000 tons with up to fifty airplanes on board—the light aircraft carrier, often built using sleek cruiser hulls and powerful turbine engines—also grew in importance during these years, but French staff kept pressuring the Fénard Mission in Washington to secure the larger platform. As noted by French historian Alexandre Sheldon-Duplaix, such ambitions were clearly misplaced as the United States had yet to transfer a fleet or light carrier to any of its allies, agreeing at most to provide escort carriers to Great Britain.[30] Often built using converted commercial ships, these vessels were too small, embarking fifteen to thirty aircraft, and too slow, at less than twenty knots, to operate with fast task forces. They played a critical role, though, in augmenting air cover during amphibious landings and substituting for larger carriers in the North Atlantic and Indian Ocean.

Seemingly as a result of Admiral Fénard's relentless lobbying, the Combined Chiefs of Staff relented in February 1945 and agreed to transfer one escort carrier to the Marine nationale. The vessel selected was the former passenger cargo ship *Rio Parana*, launched in 1940 and acquired by the U.S. Navy the following year for conversion to the carrier role. Leased to Great Britain in 1942 as HMS *Biter*, the small escort carrier first deployed for Operation Torch where, ironically, her complement of Sea Hurricanes contributed to the destruction of more than twenty French aircraft based in Oran. *Biter* then served on North Atlantic convoy routes but suffered damage in November 1943 when a Swordfish crashed into the sea on its final approach, releasing a torpedo that struck the ship's stern. More damage ensued as a result of a fire in August 1944, and she was placed in reserve in January 1945.[31]

The vessel was in poor condition when taken over by the French on 9 April 1945, subject to strict conditions from the CCS. The soon-to-be renamed

Dixmude—commemorating the heroic stand by a brigade of *fusiliers-marins* in that Belgian town in October 1914—was meant for employment as a humble aircraft transport, not an aircraft carrier, and could only be refitted using French resources.[32] Shipyard workers from Brest arrived in Faslane, Scotland, in the summer of 1945 to assist the Marine nationale crew making the ex-*Biter* fit to operate at sea (including the installation of a 10,000-liter wine tank!) but even such a scaled-down project proved a challenge for France. *Dixmude* did not resume her role as an actual aircraft carrier until January 1947, when she left Europe for a first deployment to Indochina.[33]

The transfer of *Dixmude* to the French navy took place under new Allied rearmament channels instituted in the fall of 1944 as a result of the liberation of France. General Henry Maitland Wilson of the British Army had succeeded Eisenhower at Allied Forces Headquarters (AFHQ) in Algiers on 8 January 1944, taking on the title of Supreme Allied Commander for the Mediterranean. In the lead-up to Operation Dragoon, Wilson recommended to the Combined Chiefs of Staff that the provisions of CCS 358 (Revised) "be extended to the ports expected to be captured in the forthcoming operation and to the French warships and naval personnel likely to be operating outside direct [U.S.] and British control."[34] The CCS approved this measure on 21 September but carefully worded their support, given the reluctance to contribute to France's postwar plans. They directed that "the supply of repair equipment and materials, ships, and stores to the French Navy in its home ports and to the ports themselves for their rehabilitation be limited to the extent required for the support of operations."[35]

By the fall of 1944, greater coordination became necessary between AFHQ—still responsible for rearmament of those French forces based in North Africa—and Supreme Headquarters Allied Expeditionary Force (SHAEF, Eisenhower's headquarters in London), which assumed a similar role for units and bases in metropolitan France. The latter took the leading role in handling discussions with de Gaulle's provisional government, by then installed in Paris, regarding the rearmament of all French military forces. Eisenhower had already ordered the establishment of the SHAEF mission to France on 3 September under U.S. Army Major General John T. Lewis to "provide liaison between the French Government and Supreme

Headquarters and to furnish a staff to aid the French in dealing with civil affairs in liberated France."[36] In turn, Brigadier General Harold F. Loomis, USA, was appointed on 3 October 1944 as head of the Rearmament Division of the SHAEF mission to France, bringing to Paris the larger part of the Anglo-American staff until then employed in Algiers with AFHQ's Joint Rearmament Committee.[37] The mandate of the team evolved throughout the fall, including an extension of its responsibilities to the rearmament of other European allies (Belgium, Holland, and Denmark) until SHAEF more clearly delineated its duties, as depicted by American historian Forrest Pogue:

(1) to set up and implement ground and air rearmament programs which the Combined Chiefs of Staff had approved or might approve in SHAEF's sphere;

(2) to provide inspection and training groups for the formation of approved units;

(3) to co-ordinate within SHAEF and with the nation concerned all demands for rearmament of units not in approved rearmament programs; and

(4) to keep the staff sections of SHAEF and missions to foreign governments informed regarding rearmament programs and proposals for rearmament put forward by various nations.[38]

Another reorganization at the end of December resulted in the stand-up of independent naval and air divisions, established under the jurisdiction of SHAEF mission to France in parallel to the Rearmament Division, which would focus solely on building up ground forces. Captain Dallas D. Dupre, USN, took command of the Naval Division in Paris, overseeing the continued rehabilitation of the Marine nationale under the guidance of Vice Admiral Allan G. Kirk, USN, head of the U.S. Naval mission at SHAEF in London.[39] Following the surrender of Germany, SHAEF was dissolved on 14 July 1945. Its contingents returned to their respective national authorities, including the Americans who formed U.S. Forces European Theater, headquartered in Frankfurt with Eisenhower remaining in command until his appointment as U.S. Army chief of staff in November.[40] American personnel continued their work in rearmament, naval, and air divisions transferred directly to U.S.

Forces European Theater while the British stood up their own rearmament organization. However, on 1 November 1945, the United States formally terminated its assistance to Allied rearmament, and the Fénard Mission in Washington was disbanded on 1 January 1946, bringing that effort to an end.[41]

Allies of the United States could have foreseen this precipitated conclusion. Washington agreed to a new Lend-Lease pact signed with de Gaulle's provisional government on 28 February 1945 that included an unprecedented provision for civilian reconstruction following the cessation of hostilities.[42] However, upon Roosevelt's death on 12 April, Vice President Harry S. Truman took over the presidency and immediately came under domestic political pressure to wind down Lend-Lease. Congress passed a vote that same month prohibiting the use of the act for postconflict commitments, and Senate hearings gave rise to increasing disquiet about its future scale. Reasons to oppose Lead-Lease in the last year of the war were varied, ranging from long-standing "anti–New Dealism" in Republican circles to frustration with growing shortages and rationing on the home front. Perhaps unfairly, concerns also mounted that recipients of American aid were not pulling their full weight in the closing months of the war.[43]

On 20 August 1945, within days of the defeat of Japan, Truman instructed Leo T. Crowley, head of the Foreign Economic Administration, to cancel all contracts passed under the clauses of Lend-Lease unless countries agreed to complete them on a cash-payment basis.[44] On 5 September Truman clarified his position, stating that military lend-lease was terminated but that the United States would continue providing Allied troops with those medical supplies, rations, and shelter that countries could not yet supply. In December he renewed the provision of civilian aid through the harsh winter months but held firm on terminating all outstanding contracts no later than 30 June 1946.[45]

Meanwhile, bilateral talks between Washington and Paris took place to arrange a final settlement, concluding on 28 May 1946. Negotiators determined that France's wartime debt to the United States amounted to $720 million. They eventually agreed on this figure through arduous debates to define an extensive list of goods and services that would not need reimbursement as well as defining what amounted to reciprocal aid—for example, French goods and property provided for free to U.S. forces operating in North Africa and major items such as the ocean liner *Normandie*, seized by American authorities in 1941 but lost to a fire in February 1942.[46] These sums were deducted from the aid provided by America to all French parties since 1941 (Vichy, the Free French, the Giraudists, the Algiers' Committee of Liberation and the Provisional Government).[47] France committed to reimburse this debt, reduced to $653.3 million in March 1949 after another round of negotiations resulting from a more accurate compilation of the final bills on both sides, with a 2 percent interest rate over thirty years starting on 1 July 1951. Final payment occurred in 1980, just slightly ahead of schedule.

Lend-Lease had played a pivotal role in rehabilitation of the Marine nationale, and the end of the war left France's navy with a large fleet but the overall value of these vessels was questionable. Many of its units were obsolete, others too expensive to modernize, and the overall mix of French, British, and American designs—let alone soon-to-be delivered German and Italian war reparations—would challenge French maintainers and suppliers for years to come. The force had grown haphazardly according to allied priorities as opposed to French desires, a heterogonous assembly of *poussières navales* (literally "naval dust") in Lemmonier's view. Such a term highlighted the scale of the challenge he faced in forging a naval instrument capable of defending the national interest at home and abroad as France stood alone in the postwar era.

Planning to Rebuild Alone

Assembling an aggregate of nearly four hundred ships and submarines in September 1945, the French fleet cut a respectable figure, given the trials suffered since 1939. A previous study ranked the Marine nationale fourth in size behind the navies of the United States, Great Britain, and the Soviet Union at that time, the same rank held at the outset of World War II (behind the United States, United Kingdom, and Japan) but with even more hulls than in 1939.[48] Nevertheless, its overall tonnage counted for less than half of that making up the fleet six years earlier (350,000 tons vice 745,000), far behind the Anglo-Americans in its ability to mount large, autonomous naval operations at great distance from its homeports. The only units capable of undertaking such blue-water missions in the foreseeable future remained *Richelieu*, the four cruisers and the four heavy destroyers/light cruisers refitted

Table 4.3: Marine Nationale Vessels of French Origin, 1 September 1945

(not including vessels afloat but confined to port as depot/barrack ships, such as battleship *Paris*, or returned to France by the Allies at the end of the hostilities and placed in reserve)

Category	Vessel Name or Number of Hulls per Category	Combined Tonnage	Remarks
Dreadnought battleship	*Lorraine*	23,500	Obsolete, assigned to gunnery school in Toulon
Fast battleships	*Richelieu, Jean Bart*	70,000	*Richelieu*: Operational in Trincomalee (Ceylon), soon to depart for Indochina *Jean Bart*: Not operational, in Cherbourg awaiting completion
Aircraft transport	*Béarn*	22,500	Obsolete and under repair in Casablanca, soon to depart for Indochina
Heavy cruisers (not refitted in the U.S.)	*Duquesne, Tourville, Suffren*	30,000	*Suffren*: Operational but obsolete in Toulon, departed for Indochina 21 September 1945 *Tourville*: Obsolete, in refit in Toulon, departed for Indochina 5 December 1945 *Duquesne*: Obsolete, in refit in Brest, departed for Indochina 22 December 1945
Cruisers (refitted in the U.S.)	*Gloire, Montcalm, Georges Leygues, Émile Bertin*	21,900	*Gloire*: Operational in Brest, departed for Indochina 21 September 1945 *Montcalm*: In refit in Toulon (June 1945–February 1946) *Georges Leygues*: In refit in Casablanca (June 1945–January 1946) *Émile Bertin*: In refit in Toulon, departed for Indochina 11 October 1945
Light cruiser (not refitted in the U.S.)	*Duguay Trouin*	8,000	Operational but obsolete in Algiers, used as a troop transport in the Mediterranean
Training cruiser (not refitted in the U.S.)	*Jeanne d'Arc*	6,500	Operational but obsolete in Beirut, soon to return to at-sea training role for naval cadets
Light cruisers (former destroyers modernized in the U.S.)	*Le Fantasque, Le Terrible, Le Malin, Le Triomphant*	10,400	*Le Fantasque*: Operational in Toulon, soon to depart for Indochina *Le Malin*: In postcollision refit in Toulon *Le Terrible*: In postcollision refit in Bizerte *Le Triomphant*: Operational in Trincomalee (Ceylon), soon to depart for the Pacific with *Richelieu*
Destroyers (fitted with U.S./U.K. equipment in Bermuda or North Africa)	*Tempête, Simoun, L'Alcyon, Le Fortuné, Forbin, Basque*	8,910	*Tempête*: Operational in Toulon, employed as troop transport in the Mediterranean *Simoun*: Operational in Toulon, dispatched for occupation duties in Wilhelmshaven *L'Alcyon*: Operational in Toulon, employed as troop transport in the Mediterranean *Le Fortuné*: In refit in Casablanc *Forbin*: In refit in Bizerte *Basque*: In refit in Toulon

(continued)

Table 4.3 *(continued)*

Category	Vessel Name or Number of Hulls per Category	Combined Tonnage	Remarks
Destroyers (not modernized)	*Tigre, Albatros*	4,500	*Tigre*: Operational but obsolete, employed on occupation duties in Kiel *Albatros*: Obsolete, still in refit in Casablanca after heavy damage during Operation Torch
Submarines (refitted in the U.S.)	4 × 1,500-ton types 2 × 600-ton types	7,200	*Archimède*: Operational in Oran, scheduled for transfer to the Pacific but deployment cancelled *Le Glorieux*: Operational in Oran, scheduled for transfer to the Pacific but deployment cancelled *Centaure*: Operational in Oran, training duties *Casabianca*: Operational in Oran *Amazone*: Operational, employed on training duties at Fleet Sonar School, Key West, Florida *Antiope*: Operational, employed on training duties at Fleet Sonar School, Key West, Florida
Submarines (not modernized)	5 × 600-ton type	3,000	*Orphée*: Operational, training duties in Oran *La Vestale*: Operational, training duties in Dakar *La Sultane*: Operational in La Pallice *Junon*: In reserve, scheduled for refit in Brest *Iris*: Operational but still detained in Cartagena, Spain, after escape from 1942 Toulon scuttling
Colonial sloops	3 × 2,000-ton types	6,000	*Dumont d'Urville*: Operational, modernized in Charleston, South Carolina, in 1943 *Savorgnan de Brazza*: Operational but obsolete, soon dispatched to Indochina *Ville d'Ys*: Operational but obsolete, operating in French Polynesia
Minesweeping sloops	12	7,560	Operational but obsolete
Submarine chasers	11	1,430	Operational but obsolete
Submarine tender	*Jules Vernes*	4,350	In Algiers, soon to depart for Indochina
Gunboats	*Frézouls, Crayssac*	1,200	Operational but obsolete in Indochina
Totals	**65**	**236,950**	Only 18% of the total number of hulls but 68% of the total tonnage in 1945

Table 4.4: Marine Nationale Vessels of Foreign Origin, 1 September 1945

Category	Vessel Name or Number of Hulls per Category	Combined Tonnage	Remarks
Aircraft transport	*Dixmude*	8,200	Operational but obsolete in Brest, employed as troop, cargo, and aircraft transport
U.S. destroyers	6 Destroyer escorts	10,440	Operational and modern: *Sénégalais, Algérien, Tunisien, Marocain, Hova, Somali*
British frigates	6 River class	9,000	Operational and modern: *La Découverte, L'Aventure, L'Escarmouche, La Surprise, Croix de Lorraine, Tonkinois*
British corvettes	7 Flower class	8,050	Operational but obsolete: *Lobélia, Aconit, Renoncule, Commandant Detroyat, Roselys, Commandant Drogou, Commandant d'Etienne d'Orves*
British submarines	3 V class	1,950	Operational and modern: *Curie, Doris, Morse*
Italian submarine	*Narval*	710	Operational but obsolete
British minesweepers	15 105-ft motor minesweeper class 6 126-ft motor minesweeper class	4,080	Operational and modern
U.S. minesweepers	30 YMS1 class	8,100	Operational and modern
U.S. submarine chasers	50 SC497 class	5,000	Operational and modern
U.S.-built patrol craft	32 PC451 class	12,000	Operational and modern
Motor launches and motor torpedo boats	32 various classes	1,920	All operational but a mix of modern and obsolete material
Auxiliaries	120 landing crafts and auxiliaries	43,600	Most operational but a mix of modern and obsolete equipment
Totals	309	113,050	82% of the total number of hulls but only 32% of the total tonnage in 1945

in the United States, and the dozen or so modern escort vessels leased from the Americans and the British. Even the submarines transferred to the Free French by Great Britain and those refitted in the Philadelphia Navy Yard verged on obsolescence.

As concerning for French admirals, the last two years of the war had put a dramatic end to the short-lived rise of the navy in the consciousness of the French people. Unlike the Marine nationale, the army had seemed to bear a very large part of responsibility for the humiliating armistice, momentarily losing the respect that had endured through centuries of European warfare, regardless of victory or defeat on the battlefield. Filling this momentary void from 1940 to 1942, both de Gaulle and Pétain used their respective fleets to sustain political legitimacy and negotiate adroitly with the Allies and the Axis. But, after Operation Torch, the army came back to the fore. Soldiers from the *métropole* and across the empire fought and died in Tunisia, Italy, France, and Germany—with more to follow in Indochina—while action at sea received less and less coverage in the papers. By 1945 de Gaulle was known colloquially as le Général while Juin, Leclerc, Jean de Lattre de Tassigny, and Marie-Pierre Koenig were household names familiar to all citizens of France, unlike senior leaders of the French navy.

The most well-known French admiral of World War II remained the collaborationist Darlan, with the rebellious Muselier but a faint memory and the bland Lemonnier an obscure figure even while still in command. Despite the *épuration* (purification) commenced by the Gaullists after the 1943 fusion, the navy remained populated by former Vichysts since not enough experienced personnel could be found from within the small Free French navy alone. Within a few years, former Vichy senior officers were again reaching flag rank.[49] Regardless of their past records, these officers would have to convince government and their fellow citizens of the continued importance of sea power in the postwar era and the requirement to invest vast sums to regenerate a modern fleet—not that they had waited for the end of the hostilities to ponder these issues.

While continuing to arm and modernize anything that could float and fight after the fusion of August 1943, Lemonnier rapidly built on the initial work of his predecessor, Michelier, and submitted in September a vision for a postwar navy worthy of a rejuvenated France with great power ambitions. He proposed a fleet structured to defend the *métropole* and the empire independently of the Allies, capable of operating autonomously around the world, built around several task forces—each pairing one fleet aircraft carrier and one battle-ship and a suite of escorting cruisers, destroyers, and replenishment vessels, as practiced by the Americans in the Pacific. The navy would also require groups composed of smaller escort carriers and escorts vessels for the likely replay of the Battle of the Atlantic, as well as long-range attack submarines.

Meanwhile, ongoing littoral operations in Europe and Asia showed the need for an eclectic mix of amphibious vessels, fast motor torpedo boats, smaller coastal submarines, and minesweepers.[50]

Lemonnier submitted this initial assessment to the French Committee of National Liberation in preparation for the plea Giraud and de Gaulle addressed jointly to the Allies on 18 September 1943.[51] Laying out ambitious demands for rebuilding their newly unified forces, it was answered regarding naval matters through the previously discussed CCS Directive 358 (Revised). Strategic and practical realities dramatically circumscribed Lemonnier's original vision. The committee's request only included the completion of *Jean Bart* and acquisition of a single aircraft carrier in terms of capital ships, while the CCS reply eliminated any reference to such large vessels, focusing support on the regeneration of escorts and minesweepers in addition to a few cruisers and submarines. While France's naval planners did not abandon their original ambitions once they moved back into the old Admiralty on the Rue Royale in Paris in September 1944, they also realized the need to plan for a humbler *flotte de transition*, a postwar transition fleet based on a sober assessment of the conditions likely to prevail after the defeat of Germany.

The Navy General Staff submitted another study on 6 November 1944 to Minister of the Navy Louis Jacquinot. It highlighted four concerns that would impede France's capacity to regenerate the fleet in the coming years.[52] First and foremost was the widespread destruction of naval dockyards and civilian shipyards in the *métropole* as a result of German sabotage and Allied bombings. Compounding this issue was the loss of several key industrial facilities and dispersal of workers through the war years, particularly those required for production of specialized marine equipment—heavy guns and munitions, main engines and propulsion trains, advanced welding for submarine high-pressure joints, and so on. Also lost was the industrial base and experience to produce modern aircraft necessary to renew an indigenous Aéronavale, both long-range shore-based patrol planes and those to embark in some future aircraft carrier. Last, and as concerning, was the absence of domestic expertise in the scientific and technical fields that had assumed so much importance in such a short time during the war at sea—radars and sonars, and encryption, as well as fire-control and electronic warfare systems.

Given these crippling factors, Lemonnier estimated that France would not be able to build new warships domestically, other than small patrol craft and auxiliaries, before the end of 1947 at the earliest. The report assumed that the hostilities would be over by then and that Allied assistance would come to an end with no transfer of British or American vessels other than those already approved by the CCS in 1944. Several Marine nationale units would reach their *limite d'âge* (end of service life) by the end of 1947, requiring their paying off and leaving a fleet of barely 100,000 tons made up of the *Richelieu*, five cruisers, four light cruisers, five submarines, and a handful of frigates, corvettes, and torpedo boats. The transition plan laid out very conservative ambitions in the short term: no new constructions in 1945 with resources focused on maintaining existing vessels and bringing into service the ships and submarines transferred by the Allies; the completion in 1946 of vessels abandoned in French yards in 1940 while still under construction (essentially five submarines, three destroyers, and a handful of torpedo boats); and, in 1947, construction of the first light units ordered as part of this new transition fleet as well as completion of the battleship *Jean Bart*. Additionally, Lemonnier recommended adoption of British and American calibers for all new armaments in order to facilitate acquisition of munitions on the international market.

In contrast to such immediate restraint, the chief of the Navy General Staff also proposed launching a series of studies forthwith so that plans for building up a much larger fleet—a *plan de base*—would be available when France's shipbuilding capacity was restored, after 1947 presumably. It called for four fleet aircraft carriers of 22,000 tons each, all of French construction or a mix that would include the acquisition of light or escort carriers from overseas. A minimum of two should nevertheless be built in France to develop a domestic capability and ensure inclusion of the latest lessons learned from the war. Large cruisers would be required at a rate of one new build per year, while two smaller cruisers a year were warranted. The current mix of destroyers, frigates, corvettes, and *avisos* would be replaced by only two classes, a large one of 1,500 tons and a smaller one of 300 tons, while only one type of submarine would remain at 750 tons. One large and one small escort as well as one submarine would be launched every six months to effect the timely replacement of existing platforms. The report concluded that such tremendous increase in production would require the specialization of shipyards. Designated yards would each produce an assigned category of vessel while production rates would continue until peace and the reassessment of international conditions allowed a better definition of the post-transition fleet.

The naval staff expanded on these ambitions in a follow-on report submitted by Admiral Lemonnier to Minister Jacquinot on 11 April 1945.[53] This document provided a more fulsome picture, moving beyond the types and number of vessels that warranted building to take into consideration likely future missions for the Marine nationale as well as the personnel and the framework of bases required to support the fleet. It described the minimum navy tasks as the defense of the metropolitan territory and essential sea lines of communications (in particular, that between Europe and North Africa), policing the empire, and contributing a credible force to some sort of international security organization. Such missions would require no less than two battleships, four fleet aircraft carriers and six escort carriers, twelve cruisers (six heavy and six light), thirty destroyers, and thirty large submarines. This main force was to be augmented by patrol craft and minesweepers as well as smaller coastal submarines; a training flotilla of large ships and auxiliaries; thirty squadrons of shore-based and carrier aircraft; and a sufficient number of tankers, maintenance ships, and auxiliary vessels. The fleet would reach 400,000 tons—150,000 tons of which would be aircraft carriers—supported by a vast network of bases stretching across the colonial empire.

Planners also recommended continuing the prewar practice for the Marine nationale to exercise responsibility for local defense of its shore installations, thus the requirement for additional shore-based aircraft, artillery, and troops. This plan would bring total personnel demand to 70,000 officers, sailors, naval aviators, and *fusiliers-marins* (regulars and conscripts alike: 20,000 embarked in ships and submarines, 20,000 for the *Aéronavale*, 20,000 ground troops, and 10,000 shore personnel). This proposed number for the peacetime navy was ambitious given that the navy's wartime ranks peaked at 93,000 on 1 June 1945 (5,500 officers, 78,500 ratings, 1,100 women of the female service, 2,000 auxiliaries, and 5,900 support personnel).[54] Lemonnier's shipbuilding plans seemed even more aggressive, aiming to launch 60,000 tons' worth of warships per year, double the output of French yards during the interwar period.[55]

For the more immediate term, it was believed that France would dispatch a large expeditionary force to the Pacific to fight Japan, leading Minister Jacquinot to endorse the navy's proposal and more on 28 June 1945.[56] In addition to the April plan, the draft legislation meant for submission to de Gaulle's provisional government included the immediate overhaul of the seaplane carrier *Commandant Teste* and the completion of the cruiser *De Grasse*; the destroyer *L'Aventurier*; submarines *La Créole, L'Africaine, L'Astrée, Artémis, Andromède,* and *L'Antigone*; and the submarine minelayer *Corail*, all vessels that had been under construction but not yet completed at the time of the armistice. The draft proposed the purchase of three new destroyers from Great Britain as well as the transfer from Germany of six surrendered Type XXI submarines, six large Narvik-class destroyers, and six modern motor torpedo boats. Two large submarine tenders, one hospital ship, and three cargo ships would be required to provide logistical support to the fleet expected to deploy to the Pacific in the coming months. Finally, it included provisions for the immediate formation of four new Aéronavale squadrons and aimed to retain a total of 83,500 personnel in the service.

But even before Jacquinot could bring this proposal to the cabinet, dramatic developments that summer—namely, the surrender of Japan and the end of military Lend-Lease—led him and Admiral Lemonnier to reconsider the plans. A new draft legislation dated 17 September 1945 differed considerably from the previous one, starting with the admission that efforts to define the structure of a long-term, post-transition fleet—another *plan de base*—would be in vain at this point given the prevailing uncertainty with regard to future technological developments, France's geostrategic commitments, and budget allocations in future years.[57] The new draft limited itself to promulgating a plan for the year 1946, starting with much lowered ambitions, closer to the *flotte de transition* envisioned in November 1944, starting with personnel figures dropped to 72,000 (of which 58,000 would be embarked crews).

Navy missions were also reorganized, with that of reestablishing French sovereignty over Indochina ranking first and necessitating the reapportionment of ships to form the Far East Naval Force (battleship *Richelieu*, one heavy cruiser, six cruisers, and four colonial sloops); an Indochina flotilla (three destroyers, six frigates, and three minesweepers) and the resources to put back into service the naval bases in Saigon and Cam Ranh; a transport force using all suitable warships in the absence of dedicated troop transports (initially four cruisers, the carriers *Béarn* and *Dixmude*, and the submarine tender *Jules Verne*); and a brigade of 2,400 *fusiliers-marins*. Forces tasked with missions closer to Europe (such as occupation duties in Germany and a flotilla in the Levant) would be minimal in view of that effort, with the exception of those required to continue minesweeping the French shores with no less than 112 vessels dedicated to that undertaking, including several confiscated from Germany.

Thus, from the fall of 1943 up to the end of 1945, French postwar naval rearmament plans underwent considerable reassessments, from rather grandiose in September 1943, to humble in November 1944, to even more ambitious in April and June 1945, to a pale shadow of themselves in September 1945. These developments did not occur in a vacuum. In addition to the developments on the international scene (the defeat of Germany, the surrender of Japan, the cessation of Lend-Lease), Admiral Lemonnier and Navy Minister Jacquinot had to take into account directions from their government and answer conflicting views voiced in the quasi legislature, the Assemblée consultative provisoire (Provisional Consultative Assembly). And debates over budget allocations would only grow more acrimonious through the fall of 1945 as French leaders now had to resolve the fundamental quandary laid out in the newspaper *Le Monde* the week after the bombings of Hiroshima and Nagasaki: "[Until recently], it was understood that all of our energies had to be dedicated to the liberation of the metropole and Indochina. This was the necessary price to regain our independence and our honour, and our territories overseas. But the surrender of Germany yesterday and that of Japan today changes this perspective. We must win the peace now. And without delay we must ask ourselves what policy must follow these victories: can we simultaneously rearm and rebuild?"[58]

Budgeting for Peace

With Churchill committed to subsidizing *la France libre* since August 1940 and the Roosevelt administration taking on the rebuilding of Giraud's forces after November 1942, the matter of financing military rearmament had not weighed heavily on the Algiers Committee in 1943. This seeming laissez-faire came to an abrupt end in the fall of 1944 after de Gaulle's provisional government moved to Paris. Both British financial support and American Lend-Lease involved reimbursements at the end of the hostilities, two important contributors to the postwar debt about to balloon as the extent of the damage inflicted on the country's civilian infrastructure became evident. In the more immediate term, government expenses for fiscal year 1945 were expected to reach a staggering 465 billion French francs, with revenues of barely 222 billion. Industrial output that year would amount to 38 percent of the 1938 level, while production of wheat that summer was half that of 1939.[59] Six million inhabitants were homeless, 635,000 citizens (military and civilians) had perished, and 585,000 veterans from the three services and the Resistance returned home as invalids.[60] As in every war-torn country, inflation was rife and the black market thrived, bringing the matter of postwar finances to the forefront even as the Allies had yet to defeat the two remaining Axis powers.

Although seized with these issues, de Gaulle also remained dedicated to restoring France's grandeur for the longer term, and credible armed forces were central to that project: "To regain her status was not all. France must also be able to maintain it."[61] The rebuilding of the Armée d'Afrique continued unabated. Eight army divisions were fully equipped in the fall of 1944, with three more under refurbishment. As part of the summer of 1943 fusion, de Gaulle and Giraud had established the Comité de Défense nationale (CDN, or National Defense Committee) tasked with overseeing the higher coordination of the armed forces. Supported by its own military secretariat, de Gaulle presided the committee, and the membership included Giraud and the commanders of the army, navy, and air force. Following Giraud's eviction as *commandant en chef* in April 1944, the CDN's secretariat grew in stature, becoming the État-major de la Défense nationale (National Defense Staff) and then the État-major général de la Défense nationale (National Defense General Staff) on 24 October 1944. Its first chief was General Antoine Béthouart (who had returned from Washington) until replaced by General Juin, appointed in August 1944 as *chef de l'État-major général de la Défense nationale* (chief of the National Defense General Staff).[62]

Juin informed the CCS in September that Liberation had opened up a vast pool of recruitment in metropolitan France, which would allow building up beyond the Anfa targets. General Marshall replied that the CCS were committed to meeting Roosevelt's pledge of eleven divisions but no more. Any additional U.S. equipment transferred in the forthcoming months should be directed to replenish existing formations—namely, those deployed on the front lines, which were then experiencing grievous losses.[63] This stance caused planners in Paris to look at meeting future national military needs autonomously of the Allies. The divisions built up under the Anfa Plan were structured and equipped in accordance with U.S. Army regulations and doctrine, which often sat uncomfortably with the French army experience and principles. The extent of the supply corps attached to each formation was particularly dismaying to the French. De Gaulle soon denounced undue foreign influence over the growth of France's armed forces: "The exclusive control exercised today by the Americans on French rearmament, in terms of quantities and formations, is not acceptable. We need to take stock of our own possibilities and create a certain number of divisions and army corps, structured as required for our own needs. . . . I am looking forward to receive recommendations from the National Defense Committee in order to commence laying out the foundations of new and enlarged units taking into account resources currently available and the production expected from national industries in the future."[64]

In order to guide the committee's study, de Gaulle outlined three fundamental missions for France's armed forces in the postwar era: (1) project a high-readiness force beyond the country's borders in response to a specific crisis (*capacité d'intervention immédiate*); (2) defend the *métropole* and overseas possessions (*sécurité du territoire*); and (3) train the reserves (*instruction des réserves*) for the eventuality of another extended war in Europe.[65] Juin submitted his first proposal to the CDN on 2 October 1944: an intervention force of twelve divisions; a "sovereignty force" of 150,000 troops for the empire; a large metropolitan army of regulars and trained reservists, which assumed a two-year commitment for conscripts; an air force of 2,500 planes; and a 500,000-ton navy. Seized of the coming budget crunch, de Gaulle sent the team back to the drawing board, limiting the intervention force to ten divisions, aviation to 2,000 planes, and the navy to 300,000 tons, also stating that the nation would not support conscription beyond one year.[66]

There followed repeated exchanges between Juin's staff and the committee, where de Gaulle continued to reject overly ambitious plans on the part of his military chiefs. Although an army man and committed to France's grandeur, the head of the Provisional Government had become cognizant of the fiscal burden that unrestrained military ambitions would impose on the nation. Prospects became especially dire when cancellation of Lend-Lease in August 1945 informed these debates. De Gaulle promulgated an additional constraint on 13 September 1945 whereby defense expenditures could amount to no more than one-third of the state's financial outlays.[67] With this momentous decision, the debate changed from what kind of armed forces France ought to have to what quantity the country could afford as the government focused on finalizing its budget for fiscal year 1946.

For Minister of Finance René Pleven, this policy meant a defense budget of 120 billion francs, and yet the project submitted by Juin to the National Defense Committee on 4 December 1945 still required 157 billion francs.[68] De Gaulle compromised, endorsing a defense budget of 137 billion after having shaved 4 billion from the air force proposal, 5 billion from the navy's, and 11 billion from the army's, accepting a *force d'intervention* of only seven divisions.[69] But this decision was not the end of the discussion, as the national budget required approval by the assembly elected in October 1945, dominated by the Left with the Communists controlling 26 percent of the seats and the Socialists, 24 percent. The Right (or the Center-Right, to be more accurate) was primarily represented by the Mouvement républicain populaire (Popular Republican Movement), which stood at 25 percent.[70] The latter hardly considered themselves Gaullists, however, and le Général could not expect them to support his policies blindly if differences arose between the executive authority and the legislative body, a likely prospect at the time.

The conflict came to a head during a marathon debate on 31 December lasting into the night as the budget legislation had to be voted in time for the new fiscal year (same as the calendar year in France). Socialists tested the balance of power by seeking to impose further cuts to the defense estimates presented by the government, which de Gaulle refused to accept. Addressing the assembly in person on 1 January 1946, le Général made an imperious plea, and the budget bill passed as proposed later that day but by a narrow margin. De Gaulle had succeeded in preserving the primacy of the executive for the time being, although this last altercation seemed to leave him broken. He resigned three weeks later, denouncing the resurgence of self-serving party politics. The perceived authoritarian willingly abandoned power as the assembly elected the Socialist Félix Gouin to the presidency of the Provisional Government of the French Republic on 26 January.[71] Months of acrimonious debates followed about the future political regime of France and her place in the world, just as the wartime alliance faded away while conflict in Indochina and a budding Cold War in Europe threatened the prospects of a long-lasting peace.

These uncertain circumstances left Admiral Lemonnier in a difficult position to uphold the interests of the Marine nationale and plan a credible fleet for the future. The navy had done well in combat given the challenging circumstance its officers and sailors had faced, but the commitment of a large majority of naval officers to Vichy—or at least to Darlan until November 1942—had left the institution divided and bruised politically. The end of the wartime alliance and the damage inflicted on France's shore installations left it unable to acquire new ships or submarines from former allies and incapable of generating new construction of its own. Geopolitical uncertainty on the international scene and tactical confusion regarding the future of war left planners unable to identify a clear enemy and delineate the means to fight at sea in the new atomic era. Even under a political leader as dedicated to restoring France's grandeur as de Gaulle, Lemonnier had to scale down his grandiose plans for a full-fledged blue-water fleet.

Budget constraints also tramped national ambition and strategic thought in shaping the future fleet, leaving it to the ministry of finance to determine what navy France could afford. Admittedly, nobody lamented "what good will a navy be to us now?" Both Pétain and de Gaulle, each under dramatically different circumstances, had demonstrated the political value of the fleet for national leaders. Indochina and troubles in other corners of the empire would soon demonstrate the contribution that ships and aircraft operating from the sea could make to fighting new forms of insurgencies. Meanwhile, the Iron Curtain soon to descend across Europe would show that another foe much closer to home also warranted building up forces on land *and* at sea for containment and deterrence. A new association between the Western powers ensued, soon to bring renewed possibilities for naval cooperation and fleet growth.

Nevertheless, French admirals were bound to approach such collaborative opportunities warily. Wartime experience—both for the FNFL veterans who dealt directly with the British and those from the FMA in negotiating with the Combined Chiefs of Staff—revealed that support of allies extended only so far as the latter's interests dictated, mostly at the expense of the junior partner. This dichotomy would repeatedly come to the fore as Lemonnier sought to continue leveraging Anglo-American support in developing a nascent Aéronavale while his political masters came close to surrendering France's naval autonomy in adopting a military policy shaped by one overriding objective: the defense of the Rhine.

CHAPTER 5

FACING OPPORTUNITIES, THREATS, AND UNCERTAINTIES

La défense du Rhin

The aircraft carrier *Dixmude* arrived off Cape St. Jacques at the mouth of the Donnai River, the waterway leading from the South China Sea to Saigon, late in the afternoon of Monday, 3 March 1947.[1] Once the ship maneuvered to the flying course (the heading and speed required to provide a relative wind suitable to launch aircraft), nine American-built Douglas SBD-5 Dauntless dive-bombers flew off the ship and rose into the setting sun. They headed to Tan Son Nhut, the airfield that served both as a civilian airport for the city and a French air force base, while *Dixmude* resumed course and transited up river to enter the Saigon naval base later in the evening. What seemed a routine evolution at the time—aircraft transferring to a base ashore so they could perform flying missions while the carrier was in port—actually marked a momentous event on that particular day. It was the first time in history that Aéronavale planes launched from a French carrier deployed in a theater of war ready for combat operations. At the outset of World War II, the squadrons of the older *Béarn* had flown from airfields in northern France while the carrier remained in the Mediterranean. Since then *Dixmude* (after 1945) and *Béarn* had only served as troop and aircraft transports.

This pivotal event had to be qualified, though, as the Marine nationale continued struggling through the uncertainties of the postwar era. *Dixmude* was arriving from France but had been unable to conduct flying operations during the five-week voyage. Although meant to operate as a carrier once in theater, whiffs of her humble transport days followed as authorities used this transit to transfer to Indochina twenty-nine air force planes (seventeen Morane-Saulnier Criquet for liaison and reconnaissance and twelve British-made Spitfire fighters, all dismantled in crates), 360 tons of additional matériel, and thirty-six passengers, mostly personnel from the Armée de l'air (French air force). The cargo blocked part of the flight deck so that the ship's dive-bombers could be launched but not recovered, thus staying on board until off Cape St. Jacques. The air force badly needed such reinforcements as it only counted in the whole of Indochina three squadrons of fighter-bombers (two flying Spitfires, the other equipped with Mosquitos) and two transport groups (one operating C47s and the other Amiot Toucans). These limited assets became severely strained when the Vietminh resumed a violent guerrilla campaign after negotiations with the French government failed in late 1946.

Dixmude returned to sea on 13 March for four weeks of reconnaissance and bombing missions in support of troops deployed in the coastal areas from Cochinchina to the Tonkin.[2] This small but important effort—given the growing role of air power in fighting the insurgency—truly marked the renaissance of an operational Aéronavale. As put succinctly by Admiral Robert Battet, commander of the Forces maritimes d'Extrême-Orient (Far East Maritime Forces): "A carrier-borne squadron has performed success-fully in wartime conditions."[3] By then the British government had already agreed to transfer another aircraft carrier, HMS *Colossus*, to serve under the tricolor as the *Arromanches*. A light fleet carrier of 13,500 tons, 700 feet in length, and capable of embarking about forty aircraft, this was a "real" carrier, and the Marine nationale could again call itself a carrier navy, at least periodically based on the availability of the *Dixmude* and *Arromanches* between maintenance cycles.

This renaissance showed the opportunities, threats, and uncertainties that the postwar years presented to the navy. Although France seemingly stood alone in the new peacetime era, French concerns with the potential for Germany to rise again soon merged with that of the former Anglo-American allies regarding a belligerent Soviet Union. The military alliance had come to an end, but economic and material aid from the United States and Great Britain resumed in different forms. Nevertheless, naval planners on the *Rue Royale* struggled in trying to pay off obsolete vessels and build up a fleet worthy of a great power at the dawn of the nuclear age. They welcomed assistance from London and Washington but actively resisted their influence in shaping the future Marine nationale while working warily with a political class divided over national priorities. The moment of greatest danger for Admiral Lemonnier would come in the fall of 1948. Minister of National Defense Paul Ramadier then proclaimed the primacy of the "defense of the Rhine," sacrificing naval growth to build up an army and air force focused on France's greatest vulnerability as a continental power, its land border. This dramatic turnaround stood in stark contrast to the promising symbolism of the rebirth of French naval air power launched just a few years earlier.

Rebuilding the Aéronavale

Despite his limited experience with naval aviation, Lemonnier fully adhered to the policy of regenerating the fleet around task forces centered on the combination of aircraft carriers, battleships, and a retinue of escort and replenishment vessels. He was supported in that vision by Rear Admiral Henri Nomy, commander of the Aéronavale since June 1944. The latter would play a pivotal role in the regeneration of French naval aviation in these early years and shaping the larger Cold War navy, serving as chief of the Naval General Staff from 1951 to 1960.

Nomy had missed the Great War when he graduated from the École navale in 1918 but manifested an early interest in flying. He obtained his wings in 1924 and qualified as a fighter pilot in 1927 before serving with the Air Ministry in the early 1930s. There followed several years of service with large seaplanes, conducting long-range cruises in the Baltic and the Eastern Mediterranean as well as one of the first crossings of the South Atlantic in 1934. He eventually rose to command the seaplane squadron embarked in *Commandant Teste* in 1936 and then the naval air station in Berck, on the Channel, where one of *Béarn*'s dive-bomber squadrons was relocated in the fall of 1939. Coordinating an orderly fighting retreat on land ahead of approaching columns of German panzers in June 1940, Nomy was captured in Boulogne and remained a prisoner of war until his liberation a year later in the wake of the Paris Protocols. Darlan appointed him commander of the Port Lyautey naval station in Morocco, but Nomy had already left that post by the time of the North African landings. As his faith in the Vichy regime quickly faltered, he resigned his command in June 1942 and returned to the *métropole*, where he went into dissidence and joined the Resistance. Nomy rallied North Africa in August 1943, soon to take command of the newly reunited Aéronavale.[4]

Nomy managed the wartime rebuilding of French naval aviation with the aid of the Allies and contributed studies in support of Lemonnier's planning for a postwar fleet, culminating with a report submitted to the Conseil supérieur de la Marine (CSM) on 27 June 1945.[5] The study depicted the current state of the Aéronavale in bleak terms: eight shore-based squadrons flying barely one hundred obsolete and heterogeneous planes of French, British, and American origin, manned by 6,400 personnel, and with only two obsolete aircraft transports—*Béarn* and *Dixmude*. He acknowledged the objective endorsed previously by the Comité de Défense nationale to acquire up to four hundred aircraft by 1950 and proposed a two-step plan given the paucity of French resources at the time: a stopgap measure through the purchase or leasing of modern aircraft from overseas in 1946–47, and then completing the growth to four hundred planes through domestic production from 1948 to 1950.

Nomy added that *Béarn*, *Dixmude*, and the old seaplane tender *Commandant Teste*—even if fully refitted as aircraft carriers—could only operate one or two squadrons each, and the ships' slow speed limited their operational effectiveness. Given that France was unlikely to gather the means to build a fleet carrier before 1950, he proposed that existing large "gun carriers" be converted as quickly as possible: battleship *Jean Bart*, to embark three squadrons, as well as cruisers *Duquesne* and *Tourville* with one squadron each. This would provide the Marine nationale with three fast carriers capable of deploying as elements of a task force while the older three would remain in the *métropole* and North African waters for training and convoy duties. Minister Jacquinot endorsed the outline of a four-hundred-plane Aéronavale on 5 July 1945.[6] Embarked aviation would be divided in four squadrons of fighters and four squadrons of torpedo-bombers (also capable of surveillance and reconnaissance) as well as five more squadrons based ashore but equipped with similar aircraft in order to provide training, rotation between deployments, replacements, and spares. These thirteen formations would be complemented by five squadrons of shore-based, long-range patrol planes and two transport units, for a total of twenty squadrons.

Ship-wise, however, economic realities in the latter half of 1945 and the acceptance of a much humbler *flotte de transition* for 1946 considerably affected the renewal of an operational seagoing aviation. Plans to refit *Commandant Teste*, *Duquesne*, and *Tourville* as aircraft carriers were quickly abandoned, while the overriding need to dispatch troops and equipment to Indochina meant that *Béarn* and *Dixmude* would continue to operate in the transport role without modernization for some time.[7] As for *Jean Bart*, the debate grew increasingly bitter within the highest ranks of the Marine nationale whether the ship should be completed as a battleship or an aircraft carrier. The CSM membership reviewed plans for both options but realized that conversion to the carrier role would necessitate nearly as much time and money as that required to build an entirely new vessel. Worse, it would only provide a limited carrying capability—at most forty aircraft ready for operations with fourteen more slung from the hangar deck head—and likely would prove obsolete by the time the ship entered service. Minister Jacquinot endorsed on 21 September 1945 the recommendation of Admiral Lemonnier to complete *Jean Bart* as a battleship, although dissenting voices would continue to be heard in the following months.[8] A typical statement was that proffered at the time by Rear Admiral Pierre Barjot, another veteran of the Aéronavale: "It was surprising in 1945 to see the Naval General Staff supporting the cause of the battleship against that of the aircraft carrier. This attitude, which dominated the discussions of 21 September 1945, clearly reveals that despite the experience of the war the mythology surrounding the big guns continues to rule our naval thinking."[9]

Barjot was disingenuous in presenting a one-sided view of the minister's decision. While Aéronavale proponents had long argued for converting *Jean Bart* into an aircraft carrier—Barjot authored a study to that effect back in the fall of 1943[10]—her completion as a battleship did not equate to a slavish commitment to the gun carrier. Indeed, Lemonnier also ordered that staff develop plans for three new prototypes of aircraft carrier, presented to the CSM on 2 October 1945.[11] All three would be capable of a maximum speed of thirty-two knots and embark a similar number of aircraft. The main difference in price and weight would be found in the level of protection afforded to the ships, in terms of an armored flight deck and additional antiair batteries. One outstanding concern remained, however, given the inability of French shipyards to deliver a first platform until 1950 at the earliest, regardless of which prototype was selected.

Acknowledging such delay, the CSM settled on a recommendation to initiate the construction of two light aircraft carriers as soon as possible (the cheapest, least protected PA-28 variant) while seeking the acquisition of heavier platforms from overseas in order to fill the more immediate gap. Minister Jacquinot endorsed these recommendations, and Admiral Nomy took the lead in the search for a carrier from foreign source, which would merge with his ongoing initiative to acquire new aircraft from France's former allies.[12] This new mission took place in a context dramatically different than before as the wartime mechanisms for military aid no longer existed in the new peacetime era.

Military Aid in Peacetime

France did not quite stand alone after World War II, but the end of military Lend-Lease in August 1945 seemed to cut off access to Allied resources. De Gaulle had secured a position of prominence at the United Nations with a permanent seat on the Security Council but the organization's charter did not provide channels for signatories to assist another member in growing its military strength. Visiting Moscow in December 1944, le Général had signed the Franco-Soviet Treaty of Alliance and Mutual Aid, turning to the Soviets as he doubted the Anglo-American commitment to containing Germany in the future, which he expected to reemerge as a perennial threat to France.[13] The bilateral agreement remained in effect in the immediate postwar period, but it did not address the matter of military aid in peacetime, and French leaders did not consider the Soviet Union a viable source of modern armament in any case. This left the United States and Great Britain as the most likely sources of assistance to a France struggling to rebuild its economy while restoring its military power.

The United States quickly terminated Lend-Lease in 1945 but did not quite abandon France and the other Allies altogether. The dire state of the European economies caused the administration of President Harry S. Truman to focus on economic assistance, not military means, to ensure continued peace. The Bretton Woods system of monetary management, agreed to in July 1944, rested on integration of functioning economies after the war. The United States took it upon itself to coordinate important peacetime money transfers to several Western European countries, including $650 million to France in May 1946.[14] This agreement, concerned as it was with civilian reconstruction and industrial revitalization, did not apply to military acquisitions and seemed to eliminate the United States as a source of support to regenerate the French Aéronavale, at least in the short term.

Rear Admiral Nomy visited Great Britain several times through the winter of 1945–46 to negotiate transfer of aircraft carriers, warplanes, and ancillary equipment. A first round of discussions took place in London from 30 October to 13 November 1945, leading to purchase by France of the material required to complete the refit of *Dixmude* into an operational aircraft carrier.[15] The transaction worth £12,800 provided mainly for radars, advanced communication gear, and spares, although operational priorities delayed the ship's modernization until the fall of 1946. At the same time, Nomy secured another contract for £450,000 to procure twenty-four Seafire fighters, twelve Sunderland patrol planes, and twenty Wellington bombers—as well as an appropriate supply of spare parts and ammunition and another twenty Spitfires, twenty Wellingtons, and twenty-six Anson multirole aircraft, all older versions configured for training.[16] Nomy also obtained that a first group of eight Aéronavale officers take carrier pilot and deck landing officer training at the Fleet Air Arm School located in East Haven, Scotland.

Returning to London in January 1946, Nomy obtained a five-year lease for a modern light aircraft carrier.[17] Not quite in the same league as the fleet carrier long sought by the French admiralty, HMS *Colossus* was nevertheless a step clearly above the converted *Biter/Dixmude*. Launched in September 1943 as the lead ship of her class, the light carrier included the early lessons learned by the British in the Mediterranean and the Americans in the Pacific. Soon renamed *Arromanches*, she could sustain a maximum speed of twenty-five knots and embark two squadrons of Seafires and one squadron of Dauntless dive-bombers. Following service with the British Pacific Fleet, the vessel refitted in South Africa and returned to Portsmouth in July 1946. Barely two weeks later, on 6 August, a French crew took possession and soon set sail for Toulon, her new home port.[18] Thanks to Great Britain, France had acquired her first purpose-built aircraft carrier since the launch of *Béarn* in 1928. But what was behind such generosity toward the French on the part of "perfidious Albion," especially when several contentious issues strained relations between London and Paris in the early postwar era?

Whether under Prime Minister Churchill or his successor, Clement Attlee, after July 1945, Whitehall officials fretted over the ambitions of French politicians in the Levant, the harsh treatment Paris wished to impose on defeated Germany, and the presence of influential Communists in the Provisional Government of France and early Fourth Republic cabinets. Nevertheless, British and French leaders also shared common concerns at the time. They ranged from disquiet over the looming withdrawal of American forces from continental Europe to maintaining control over their respective empires despite growing pressure at the United Nations to accept some form of Rooseveltian trusteeship over their colonies on the way to eventual independence.[19] Of great interest as well, defense industries in Great Britain, struggling with the sudden halt of domestic military orders, would profit from continued sales to France. Finally, the Admiralty perceived the adoption of RN equipment, standards, and practices as conducive to greater interoperability (and influence) with her sister navy.[20]

Goodwill continued in the following months, with sixty-three Aéronavale pilots and sixty radar operators and technicians attending training in Great Britain in 1946. That same year the Royal Air Force transferred fifteen Spitfires from a squadron crewed previously by Polish nationals in Italy.[21] Training and that last transaction came for free, as did the initial two years of the five-year lease of the aircraft carrier *Colossus*. Nevertheless, continued support to France's navy also provided revenues to the British government as all other commitments were conducted through cash transactions, not long-term loans or previous wartime mechanisms that postponed payment to some future date. From the French point of view, these arrangements—as valuable as they were, given the paucity of armament industries in France at the time—also meant that an inordinate portion of the naval budget went to growing the Aéronavale.

Such a commitment would severely hamper Admiral Lemonnier's ability to rejuvenate a surface fleet worthy of the vision outlined in earlier building plans.

The Shrinking Fleet and Dwindling Budgets

In a December 1946 note addressed to the defense ministry, the Naval General Staff provided a summary of French and foreign-built vessels that had been condemned or mothballed as a result of obsolescence, wartime damage, and prohibitive maintenance costs: three former Vichy battleships, one aircraft transport (*Commandant Teste*), two cruisers, fourteen destroyers, twelve sloops, one British corvette, twenty-seven submarine chasers, eight torpedo boats, eighteen motor torpedo boats, ten armed trawlers/gunboats/patrol craft, four miscellaneous support vessels (tankers, tenders), and no less than twenty-five submarines.[22] A similar decrease took place in terms of personnel with a precipitated decline from the June 1945 peak of 93,000 officers and sailors past the postwar objective of 72,000 proposed by Lemonnier in September 1945 to the ceiling of 45,000 imposed by the Provisional Government in January 1946. Admittedly, this last figure was alleviated by a temporary reprieve of 5,000 additional sailors assigned to minesweeping duties in the *métropole* and North African waters as well as 5,000 more serving with the Indochina fleet, the latter paid by the Ministère de la France d'outre-mer (Ministry of Overseas France, the former department for the colonies). This situation left the Marine nationale with a temporary strength of 55,000 personnel pending the completion of these tasks.[23]

All postwar navies faced dramatic retrenchment in terms of hulls and personnel, but what worried French admirals was the shrinking share of naval appropriations in the overall national defense budget. These figures reached a low of 14 percent in 1946, in contrast to the interwar period, when it hovered at 20–25 percent. The navy minister's ability to fund new constructions or refit existing vessels while subsidizing the rejuvenation of the Aéronavale through direct purchases overseas was severely constrained.[24] Although the battleship *Jean Bart* arrived in Brest on 12 February 1946 to commence an extensive period of repair and to complete her armament as a modern "task force flagship, heavy AA vessel, and fire-support ship for shore bombardment," work would only progress at a glacial pace through the following years due to the limited funding allocated to that project.[25] Efforts to finish those prewar constructions found relatively intact on French slips after the Liberation were mostly suspended, including that of the cruiser *De Grasse* and destroyer *L'Aventurier* as well as submarines *Artémis* and *Antigone*.[26] Work continued on three other submersibles as well as four small *avisos*/sloops, but this was the extent of new builds expected to join the French fleet in the coming years.

Transfers from the defeated Axis powers could provide another source of growth, but the "Big Three"—the United States, Great Britain, and the Soviet Union—sought to limit such ambition in the closing months of the war. The subject of German war reparations was fiercely debated at the Potsdam Conference (17 July–2 August 1945), but, to de Gaulle's great frustration, France did not have a seat at that table. Regarding naval war reparations, the text of the final agreement promulgated unequivocally that the "total strength of the German surface navy . . . shall be divided equally among the U.S.S.R., U.K., and U.S."[27] The lesser Allies could not avail themselves of any such vessels, and another provision stated: "The larger part of the German submarine fleet shall be sunk. Not more than thirty submarines shall be preserved . . . for experimental and technical purposes." Nevertheless, France succeeded in capturing a number of ships and submarines abandoned in metropolitan ports and across the Rhine as German forces withdrew in 1944–45. Great Britain also agreed in 1946 to transfer some of its own seizures and war reparations to the Marine nationale. In total, acquisition of German vessels amounted to four U-boats seized in France and two more transferred from Great Britain, thirteen minesweepers captured in Germany, and nine German destroyers obtained from the Royal Navy.[28]

Following negotiations that dragged on until July 1948 to finalize the naval clauses of the February 1947 peace treaty between Italy and the Allied powers, the French navy also took on two Italian light cruisers, four destroyers, one sloops, two motor torpedo boats, one tanker, and nine auxiliaries.[29] Although welcome in terms of numbers, all of these acquisitions from Germany and Italy would not make much of a contribution given this paltry 1950 assessment by the Amirauté: "The German vessels were built during the hostilities in a harried manner with material of an inferior quality. Their continuous service during the war and their abandonment after the conflict aged them prematurely. The Italian ships, built before the war, also suffered a long period out of service after the hostilities. Their equipment is obsolete, especially their electronics, which would require an extensive period of refit and modernization to restore to operational status."[30]

Another challenge to rejuvenating a fleet of modern warships was the priority accorded to the rehabilitation of France's merchant navy. Even before the Liberation, powerful voices within the Provisional Government warned that the wartime loss of half of the country's capacity to transport passengers, solid cargo, and oil products by sea grievously constrained the country's capability to rebuild national infrastructure as well as provide for the food and sanitary needs of the people in the *métropole* and overseas. The end of the hostilities resulted in an overabundance of merchant shipping from other nations available for hire, lease, or outright purchase, but such transactions would drain the limited amount of foreign currencies available in Paris. René Pleven, de Gaulle's minister of the economy and finance, proved especially vehement in that regard, joined as he was by influential figures such René Meyer, the minister of public works and transport, and René Coty, soon to be appointed minister for reconstruction and urbanism.

Coty reported to the National Assembly in December 1945 that the costs to charter foreign shipping would rise to US$350 million in 1946 alone.[31] Within months, as French commercial yards became available, they were set to build merchant ships of all types, much cheaper by the ton, simpler in design, and quicker in production than complex men-of-war.[32] Marine nationale dockyards also contributed to this effort, with Brest first laying the keel of the *Penlan* on 29 July 1946, a collier of 4,700 tons launched the following February, even as work on the battleship *Jean Bart* languished in the next dock over. Brest and other naval yards in Lorient, Cherbourg, and Toulon, would go on to repair 22 liners, 129 freighters, and 37 fishing boats through 1946–47, receiving additional orders for building 60,000 tons of new merchant vessels, 4,500 train cars, and other heavy equipment for civilian use.[33] This orientation toward civilian production proved controversial, perceived as it was by the political Right and among some naval circles as a misappropriation of naval resources to poach contracts from privately owned yards at the expense of work in support of the Marine nationale.

However, Communist minister for the armaments Charles Tillon, who promoted such policy, repeatedly pointed out, quite rightly, that this effort actually contributed to rejuvenation of the navy's shore infrastructures during a period when the French government could not subsidize any more work on warships. Trained workers with rare specialist skills dispersed during the course of the war returned to their former jobs, and civilian commitments allowed those naval dockyards to upgrade their facilities and building techniques while making an important contribution to the national effort of reconstruction.[34] French admirals also appreciated that resources dedicated to reconstituting the merchant navy would contribute to the nation's sea power in the long run, even if at the expense of the naval fleet in the more immediate term.[35] It remained, though, that Admiral Lemonnier could only use limited credits and dockyard space during that time to mitigate the steady decline of the fleet rather than initiate a genuine renaissance, thus far limited to the Aéronavale. Even in that case, success rested entirely on the lease of the carrier *Colossus* and the continued procurement of British planes as French firms failed to develop new aircraft prototypes.

The chief of the Naval General Staff communicated a bleak assessment to newly appointed minister for the armed forces, Pierre-Henri Teitgen, in November 1947.[36] Starting on a positive note, he stated that the Marine nationale could meet its current missions, starting with the most fundamental one of defending the national territory and that of the Union française (as the former colonies were designated in the constitution of the Fourth Republic).[37] Then the navy needed to maintain the ability to contribute a naval task force for service under the United Nations when mandated in peacetime. Finally, it had to ensure the security of France's critical sea lines of communications in wartime—namely, between the *métropole* and North Africa in the Mediterranean and from Brest to Dakar in the Atlantic.

However, Lemonnier also expressed his concern that continuously paying off obsolete vessels without new procurements would lead the French fleet into oblivion with only one battleship, two aircraft carriers, two cruisers, three ocean escorts, and four submarines left in 1959, all of them obsolete, for an overall fleet tonnage of barely 70,000 tons. This emotional outburst came on the heels of a fateful decision by the political authorities. Although funding for the light aircraft carrier PA-28 (tentatively named *Clémenceau*) was included in the 1948 defense estimates approved by the National Assembly on 14 August 1947, a cabinet decree put that project on hold on 9 October as a result of the ongoing budgetary crisis facing the flailing government of Paul Ramadier, which would fall in November in the face of widespread worker strikes and civil unrest.[38] The blow badly undermined Lemonnier's aspirations for the Marine nationale to move up from the status of a nominal carrier navy to that of a credible one in the near future.

As dire as that development may have seemed, it should be kept in perspective. French historian of the Fourth Republic navy Philippe Quérel noted astutely that no country in the world commenced building a new aircraft carrier during the period 1945–50. The British slowly advanced work on four Centaur-class carriers begun in 1944–45. All carriers commissioned into the U.S. Navy from the defeat of Japan to beginning of the Korean War had been laid down during World War II, and the United States–class "supercarriers" were abruptly cancelled in 1948 amid a bitter debate over the roles of the strategic bomber and naval aviation in a nuclear world.[39] Indeed, French strategist Hervé Coutau-Bégarie observed that the decision to suspend work on the PA-28 was actually a blessing in disguise: the project would have engulfed huge sums to deliver an obsolete platform of limited capacity sometime in the far future based on the very slow rate of progress then observed for completion of the battleship *Jean Bart*.[40]

As importantly, the cabinet decision of October 1947 did not signify that the political class disavowed the idea of the Marine nationale as a blue-water carrier navy. The decree was not aimed specifically at the PA-28 as it froze all new military projects. Instead, this development underlined the continued dilemma government faced in establishing priorities between civilian reconstruction and rearmament in the postwar era. Debates in the National Assembly that had led to the budgetary approval of the previous August did not give rise to many attacks against the concept of the aircraft carrier itself nor that of strong French navy, but the economic argument eventually prevailed. As reported by the Finance Commission on 6 August 1947: "Several members, without denying the importance of aircraft carriers in general or the value for France of acquiring a modern one, assess that, given the current economic and financial circumstances, it would not be reasonable to incur such a large outlay. . . . Such commitment would also result in reallocating precious resources away from other valuable and necessary endeavors in support of the rehabilitation of the national economy, including skilled technicians, experienced workers and considerable quantities of material, resulting in dire consequences that appear unacceptable for the time being."[41]

In other words, the fundamental principle that France needed a navy did not come under attack in the National Assembly. Instead, the eventual fate of the still-born *Clémenceau* showed a considerable gap in the level of ambition entertained by the successive governments of the early Fourth Republic and that of the Amirauté. Indeed, Lemonnier completed his November 1947 report to Minister Teitgen with a new transition plan, the Plan transitoire de 1947. He proposed relaunching work on the aircraft carrier PA-28; initiating the immediate building of six generic escort vessels of 2,500 tons as an initial step to commence replacing the light cruisers, destroyers, and corvettes that would all become obsolete by 1954 (with a second tranche to bring the total number of escort to sixteen by 1958); complete the submarines *Artemis* and *Antigone* (found on slipways at the Liberation) as well as start building a new submarine of 1,200 tons inspired by the revolutionary German Type XXI; and progress the completion of *De Grasse* as an all antiaircraft gun cruiser.[42] However, circulated just as the Ramadier government was about to fall on 19 November, the report went nowhere.

Having failed to get a short-term proposal through, the navy adopted a different approach under the new Robert Schuman government, presenting in the spring of 1948 a larger, more fulsome Plan de base 1950, seeking to shape the rejuvenation of the entire fleet for the longer term.[43] This "basic plan" proposed a Marine nationale capable of deploying two task forces on a permanent basis while maintaining the necessary assets to defend metropolitan and Union française territories as well as securing the strategic sea lines of communications in time of conflict. It necessitated a large number of vessels: two battleships, four light carriers and three escort carriers, six cruisers, forty destroyers and smaller ocean escorts, fifteen to twenty submarines, and forty other auxiliaries (amphibious vessels, minesweepers, etc.). The plan provided for a fleet of 400,000 tons requiring 20,000 to 30,000 tons of new builds per year and maintained an objective of four hundred aircraft for the Aéronavale divided among twenty squadrons. Lemonnier submitted a more refined version on 9 April 1948, which was endorsed by Secretary of State for the Navy Joannès Dupraz on 13 May.[44]

Dupraz then put up a valiant fight to have this vision accepted in cabinet, but the budget presented in the summer of 1948 only included a one-year tranche providing for work on the *Jean Bart*, completion of the submarines *Artémis* and *Antigone*, and construction of small amphibious vessels for Indochina. By then the navy's ambitions for either a transitory proposal à la 1947 or a more fulsome Plan de base 1950 had been defeated. But cabinet instability that summer was not wholly responsible for this dire conclusion. As importantly, even had the Marine nationale been appropriated such sums, the national shipbuilding capability was just not available to meet the intended objectives along the ambitious timelines delineated in both documents.[45] Alternatively, the Amirauté could have considered another possibility, that of acquiring new vessels overseas. Although not an option until then, dramatic developments on the international scene were about to bring such a course of action to the fore. Once again Lemonnier and his colleagues would be called upon to consider the range of opportunities and frustrations that working with allies entailed, in a manner very similar to that observed during the previous conflict.

The Budding Cold War and Return of the Alliance

Admiral Lemonnier's efforts to rebuild the Marine nationale did not take place in a geostrategic vacuum, and the fleet had been quite busy since the end of the war. Indeed, one of the pitfalls he faced in trying to "sell" the dire state of the navy to political authorities was the continued success of his officers and sailors in meeting their assigned missions. Their tasks spanned a wide range of postconflict, peacetime, and active combat duties. Even before the end of the war, France stood up the Forces maritimes du Rhin (Rhine Maritime Forces), which was soon integrated in the larger occupation force maintained in Germany, reaching a peak of eight hundred sailors and one hundred vessels in 1956.[46] Reconstruction of shore infrastructure and minesweeping in the *métropole*, North Africa, and Indochina continued unabated throughout the late 1940s. Sovereignty patrols resumed in Europe and throughout the Union française, as did periodic deployments in support of the Newfoundland fisheries, while the prewar network of bases, ships, and aircraft dedicated to *sauvetage aéro-maritime* (air and sea search and rescue) was reconstituted. Meteorological work as well as scientific missions and hydrographic surveys commenced anew in 1947, including deployments to isolated outposts abandoned during the war.

But one overriding operational commitment dominated the fleet's employment through the immediate postwar years: contributing to the control of restive populations in the Union française. What was expected at first to constitute a temporary commitment would soon consume an inordinate amount of personnel and resources for the French navy and the other services. It commenced with a bloody precedent in Algeria on the very day of the end of the hostilities in Europe. Victory celebrations in the provincial capital of Sétif on 8 May 1945 turned violent, with Algerian nationalists killing more than one hundred *pieds noirs* (settlers of European descent) that day. French authorities launched a brutal repression campaign that spread across eastern Algeria in the following weeks and claimed several thousands of victims.[47] Heavy cruiser *Duguay-Trouin* and smaller units participated in these violent reprisals, landing detachments of sailors and *fusiliers-marins* to assist army troops, and carrying indiscriminate shore bombardments of coastal villages "to intimidate the rebels."[48] The Algerian episode was short-lived, but more troubling events spread to other territories, including a large-scale campaign of terror that commenced in Madagascar in late 1946, with natives torturing and murdering French officials, *colons*, and Madagascans working for the colonial administration.

The movement quickly gathered speed and turned into a full-blown insurgency in March 1947, leading to another campaign of violent repression by French troops that continued into the following year. The Marine nationale was called upon to participate in the reinforcement of the island's garrison by ferrying troops from the *métropole* and North Africa as well maintaining a potent naval force of destroyers and colonial sloops in the region to provide fire support and put landing parties ashore. The cruiser *Duguay-Trouin* transported a troop of naval commandos from Toulon in May 1947 and remained on station until October.[49] The ship once again fired her heavy guns against rebel positions and coastal villages suspected of supporting the insurrection, an initial contribution that paved the way to a bloody repression that left tens of thousands of natives dead or displaced in insalubrious camps.

The Madagascar uprising was overshadowed by the larger Indochina insurgency, where the Marine nationale played an important role until the very end. Warships took on a considerable burden in transporting the Corps expéditionnaire français en Extrême-Orient (French Far East Expeditionary Corps) in 1945–46. After disembarking these troops, the ships would then provide fire support as French forces continued to grow, reaching 128,600 personnel in December 1947. Of that, up to 8,500 were provided by the navy. They included the Brigade marine d'Extrême-Orient (Far East Naval Brigade), stood up in September 1944 and eventually numbering 3,000 *fusiliers-marins* and naval commandos. Some 5,500 sailors and naval aviators also served with the ships of the Forces maritimes d'Extrême-Orient and two squadrons of shore-based patrol aircraft.[50] In addition to the usual range of missions discharged by warships employed in a counterinsurgency role (shore bombardment, security of the coastal lines of communications, interdiction of enemy supply traffic at sea), sailors and aviators of the Marine nationale distinguished themselves in two particular roles during that conflict, riverine warfare and the provision of air support from the sea.

Following the initial campaign of *Dixmude* in March–April 1947, the ship returned to Indochina in October, providing seaborne air support until she set sail for France in April 1948.[51] The *Colossus*, officially redesignated *Arromanches* through ministerial decree on 4 March 1947, undertook her first deployment to Indochina in the fall of 1948 with ten Dauntless dive-bombers and two Seafire fighters embarked. The carrier arrived off Cape St. Jacques at the end of November and departed theater in early January 1949.[52] *Dixmude* and *Arromanches* completed valuable service in augmenting France's understrength air power, but their contribution was often limited by the small number of aircraft they could operate (on average, six for the former and eight for the latter due to maintenance, equipment breakdown, etc.). As problematic, the two ships could not maintain a constant rotation in the region as a result of refit cycles and other missions in Europe, despite the growing scale of the Vietminh insurgency.

The presence of the French navy on Indochina's numerous waterways would prove much more enduring. Heterogeneous flotillas of self-propelled barges, Japanese launches, and even motorized junks were assembled hastily in 1945–46.[53] The Marine nationale formally organized these forces, supplemented by a variety of landing craft obtained from the Americans and the British, as the Force amphibie de la Marine en Indochine (Indochina Naval Amphibious Force) in January 1947. This command coordinated a number of *divisions navales d'assaut* (naval assault divisions, colloquially known as the *dinassauts*) tasked with missions such as the routine resupply of isolated outposts and supporting autonomous raids upriver by the *fusiliers-marins*. They also played an important role during larger operations with the army, taking part in simultaneous assaults of enemy strongholds by amphibious and airborne troops. Sailing in vessels of all types that often lacked regular maintenance and looked most unusual as a result of the mounting of armor plating and armament that ranged from small machine guns to heavy mortars and even tank turrets—depending on the size of the platforms and the resourcefulness of their crews—the *dinassauts* sailors developed a reputation for mischief but unparalleled esprit de corps during these years.[54] They delivered critical support until the very end of the Indochina war, and the U.S. Navy would replicate that experience in Vietnam a decade later.

Although American advisers and military aid were not yet bound for Indochina in 1948, French authorities had already taken pains to frame the colonial conflict as part of the budding Cold War. De Gaulle's successors, still concerned with the prospect of a resurgent Germany and eager to maintain a seeming balance between the two superpowers in the immediate postwar era, complemented the 1944 agreement with Moscow with another pact of "alliance and mutual aid" through the Treaty of Dunkirk signed with Great Britain on 4 March 1947.[55] At that very moment, however, the German threat receded behind that of an increasingly belligerent Soviet Union. Western anxieties grew as a result of Moscow's forceful imposition of friendly regimes in Eastern Europe, its reluctant withdrawal from Iran and Manchuria, the continued occupation of North Korea, Stalin's incessant pressure on Turkey, and his active support to Communist insurgents in Greece.

Photographed at Villefranche-sur-Mer in late 1938 or early 1939, ships from three classes that formed the backbone of the interwar fleet and met dramatically different ends. Destroyer *Vauban* (*foreground*) was scuttled in Toulon on 27 November 1942. Battleship *Courbet* (*left background*) served as flagship of the fledgling Free French fleet in 1940–41 but was sunk off the Normandy coast in June 1944, part of a breakwater for a Mulberry harbor. One of the three *Duguay-Trouin*-class light cruisers appears in the right background. One survived the war and served into the 1950s, one was sunk by Allied bombers in Indochina in 1945, and one met a fiery end during a doomed sortie against the USN fleet covering the landings in Morocco in November 1942. *Naval History and Heritage Command (NH 93575)*

General Charles de Gaulle, leader of the Free French movement (*center*) visits the destroyer *Le Triomphant* in a naval port in Great Britain in the fall of 1940. On the left stands Vice Admiral Émile Muselier, head of the Free French navy until he lost his post due to repeated disagreements with de Gaulle. The ship's captain, Commander Philippe Auboyneau, is at right. De Gaulle put him in command of the Free French navy after firing Muselier in March 1942. *Imperial War Museum (A 2176)*

Two views of a Flower-class corvette (ex–HMS *Lotus*) being refitted in a British port for service with the Free French navy as *Commandant d'Estienne d'Orves* in the spring of 1942. She was one of the nine corvettes transferred from the Royal Navy during the war, all of which made significant contributions in the Battle of the Atlantic. *Naval History and Heritage Command (NH 81797)*

French battleship *Richelieu* photographed in Dakar, Senegal, on 25 July 1940, where she found refuge and remained in Vichy service after the armistice. This angle does not show the damage inflicted by British aircraft, which struck her stern during Operation Catapult on 8 July 1940, but it does illustrate the clear field of fire the berth afforded her to engage Free French and RN units during Operation Menace in September of the same year. Also note the buoys for antitorpedo nets around the ship. *Naval History and Heritage Command (NH 55781)*

U.S. ambassador Admiral William D. Leahy, USN (Ret.) (*right*), pays a farewell call on French Chief of State Marshall Henri Pétain on 27 April 1942. Recalled to Washington, Leahy would put his naval uniform back on to serve as chief of staff to the commander in chief (effectively head of the Joint Chiefs of Staff) until 1949. Placed under house arrest after the North African landings, Pétain remained a puppet of the Germans until he turned himself over to the French provisional government in April 1945. Tried and imprisoned for life, he passed away while still in detention in 1951. *Naval History and Heritage Command (NH 89478)*

The incomplete battleship *Jean Bart* at Casablanca, Morocco, on 16 November 1942, showing damage from 16-inch shells and 1,000-pound bombs inflicted in action with U.S. Navy forces on 8 November. The large hole and upended deck structure by her hangar appear to have been caused by a bomb. Note the antitorpedo barrier off *Jean Bart*'s port side and the 1,500-ton destroyer in the distance off her bow. *Official U.S. Navy photograph, now in the collections of the National Archives; Naval History and Heritage Command (80-G-31605)*

A portion of the Vichy fleet on 28 November 1942, the day after the scuttling in Toulon. Smoke and shadows obscure part of the scene, testifying to the thoroughness with which the French sailors carried out their bitter task. *From bottom to top*: battleship *Strasbourg*, heavy cruisers *Colbert* and *Algérie*, and light cruiser *Marseillaise*. *Strasbourg*—which had escaped the British attack on Mers-el-Kebir without damage in 1940—looks deceptively intact but has settled upright on the shallow bottom. *Library of Congress Prints and Photographs Division (LC-USW33-026496-D)*

Allied leaders meeting at the presidential villa at Casablanca, Morocco, January 1943. Present are (*left to right*): General Henri H. Giraud; President Franklin D. Roosevelt; General Charles de Gaulle; Prime Minister Winston Churchill. *Official photograph from the National Archives & Records Administration. Naval History and Heritage Command (80-G 38546)*

Destroyer escort *Tunisien* (ex–USS *Crosley*) off the Philadelphia Navy Yard, 18 April 1944. She was one of six Cannon-class DEs transferred to France in 1944 under Lend-Lease arrangements. Eight more would be reactivated and transferred in 1950–52 as part of the Mutual Defense Assistance Program. *Official U.S. Navy photograph, now in the collections of the National Archives. Naval History and Heritage Command (19-N-65941)*

The commander of the reunited French navy, Vice Admiral André Lemonnier (*center*), receives Vice Admiral Alan G. Kirk, Commander, U.S. Naval Forces, France (*left*) and Admiral Harold R. Stark, Commander U.S. Naval Forces, Europe at his Rue Royale headquarters in Paris on 6 October 1944. Despite their friendly demeanor, tensions were already prevalent between American and French naval commanders as to the future extent of U.S. support to the Marine nationale. *Official U.S. Navy photograph, now in the collections of the National Archives. Naval History and Heritage Command (80-G-286736)*

French aircraft carrier *La Fayette* (ex–USS *Langley*) in Indochinese waters, 1953. On deck can be seen one Sikorsky H-5 helicopter (*forward*) as well as several Douglas SBD Dauntless dive bombers (ranged along the port side with wings folded vertically) and Grumman F6F-5 Hellcat fighters (ranged along the starboard side with wings folded horizontally). *Naval History and Heritage Command (NH 79384)*

A typical mix of riverine craft forming a *division navale d'assaut* (colloquially known as the *dinassaut*). LCMs *Monitor* and *Normale* lead other LCMs and infantry landing craft deep into Vietnamese territory, 1954. Note the intimidating twin-barreled, turret-mounted machine guns forward of the lead LCM as well as the jury-rigged crow's nest to extend visibility beyond reeds and other river vegetation. *Naval History and Heritage Command (NH 79375)*

Admiral Henri Lomy photographed on 24 June 1960 after being presented with the prestigious Médaille militaire (Military Medal) for his nine years of service as commander of the French navy. He retired the following month, having played a pivotal role in the rejuvenation of French naval aviation in the immediate postwar years and the renaissance of the larger Marine nationale through the first decade of the Cold War. *Alamy*

Fifth meeting of the Chiefs of Staff Committee of the North Atlantic Ocean Regional Planning Group at the Navy Department, Washington, D.C., on 6 February 1952. The group's insignia is on the wall, flanked by flags of participating nations. The chairman, Admiral Lynde D. McCormick, USN, is seated at center. Seated (*left to right*): Rear Admiral George Cabanier (France); Admiral Sir Cyril Douglas-Pennant (U.K.); Admiral McCormick; Vice Admiral E. R. Mainguy (Canada); Rear Admiral Jonkheer H. A. Van Foreest (Netherlands); and Rear Admiral Johs E. Jacobsen (Norway). Standing (*left to right*): Rear Admiral Svent Ramlauhansen (Denmark); Brigadier A. A. Ferreira (Portugal); Lieutenant Colonel J. Ducq (Belgium); and Mr. Peter Eggerz (Iceland). *Naval History and Heritage Command (80-G-438921)*

As observed by one British historian, the vague wording of the Treaty of Dunkirk regarding Germany had resulted "in a pact of which the principal value was the purely technical, and arguably redundant, one of normalising Anglo-French relations."[56] But the immediacy of the Soviet threat soon concentrated minds in London and Paris. Another round of negotiations got under way to arrive at a more extensive agreement that included the Low Countries or "Benelux" (Belgium, the Netherlands, and Luxemburg), leading to signing on 17 March 1948 the Treaty of Economic, Social and Cultural Collaboration and Collective Self-Defense, otherwise known as the Brussels Pact.[57] Although still cognizant of the German problem in committing the signatories to "take such steps as may be held to be necessary in the event of a renewal by Germany of a policy of aggression," the agreement was in fact a response to the Soviet threat and incorporated several important precedents. It introduced such notions as standing arrangements for a joint defensive system in peacetime, strengthened economic and cultural ties as elements of collective defense, and the establishment of "a Consultative Council, which shall be so organised as to be able to exercise its functions continuously."[58]

Political and military leaders dedicated the following months to developing the peacetime machinery that would allow pact members to provide a signatory "under armed attack in Europe . . . all the military and other aid and assistance in their power."[59] A sense of urgency propelled these talks as Communists forcefully seized power in Czechoslovakia in February 1948 and Moscow launched the blockade of West Berlin in June. The Consultative Council consisting of the five foreign ministers stood as the supreme body of the new alliance, and the subordinated Western Union Defense Committee allowed the defense ministers to provide coordinated political direction to their military chiefs. Further deliberations resulted in standing up the Western Union Defence Organisation in September, the military arm of the Brussels Pact led by combined chiefs of staff overseeing the Permanent Military Committee of the Western Union.[60] Field Marshal Bernard L. Montgomery, then Great Britain's chief of the Imperial General Staff, was appointed permanent chairman of the Land, Naval and Air Commanders-in-Chiefs Committee, with headquarters in Fontainebleau, on the outskirts of Paris. Another British officer, Air Chief Marshal Sir James Robb, took the role of commander air forces, while France appropriated the two other key posts with the appointment of General Jean de Lattre de Tassigny on the army side and Vice Admiral Robert Jaujard for the naval forces.[61]

The Brussels Pact and the Western Union Defence Organisation were viewed positively in the French navy. The appointment of Jaujard would provide the Rue Royale with an influential voice within the organization, especially as the sailor proved much more effective in that collaborative context than de Lattre de Tassigny, who quickly developed an acrimonious relationship with Montgomery. Another positive prospect arose when leaders from the five powers met in London in April 1948 "to study their military equipment needs, with a view to determining how much they could meet from their own production and how much supplementary aid should be requested from the United States."[62] From July on, American and Canadian representatives joined these talks, providing a venue for France and her allies to supplement their struggling industries with an alternative source of production to rejuvenate their army, air, and naval forces.[63] French naval planners welcomed this initiative as they continued struggling to find a way to acquire new construction for the fleet. Little did they know that the prospect of renewed foreign assistance would also entail a dramatic realignment of national priorities in September 1948.

Putting the Fleet on Hold

Containment was first envisioned as an economic endeavor in Washington. President Truman announced to Congress in March 1947 that the United States would commence disbursing assistance to "free peoples who are resisting attempted subjugation by armed minorities or by outside pressure . . . primarily through economic and financial aid which is essential to economic stability and orderly political processes."[64] The Marshall Plan followed in June, disbursing aid to European powers willing to coordinate the recovery and reconstruction of their shattered economies within the Bretton Woods framework.[65] Within a year, though, it became evident that Western Europe would require a considerable influx of equipment from overseas to build up the modicum of a credible deterrent against the Soviet threat, as acknowledged in secret talks between American, British, and Canadian representatives in

March 1948.[66] Instituting mechanisms to disburse such aid would be fraught with difficulty amid a presidential election in the United States.

Administration officials were especially aware of the need to conciliate "America First" voices in Washington by avoiding connotations reminiscent of the wartime Lend-Lease and alleviating a debilitating impact on America's own rearmament. Republican senator Arthur H. Vandenberg, chairman of the Senate Foreign Relations Committee and once a leading light of the isolationist movement, accepted to clear an initial path for that purpose. He pushed a resolution through on 11 June that encouraged the "association of the United States, by constitutional process, with such regional and other collective arrangements as are based on continuous and effective self-help and mutual aid, and as affect its national security."[67] But even this growing bipartisanship in support of greater cooperation did not mean that military aid would flow immediately and freely. The Europeans needed to help themselves first. Then, and only then, would Washington meet carefully defined and prioritized needs as stated in a National Security Council report endorsed by President Truman in July 1948:

> (1) They [Western Union states] must first plan their coordinated defense with the means presently available, (2) they must determine how their collective military potential can be increased by coordinated production and supply, including standardization of equipment, (3) we would then be prepared to consider and screen their estimates of what supplementary assistance from us was necessary, (4) we would expect reciprocal assistance from them to the greatest extent practicable, and (5) legislation would be necessary to provide significant amounts of military equipment but the President would not be prepared to recommend it unless the foregoing conditions have been met.[68]

Major General Lyman Lemnitzer, USA, delivered this blunt message to Western Union officials later that same month when he arrived in Great Britain at the head of his country's delegation of observers.[69] The five powers had commenced vague discussions in April 1948 on the matter of coordinating the production and standardization of equipment, but the American approach clearly put the onus on them to initiate a new process of peacetime military aid. A major conference of the Union's defense ministers was called for 27–28 September to address this fundamental issue. Ironically, it was to take place in Paris, but the gathering was ill timed for France.

The country had just gone through a severe period of instability with the successive falls of prime ministers Schuman, Marie, and Schuman again. Radical Henri Queuille finally gained the confidence of the National Assembly to form a more lasting government on 11 September, but his overriding priorities were clear: the restoration of domestic order as violent workers strikes continued across the country and the protection of the French franc through a range of austerity measures designed to bring inflation under control, including new cuts to the defense budget.[70] Retaining the finance portfolio for himself, Queuille appointed the former socialist premier Paul Ramadier as minister of national defense who had two weeks to get ready for the next ministerial meeting of the Western Union.

Ramadier immediately ordered the three services to collaborate on the elaboration of an urgent plan for the "reconstitution of the overall military forces of France" (Plan de reconstitution de l'ensemble des Forces militaires françaises).[71] This plan expanded on the approach that had emerged during the summer sessions of the Western Union's Military Committee: the pooling and specialization of national resources, augmented by military aid from allies overseas, to ensure the common defense of Western Europe. For Ramadier, the greatest and most effective contribution France could make to this framework was the establishment of a powerful *force aéroterrestre*. Prepositioned at high readiness east of France's land border, this joint air–land force would blunt an enemy offensive toward the Rhine on the very first day of the war.

While acknowledging that the defense of the larger Union française also necessitated additional forces, Ramadier placed *la défense du Rhin* (the defense of the Rhine) at the apex of France's interests, trumping all other concerns in the reconstitution of the French military.[72] This effort required, first and foremost, the expansion of heavily mechanized land forces in Europe as well as the development of an air force focused on air defense and close air support to the army. Within this construct, the role of the navy would be limited to maintaining "essentially light escort forces and shore infrastructures in Africa."[73] For Lemonnier and his fellow admirals, this situation was 1943 all over again, with one important difference: the Allies would assist in rebuilding the French fleet at the cost of restraining it to subordinate secondary missions, but the concept was promoted by the French government itself this time.

Secretary of State for the Navy Joannès Dupraz replied two weeks later with a sharp rebuttal to this *mise en parenthèse de la flotte*, placing naval rearmament on hold ("in parentheses").[74] He recognized the importance of preparing for battle east of the Rhine but decried the reductionist approach to the navy's fundamental missions and the sacrifice of the means required for defense of the Union française. Dupraz's letter included a reminder of the intrinsic value of sea power to France as a country with worldwide interests and an emotional appeal for the constitution of balanced armed forces in support of a viable national defense in the postwar era. He once again presented the detailed submission provided earlier by Admiral Lemonnier in support of his proposal for a Plan de base 1950 and expanded on how such a vision for a balanced, blue-water fleet fitted in a strategy focused on the defense of the Rhine.

While the army and the air force would focus on the battle in Europe, the navy could make an essential contribution by discharging vital missions inside and out of that theater. The Marine nationale would secure the strategic sea lines of communications with the Union to ensure the safe arrival of personnel and material reinforcements from overseas. Its footprint across the Union française would reduce the necessity for the other services to maintain assets outside metropolitan France. It would continue its assigned tasks in defense of commercial ports and naval bases in the *métropole*, negating the need to divert army and air force resources for that purpose. The fleet's mobility would cause the enemy to disperse forces away from the European battlefield by threatening offensive actions on the flanks of Eurasia in cooperation with allied navies. And the navy could make a direct contribution east of the Rhine by deploying Aéronavale planes and *fusiliers-marins* units on the front line were such reinforcements requested by the army.

The impact of Dupraz's dispatch at that early stage is difficult to gauge. Dated 27 September, one must assume that Ramadier did not receive it in time to shape his input at the Western Union defense ministers' meeting, which started that same day. Regardless, these proceedings turned into somewhat of a non-event as the participants had not yet had enough time to define their defense needs to the level of refinement expected by the Americans.[75] Similar meetings continued through the fall, but the Wester Union military chiefs struggled to come up with a united rearmament plan, as observed by NATO historian Lawrence S. Kaplan: "No movement had been made to pool inventories and production resources in order to draft a balanced program, and even the list of deficiencies was incomplete and unsatisfactorily screened. . . . It was obvious that they were superficial and drawn according to the needs of national rather than European defense."[76]

Regardless of the lack of results at this stage, these discussions confirmed the adherence by the Brussels Pact members to the concepts of pooling resources and specialization among their armed forces. Such ideas were also likely to carry over in the framework of the expanded North Atlantic Treaty then under negotiation. Acceptance of this approach by France's minister of national defense put great strain on his relations with the secretary of state for the navy. Ramadier implicitly accepted that the Allies—namely, the Anglo-American navies—could be relied upon to secure Western Europe's sea lines of communications and interests overseas, allowing the French to focus limited resources on making a large and influential contribution to the land battle east of the Rhine. But Dupraz expressed severe doubts about this fundamental assumption in his original missive of 27 September 1948, a reflection of a deeply held belief among the country's admirals that would be reiterated persistently in the coming months and is worthy of a lengthy citation here:

> It would be a grievous mistake to believe that we can rely on foreign navies to discharge these heavy tasks. There is no doubt that their assistance would be essential and would grow during the hostilities but, at the outset of the conflict, during those weeks when the fate of the nation would be at stake as occurred in 1914 and 1940, we would likely have to count on our own resources only, as each nation would be hard-pressed to meet their own military requirements at sea. Allied navies would dispose of limited means at the beginning of the war, only those means maintained in peacetime. These are sparse capabilities given the length of the sea lines of communications and the distance

to the theatres of operations where their interests would be threatened. Would we really accept depending on the will of our Allies at such dire hour? Allies who can have dramatically different views from that of the French government on the strategy to adopt in the defense of France's soil and families in the *métropole*? Can we abandon to foreign authorities the responsibility for our ports, be they on the continent or overseas?[77]

Nevertheless, the secretary of state and Admiral Lemonnier could not allow such distrust to blind them to the fact that the French navy remained in dire need of assistance to build up a credible Cold War fleet. By late 1948 French yards had not been able to launch a new warship or submarine of large tonnage since the battleship *Jean Bart* had escaped Saint-Nazaire in 1940. The Aéronavale was growing in size—from eight to ten squadrons, including three carrier-based formations, though still well short of the target of twenty squadrons—but all aircraft remained World War II designs acquired from the British and the Americans.[78] The Queuille government would soon cancel the carrier project PA-28 altogether and, in June 1949, postpone completion of *Jean Bart* to an ill-defined future date.[79] By then the Amirauté had already accepted that the cruiser *De Grasse* would not be completed until 1953 at the earliest, given the inability of French industry to produce heavy naval guns.[80] Of the nine cruisers that had survived the war, four were still operational, but three were confined alongside as floating barracks while the aging *Émile Bertin* and *Jeanne d'Arc* found themselves restricted to training tasks, one with the gunnery school in Toulon and the other with the École navale in Brest.[81]

Alleviating some concerns, the Americans announced that they would no longer seek the return of vessels loaned to France under the terms of the Lend-Lease program, and the integration of German seizures and Italian war reparations continued in 1948. Even then, the following year witnessed the continued shrinking of the seagoing navy as a result of the incessant withdrawal of aging units.[82] By January 1950 the fleet presented a complex picture of achievements and unfulfilled ambitions on the part of Marine nationale through the challenging years of the early postwar era. With 257 warships and submarines and a combined tonnage of more than 400,000 tons, the fleet remained the largest in continental Europe, a potent force that continued discharging all of the missions expected of it by the nation, in metropolitan waters and across the Union française. However, even when applying a very loose standard as to which vessels could still be considered "modern" and "operational"—whether modernized prewar French cruisers, the converted aircraft carrier *Dixmude*, or other Allied and Axis transfers—the ability of the French navy to conduct large-scale, autonomous blue-water missions was dramatically limited.

This was obvious when considering the standing commitment to provide a task force when called upon to support a United Nations response to a crisis overseas. The Amirauté defined such a formation as one aircraft carrier, one battleship, three cruisers, and a complement of escort ships, supply vessels, and submarines depending on the mission at hand. The French navy would only be able to dispatch such a force during those limited periods when both aircraft carrier *Arromanches* and battleship *Richelieu* were available simultaneously, always an uncertain combination given the requirements for refits, training, and other national tasks. As well, with only 232,000 tons of ships and submarines actually operational (and nearly half of those vessels small patrol boats and auxiliaries), the fleet fell quite short of that sought by French admirals, who continued to target a mix of 300,000 tons in warships and another 100,000 tons in patrol craft and auxiliaries to meet France's national needs.[83] Virtually all work to complete those ships and submarines found intact in France after the war had been suspended by the Queuille government, a long way from the 20,000-ton a year in new construction advocated by the Rue Royale since 1946. Perhaps a return to the alliance system could provide some reprieve?

Negotiations proceeded apace in 1948–49 for signatories of the Brussels Pact to join forces with the United States, Canada, Iceland, Norway, Denmark, Italy, and Portugal within a new peacetime organization seeking to secure Western Europe and North America against the Soviet threat. Clearly, such combination would result in more opportunities, threats, and uncertainties for the French navy. The Amirauté could expect that the Alliance would initially exercise a clear naval superiority in the North Atlantic but under Anglo-American leadership, with little room for a French voice in shaping maritime strategy. Minister Ramadier would likely continue pursuing a policy centered on the defense of the Rhine, propounding that resource pooling and mission specialization decreased the need for France to maintain a large blue-water fleet. Simultaneously, France's admirals would strive to keep alive the hope of rebuilding a modern fleet capable of exercising some influence at sea; thus, they had to once again step warily into the embrace of the Anglo-Americans to make up for the continued weakness of the nation's industries and ongoing budgetary woes.

As experienced during World War II, foreign assistance would likely result in an uncomfortable dependence and relegation to the subordinate missions of convoy escorts and coastal defense. French historian Philippe Vial later illustrated this ambiguous development in the following terms, setting the tone for the next stage in the rearmament of the Marine nationale: "Hopes for allied help were explicitly stated in justifying renewed ambitions to restore France's rank. . . . Here lay the paradox: the desire to avoid another episode of subordination led the men of the Rue Royale to plan on assistance that would necessarily generate dependency! A vicious circle could not be avoided as the international conjecture evolved quickly and the state of the fleet required urgent decisions."[84]

CHAPTER 6

RETURNING TO A STRATEGY OF ALLIANCE

A Beautiful Friendship or Bitter Déjà Vu?

T he sun shone brightly over the Philadelphia Navy Yard on Saturday, 12 August 1950, seven years after the cruiser *Montcalm* had completed her refit in the same USN shipyard. As the wartime support provided by the United States in rebuilding the French fleet came to a sudden halt in 1945 and France's own dockyards had yet to demonstrate the capacity to build new warships, the scene taking place that day was powerful in its symbolism. Two American-built Cannon-class destroyer escorts (DE) were lying alongside each other, flying the U.S. flag for the last time. Following a short ceremony, USN sailors hauled down the colors and two *pompons rouges*—French sailors so called for the ball of red wool sewn atop their headdress—hoisted the tricolor at the stern of the former USS *Samuel S. Miles* (DE 183) and USS *Riddle* (DE 185), signifying their formal transfer to the French navy under new names, *Arabe* and *Kabyle*.[1] They were the first two of six DEs that the United States would hand over to France in the coming months, only one element of the wide-ranging Mutual Defense Assistance Program (MDAP) authorized under the premise of the Mutual Defense Assistance Act signed by U.S. president Harry S. Truman on 6 October 1949. As the Cold War turned increasingly tense in the late 1940s and early 1950s, the MDAP played a significant role in the rejuvenation of French sea power. However, it also exposed the same ambivalence that had qualified similar support during the previous conflict as Washington and Paris continued holding conflicting visions as to the role of France and its navy in the renewed Atlantic Alliance.

The two DEs certainly looked smart and trim, sporting a fresh paint scheme and a good assortment of weaponry and sensors for their size, with four diesel engines driving two shafts to propel their 1,300 tons at speeds up to twenty knots.[2] And yet they were no more modern or powerful than the six other Cannon-class DEs transferred to France in 1944. *Samuel S. Miles* and *Riddle* were cheap wartime constructions, built in less than four months each. They had seen hard service in the Pacific, including a kamikaze hit that inflicted serious damage on the latter. Both were quickly decommissioned after the war, suffering the vagaries of tropical heat and humidity while mothballed up the St. Johns River, outside Green Cove Springs in northern Florida, until towed to Philadelphia for a short refit in the summer of 1950.[3] The ships would augment the capacity of the Marine nationale but under the terms of the MDAP, which itself followed the signature of North Atlantic Treaty on 4 April 1949. They were meant to be employed in NATO's area of responsibility. France was not to deploy them for national commitments beyond the purview of the Alliance, such as the defense of Union française territories, an important military concern for Paris at the time, given the desperate struggle then ongoing in Indochina.

As in 1943, resumption of American assistance to France was greeted warmly but left many questions unanswered for French admirals and politicians alike. The explosion of a first Soviet atomic bomb on 29 August 1949 was followed by the proclamation of the People's Republic of China by Mao Zedong in October of that same year, and the North Korean offensive across the thirty-eighth parallel on 25 June 1950 certainly brought an added level of urgency in the delivery of aid from North America to the European allies. Nevertheless, the awkward experience of World War II, when help sought to restore France's armed forces had resulted in dependence and subordination, remained a burning memory at the Rue Royale.

American aid recommenced flowing in a variety of forms while French shipyards, industries, and research centers soon started making a direct contribution to building up the country's general defense, particularly its navy. This situation was a far cry from the moment of greatest danger of just a few years earlier when Minister of National Defense Paul Ramadier promoted a single focus on the defense of the Rhine and accepted a seemingly unavoidable *mise en parenthèse de la flotte.* Still, it was this return to a strategy of alliance that had permitted Ramadier to advocate for a powerful *force aéroterrestre* at the expense of the fleet, a course of action that successive governments could continue if they chose to do so. French admirals demonstrated great sagacity in embracing NATO, but they would continue confronting that inescapable paradox, unsure whether the strategy of alliance would beget a beautiful friendship with the American ally in peacetime or turn into bitter déjà vu reminiscent of the wartime strains.

From the Western Union to NATO

French views proved remarkably consistent during the multifaceted negotiations that led to signing of the North Atlantic Treaty in April 1949. Successive cabinets holding power from the conclusion of the Brussels Pact in March 1948 to the founding of NATO a year later all favored closer military links with the United States and Canada as the Western Union did not assuage French security fears. The three Benelux allies could provide little in terms of actual armed might in support of the defense of Western Europe, while Great Britain remained reluctant to commit forces to the Continent in advance of a Soviet offensive.[4] As perceived in Paris, the French army would bear the brunt of the bloody fight necessary to keep the assailant from crossing the Rhine into the *métropole*. The United States and Canada declared solidarity with the Western European Union, and the launch of the Marshall Plan boded well for further cooperation, but memories of 1914 and 1939 left French leaders skeptical of ambiguous professions of good faith on the part of potential allies.

What they sought was a formal pledge of armed assistance in peacetime, and the Truman administration agreed to initiate such discussions as it would place the defense of Western Europe within a more effective Atlantic security system.[5] By and large, French admirals approved of this commitment to a wider alliance even though the leading voice assumed by the Marine nationale within the Western Union Defence Organisation would likely diminish in the face of American leadership in shaping NATO's maritime strategy.[6] The expected prize in return for this concession: immediate access to direct material assistance from the United States.

Distribution of American assistance to Cold War allies did not take place strictly within the confines of the North Atlantic Treaty. Negotiations with other nations got under way to discuss economic and military aid in parallel to the talks already taking place with the Western Union. These developments gave rise to concerns that so many uncoordinated initiatives could become self-defeating, as observed by historian Chester J. Pach in reference to a late 1947 report from the U.S. Army Plans and Operations Division: "Emergency assistance on a country-by-country basis . . . prevented systematic efforts to balance commitments against resources and postponed considerations of permanent solutions to foreign armament needs. The deletion of surplus mate-rial, the sharp contraction of munitions industries since 1945 . . . threatened not only current programs but also future efforts to arm foreign nations. . . . Drastic reforms were needed to maintain military assistance as an effective, continuing instrument of national policy."[7]

As recommended in a National Security Council report submitted during the NATO Treaty negotiations, the Truman administration set about lobbying Congress for not only "a North Atlantic arms bill but a broader measure that would provide the president with the general authority and funds he lacked to arm foreign nations . . . [and] establish an integrated, worldwide program for military assistance."[8] On 25 July 1949, the same day that President Tru-man formally ratified the North Atlantic Treaty, the House Committee on Foreign Affairs started examining an ambitious White House proposal to shape the distribution of aid through three channels: transfer of equipment (so-called end items), direct financial aid (to finance the production of military equipment in North America for the Allies and to assist the Europeans in acquiring the means to increase their own production capacity), and access by allied personnel to school and production facilities in the United Sates as well as the dispatch of U.S. experts to allied countries to train and advise in the production, use, and maintenance of American equipment.[9]

The draft legislation came under close scrutiny and raised concerns in Congress, but laborious negotiations led to enactment on 6 October of the Mutual Defense Assistance Act.[10] Aid to NATO members became the pur-view of the interdepartmental European Coordinating Committee, established in London under the American ambassador to the United Kingdom. The European Coordinating Committee acted as the political, military, and economic coordinating agency for the program in the European area. A similar approach—the distribution of economic and military aid both controlled by diplomats—shaped the Military Assistance Advisory Group (MAAG) set up in each recipient country. They operated under direction of the local ambassador as part of a country team that included political, economic, and uniformed personnel. Military assistance reached recipients through army, navy, and air force sections in each MAAG.[11] By late 1949 the MDAP framework was in place and ready to commence disbursing aid to the NATO allies subject to two requirements that needed implementation before the appropriation of funds as specifically stated in the Mutual Defense Assistance Act: adoption of a single strategic concept for the integrated defense of the North Atlantic area and bilateral agreements to define the assistance provided to each country.

A comprehensive framework was necessary to shape the development of allied military forces in the coming years based on missions assigned by the Alliance to national forces. The NATO strategic concept developed under the purview of the Alliance's Military Committee through the fall of 1949 made for sober reading in view of the overwhelming superiority of the Soviet Union in conventional forces. It emphasized the challenges of defending against a Communist offensive and reinforced the concept of specialization promoted by the Americans. Reduced to its core, the document stated that the United States would conduct strategic bombing in the enemy's rear and be ready to use tactical nuclear weapons on the central front; the U.S. Navy and the Royal Navy would look after the transoceanic sea lines of communications; and the continental allies—foremost France—would provide the bulk of the troops deployed east of the Rhine to take on the Red Army.[12]

This division of labor required France and her neighbors to expand their ground forces quickly and develop complementary capabilities in terms of air defense and tactical air support as well as coastal and harbor defense.[13] Unstated was the dire cost the European partners would pay in resisting a Soviet onslaught—on the front lines and at home, given the enemy's capability to conduct an air offensive across the length of the Continent. Meanwhile, the United States and Canada would remain relatively safe beyond the Atlantic, at least until the Soviets developed a capability for intercontinental bombing.[14] But at that juncture the Europeans could only agree to these terms in order to secure North American assistance.

The NATO Defense Committee endorsed this approach on 1 December 1949 and forwarded it for acceptance by the North Atlantic Council on 6 January. President Truman approved the concept on 27 January, the very day that the United States concluded bilateral agreements implementing aid programs with each of the eight European allies that had requested military assistance, including France.[15] Both chambers of the French parliament ratified this accord on 15 March 1950. By then, the old *Dixmude*, once again employed as a humble aircraft transport, had already arrived in Norfolk, Virginia, to embark a first consignment of American aid. Washington and Paris publicized the event as the dawn of an unprecedented Franco-American friendship that promoted peace through deterrence. The ship left with great fanfare on 18 March, bursting at the seams with twenty-two Grumman F6F-5 Hellcat fighters, twenty-two Curtiss SB2C-5 Helldiver dive-bombers, 145 tons of aircraft spares, and 276 tons of miscellaneous materials.[16] Boasts about the delivery of naval equipment as the first milestone in the provision of assistance should not be misinterpreted, however.

The priority allocated to France in the overall MDAP appropriation was clear. The bulk of the US$900 million initially budgeted for fiscal year 1950 was directed to the NATO allies, and France received fully half of that allocation. But that was primarily in support of Paris' commitment to provide 55 percent of the ground troops to be deployed in West Germany and the determination to pursue a rapid buildup of the country's tactical aviation, leaving only a marginal portion to the Marine nationale.[17] French admirals may well have considered the launch of peacetime U.S. military assistance under Truman eerily reminiscent of the wartime program agreed to by Roosevelt at Anfa in early 1943, focused as it was on building up Giraud's North African army. The French government having endorsed these priorities, *la défense du Rhin* looked set to continue dominating formulation of defense policy in the *métropole*. This stance left France's navy in a difficult position when trying to avail itself of a greater share of American aid and outlining its potential contribution to defeating a land offensive across the Iron Curtain.

Apportioning U.S. Assistance to France

Planning for resumption of American aid to the Marine nationale took place in a context of considerable acrimony in Paris. Rue Royale officials spent the greater part of the Queuille government's time in office (September 1948–October 1949) arguing over the place of sea power in the vision of Minister for National Defense Paul Ramadier. He focused on the defense of the Rhine in a context of great fiscal restraint. French leaders had resumed a strategy of alliance at the dawn of the Cold War—first through the Dunkirk Treaty, then the Western Union, then NATO—and could look forward to the commitment by the United States of considerable resources to France's recovery through the Marshall Plan and MDAP. Nevertheless, the government's priority remained that of salvaging the value of the French currency as part of the ongoing battle against a rising inflation that still threatened the social and economic fabric of the country. Key to the effort was decreasing national military expenditures, which consumed a quarter of the government's budget in 1948–49.[18]

To this end, Ramadier sought to implement important reductions in manpower across all three services. Prevailing conditions—namely, building up forces for the defense of the Rhine while maintaining an adequate contingent fighting in Indochina—conspired to minimize gains on that front. The only alternative was imposing economies on the matériel side. Ramadier initially experienced more success in that area by restraining modernization and growth of a heavy bomber aviation and limiting naval constructions (recalling the suspension of work on the *Jean Bart* and PA-28 in the spring of 1949), even at the cost of increasingly bitter relations with the secretaries of state for the air force and the navy as well as their senior military staff. Of note, the growing fracture among the political figures overseeing the military establishment developed in parallel to the decrease in influence of the *État-major de la Défense nationale* (National Defense Staff), marking the decline of another unifying voice in defense.[19] Its influential wartime commander, General Alphonse Juin, left in May 1947, only to be replaced by a succession of lesser-known figures, a trend no doubt encouraged by generals and admirals who foresaw that the budget battles ahead would necessitate strong service voices.

The thin veneer of collegiality at the top of France's defense establishment seemed to crack at the very moment when distribution of material assistance from the United States necessitated unified input from the Allies. U.S. frustrations had come to the fore as a result of the inability of Western Union members to forge united requests for assistance in Alliance terms, and the signing of the North Atlantic Treaty did not alleviate this concern. France's first NATO submission was typical in that regard, mixing up demands for equipment necessary to bulk up its strength in Europe, North Africa, and Indochina rather than clearly underlining how these would contribute to the Alliance's division of labor.[20] Surprisingly, given later disagreements that would arise as to the role of the French navy within NATO, the list submitted by Rue Royale planners on 5 March 1949 as part of the larger national inventory seemed notably restrained and suitably adapted to the Alliance needs.

It included requests for one light aircraft carrier (meant to replace the small *Dixmude* to form the nucleus of an antisubmarine "hunter-killer group"), 6 DEs, 24 minesweepers, and 120 aircraft as well as a mix of upgraded equipment (minesweeping suites, radars and sonars, modern gunnery) and various ammunition.[21] But the Queuille government had not yet suspended work on *Jean Bart* and PA-28 by that point. One could begin to see in these initial talks the approach the French navy would adopt for most of the 1950s in dealing with Allied assistance: focus demands for foreign aid on those instruments necessary for subordinate missions attributed to France by the Allies so that national resources could be dedicated to forging the means of a true blue-water navy.

This approach came to a grinding halt within months in the face of higher economic and social priorities. Ramadier forced suspension of work on France's two new capital ships while limiting metropolitan shipyards to work already under way for a few escorts, submarines, and amphibious vessels. The first tranche of assistance for U.S. fiscal year 1950 (1 July 1949 to 30 June 1950) included funding for delivery of six DEs, spare parts, and munitions as well as requested aircraft (sixty F6F-5 Hellcats and sixty SB2C-5 Helldivers) and provision of training in the United States for pilots. However, only six YMS minesweepers, less than a quarter of those demanded originally, hoisted the tricolor in the following months while the request for an aircraft carrier was ignored altogether. The U.S. Navy elected instead to prorogue the lease on

Dixmude at no cost, a small consolation for French admirals.[22] Meanwhile, the proportion of the French defense budget allocated to the Marine nationale decreased to 15.3 percent, in contrast to the 20–25 percent figure that had prevailed in the decades leading to World War II.[23] There appeared the great paradox of 1949: the prospect of increased allied assistance allowed Ramadier to decrease national expenditures dedicated to the navy while U.S. aid would neglect French naval rearmament, at least initially.

The Queuille government fell on 5 October, after thirteen months in office, to be followed by a renewed period of short-lived cabinets and ministerial instability at the very moment that Lemonnier's long reign at the helm of the French navy came to an end. Selected for the post of naval deputy to NATO's Supreme Allied Commander Europe, Lemonnier was succeeded on 31 May 1950 as chief of the Naval General Staff by Vice Admiral Robert Battet, a naval aviator close to Darlan until he rallied to de Gaulle after the 1942 North African landings. Battet commanded the Far East maritime forces in 1947–48 and then took charge of the navy's training schools. His choice to lead the navy was widely praised given the admiral's operational experience and professional credibility, but his tour turned short when he passed away on 15 July 1950 after a few weeks of acute illness.[24] Appointed to the same post on 18 August, Vice Admiral Roger Lambert lasted less than a year, felled as he was by his own shortcomings, a superb mariner and warrior but prone to bouts of drunkenness and patent Anglophobia.[25]

Following a grave incident in the presence of shocked NATO naval attachés who witnessed both symptoms during a lively lunch hosted on board the cruiser *Émile Bertin*, Lambert was effectively fired on 1 June 1951 and replaced by Vice Admiral Henri Nomy, who had already played a key role in the resurrection of the Aéronavale in 1943–47.[26] Since then, Nomy had served as vice chief of the Naval General Staff (1947–49), inspector general of naval aviation (1949), and inspector general of the navy (1950).[27] His appointment as head of the navy—and that of Battet previously—underlined the rise in influence of naval aviators in the Marine nationale and brought much renewed focus and steadiness to the post, as Nomy remained in that role until July 1960.

Naval planners in Paris certainly welcomed such renewed focus and steadiness, especially in the wake of a dramatic occurrence in Asia a year earlier, with deep repercussions that rippled all the way to France. Although taking place halfway around the world, the sudden march of North Korean troops across the thirty-eighth parallel on 25 June 1950 immediately resulted in increased tensions in Europe, with many observers decrying the event as the precursor to a general Soviet offensive against NATO. This premise gave greater urgency to the need for the provision of military aid from North America to Europe. It also boosted allocation of France's own resources to national defense despite the Fourth Republic's unfinished effort at civilian reconstruction and the deepening quagmire in Indochina. Through this crisis another opportunity arose for the Marine nationale to renew its approach of leveraging foreign assistance to acquire the means to discharge its subordinate alliance missions while maximizing national resources to develop a credible blue-water fleet. But it remained to be seen whether Battet and Lambert would seize the moment during their unexpectedly short-lived tenures.

Setbacks in Asia, Renewed Assistance in Europe

Another war brought another paradox. The outbreak of the Korean conflict imposed further military burden on an overstretched France but also greatly increased the perceived threat against Western Europe, resulting in a marked boost in NATO's military preparedness and increased foreign assistance within the Atlantic Alliance. The circumstances behind hostilities on the Korean peninsula are well known, but one must also place them in parallel to the degrading situation facing the French in Indochina. Following years of low-level guerrilla warfare, the Vietminh inflicted a humiliating defeat on the French army during the Battle of Route Coloniale 4 (RC4, or Colonial Highway 4) in October 1950, France's "greatest colonial defeat since Montcalm had died at Quebec."[28] French commanders had decided to evacuate isolated northern border posts, mostly by foot using the RC4—nothing more than a single-lane jungle track. Swooping in on these walking contingents, insurgents killed or captured more than five thousand French and colonial troops in three bloody weeks of jungle fighting. Barely seven hundred survivors made their way to safety in small and harried groups, leading the public in France—and the Allies—to realize for the first time that the French army could lose the Tonkin within months. Indochina itself could very well fall, especially as Communists troops of Mao's People's Liberation Army by then stood victorious across the border.[29]

The tragic defeat along the RC4 resulted in part from the lack of air support in theater, a factor worsened at the time by absence of an aircraft carrier as *Arromanches* was in Toulon, getting ready for another refit and exposing the limitations of a single-carrier navy.[30] Meanwhile, U.S. general of the army Douglas MacArthur had succeeded in turning the situation in Korea and started his push north of the thirty-eighth parallel. Within weeks, Chinese troops crossed the Yalu River and launched a devastating assault in November, forcing the Americans into retreat and causing a despondent MacArthur to call for a campaign of strategic bombing against targets in Manchuria. But these setbacks in Asia only reinforced in American minds the importance of the Soviet threat in Europe.

On 19 July 1950 President Truman had already declared that "free nations of the world must step up their common security program. . . . In the case of the North Atlantic area . . . I shall lay before Congress a request for such funds as are shown necessary to the attainment and maintenance of our common strength at an adequate level."[31] In September, having approved the buildup of U.S. forces in Europe, Truman formally endorsed National Security Council Report 68 (NSC 68), which promoted the primacy of the military dimension of containment, turning away from the priority allocated to economic aid since 1947.[32] Meanwhile, the $1.225 billion MDAP bill for 1951 was increased by $4 billion, of which $3.504 billion went to NATO when the president signed the supplemental appropriation bill on 23 September 1950.[33] The next, harder step was quickly apportioning the money among the Allies, as time was of the essence in the U.S. view.

Secretary of State Dean Acheson peremptorily asked the European members of NATO on 22 July 1950 for statements within the following two weeks detailing their commitment to a similar increase in their own defense effort as well as their views on the distribution of increased MDAP funding.[34] On 5 August the newly installed government of René Pleven replied with an ambitious three-year plan seeking to increase the defense budget by 19 percent in 1950, from 420 billion French francs (FF) to 500 billion FF and another 16 percent in 1951 to reach 580 billion FF, not including the cost of fighting in Indochina and defending the rest of the Union française, an expenditure of 220 billion FF per year. An additional 2,000 billion FF was specifically allocated under a stand-alone rearmament bill to fund twenty army divisions in Europe (ten in 1951 and five each in 1952 and 1953), compress a five-year air force expansion plan into three years (to stand up twenty-eight new fighter squadrons and another twenty-four for tactical air support), and increase funding for convoy escort and coastal defense.[35] A month later, Pleven extended the duration of compulsory service from twelve to eighteen months, an important boost to the defense of Europe, as conscripts could only be made to serve on the Continent unless they volunteered for overseas service.[36]

France's North Atlantic Allies certainly welcomed Pleven's ambitious plan, although many doubted his ability to finance it without triggering another wave of devastating inflation.[37] To alleviate such concerns and in response to recommendations submitted by the MDAP South East Asia Survey Mission—dispatched on 4 July to study defense requirements in Indochina, Indonesia, Malaya, Burma, and Thailand—the Truman administration agreed in September 1950 to stand up a dedicated MAAG in Saigon.[38] Washington had already initiated the provision of economic assistance to Indochina in February by redirecting funds previously assigned to the Chinese Nationalists, now defeated and isolated on the island of Taiwan.[39] Direct military aid followed in July, and the Truman administration agreed in December to a stand-alone MDAP agreement dedicated to Indochina, an effort funded and administered in addition to and independently of the program managed by MAAG France.[40]

In naval terms, MDAP Indochina provided a welcome reprieve to the Marine nationale. It lessened the burden of directing a continuous flow of amphibious vessels and river patrol craft to the Far East, as well as the necessary fuel, spare parts, and ammunition necessary to support operations. French admirals could also leverage the American commitment to the fights in Korea and Indochina to support their narrative whereby France's security, and that of the North Atlantic Alliance itself, extended beyond a narrow focus on the European central front in the context of the larger Cold War. However, disagreements still existed in defining the role the French navy was meant to play in the coming years and the means it required to discharge its assigned missions. Regardless of America's newfound largesse toward France, differences in priorities between Paris and Washington continued hampering the formulation of mutually agreed vision.

Conciliating Differing Naval Visions

The Medium Term Defense Plan adopted by NATO's Defense Committee in the spring of 1950 accepted the strategy promoted by the continental Allies seeking to "hold the enemy as far to the east in Germany as possible," but it also confirmed the relegation of their navies to the roles of local convoy escort and coastal defense.[41] Although the plan had established immediate national force objectives for July 1951, the outbreak of the Korean War forced a revision of several aspects of Medium Term Defense Plan within months of its adoption, especially in terms of accelerated production objectives for 1954. The Truman administration intimated that the decision to dispatch additional American forces to Europe would be contingent on the rearmament of a newly united West Germany—the U.S., British, and French zones of occupation having been amalgamated into the Federal Republic of Germany on 23 February 1949, the Soviets reacting with the instauration of the German Democratic Republic in October.[42] While the prospect of a buildup of American strength on the Old Continent was welcome in France, that of rearming the former enemy met with firm opposition.

Washington and Paris agreed on the requirement to urgently increase the defense effort in Europe, but they disagreed on the means to achieve this aim. The disagreement took on a very public face during the North Atlantic Council meeting, which took place in New York on 18 September 1950. Secretary of State Acheson formally proposed to integrate a large contingent of West German ground troops in what would become NATO's Allied Command Europe the following year. The explosive news forced a recess to allow national representatives to consult with their respective governments. In France, many within Pleven's cabinet were leery of the U.S. initiative, largely reflecting a public opinion vehemently opposed to the concept. Minister of Foreign Affairs Robert Schuman put up a ferocious fight in defending the French position when the parties reconvened on 26 September. Paris could agree, at most, to a light and mobile paramilitary police force to discharge security duties in Germany in wartime and the employment of "civilian construction battalions" to assist in expanding NATO infrastructure beforehand. Although isolated by the end of the conference, Schuman succeeded in delaying an official decision, to Acheson's great frustration.[43]

German rearmament did not directly impact naval matters as the American proposal was purely concerned with ground troops; it did not envision the formation of a West German navy or an air force at that stage. But French obstructionism on that specific question dramatically affected Franco–U.S. relations in the fall of 1950. Among others in the United States, the U.S. Joint Chiefs of Staff repeatedly stated their dissatisfaction that France actively opposed mobilizing German resources in support of the defense of Western Europe and yet struggled to raise but a fraction of the one hundred divisions it fielded in 1940, just a decade before.[44] Such predispositions did not bode well for the upcoming visit to Washington of a French ministerial delegation co-led by Minister of National Defense Jules Moch and Minister of Finance Maurice Petsche. Talks took place 13–18 October 1950 with the aim of discussing future rearmament plans in view of the supplemental assistance approved by Congress in September. The visit would come just in time to assist France's government to prepare its budget submission due to the National Assembly before the end of the year.

Concerned as the Americans were with building up ground and air forces in Europe while the French camp was preoccupied with the desperate jungle fight along the RC4 then under way in Indochina, not much time was spent discussing naval issues that week.[45] Tellingly, no naval officer was present among either delegation. Nevertheless, the subject of support to the Marine nationale did come up on the first day to discuss the bid formulated earlier by the Amirauté for inclusion in the supplementary MDAP allocation announced by Truman in August 1950. As in 1949, navy planners formulated a request that seemingly reflected Alliance priorities and common defense requirements: one antiaircraft cruiser, three large fleet destroyers, sixteen smaller DEs, forty-one minesweepers; the necessary equipment, spares, and ammunition necessary for operating these units; additional aircraft, including jet fighters of the type being introduced for service on board USN and RN carriers; and additional training billets in the United States for ground and air crews.[46]

The continued need for minesweepers and DEs was evident in terms of the NATO-assigned missions of coastal defense and convoy operations. One could also justify the antiaircraft cruiser, fleet destroyers, and jet fighters as necessary for the defense of a carrier-centric antisubmarine warfare (ASW) hunter-killer group, but this last step did not square with the American position on French naval armament.

U.S. representatives—including Secretary of State Acheson and Secretary of Defense Marshall—endorsed France's proposal to a degree on 13 October: "With regards to naval vessels, the French production program, from the point of view of timing, appears reasonable."[47] But they proved much more guarded in their approach to the subject of naval aviation: "Secretary Marshall said . . . the French should economize by making only anti-submarine carrier-based aircraft and delete the fighter aircraft."[48] This perspective prevailed in the following weeks as further negotiations resulted in the dismissal of the request for the cruiser and fleet destroyers (perceived in the United States as adequate for integration in attack carrier formations rather than the humble ASW hunter-killer groups), the destroyer escorts (those would have been in addition to the six DEs already included in the original MDAP 1950 appropriation), and the jet fighters (limiting French hopes to more wartime propeller aircraft). In contrast, negotiations for naval allocations within the new MDAP Indochina agreement proved more promising.

In this case, the United States undertook the delivery of six landing ship support large (heavy gun- and rocket-carrying amphibious vessels designed to provide close fire support to troops already ashore or in the process of landing from other craft), thirty-six landing craft vehicle and personnel (also wartime craft but used for the actual landing of troops and vehicles), and fourteen Supermarine Sea Otter amphibian patrol aircraft (a variant of the proven Walrus biplane design, to be purchased from the British using MDAP funds).[49] While urgency contributed to the seeming generosity of the MDAP Indochina transfers, the relative paucity of the 1950 supplemental plan regarding the French metropolitan fleet was telling of American priorities. France needed to build up her *corps aéroterrestre* in West Germany immediately, especially as Paris promoted a strategy of forward defense while blocking the rearmament of her neighbor to the east. As far as Truman administration officials were concerned, the time was not opportune to divert precious allied resources to purely national ambitions.[50]

Perhaps, but the United States also seemed reluctant to fill France's demands regarding coastal defense tasks and convoy duties within the MDAP supplemental bill, especially in terms of minesweepers and DEs. Practical concerns prevailed in that regard. By the fall of 1950 increasing reactivation work of ships maintained in reserve since the war imposed a tremendous burden on American shipyards in response to the widening demand from the United States and overseas. The importance of the lowly minesweeper truly came to the fore that year, especially in the wake of the Wonsan landing in Korea, which reminded naval planners of the debilitating effect mines could impose on the freedom of movement at sea and the scale of resources needed to defeat that threat. This demand led to serious bottlenecks as the U.S. Navy sought to grow its own mine warfare assets for deployment to Asia at the very moment the European allies clamored for more transfers.[51] As for destroyer escorts, two of the six DEs ordered the previous year were yet to be delivered, and consideration for additional transfers to France were postponed to future MDAP iterations.[52] As limited as end-item deliveries may have seemed, one must acknowledge that American aid also took different forms that would prove as relevant in the long term.

MDAP legislation allowed for two conduits to provide equipment: material in the form of end items (finished military goods ranging from bullets to tanks, ships, and aircrafts) and direct financial aid. The latter could be disbursed as additional military production (AMP) or offshore procurement (OSP). AMP allowed the United States to subsidize defense production in Europe through "the provision of dollar financing of materials (both raw materials and components), machine tools, technical services, licenses and prototypes."[53] Instead of restricting military goods to wartime stocks and industrial production in America, AMP "was designed to enhance production in the NATO countries of certain specified military items."[54] Washington contributed funds to develop military industries in a given country and to subsidize the local production of armament for use by that country's armed forces.

OSP, on the other hand, provided an avenue to "pay foreigner [sic] countries to build armaments for the United States and western Europe, both for those nations that built the armaments and for transfer to other NATO countries."[55] In other words, the United States funded the production in Europe of goods for use by the producing country or a third party within the Alliance (say, building ships in the Netherlands for the Portuguese navy). OSP did not play much of a role in the early years of MDAP, but AMP is quite relevant to this discussion as French dockyards and industry finally showed the potential to undertake new naval constructions on a larger scale in the early 1950s.

France's naval dockyards and commercial shipyards had focused mostly on civilian production and refurbishment of existing naval units since the end of the war. Meanwhile, the Direction centrale des constructions et armes navales (Central Directorate of Constructions and Naval Armaments), under the energetic leadership of Louis-Lazare Kahn, undertook several studies of new models in all classes of ships in preparation for new building programs. Prime Minister Pleven's announcement of an accelerated three-year rearmament plan allowed Admiral Lambert—appointed head of the navy just days earlier—to submit a proposal developed during the few weeks his predecessor (Battet) had spent in office with a view to initiate new constructions in French shipyards through the years 1951, 1952, and 1953.[56] Minister of National Defense Moch eventually endorsed a final plan that provided Lambert with the guidance required to outline a five-year building program of 50,000 tons, at an average of 10,000 tons a year, to launch the following vessels:

- One new antiair cruiser, in addition to completing *De Grasse* for that same role;
- Four fleet destroyers (the new type T-47);
- Seven DEs (the new type E-50);
- Seven 600-ton coastal patrol craft;
- Twelve 150-ton harbor patrol craft;
- Twenty-one coastal minesweepers;
- Four *Narval*-class submarines (based on the German Type XXI); and
- 4,600 tons of amphibious vessels of various classes.[57]

Dated 16 October 1950, Lambert's submission conveyed both restraint and ambition. In terms of capital ships, the proposal did not dispute the previous cancellation of the carrier project PA-28, nor did it promote increased funding for battleships. At the time, *Richelieu* was in the middle of a refit commenced at Brest in January 1950, an important investment of resources to refurbish the machinery, main gunnery, and the miscellany of auxiliary systems found on that tired vessel. Plans to complete the once hoped-for modernization of electronic sensors and antiair weapons, however, were abandoned. Meanwhile, *Jean Bart* left Brest following the slow repair of her wartime damages in 1946–47 and the fitting out of her remaining main armament and auxiliary machinery, completed in the spring of 1949.[58] Thereafter, she was restricted to peacetime maneuvering with the fleet, awaiting further funding to install the modern radars and antiair gun batteries required to allow her deployment in harm's way. In another sign of restrained ambition, Lambert proposed "downgrading" *Châteaurenault* and *Guichen*, the two former Italian light cruisers, to the role of ASW command destroyer. However, he reiterated his concern with the fact that the remaining cruisers—*Émile Bertin*, *Georges Leygues*, *Montcalm*, and *Gloire*—were nearing the end of service lives without plans for their replacement.[59]

The report also welcomed the contribution of a rejuvenated aeronautical industry. This renewal allowed for the acquisition in 1951 of eighteen newly designed Nord 1400 long-range flying boats (the Noroit, a twin-engine monoplane with an enclosed cabin for a crew of seven that first flew in 1949) and thirty-five Nord 1002 Pingouin, single-engine monoplanes capable of embarking four personnel. Although modeled after the old German Messerschmitt 108 and unable to operate from a carrier, the latter proved highly useful for initial aircrew training, an important need as the Aéronavale was quickly expanding to meet increasing MDAP aircraft deliveries.[60] Left unstated was the likely ambition that the acquisition of an antiair cruiser, fleet destroyers, and another tranche of DEs from the United States, as well as the provision of AMP funding to subsidize the building of smaller vessels in French shipyards, would leave room for directing national funds to more ambitious naval projects in future budgets. As in 1949, such hopes did not endure.

American deliveries of naval end items (other than aircraft) fell well short of those envisioned by Lambert while the final defense budget and rearmament plan adopted by the Assemblée nationale on 8 January 1951 did not make up for these shortfalls. Overall French military expenditures grew from 559 billion FF in 1950 to 881 billion FF in 1951 (from 25.5 to 36.4 percent of the national budget), with MDAP transfers adding 140 billion FF in 1951.[61] The share of the navy's appropriations in the national budget grew from 15 to 18.3 percent over these two years and, of the 35 billion FF invested by the United States for the production of military goods in France in 1951, 9.3 billion FF went to naval rearmament.[62] These investments played a critical role in the modernization of French shipyards. They also subsidized the immediate start of construction programs for the T-47 destroyers, the E-50 escorts, and new coastal minesweepers; the conversion of the cruisers *Châteaurenault* and *Guichen* into powerful *escorteurs d'escadre* (squadron escorts—the original vision of ASW command destroyers but augmented with a potent antiair warfare capability); and the ability of French industries to commence producing modern electronics (radars, sonars, etc.), naval guns, and munitions. Nevertheless, even though the term "defense of the Rhine" had been erased from policy documents since the departure of minister Ramadier in October 1949, NATO's adoption of a strategy of forward defense in Germany, promoted by successive French governments, did not bode well for an end to the *mise en parenthèse de la flotte.*

By then the Americans had already announced that MDAP naval deliveries would not meet the numbers and capabilities requested by the French. End items, including aircraft for the Aéronavale, remained limited to wartime stocks or similarly aging designs built after the hostilities, such as British Sunderlands and Lancasters soon to be acquired for long-range maritime patrols.[63] Although ministers Moch and Petsche had fought for Admiral Lambert's October requests in Washington, they admitted defeat as this effort did not warrant threatening support from the United States for the buildup of the army and tactical aviation in Europe. Appearing before the National Assembly's Commission de la défense nationale in the weeks leading up to the vote on the forthcoming rearmament bill, Moch made a telling statement:

> If we had unlimited funds, I would gladly make an additional effort for the navy but the problem is not that. The problem, as resources available are few, is to design a plan that best uses these limited funds to meet our most immediate needs. There is no doubt that, given the current

geopolitical context *and the fact that the biggest navies are with us while our frontier to the East remains undefended,* the first military duty of France is to assemble a formation of ground troops with the complement of tactical aviation necessary to protect that force. . . . As much as politics is the art of choosing the lesser evil, so is the role of the defense minister in resolving the most pressing problem at hand while respecting existing budgetary constraints. . . . We have an imperious duty to make a massive effort on behalf of the army and, if I had another 50 billion FF to divide between the three services this year, *the part of this increase that would go to the navy would still be minimal.*[64] [Emphasis added.]

So, the World War II paradoxes that reappeared when France resumed a strategy of alliance in 1948 seemed likely to persist into the following decade. On the one hand, France joined NATO and gained access to the wealth of resources the United States made available through MDAP at the very moment when French government brought rearmament back on an equal footing with civilian reconstruction. This moment presented the Marine nationale with a unique opportunity for unprecedented regeneration. Admirals Lemonnier, Battet, and Lambert—with the active support of their respective naval ministers—tried to make the best of this opening, quickly leveraging any U.S. and French resources that became available. On the other hand, the Soviet threat on the Alliance's eastern border drove the United States to demand that the continental Allies urgently build up a credible *force aéroterrestre* for deployment on the central front. And successive French governments readily endorsed this focus, especially when Secretary of State Acheson made it clear that failure to do so would lead to the rearmament of France's former foe, West Germany.

If anything, the focus on the central European front gained momentum in the following months. Fighting in Asia, so dire in the closing weeks of 1950 with the UN forces pushed back by the Chinese and the French still reeling from their humiliating defeat along the RC4, subsided in the new year. General Matthew Ridgway replaced the frantic MacArthur and stabilized the Korean front back along the thirty-eighth parallel by the spring of 1951. Earlier on, in December 1950, famed General Jean de Lattre de Tassigny had come to the rescue in Indochina, immediately restoring morale within the expeditionary corps and quickly inflicting several bloody defeats on overly confident Vietminh troops.[65] These victories in Asia—or at least turning defeats into less pressing military draws—reemphasized the centrality of the Soviet threat in Europe, confirming NATO's strategy of forward defense and the subordinate role of France's navy in that context. The 8 January 1951 French rearmament bill and continued U.S. support through MDAP provided the Marine nationale (and French naval industries) with increasing capacities but left ambitions for a capable and credible blue-water fleet in abeyance. Unresolved in this paradoxical period was whether the years ahead would see the triangle of conflicting interests and priorities between the French government, the Rue Royale, and Washington evolve into an agreeable construct of mutually supporting objectives or disintegrate further into a flux of renewed and bitter confrontations.

CHAPTER 7

BUILDING A BLUE-WATER FLEET

Clashing Visions at Home and Abroad

The sun had yet to rise over the horizon, but a pallid glow already silhouetted the aircraft carrier *La Fayette* as it turned to the flying course in the predawn hours of Thursday, 1 November 1956. Gathering speed through the warm waters of the Eastern Mediterranean, the French ship launched several American-built Chance Vought F4U-7 Corsair fighter-bombers, which formed up and flew due south to complete their assigned mission: sinking the Egyptian warships based in the port of Alexandria. The strike was a small part of the much larger Opération 700, better known by its British designation, Operation Musketeer. Following the Israeli invasion of the Sinai in the previous days, Great Britain and France planned to seize the Suez Canal Zone with a combined force of airborne and amphibious troops to turn back the nationalization of the Suez Canal ordered by President Gamal Abdel Nasser earlier in July. For the first time since the end of World War II, pilots of the Aéronavale prepared to carry out what they considered the core mission of carrier aviation, striking at the enemy's fleet. The moment had been long awaited for, but the feverish excitement that reigned on board *La Fayette* during these early morning hours—as well as in the carrier *Arromanches* and the rest of the Force navale d'intervention (Naval Intervention Force) assembled for the expedition—turned to frustration as a result of the interference of a key ally, the United States.

Concerned with the reaction of the Warsaw Pact as well as the nascent Non-Aligned Movement at the United Nations and the Arab world at large,

President Dwight D. Eisenhower disapproved of the Anglo-French-Israeli offensive against Egypt.[1] His administration had already launched a wide range of diplomatic and military measures since the summer, including concentration of the U.S. Sixth Fleet to shadow the movement of Anglo-French forces in the Eastern Mediterranean as well as positioning naval assets off the coast of Egypt to dissuade further escalation.[2] Conscious that mistakenly firing upon American units would entail dramatic consequences, French and British authorities severely restricted the ability of pilots to engage warships, requiring stringent visual identification of vessels larger than patrol boats. Although later sorties against Egyptian airfields and troop concentrations inland proved decisive in preparing for an airborne drop on 5 November and an amphibious assault the following day, the presence of American ships, aircraft, and submarines off shore as well as in Alexandria and Port Said greatly restrained the effect of French and British naval air sorties during that fateful week.[3] Renewed U.S. pressures—namely, denying a request from London to the International Monetary Fund for financial assistance—and threatening gestures from Moscow led to a cease-fire on 7 November and a humiliating withdrawal the next month.

The irony was clear when looking at the composition of France's naval task force, the United States having provided the bulk of those means. The French naval commander for Opération 700, Rear Admiral Pierre Lancelot, sailed in the cruiser *Georges Leygues*, modernized in Philadelphia in 1943. *La Fayette* had been transferred to the Marine nationale from the U.S. Navy in 1951. The carrier group commanded by Rear Admiral Yves Caron included T-47 fleet destroyers and E-50 destroyer escorts built in French yards but subsidized with American funds through the additional military production (AMP) channel. Other units had been delivered from America as end items under the Mutual Defense Assistance Program (MDAP), including the eight Cannon-class destroyer escorts acquired in 1950–52, a miscellany of amphibious vessels and minesweepers, and all of the aircraft embarked in *La Fayette* and *Arromanches*. Preparations for Suez had also shown the French armed forces wanting in their ability to mount a large-scale expeditionary operation, of which a credible world power should be capable.

The mid-1950s would stand as a period of paradoxes in the maturation of the postwar Marine nationale. Successive governments realized that the previous fixation on the defense of the Rhine and a strategy of forward defense as far east in Germany as possible would not be enough to meet the country's political ambitions and military needs in the context of the Cold War. On the one hand, allied material and monetary assistance combined with renewed prosperity at home to generate the means to build ships, submarines, and shore infrastructure at a tremendous pace. By then France had suffered defeat in Indochina, and the Algerian struggle was already turning desperate but the French navy performed well through both conflicts and counted as an increasingly respected voice in allied naval circles and within the national defense establishment. On the other hand, the Suez embarrassment also showed the limits of France's influence on events overseas and the continued inability of the fleet to operate autonomously in support of national interests and ambitions. These circumstances illuminate the development of two successive documents that would come to shape decisively the regeneration of the navy for decades to come: the Statut naval de 1952, which set the path for a credible blue-water surface fleet and the 1955 Plan bleu. The latter sought to elaborate a longer-term vision of a mature navy capable of upholding France's grandeur through the complex peacetime circumstances of the Cold War and standing ready to fight in the unprecedented conditions of the nuclear era.

The Continued Challenge of Clashing Naval Visions

As a committed building effort had only been launched the summer before, France's naval fleet was still very much in transition in the summer of 1951 (see table 7.1). Figures show a total of 256,000 tons (300,000 tons if one included various auxiliaries and amphibious vessels), but the fleet remained an assemblage of French prewar construction, allied transfers of World War II stocks, and Axis trophies of war. The T-47 destroyer *Surcouf* was the only genuine postwar unit, and her construction had barely begun. The French navy did not have the ability to maintain a carrier task force available to respond to a national crisis or a sudden UN commitment, nor did it provide NATO with at least one ASW hunter-killer group on a continuous basis.

The smaller destroyer escorts, minesweepers, and patrol craft were operating at full capacity, dispersed as they were on operations that ranged from the *métropole* to the antipodes of the Union française, especially as the fight in Indochina called on ever more resources. The submarine force could not conduct operations of its own, dedicated as it was to supporting the ASW training of the surface fleet. This portrait made for a bleak assessment of the Marine nationale's operational capability six years after the end of World War II.

The Aéronavale had yet to join the jet age, with all of its carrier- and shore-based squadrons flying proven but obsolete aircraft designs from the previous decade. However, such a bleak reading of conditions at the time could be misleading. Naval aviation had already come to dominate planning at the Rue Royale when Admiral Henri Nomy, the navy's senior pilot, took over from the boisterous Lambert as *chef de l'État-major général de la Marine* in June 1951. If any doubt still lingered in the immediate postwar era, the "gun carriers versus aircraft carriers" debate had since been resolutely concluded, with the latter the reigning capital ship, key to exercising sea power in the coming decades.[4] Nuclear weapons would soon become small enough for delivery by carrier-based aircraft, while flexible carrier wings could discharge the full range of missions through the Cold War, from forming the nucleus of ASW hunter-killer groups to the provision of air defense at sea and in the littoral as well as mobile fire support to forces ashore, as demonstrated in Korea and Indochina. By 1951 the Marine nationale had also completed a resolute turn away from the Royal Navy toward the U.S. Navy in its approach to carrier operations—whether in terms of doctrine, procedures, and equipment—and could envision continued growth through the provision of American aid.

The purchase of *Arromanches* from Great Britain represented the final act in the postwar RN assistance to French naval aviation. London had agreed in 1946 to lease the former *Colossus* to France for five years, but the French government elected in March 1951 to buy her outright for 1.5 million British pounds.[5] From then on, the Aéronavale embarked on a decided course of "Americanization." Admiral Lemonnier had already approached the U.S. Navy for transfer of a light carrier, citing the 1949 decision by the French government to cancel the PA-28 project and the (then-) expected termination

Table 7.1: Main French Fleet, 1 July 1951
(does not include oilers and auxiliaries, amphibious craft, planes, and submarine tenders)

Numbers of Hulls per Category	In Service, Capable of Combat in Modern Conditions	In Service or in Refit but Obsolete	Under Construction / Completion / Modernization	Remarks
Battleships (2)	0	1	1	*Richelieu* in refit in Cherbourg, limited to training role at gunnery school *Jean Bart* in service but back in dry dock in November 1951 for final completion
Aircraft carriers (2)	1	0	1	*Arromanches* operational *La Fayette* still in the United States but with French crew working up
Aircraft transport (1)	0	1	0	*Dixmude* in service
Cruisers (6)	3	2	1	*Gloire, Georges Leygues,* and *Montcalm* operational *Émile Bertin* and *Jeanne d'Arc* on training duties *De Grasse* in reserve in Lorient, to be towed in the fall of 1951 to Brest for completion
Fleet Destroyers (11)	5	2	4	*Kleber, Marceau, Alsacien, Lorrain* (modernized former German destroyers) operational *Le Malin* (prewar *contre-torpilleur* / light cruiser recommissioned on 1 July 1951 to deploy to Indochina with *Arromanches*) operational *Alcyon* and *Albatros* (prewar *contre-torpilleurs*) on training duties at the gunnery school *Surcouf* (first of the T-47s) laid at Lorient shipyard July 1951 *Châteaurenault* and *Guichen* (former Italian cruisers) in La Seyne shipyard for conversion to ASW command destroyers *Hoche* (former German destroyer) in refit for conversion to trial ship role
Destroyer escorts (18)	12	6	0	12 former U.S. Cannon-class (*Algérien, Sénégalais, Somali, Hova, Marocain, Tunisien, Touareg, Soudanais, Kabyle, Arabe, Bambara, Sakalave*) operational 6 former U.K. River-class frigates (*Croix de Lorraine, L'Aventure, L'Escarmouche, La Découverte, La Surprise, Le Tonki*nois) operational

(continued)

Table 7.1 (continued)

Numbers of Hulls per Category	In Service, Capable of Combat in Modern Conditions	In Service or in Refit but Obsolete	Under Construction / Completion / Modernization	Remarks
Corvettes / sloops (24)	0	24	0	La Grandière, Savorgnan de Brazza, and Dumont d'Urville (colonial sloops) obsolete but adequate for Union française Francis Garnier (former Italian colonial sloop) obsolete but adequate for Union française missions 10 Élan-class and 6 Chamois-class prewar avisos-dragueurs, obsolete but adequate for metropolitan and Union française missions 4 U.S. Tacoma-class frigates employed as unarmed weather ships (Mermoz, La Place, Le Brix, Le Verrier)
Minesweepers (38)	Various			9 oceangoing and 29 coastal sweepers, even mix of modern and obsolete builds
Coastal patrol craft (35)	Various			Mostly obsolete but adequate for metropolitan and Union française coastal patrol tasks
Submarines (11)	3	6	2	La Créole, L'Africaine, L'Astrée (laid in 1939–40, completed in 1949–50) operational Junon (in service 1937), employed in the training role Former U-boats Roland Morillot, Blaison, Millé, Laubie, Bouan employed for training and experimentation Andromède and Artémis (laid in 1939–40, work interrupted by World War II) still under construction
Total	24	42	9	75
Tons	76,100	102,900	77,000	256,000 Not including ships in reserve, used as barracks, schools, etc.

of the British lease of the *Arromanches*. Lengthy negotiations ensued, leading in October 1950 to the lease at no cost of an Independence-class light carrier as part of the next MDAP tranche.[6] Although a dated platform from the early years of World War II, USS *Langley* provided the French navy with a tremendous asset, capable of sustained speeds of thirty knots and embarking thirty aircraft. Originally planned as a Cleveland-class cruiser, she and eight of her sister ships were designated for conversion to the light carrier role while under construction in 1941–42, retaining their sleek hulls and powerful engineering plant. Laid as the USS *Fargo* (CL 85) in April 1942 but commissioned as *Langley* in August 1943, the ship saw active combat in the Pacific in 1944–45. Employed to repatriate troops from Asia and Europe in 1946, *Langley* was paid off in Philadelphia in February 1947, where she remained mothballed until selected for reactivation and transfer to France in early 1951.[7]

As in the case of the Cannon-class destroyer escorts delivered the previous year, Washington insisted that the newly renamed *La Fayette* be employed exclusively for ASW missions in the North Atlantic treaty area. Nevertheless, her arrival in European waters freed up *Arromanches* for several years of nearly continuous service in Indochina. Having completed an extensive refit in late 1950 and early 1951 and an intense working up period until the summer months, the former British carrier set sail at the end of August. This second deployment to the Far East (having first served there from October 1948 to January 1949) had been anxiously awaited by French authorities in Indochina. As demonstrated during the Battle of Route Coloniale 4 in October 1950, the absence of carrier-based air cover could severely impede operations ashore, given the paucity of air fields in Indochina and the limited number of shore-based aircraft in theater. The Armée de l'air would still only have 360 combat planes dispersed through the whole of Indochina by 1954, with a third of those often unavailable due to maintenance and repair.[8] *Arromanches'* complement of twenty-five aircraft could make a significant difference when dedicated to any single operation taking place in a given sector.

Meanwhile, the older *Dixmude* reverted to her less glamorous but essential transport role. Transferring large number of aircraft around the world had indeed assumed a critical importance. The Marine nationale was tasked to support the buildup of French air strength in Indochina and ferrying an increasing rate of MDAP transfers from America to the *métropole* in 1950–54.[9] The sheer scale of deliveries taken on by *Dixmude*—and many more carried in civilian hulls through the same period—clearly showed the commitment of resources by the United States to the rearmament of France in the early 1950s. The nature of the material being transferred to the French navy, though, also revealed a continued reluctance in Washington to endorse the level of ambitions contemplated at the Rue Royale. Requests for jet aircraft were denied and *Dixmude* embarked World War II piston-engine Corsairs and Avengers as late as 1957 for delivery to France. AMP funding played a pivotal role in quick-starting naval construction in French yards, but the provision of U.S. dollars remained carefully restricted to building, in addition to minesweepers and amphibious craft, those T-47 and E-50 destroyers required for the escort of ASW hunter-killer groups and slower merchant convoys, not some future French carrier strike group.

Even discussions of items of common interest could give rise to serious disagreements. Following the adoption by the Assemblée nationale on 8 January 1951 of a new defense budget for the current fiscal year and a longer-term rearmament policy, Minister of National Defense Jules Moch addressed to the U.S. government a comprehensive plan to implement the legislation. This note having been circulated in Washington, the U.S. Embassy in Paris relayed to French authorities an aide-mémoire providing the consolidated feedback of various agencies "with a view to increasing the effectiveness of the present Franco-American efforts to strengthen the combat effectiveness of the French military establishment."[10] The section concerned with naval matters attributed a low priority to the construction in France of carrier planes as well as the purchase of long-range patrol aircraft from Great Britain (Lancasters and Sunderlands). It recommended, instead, that greater emphasis be placed on the production of minesweepers, vehicle and personnel landing craft, and destroyer escorts.

This view drew a sharp reply penned by chief naval architect Louis-Lazare Kahn, who stated that the French plan was designed to satisfy national imperatives as well as alliance requirements.[11] Although they were in short supply, increasing the production of minesweepers in France would impact the construction of new fleet destroyers and the completion of the cruiser *De Grasse*. Kahn also decried the proposal submitted in earlier U.S. correspondence that an American minesweeper design be adopted for construction by French shipyards for the purpose of equipment standardization within NATO. Kahn stated that contracts had already been let for the construction of what he believed to be a "superior" French model and the fact that the British were still building their own design provided a precedent which could not be ignored.

Submarines also proved contentious in 1951. Later that spring, MAAG authorities in Paris suggested that France should put plans for construction of six new *Narval*-class submersibles on hold and concentrate national resources on building surface units. American skepticism regarding French ambitions in reconstituting a modern submarine fleet was twofold: operational and technical.[12] First, NATO war plans did not call for France to provide a large contribution of submarines beyond some capability for coastal patrol off the *métropole*. Second, the record of French shipyards in tackling the considerable challenges involved in the construction of submersibles capable of the performance required in the postwar era (extreme depths, higher speeds, improved autonomy, quieter hulls) appeared weak.

Although three submarines first laid before the war had entered service in 1949–50 (*La Créole*, *L'Africaine*, *L'Astrée*), they were largely completed along their original prewar drawings, while two more (*Andromède*, *Artémis*) remained under construction.[13] Delays continued to plague work on the latter as a result of repeated attempts to incorporate new designs and equipment based on lessons from the previous conflict and the study of German U-boats (enclosed sail for increased speed and quiet, air-breathing snorkel, improved combat information center, and torpedo arrangements). These challenges did not deter the French, however, and they presented some valid arguments in justifying their continued pursuit of submarine construction.

Within the context of the Alliance, the provision of an effective escort force demanded that ships and aircraft be provided with the opportunity to train against realistic targets. Only modern submarines could replicate the tactics and technical performance of the Soviet submarines that NATO fleets would be called upon to defeat in war. Dedicating national resources to building such modern platforms would also contribute to developing unique capabilities and expertise in French shipyards that the Alliance could leverage in the longer term, making these facilities as valuable as the vessels they would launch.[14] The debate was short-lived, however, as French admirals elected to dedicate purely national resources to their submarine projects, securing the inclusion of *projet E-48* in the 1951 national rearmament plan instead.[15] These *Narval*-class vessels—fruit of extensive postwar studies and practical experimentation using the German Type XXI *Roland Morillot* (the former

U-2518)—would not enter service for some time, however, and the Amirauté covered the training gap by leasing vessels from Great Britain. Paris and London agreed in December 1951 to transfer four wartime S-class submarines for four years at a cost of 245 million FF, soon renamed *La Sibylle, Le Saphir, La Sirène,* and *La Sultane*.[16]

The French navy also proposed another class of submersible, designed to kill its own kind. First raised in Conseil supérieur de la Marine (CSM) in 1948, the idea of a submarine specifically intended to attack other submarines quickly gained support and Lemonnier ordered a first study the following year.[17] It was inspired in part by a similar effort in the U.S. Navy—leading to the commissioning of USS *Barracuda* in November 1951—and the German Type XXIII, a small coastal U-boat conceived to patrol in shallower and enclosed waters such as in the North Sea and the Baltic. The CSM endorsed *projet I-53* in 1952, a *sous-marin de chasse* ("hunting" or attack submarine), larger than the Type XXIII but smaller than the *Narval*, for employment in the Mediterranean.[18] Based in Mers el-Kébir and Bizerte, vessels of the *Aréthuse* class would guard against Soviet submarines seeking to threaten the strategic lines of communications between North Africa and the *métropole*.

Their small size, short endurance, and narrow specialization later proved liabilities, and their operational careers were short-lived. Still, building upon the developmental work and experimentation required for the launch of *Aréthuse* and her three sister vessels eventually led to the design of the larger and more polyvalent *Daphné* class.[19] But such success still lay well into the future as the specter of differing naval visions held in Paris and Washington continued to challenge the more immediate development of the Marine nationale. Laborious negotiations over a French request submitted on 5 March 1953 for the lease of two modern American submarines were symbolic, denied a year later for not meeting Alliance needs as viewed by the U.S. Navy.[20] Nevertheless, military assistance had largely overtaken economic aid as the most effective means for the United States to sustain its containment policy and its strategy of deterrence in the West. Combined with the resurgence of France's economy, the stage would soon be set for French admirals to overcome the challenge of clashing visions within the Alliance to achieve the revival they had sought since the war years.

Setting the Path for a Blue-Water Fleet

The militarization of American aid to Europe and other allies around the world, launched with the enactment of the Mutual Defense Assistance Act in 1949 and accelerated in the months that followed the start of the Korean War, was signed into law on 10 October 1951 by President Truman. Building up on recommendations first made by White House adviser Gordon Fray in the fall of 1950 to amalgamate military and economic aid in support of the fight against Communism, the Mutual Security Act abolished the Economic Cooperation Administration, which had managed the Marshall Plan, as well as the Office of the Director of Mutual Defense Assistance, until then appointed under the authority of the secretary of state. In their stead, a single authority—the Mutual Security Agency—would administer a unified program of military, economic, and technical aid to "assure that the defensive strength of the free nations of the world shall be built as quickly as possible on the basis of continuous and effective self-help and mutual aid."[21] The primacy of the military component within the program was evident in the appropriation for fiscal year 1951. Of the $6 billion allocated to Western Europe (out of a worldwide total of $7 billion), $5 billion went to military aid and only $1 billion to economic assistance.[22]

As before, the Americans attributed the larger share of the European allocation to France. Secretary Acheson and Minister Schuman signed a bilateral agreement on 25 February 1952 that provided for, in various forms, the equivalent of 15 percent of France's 1.4 billion FF defense budget for the 1952 fiscal year.[23] In addition, the practice of providing direct military support to the fight in Indochina continued, with a commitment of $150 million that year and a steady expansion until the conclusion of the Geneva Accords. By the summer of 1954, the United States had disbursed an estimated $2.6 billion in combined military and economic assistance to the French effort in Indochina. The delivery of 150,000 tons of matériel included 1,800 combat vehicles, 30,887 transport vehicles, 361,522 small arms and machine guns, and about 500 aircraft, providing for 80 percent of the costs of the conflict in its last year.[24]

As reflected in table 7.2, naval transfers only amounted to a small fraction of the U.S. commitment, mainly in the form of amphibious vessels and patrol aircraft. Nevertheless, this support played a crucial role in alleviating the material burden the conflict imposed on the Marine nationale—although not the human costs as the navy maintained as many 12,000 sailors, marines, and aviators in that theater and more than 1,000 never returned.[25] And through it all Admiral Nomy and his staff could not ignore the European front as they shaped plans to meet the ambitious goals agreed to at the meeting of the North Atlantic Council in Lisbon, Portugal, on 20–25 February 1952.

The Lisbon summit constituted an important milestone in NATO's history. Decisions taken at that time consolidated the organization's peacetime infrastructure (with the adoption of a civilian secretary general and a permanent international staff as well as consolidation of its various military commands), launched a first round of enlargement (with the inclusion of Greece and Turkey), and set ambitious national force goals for the long term.[26] Most importantly, the council confirmed the commitment to build up a credible deterrent of conventional forces in Europe, bolstered by the American nuclear shield. At the time, the Soviets and their satellites were believed to have no less than 175 active divisions west of the Urals while General of the Army Dwight D. Eisenhower, appointed as the Alliance's first Supreme Allied Commander Europe (SACEUR) in April 1951, could only count on twenty-one, including those in reserve or subject to a lengthy mobilization process at the start of the hostilities. In Lisbon, NATO members promised to increase their ground forces to forty-one active divisions by 1954, with another forty-nine capable of mobilization within thirty days, supported by nearly 10,000 aircraft. Canada and the United States would provide eleven of those ninety divisions earmarked for service on the central front (i.e., excluding those of Greece and Turkey), while France, which had previously pledged ten, agreed to increase its obligation to thirty.

Promoted forcefully by the Americans to urge the Europeans to take on a larger share of the Alliance's conventional deterrent, the force goals adopted in Lisbon proved stillborn. The economies of Western Europe, even with subsidies from the United States, just could not sustain such a dramatic buildup. Senior NATO military leaders—including U.S. Army General Matthew Ridgway, who replaced Eisenhower as SACEUR in May 1952—remained skeptical of the sincerity of the politicians who had agreed to

Table 7.2: U.S. Naval Transfers to Indochina, 1950–53

French Fiscal Year	End Items	Value (Millions FF)
1950	6 LSSL*, 36 LCVP†, 14 Sea Otter Flying Boats	2,490
1951	6 patrol craft, 1 submarine chaser, 3 LSIL‡, 31 LCM§, 45 LCVP, 1 maintenance ship, 1 tanker ship, 14 tugs, 10 Consolidated PB4Y-2 Privateer patrol planes	10,013
1952	27 coastal patrol vessels, 6 river craft, 2 LSV#, 1 LSD**, 1 LSIL, 19 LCM, 44 LCVP, 24 assault rafts; 1 PB4Y-2 patrol plane, 12 Grumman JRF5 amphibian planes	8,370
1953	1 LSSL, 4 LSV, 36 LCM, 42 LCVP, 48 assault rafts, 2 PB4Y-2 patrol planes	11,314

* landing ship, support large	† landing ship, infantry large	# landing ship, vehicle
† landing craft, vehicle and personnel	§ landing craft, mechanized	** landing ship, dock

these targets, believing instead that the goals had been merely accepted as the basis for future negotiations.[27] Regardless of such suspicions, however, NATO leaders had also agreed to ambitious naval figures in MC 26/1, "Militarily Desirable Goals for Planning Purposes beyond 1954," the document approved in Lisbon on 23 February 1952. As politically savvy as ever, Admiral Nomy saw an opportunity and seized it.

As reported in a note from the Conseil de la Marine, this policy did not radically alter the fundamental tasks assigned to the French navy, defined as (a) the defense of the country's vital sea lines of communications (those linking the *métropole* with North and West Africa as well as the arrival points in France of the Alliance's transatlantic convoy routes); (b) the defense of French harbors and naval bases, and their seaward access; and (c) the provision of support from the sea to NATO ground and air forces operating in French zones of responsibility.[28] As before, these missions entailed the provision by France of ASW hunter-killer groups, convoy escorts, and coastal defense assets but in much larger numbers than contemplated before by NATO:

- 3 aircraft carriers
- 4 cruisers
- 31 fleet destroyers (*escorteurs de 1ère classe*)

- 62 destroyer escorts (*escorteurs de 2ᵉ classe*)
- 20 coastal escorts
- 24 high seas minesweepers, 170 coastal minesweepers, 31 shallow-water minesweepers
- 10 operational submarines (i.e., not including those committed to the training role)

This vision, an aggregate of 400,000 tons to be made available for NATO service in European waters at the outset of a conflict, entailed a dramatic demand for resources, especially when contrasted with the current state of the French navy. The fleet continued to shrink in the early 1950s as old vessels were retired at a faster rate than new constructions and MDAP end items could enter service. Rue Royale planners expected that 47,000 tons of obsolete ships and submarines would be decommissioned in 1952–54, and then another 121,500 tons through to the summer of 1958. Meanwhile, French shipyards struggled to launch 10,000 tons of new constructions in 1950 and 1951.[29] As well, the NATO figures did not include purely national requirements such as the defense of Union française territories or the provision of support to UN missions. Nevertheless, MC 26/1 offered a framework that Admiral Nomy intended to leverage quickly in order to obtain a formal commitment on the part of his political masters to accelerate the rejuvenation of the fleet.

This initiative on the part of the navy did not take place in a void, as Nomy could leverage a third element, in addition to militarization of American aid and promotion of ambitious force goals by NATO, to bolster support for his plans. Even as France struggled to fulfill its army commitments on the European central front and in Indochina, a growing chorus of voices within the political class came to support increased allocations for the navy. Such voices were not entirely new. Ever since 1945 a number of elected representatives, in government and from the opposition, within the secrecy of cabinet debates and more public fora such as the National Assembly's defense and finance commissions, clamored for France to rebuild her strength at sea. Such argument was clearly on display during the debates over the aircraft carrier project PA-28 and the completion of *Jean Bart*. Typical was an emotional statement by Paul Anxionnax, from the Radical Party, during a session of the Commission des finances in March 1949: "Voices always rise after France's wars to critique the navy and declare it irrelevant. We have made this mistake on several occasions before, let us not make this same mistake again!"[30] Close to more conservative circles, *Le Monde's* naval analyst Edmond Delage wrote in September 1949:

> The last war marked the triumph of the nations which mastered the seas. Another war would likely lead to the same gigantic conflict between a country dominating the larger part of Eurasia and the Anglo-American sea powers. Even if the latter are called upon to assume the majority of the burden of naval tasks during such a conflict . . . they will welcome, as they did in 1939, a maritime contribution by allies such as the Netherlands and France. As well, a dispersed body such as the *Union française* cannot dispense for its internal security and the protection of its vital lines of communications with inadequate maritime forces. These two imperatives legitimize the need for a French navy.[31]

Those voices could not overcome Ramadier's commitment to the defense of the Rhine in the late 1940s as a result of strategic uncertainties and economic realities, but later developments led to a renewed appreciation for sea power in France. Korea and Indochina demonstrated the value of the aircraft carrier, cruiser, and destroyer in projecting fires ashore and providing logistical support to land forces in the littoral. Smaller units—minesweepers, fast patrol craft—proved essential to protecting one's freedom of movement at sea while interdicting that of the enemy and cutting off insurgents from their rear bases. Frigates and other escorts, which would soon be capable of operating helicopters in all weather, provided valuable flexibility in taking on the protection of carrier groups as well as that of transoceanic convoys. Whether fighting guerrillas in Asia or the Soviets in Europe, amphibious operations would offer a unique ability to turn the main front on land and conduct supporting operations on the littoral flanks.[32] More specific to the French context, a potent navy would also provide a valuable tool in peacetime, an argument that cut across the political divide. Whether Gaullists on the Right or Communists on the Left, voices proclaimed that any tool that allowed France to make its influence felt independently of the Anglo-Americans was a worthwhile investment.

The year 1952 also proved rich in technical and operational breakthrough, alleviating many of the strategic and doctrinal uncertainties that had undermined arguments put forward by navalists promoting the continued relevance of sea power in the nuclear age. By then virtually all elements that eventually shaped the Cold War at sea were coming into being, providing a clearer roadmap in defining future navies. Both the Royal Navy and the U.S. Navy adopted the angled-deck and the steam-powered catapult to finalize the shape of future carriers able to launch large jet aircraft capable of a variety of missions.[33] Trials using a painted outline took place on board HMS *Triumph* in February 1952, and USS *Antietam* emerged from an extensive refit in December with a deck angled to port. October witnessed the first flight of the jet-powered Douglas A-3 Skywarrior, capable of conventional and nuclear long-range bombing missions, with follow-on variants fitted for airborne refueling and electronic warfare tasks.[34] Two months later the lead Grumman S2F Tracker took to the sky, the first carrier aircraft designed specifically to conduct ASW search and attack missions.[35] The keel of USS *Nautilus*, the world's first nuclear-powered submarine, had already been laid down in June, and the former seaplane tender USS *Norton Sound* fired in November a Regulus turbojet rocket, the first shipboard launch of a guided land-attack missile.[36]

The immediacy of the Soviet threat at sea also remained genuine. On 15 May 1952 the Soviet Union commissioned the cruiser *Sverdlov*. She was the first large platform launched by that country since World War II, with thirteen more coming into service over the next three years as well as a range of smaller vessels, including seventy *Skorij*-class destroyers completed in 1949–53.[37] U.S. Secretary of the Navy Dan A. Kimball announced in a press conference in Paris that the Soviet Union could deploy more than three hundred submarines at the outset of a conflict, highlighting the very high risk posed to the Alliance's transatlantic lines of communications.[38] The announcement came on the heels of Exercise Mainbrace, the first large-scale exercise conducted under the joint command of SACEUR and Supreme Allied Commander Atlantic, established in Norfolk, Virginia, in January 1952. Unfolding in September off the coasts of Norway and Denmark with more than two hundred vessels involved, Mainbrace demonstrated the importance of the maritime dimension of NATO's overall strategy.[39] However, this exercise also illuminated ongoing difficulties in rejuvenating France's navy.

While the Marine nationale deployed twenty ships for the event, there were only seven destroyer escorts, the balance consisting of smaller coastal minesweepers and patrol craft. This contribution reflected the maritime tasks assigned to France within the Alliance but drastically limited the influence of French admirals in shaping events at sea in the NATO context. Nevertheless, developments in 1952 seemed to provide renewed impetus as Admiral Nomy set about securing political support for a more structured renewal of the fleet. Former *secrétaire d'État à la Marine* Joannès Dupraz—an important voice within the Mouvement républicain populaire (Popular Republican Movement), the Center-Right party that played an influential role in the formation of all government cabinets during the years of the Fourth Republic—set the tone in a June address to the National Assembly. Strikingly, he contrasted France's immediate strategy of alliance with the long-term need to create and maintain an independent French fleet built in France to uphold the country's sovereignty, preserve the sanctity of the Union française and promote French industries:

> One can affirm that the great European and Atlantic coalition to which we belong is rich enough in naval resources and that France must tackle other priorities. But this language imposes severe limits. We have our own enduring responsibilities which we cannot abandon without ceasing to be a great nation. We have witnessed the ability of French dockyards and civilian shipyards to develop and build new prototypes. Are we willing to risk this capability? Our bases [at home and overseas] constitute strategic assets, are we willing to lower the flag flying over them? *Can we envisage being almost exclusively dependent on foreign material in ten years hence* to maintain the means to reach across the French Union and our other territories overseas? Today is the time to act as there is very little time left to correct this situation.[40] [Emphasis added.]

From the Statut Naval de 1952 . . .

Ever since the war years, Rue Royale planners, as well as their army and air force colleagues, had been laboring under the strictures of defense funding provided in the form of *tranches annuelles*. These annual budgetary allocations varied from one fiscal year to the other, and their details were the object of extensive debates in Parliament. Competing commissions of elected officials—including but not limited to the ones concerned with national defense, foreign affairs, and finances—all had a say in reshaping the budget proposals submitted by Fourth Republic cabinets before updated versions made their way to the National Assembly for a vote.[41] More public debates preceded such votes and often led to additional amendments before the ministries finally obtained their respective allocation and specific instructions for the implementation of the defense budget, most often well past the beginning of the fiscal year.

In the case of the navy, such instructions could go into much detail such as the work to be executed from year to year in completion of the battleship *Jean Bart* and the cruiser *De Grasse* (amending priorities from main armament to antiair guns, propulsion systems to electronic sensors) or the on-again, off-again lay down of the ill-fated aircraft carrier PA-28. After 1949 this cycle of annual incertitude was compounded by introduction of direct American aid. Successive MDAP allocations—whether end items or financial subsidies—were certainly welcome in France but also came as annual tranches, which could vary in nature and size. This greatly complicated planning for timely decommissioning of obsolete units, figuring out recruitment and manning goals, as well as prioritizing national allocations to support new constructions, refits and modernizations, the acquisitions of suitable spare parts and ammunition of the right caliber, and so on. As a result of these challenges, French admirals longed to propose a long-term *statut naval* for adoption by the National Assembly.

A "naval statute" or "naval bill" would secure endorsement by the National Assembly of stable financing in support of a coherent fleet for the coming decades. Past efforts had not fared well during the years of the Third Republic. The last statute ever enacted came in 1912, but it was first suspended then abandoned altogether during the Great War.[42] Vice Admiral Henri Salaün, head of the navy from 1924 to 1928, was next in attempting to push through Parliament a rational plan based on the lessons of the conflict and the treaty limits agreed to at the Washington Conference in 1922. The ambitious Statut naval de 1924 never made it to the National Assembly, but the draft was circulated widely and endorsed by influential politicians who were already worrying about the future rearmament of Germany and the powerful Italian fleet in the Mediterranean. Navy minister Georges Leygues then ensured that the statute's shipbuilding goals were achieved through the following decade by shaping the annual budgetary tranches allocated to the Marine nationale along those lines.[43] This last precedent was of particular interest to Nomy in 1952, especially as another bone of contention arose between Paris and Washington, this time on the subject of offshore procurements (OSP).

OSP (funding by the United States of commercial production of military goods in Europe for use by the producing country or a third party within the Alliance) were one of three conduits of American aid under both the Mutual Defense Assistance Act and the Mutual Security Act. The other two—the delivery of end-items and the investments of U.S. funds to develop and modernize Allied defense industries as AMP—had thus far been privileged by the Americans, as OSP could prove controversial at home. Many in Congress were particularly concerned whenever Washington contracted foreign firms to produce military goods in direct competition with U.S. companies, regardless of the political objective of building up Allied defense industries for the purpose of common security. Despite such sensitivities, French governments militated throughout 1951 for disbursement of a greater share of American aid through OSP contracts, even at the cost of reducing end-item deliveries.

This pressure led to a bilateral agreement concluded on the margins of the Lisbon Conference in February 1952, whereby Secretary of State Dean Acheson committed the United States to negotiate contracts with French firms to the tune of $200 million in 1952.[44] On 6 May, Defense Minister René Pleven made a new demand for an additional $616 million to be spent on OSP during the following three years, a commitment the Americans proved reluctant to take on.[45] Bitter negotiations ensued—the rift becoming public amid a presidential election year in the United States—and resolution could not be achieved until the newly installed president, Dwight D. Eisenhower, agreed to a compromise in April 1953 for $230 million in OSP contracts for the next two years.[46] Beyond the dollar figures, the Franco-American dispute over OSP resulted from the fact that Washington wanted to maintain a veto over the type of production subsidized through this conduit while Paris intended to use these contracts as the government saw fit to develop and shape the national defense industry. Americans referred to Alliance needs and priorities as the main criteria, but French leaders would not content themselves with the production of lower-end items such as uniforms, small-caliber ammunition, and general-purpose wheeled trucks even if those were badly needed across NATO.

Sophisticated production was also in high demand, and Paris sought to leverage this opportunity to reinvigorate industries seeking to make inroads in the challenging (and highly profitable) fields of aeronautics, electronics, and heavy vehicles such as tanks and tracked armored personnel carriers. The inclusion of 180 Sea Venom fighter aircraft in the Pleven submission of May 1952 highlighted these differences. The Americans had denied earlier requests from the Marine nationale to obtain U.S.-built jets as end items or the subsidization of research and development of a French prototype through AMP.[47] As an alternative, French negotiators then insisted on the merits of building the British aircraft under license in France as three previous domestic projects had already failed to produce a reliable carrier fighter jet. The United States eventually relented, agreeing to fund this transfer of technology and residual expertise to France.

In this context of tense Franco-U.S. relations came another encouraging note for the Rue Royale planners in the form of a letter from *maréchal* Alphonse Juin to the secretary of state for the navy. Then employed as inspector general for the French armed forces, the army's most senior officer made an impassioned plea on behalf of the navy as an essential contributor to the sovereignty of France: "As much as satisfying the engagements taken within the context of the Atlantic Alliance, our naval program must allow us to discharge, on behalf of the Union française, the duties required to uphold our position and independence in the world: maintaining order in our overseas territories, assist the Associated States, protect our lines of communications. . . . It is appropriate that the next annual tranches reach the goal of 30,000 tons as deemed indispensable by the Naval General Staff to achieve the goals assigned."[48]

Endorsement from one of the most influential French army voices—even as the services were each vying for resources—proved timely. It addressed the draft naval statute Nomy submitted to his colleagues of the CSM that same day for their review before furtherance to Navy Minister Jacques Gavini. An implied reference to the Statut naval de 1924 seemed apparent in the intent outlined by Nomy in a cover note: "The time has come . . . to determine the level of forces we must achieve in the coming years in terms of fleet and naval aviation. *Even if the results of this work may not be submitted for immediate approval in Parliament*, it is necessary that the navy establishes the fundamental directive to guide the efforts we must undertake to rejuvenate the fleet"[49] [Emphasis added].

Nomy did not propose a dramatic departure from earlier plans in terms of platforms and tonnage. He did, however, define annual building plans that delineated eight annual tranches starting in 1953 for completion of the overall plan by 1960 at a vastly accelerated pace in terms of construction in French yards. Each tranche would deliver 34,500 tons (30,000 of those dedicated to combat units) per year. It admitted that each tranche would be adjusted to reflect the level of mutual assistance provided by the United States, but it underlined that French shipyards needed to provide the balance most urgently. As importantly, it proposed the construction of an aircraft carrier in France to commence in 1954. The CSM debated Nomy's proposal over two days of extensive discussions, and minister Gavini approved the amended version on 19 July.[50] It proposed a fleet of 470,000 tons and 500 aircraft by 1960, divided as follows (not including auxiliaries and utility vessels):

- 2 battleships, 5 aircraft carriers, and 6 antiair (AA) cruisers
- 32 fleet destroyers and 73 destroyer escorts
- 80 patrol craft, 165 mine warfare vessels, and 16–20 submarines
- Various amphibious and riverine craft (20,000 tons)
- 389 combat planes, 84 patrol aircraft, and 24 transports

Fundamentally, this breakdown reflected the ambition to assemble, maintain, and supply those air, surface, and submarine elements necessary to generate (a) autonomous task forces to discharge the dual roles of long-range strike and ASW hunter-killer missions—with each task force centered on an aircraft carrier, a battleship or a cruiser dedicated to antiair defense, as well as a retinue of smaller escorts and support vessels; (b) fast and slow escorts to operate as national flotillas or within larger Alliance groups in support of local and transoceanic convoys; and (c) amphibious and coastal defense forces for operations in the littoral and riverine environments. In other words, the proposed Statut naval de 1952 outlined the detailed vision of a balanced and modern blue-water fleet capable of operating effectively in the Cold War era to discharge national responsibilities as well as the Alliance tasks promulgated in Lisbon. It remained to be seen whether this momentous commitment could be turned into reality.

. . . to the Plan Bleu de 1955

Existing records do not disclose whether Admiral Nomy and Secrétaire d'État Gavini had a plan to present the Statut naval de 1952 for consideration by the cabinet and an eventual vote in the assembly, neither of which took place in the long run. Nor do they show how the draft document was circulated, but the records of parliamentary commissions, debates in the Assemblée nationale, and newspaper coverage indicate that the highlights, if not the details, became widely known within months.[51] Either way, Gavini stated in January 1953, in a response to a query from a member of the opposition, that he would not seek the enactment of a long-term shipbuilding plan at that juncture given the ongoing cycle of negotiations with the Americans over military aid. But he did confirm that the guiding principles of the 1952 statute would shape successive allocations:

> Defining the annual naval tranches of the defense budget is not done arbitrarily as the Conseil supérieur de la Marine has already defined the composition of our future fleet, the one we must strive to achieve. However, it is not possible to plan in advance for a multi-year program as, complimentary to such a plan, there is one element that we cannot control, which is what can be expected from the Americans on an annual basis. Only once this becomes known can we plan each tranche, while taking into account the most pressing needs of the nation. . . . Nevertheless, let me assure you that the tonnage and composition of the target fleet are known and show us the objectives to achieve.[52]

He proffered this statement during a parliamentary debate on the defense budget for 1953, a year that proved auspicious for the Marine nationale. Two key decisions had already been taken. First, regarding cruisers, *De Grasse* would be completed for the antiaircraft role, fitted with no less than sixteen 127-mm guns and twenty 57-mm guns mounted in twin turrets, putting an end to the recurring debate over the ship's main armament. A technical study was also nearing completion to serve as the basis for building a true postwar AA cruiser, the future *Colbert*.[53] Second, within days of approving the 1952 naval statute, Secretary of State Gavini ordered the launch of another study to define a modern aircraft carrier, to be constructed in France and capable of launching jet aircraft in support of surface strike and ASW tasks.[54] As for 1953, the defense budget approved in the National Assembly largely reflected the statute's proposed first tranche, with funds allocated for one cruiser (the *Colbert*), five T-47 destroyers, two E-50 escorts, four minesweepers, and two *Narval*-class submarines. Funds previously voted for the (a) completion of battleship *Jean Bart* and cruiser *De Grasse*; (b) completion of twelve T-47s, four E-50s, seventeen minesweepers, and the first four *Narval*-class submarines; and (c) conversion of the former Italian light cruisers *Châteaurenault* and *Guichen* to *escorteurs d'escadre* (squadron escorts) were maintained.[55]

Admittedly, the National Assembly voted an allocation in 1953 short of that proposed in the 1952 statute, for 27,320 tons rather than the recommended 30,000 tons in combat units. But increased American aid more than made up the shortfall that year; naval allocations doubled in value from 19 billion FF in 1952 to 40 billion FF in 1953.[56] OSP contracts placed with French firms in 1952–53 would result in the delivery of an additional seven E-52A escorts (improved versions of the E-50), three coastal patrol craft, nine minesweepers, and six large net tenders (at 700 tons each) by the end of 1955.[57] End-item deliveries for that tranche included (at no cost to France) another thirteen minesweepers; fifty-four Corsair fighter-bombers and ten Helldivers; sixteen Avengers, twenty-six Neptunes, and six PV-2 Harpoon for ASW tasks; ten single-engine SNJ-4 aircraft for training; twenty larger SNB-5 transports; and four HUP-2 tandem helicopters (recognizable for their banana shape).[58] By far, however, the biggest announcement that year was the United States agreeing to lend a second aircraft carrier to France.

French sailors had barely hoisted the tricolor on board *La Fayette* in June 1951 when Rue Royale authorities expressed their wish for another USN carrier but to no avail during the remainder of the Truman presidency. Seeking to create an opening with President-elect Eisenhower, Admiral Nomy formally reiterated this request in a letter addressed to the head of MAAG France on 29 December 1952.[59] Follow-on negotiations led to an agreement in the summer of 1953, in great part as a result of the Eisenhower administration's early commitment to supporting France in repulsing the Vietminh in Indochina while reluctantly accepting a draw in Korea.[60] Although the loan of the carrier would take place under the MDAP framework as an end item for the purpose of mutual defense within the Atlantic Alliance, Washington authorized the vessel's deployment to the Far East in an agreement signed on 2 September 1953, which would come to an end either no later than six months after the end of the hostilities in Indochina or on 5 August 1958.

France took possession of the former USS *Belleau Wood* (a sister ship of *Langley / La Fayette*) on 3 September in San Francisco, promptly renaming her *Bois Belleau*. The French crew then undertook three months of training in American waters before sailing for the *métropole* and arriving in Toulon—after a short stop in Bizerte to disembark an MDAP delivery of sixteen TBM Avengers—on 23 December.[61] Placed on active service that same day, *Bois Belleau* soon proved an important force multiplier for the Marine nationale. Following extensive work-up training with her assigned aircrews in the first months of 1954, she set sail for Indochina in April, although she arrived too late to make a difference in the defense of Dien Bien Phu. Nevertheless, the addition of a third aircraft carrier finally allowed Rue Royale planners to rotate these vessels for deployments overseas on a nearly continuous basis from then on. Although the Geneva Accords of 20 July 1954 signified the end of the French presence in the Tonkin, *Bois Belleau* and *La Fayette* continued to operate alternatively in the region until the summer of 1956, when the last of France's military personnel evacuated South Vietnam.[62]

Paradoxically, the Marine nationale continued to prosper while Fourth Republic leaders confronted crisis after crisis in 1954, from the loss of Indochina to the beginning of a new insurgency in Algeria. The naval budget tranches for that year and again in 1955 closely adhered to those proposed in the 1952 statute in terms of tonnage if not composition. The 1954 budget provided for 27,700 tons (one aircraft carrier, three sloops for Union service, four submarines) and that of 1955 for 29,700 tons (another aircraft carrier, one sloop for Union service, three escorts, and three submarines). The PA-54 aircraft carrier included in each of those tranches reflected Nomy's ambitious vision endorsed by his CSM colleagues in 1953: "This is neither an escort carrier, nor an ASW hunter-killer group carrier. It is, rather, a light fleet carrier capable of providing a naval force operating within a larger allied fleet with fighter air defense as well as contributing strike support to an amphibious force ashore and deploying ASW assets when offshore."[63]

The proposed platform included most of the innovations recently developed by the American and British navies. PA-54 proposed a potent vessel of 24,000 tons (later reduced to 22,000 tons), capable of a sustained maximum speed of thirty-two knots on two shafts, fitted with an armored angled flight deck with two steam catapults and two elevators. These provided access to a hangar accommodating up to forty aircraft that could weigh as much as fifteen tons each. Eight batteries of twin 57-mm AA guns (later changed to eight single 100-mm guns) provided self-defense. The first PA-54, the *Clémenceau*, was included in the defense budget adopted on 16 March 1954.[64] Six months later, as the CSM debated the rational for proposing a second one instead of additional destroyers and escorts for the 1955 tranche, Admiral Nomy pressed urgently for another "flat top":

> Appreciating that escort forces are necessary, my preference remains for a second aircraft carrier. . . . It is urgent to develop our carrier fleet as we may soon have to return *Bois Belleau* to the United States and we must absolutely maintain two aircraft carriers available for Union française tasks. I also believe that circumstances are more suitable now that at any other time to convince Parliament. The Aéronavale has the wind in its sails thanks to its performance in Indochina. Time may be pressing. If budget cuts loom ahead and if the naval tranche is reduced to, say, 20,000 tons, then we could no longer propose an aircraft carrier over that tonnage. Is this not the last year that we can expect its inclusion in the defense budget?[65]

Nomy won the council over to his argument and Secretary of State for the Navy Henri Caillavet persuaded his colleagues in the Pierre Mendès France government to include a second PA-54 (the future *Foch*) in the 1955 budget. These achievements were significant for Nomy, but he was also justified in expressing concerns about the future. Hostilities had ended in Indochina, and the insurgency in Algeria had yet to prove as consuming in terms of military resources, perhaps prompting government to seek economies by lowering upcoming defense budgets. NATO authorities had already forfeited the Lisbon force goals as unachievable while the Eisenhower administration adopted the New Look policy based on the doctrine of nuclear massive retaliation, introducing uncertainty in the frenetic buildup of conventional forces. And Nomy's staff also realized that French naval dockyards and private shipyards could not even keep up with the generous investments already approved by the National Assembly, as reflected in the repeated delays in the delivery of vessels, submarines, and aircraft during these years.

Battleship *Jean Bart* and cruiser *De Grasse* finally entered service on 1 May 1955 and 3 September 1956, respectively, but only half of the twelve authorized T-47 destroyers joined the fleet by late 1956, and the five newly ordered T-53s would not arrive until 1958.[66] While the four E-50 escorts of the *Le Corse*–class entered service in 1954–55, the bulk of the fourteen *Le Normand* E-52s would not sail before 1958, with the last one delivered in 1960.[67] World War II submarines *Andromède* and *Artémis* only entered service in 1953 and 1954, admittedly followed by the six *Narval*s and four *Aréthuse*s in 1957–60, but the first of the *Daphné*s did not become operational until 1964.[68] Meanwhile, the World War II stocks of American and British ships, submarines, and aircraft delivered during the hostilities and as end items afterward were unlikely to remain deployable for operations beyond the end of the decade. And the relentless decommissioning of obsolete units continued unabated.

A representative of the National Defense Commission reported to the Assemblée nationale in March 1954 that 11,200 tons of combat vessels would be struck that year, 85,000 tons in 1955–58, and another 55,000 tons by 1960, arresting figures when the Marine nationale hoped to maintain a fleet of 360,000 tons in 1960.[69] Also ominous was the possibility that the Americans could demand the return of the leased *La Fayette* and *Bois Belleau* without much notice; the continued challenge of maintaining sufficient quantities of spares and ammunition for the ships, submarines, and aircraft of foreign origin; and the technical and training challenges that continued to plague the heterogeneous French fleet. By March 1955 Admiral Nomy promulgated a new directive that addressed these developments as well as the most recent technical achievements at sea.

The document, eventually known as the Plan bleu de 1955, did not replace the proposed 1952 naval statute but updated the composition of the future fleet; amended the expected timelines in terms of ships, submarines, and aircraft production; and assumed the end of American direct assistance within the course of the next year.[70] Nomy envisioned reaching the objective of a new fleet of 360,000 tons in 1963 (i.e., all vessels launched or completed after World War II) and assumed continued allocation of 30,000-ton annual tranches at least until 1961. The longer-term objective would be a Marine nationale composed of 450,000 tons in combat units, 20,000 tons in amphibious forces, and 70,000 tons in auxiliaries, for a total of 540,000 tons of postwar French production by 1970. It proposed a battle fleet (a *corps de bataille*) centered on three aircraft carriers (*Clémenceau*, *Foch*, and a third one yet to be authorized by the National Assembly), supported initially by the battleships *Richelieu* and *Jean Bart*, both to be replaced in the long run by additional AA cruisers. In addition to *De Grasse* and *Colbert*, these new cruisers (for a total of four) would provide not only air defense but also an offensive punch by taking on the role of "missile carriers."

Another cruiser would be launched as a "helicopter carrier" with the peacetime role of training cadets of the École navale in replacement of the aging *Jeanne d'Arc*, launched in 1930. The document also ordered new studies to explore the use of nuclear propulsion for surface vessels and submarines, improved defenses against the effects of atomic weapons at sea, and antiair and antisurface missile know-how as well as studies for the improvement of living quarters onboard ships for sailors and officers and the simultaneous reduction in crew size through automation technologies. Other ships would be required for the specific roles of replenishment at sea, afloat support to submarines, and provision of fleet repair services under way. Finally, the plan maintained its predecessor's vision for an Aéronavale of twenty combat squadrons of embarked fighters and strike aircraft as well as carrier- and land-based ASW aircraft, all French constructions by 1963.

Nomy expected that by then virtually all of World War II ships, submarines, and aircraft built in France and those acquired through the Allies or as enemy war reparations would be decommissioned or, at most, serve as training platforms. The Plan bleu de 1955 provided the outline of an operational fleet composed entirely of modern, postwar French constructions designed specifically to discharge national and Alliance missions within the framework of the Cold War divide and a close-knit Union française. In putting such a vision forward, based on an aggressive program of domestic shipbuilding and modern aircraft production, Nomy sought to exploit a momentary window of opportunity he knew would not necessarily last, given France's long history of haphazard interest in its navy. What he could not forecast at the time were the coming upheavals and their potential impact on the French navy. From the escalating insurgency in Algeria to the humiliation at Suez and continued political unrest in the *métropole*, events at home and abroad eventually led to the downfall of the Fourth Republic itself and the return to power of Charles de Gaulle.

These developments would test Nomy's ability to achieve the objectives laid out in the Plan bleu along the timeline envisioned therein. Nevertheless, French admirals and their successive Fourth Republic ministers could reflect with pride on their success in laying out the foundations of a credible and modern blue-water fleet in the midst of complex geopolitical factors abroad and unmitigated popular angst at home at the dawn of the Cold War. By 1958 the fleet remained a heterogeneous assembly of vessels and aircraft of varied origins but a vibrant shipbuilding industry—as well as a wider defense sector engaged in the most advanced field of sensors, guns, missilery, and aviation—clearly showed France's capacity to regain her place as a sea power of influence within the Atlantic Alliance and beyond. Operationally, lessons learned from World War II, Indochina, and Suez as well as continued involvement in the Algerian fight and NATO training provided an eclectic mix of experience. French officers, sailors, and naval aviators determined to implement them as quickly as they could be interpreted and updated to reflect the range of new technologies revolutionizing the conduct of war at sea.[71]

And one particular technology loomed large in the navy's future, as is discussed in the next chapter. Charles de Gaulle returned to power in the wake of the rebellious weeks of May 1958 and set off once again to restore the grandeur of France, but the French admiralty had already proposed exploring the last dimension of modern sea power that remained beyond the grasp of the Marine nationale. Although Nomy only referred to nuclear power as a potential means of propulsion for ships and submarines in the Plan bleu, a follow-on staff study in October 1955 pressed urgently for development and deployment at sea of French nuclear weapons, laying the stakes succinctly for the coming years: "A navy that would renounce the atomic bomb would be out of the game, even for secondary missions in war and would have no value as an ally. It would be the same as those constabulary forces maintained by Portugal or Thailand. *The future of the navy is thus tightly bound with the policy government wishes to adopt with regards to nuclear weapons*"[72] [Emphasis in the original].

CHAPTER 8

GOING NUCLEAR

Bases and Submarines

A loud Klaxon rang stridently on board the submarine *Le Redoutable* as crewmembers rushed to their diving stations on Friday, 28 January 1972. Although the end of the workweek ashore, that day marked the beginning of a new era for France and her navy. Heading out into the frigid waters of the winter Atlantic and leaving the rugged Brittany coast in her wake, the largest submersible ever built in France was setting off on her first operational patrol. The *sous-marin nucléaire lanceur d'engins* (subsurface ballistic nuclear submarine, SSBN) carried sixteen M1 MSBS (*mer-sol balistique stratégique*, or submarine-launched ballistic missile, SLBM). Each could deliver a single nuclear warhead of 450 kilotons out to 2,500 kilometers.[1] As *Le Redoutable* ("fearsome" or "dreaded") set course for the Norwegian Sea from where her missiles could reach the Soviet heartland, the Marine nationale joined a very select club of navies, the only ones that at that time maintained part of their nation's nuclear inventory hidden in the depths of the sea: those of the United States, the Soviet Union, and the United Kingdom.[2] Through silence and mobility, SSBNs provided the nearly invulnerable component of a credible and effective triad of deterrence, which included long-range bomber aircraft and land-based ballistic missiles.

The lead vessel of her class, *Le Redoutable*, could only maintain a periodic watch at sea by herself, but five others joined her in subsequent years: *Le Terrible*, launched in December 1969 and commissioned in January 1973, as well as *Le Foudroyant*, *L'Indomptable*, *Le Tonnant*, and *L'Inflexible*, which entered service in 1974, 1976, 1977, and 1985, respectively. This aggregate eventually allowed the Marine nationale to maintain up to three SSBNs deployed in different patrol areas simultaneously in order to provide even more redundancy and credibility to the country's nuclear deterrent. Commissioned in 1970, the Île Longue naval complex offered a suitable home port for the entire class, a role that continues today in support of the four *Le Triomphant* SSBNs, which succeeded the *Redoutable*s starting in the late 1990s.[3] An elongated and narrow peninsula sited across the roadstead from France's main Atlantic base, Île Longue provides at once a remote location (in case of a nuclear accident) and access to the nearby Brest industrial complex, within reach of an airfield and a large road network (to transport missile components), with easy-to-secure sea and land approaches. It took five years to build the large infrastructure needed to support operational SSBNs and conduct periodic maintenance on those in-between patrols as well as look after their nuclear arsenal. The latter necessitated elaborate facilities to assemble the missile stages built in Bordeaux (650 kilometers to the south, inland from the Bay of Biscay) and mounting their warhead (assembled in Valduc, near Dijon) before loading them on board the submarines berthed in fully enclosed and hardened docks.

By the time *Le Redoutable* set off on her first operational patrol, another element required for an effective sea-based nuclear deterrent was also in place. In addition to construction of the submarine, the missiles, and their base, the Marine nationale joined the national command-and-control infrastructure already set up to facilitate the immediate execution of presidential orders for a nuclear launch. The first air force squadron of Dassault Mirage IV jet aircraft had assumed the nuclear-ready status in October 1964, operating out of Base aérienne 118 in Mont-de-Marsan in southwest France.[4] The 1er Groupement de missiles stratégiques (1st Strategic Missile Group) was established in 1968 to operate the S2 intermediate-range ballistic missiles deployed in underground silos on the Plateau d'Albion, north of Marseille, which became operational in August 1971.[5] The president of the French republic, as head of state and commander in chief of the armed forces, exercised the nuclear executive authority for all elements through the Poste de commandement (PC, command post) Jupiter located in the official residence at the Palais de l'Élysée.[6] In the case of the sea-based component of the nuclear triad, presidential orders would be relayed via the very low frequency transmitter, capable of reaching submerged submarines from its location near the small community of Rosnay (halfway between Paris and La Rochelle).[7]

Le Redoutable's first operational deployment began on a frustrating note when an issue with the satellite navigation system Transit forced her to put into Brest for repairs within hours of leaving Île Longue. The problem was resolved overnight, and the submarine resumed her transit to the Norwegian Sea for a fifty-five-day patrol. Typical patrols would eventually be lengthened to seventy days, including deployments to the Eastern Mediterranean, within reach of targets in southern Russia and the Middle East.[8] The blue crew was on board as the Marine nationale adopted the USN model of alternate crews in order to maximize the time ballistic submarines spent at sea. Not that this was the submarine's first deployment. Laid in 1964, launched in March 1967, and manned for trials in April 1968, *Le Redoutable* finally left Cherbourg in September 1970 for eventual commissioning in Île Longue. She conducted two submerged missile firings in May and June 1971 (one for each crew), followed by a "trial deployment" to the Norwegian Sea in July with four inert missiles embarked. The blue crew conducted this first trip that allowed for testing key equipment on board as well as practice communications and launch procedures with PC Jupiter through the Rosnay transmission center. The red crew conducted a similar cruise in the fall and the submarine was declared ready for operations on 1 December 1971.[9]

The *Redoutable* class proved a remarkable technical achievement executed in great haste following Charles de Gaulle's momentous press conference of 14 January 1963, when he announced the decision to complement the nation's nuclear deterrent with ballistic missile–carrying submarines built and controlled by France alone. Standing up the Force océanique stratégique (FOST, or Oceanic Strategic Force) came at an enormous price, however. Even enabled by some technical support from the Allies in the early days, growing tensions between the French and the Anglo-Americans through the 1960s meant that France bore the entire costs and resource commitments necessitated for further research, development, and construction of the submarines and their missiles. De Gaulle's renewed interest for the Marine nationale presented French admirals with a new paradox. FOST meant huge investments in the navy, but dedicating so many resources to ballistic submarines alone gravely affected execution of the Plan bleu de 1955, Nomy's vision of an expeditionary fleet of aircraft carrier–centric *groupes d'intervention naval* and an eclectic mix of smaller conventional surface combatants and attack submarines.[10] It remained to be seen how this legacy plan and the fleet it created could be conciliated with de Gaulle's drive for SSBNs.

Another dimension of the atomic era impacted allocation of resources within the French navy. Bases needed to go underground in order to survive a nuclear exchange. While new technologies extended the autonomy of naval forces, the first decade of the Cold War also showed that blue-water fleets still required a worldwide network of support infrastructures to conduct independent operations and exercise an enduring influence in any given region. France could not have maintained an effective naval posture off the coast of Indochina for nearly a decade of combat operations without access to British drydocks in Hong Kong and Singapore, as well as commercial shipyards in Japan, to back up smaller repair facilities in Saigon.[11] But bases were more complex than in the era of coal because of the requirement to harden installations against the effects of atomic blasts, whether direct strikes, remote electromagnetic pulses, or long-lasting nuclear fallout. In this context, active defense means (fighter aircraft, ship- and ground-based missiles, and gunnery) were limited in their ability to intercept the vectors carrying nuclear bombs, necessitating reliance on a limited number of passive measures to mitigate the inherent exposure of fixed bases.

The most effective measure was also the most expensive—namely, burying installations in hardened bunkers capable of sustaining operations and accommodating personnel in the wake of a nuclear attack.[12] However, Rue Royale staff gave priority in the postwar years to reconstituting a modern fleet over rebuilding bases in the *métropole* and overseas. Thus, any examination of the French navy's turn to the nuclear in the closing years of the Fourth Republic and the turbulent transition to the Fifth Republic must include a long-delayed look at the base question to understand fully the elements that affected the rejuvenation of an autonomous fleet.

The coming end of allied support to the rearmament of France further aggravated resource pressures. Despite a momentary pause in the immediate postwar years, assistance from Great Britain and the United States had remained essential to the recovery and expansion of French military strength since the agreements between de Gaulle and Churchill in August 1940 and between Giraud and Roosevelt in February 1943. American aid, especially, had proven indispensable in rebuilding the French navy and the resurgence of a viable shipbuilding industry in France after the war. The militarization of economic assistance after 1950 allowed French admirals to leverage the provision of foreign end items and subsidies to meet short-term commitments while allocating national resources to building those ships, submarines, and aircraft more closely aligned with the national interest at sea and the defense of the Union française. But this support came at a cost, reflecting alliance priorities and imposing a tremendous supply and maintenance burden to look after the eclectic mix of prewar and wartime British, U.S., German, Italian, and French assets that still made up the bulk of the fleet in the mid-1950s. And much uncertainty reigned as the nation witnessed the fall of one republic and the rise of another under Charles de Gaulle.

Dawn of a New Republic, End of Allied Assistance

The Fourth Republic collapsed in May 1958, the result of a combination of sudden events and drawn-out crises marked by instability in Parliament, inflation and budget shortages, social unrest at home, military quagmires in Indochina and Algeria, and international humiliation at Suez.[13] With the *pieds noirs* and the Armée d'Afrique in a state of near rebellion in Algeria, Charles de Gaulle announced that he was ready to "assume the mantle of the republic," and the Assemblée nationale proclaimed his government on 1 June. Two days later Parliament voted a special law calling for a revision of the constitution. A draft document—largely reflecting de Gaulle's original vision of a strong executive presidency and reinstituting an elected senate to moderate the National Assembly—was endorsed with 82 percent support through a referendum on 28 September 1958 and enacted on 4 October. The first parliamentary elections took place in two tours on 23 and 30 November, leading to the formation of a government under Michel Debré, who officially replaced de Gaulle as *premier ministre* on 8 January 1959. That same day le Général assumed the presidency of the Fifth Republic for a mandate of seven years.

Once in power, de Gaulle's relationship with a flag officer corps largely made up of Darlan followers, who had waited for the North African landings before rallying to the allied camp, presented much potential for tension. However, the French navy had remained loyal to the government during the mutinous weeks of May 1958, maintaining at most a benevolent neutralism. Few naval officers joined the unruly *comités de salut publique* (public safety committees) that formed in Algeria and Corsica in defiance of the central government, and the fleet did not have a role in the impending paratroopers' descent on Paris planned in army and air force circles.[14] De Gaulle was also aware that few *pieds noirs* joined the navy, so concerns with the loyalty of senior officers with Algerian roots or those who had served long tours with the Armée d'Afrique were not as potent.[15] And within weeks le Général was presented with striking examples of the navy's ability to support his agenda of autonomy within the Atlantic Alliance.

As the U.S. Sixth Fleet landed Marines in Beirut to resolve the Lebanon crisis of the summer of 1958, de Gaulle learned that a French task group was already in theater, on a routine deployment to the Eastern Mediterranean. Although he did not openly disagree with the American intervention in France's former League of Nations mandate, the newly installed prime minister instructed that the force be ready to protect France's interests in the region independently of the Anglo-Saxons—Great Britain having also dispatched forces to buttress King Hussein in Jordan.[16] The American intervention was short, as the last of the U.S. troops left Beirut on 28 October, and the French force did not get involved. Nevertheless, le Général could not have failed to notice how leveraging sea power allowed the United States to resolve quickly this first test of the "Eisenhower Doctrine."[17] As importantly from the Gaullist perspective, the ships would have provided Paris with the means to make France's voice heard had he wished to do so at the very moment when the Republic was at its most impotent in the wake of the quasi-military coup of the previous weeks.

Also foreshadowing de Gaulle's interest in instruments of sea power was the correspondence he addressed to Eisenhower that same summer. On 11 August 1958 he warmly congratulated the American president for successful completion of the submerged transit of USS *Nautilus* from the Pacific to the

Atlantic, under the Arctic ice cap.[18] The world's first nuclear-powered submarine was the first vessel ever to reach the geographic North Pole. Launched as a top-secret mission but widely publicized as soon as *Nautilus* emerged from beneath the ice, the deployment was somewhat of a propaganda stunt. Washington sought to lessen the sting felt in the United States when the Soviet Union unexpectedly took the lead in the space and missile race in October 1957 by launching Sputnik, the first artificial satellite to orbit the Earth.[19] Nevertheless, *Nautilus'* feat demonstrated the capability of a nuclear submarine to roam undetected for extended periods in all oceans of the world, with the potential to bring armed might—and, soon, nuclear armed might—right up to an opponent's shores. Again, de Gaulle would not have failed to notice that any nation capable of deploying such capability would acquire powerful leverage on the international scene, whether in time of peace or war.

Of more immediate concern, however, was the termination of aid from the United States. It did not result from a single decision such as had occurred at the end of World War II, when President Truman abruptly canceled Lend-Lease. Instead, transfers petered out over the last few years of the 1950s. Stocks of wartime equipment still worthy of consideration for employment in Europe in the 1960s had been exhausted and modern weapon systems once offered at no cost became available only through cost-sharing arrangements or purchase at full price. Tensions over strategy, command relationships, basing rights, and integration of West German forces tested NATO after the mid-1950s. Relations between Washington and Paris worsened as a result of Suez and through the course of fighting in Algeria. While the Eisenhower administration condoned the French effort in Indochina, it refused to support France's approach in North Africa.[20] The American president and his advisers were convinced that the Vietminh were puppets of Moscow and Beijing in 1953–54 but they grew skeptical of the Communist credentials of the Algerian rebels. If anything, they believed that the conduct of the French military in Algeria badly undermined American efforts to counter the growing Soviet influence among the numerous countries then gaining their independence across the developing world.

Such opposing views did not make for positive exchanges in terms of American support to French rearmament after 1954. Washington argued for Paris to reinforce its conventional forces in West Germany and decried the employment of U.S. matériel to wage a colonial fight in North Africa. These bilateral tensions also took place in a context where the Eisenhower administration reassessed the value of direct assistance for the rearmament of its European allies in the late-1950s as their economies grew ever more vibrant. The Mutual Security Agency set up under the 1951 Mutual Security Act became the Foreign Operations Administration in 1953 while Congress continued passing appropriations that favored military aid over economic assistance. Nevertheless, Eisenhower instructed in June 1955 that the authority to execute each aspect be split again by abolishing the Foreign Operations Administration and establishing the International Cooperation Administration under the secretary of state while the Department of Defense resumed its role in leading the provision of military assistance.[21] Economic aid regained importance, but Washington targeted allies and friendly regimes beyond Europe for the remainder of Eisenhower's second mandate, a trend that continued with the arrival of John F. Kennedy at the White House. A provision of the Foreign Assistance Act enacted in September 1961 disbanded the International Cooperation Administration and stood up, in its stead, an independent authority with an expanded mandate of assistance overseas, the United States Agency for International Development, which continues its effort today.[22]

This renewed focus on economic assistance and foreign aid occurred just as relations between Washington and Paris turned increasingly tense. This context led to reductions of large-scale transfers of military equipment as end items and declining direct subsidies to the French armed forces and state-owned and private firms involved in the defense sector. Gradual transition to more tailored bilateral offers of assistance in specific domains followed. This new form of collaboration meant fewer dollars but remained appreciated by the European recipients. Insights into previous scientific research, technical advice, and the transfer of complex electronic systems as well as rare metals and refined material (such as plutonium) would provide an ability to "kick start" national efforts in the demanding fields of advanced sensors and weapons, jet propulsion and missilery, and—of vital importance—atomic research. Meanwhile, restoring the navy's bases in the immediate postwar years continued to bear heavily on the minds of French admirals well into the Cold War.

Bases and Shore Infrastructure

All Western fleets went through retrenchment after 1945 and then rapid expansion once the Cold War set in. The experience of the Marine nationale, however, was unique given the formidable obstacles ashore that compounded the challenges at sea. Wartime had ruined the network of bases and shore infrastructures established at home and across the empire through the previous century.[23] German sabotage and allied bombing proved particularly devastating during the Liberation. Key facilities—piers and jetties, floating and graving docks, hangars and machine shops, fuel and ammunition depots—in metropolitan bases such as Toulon, Brest, and Cherbourg were destroyed. The approaches and roadstead of larger civilian ports and naval bases were encumbered by all sorts of wrecked vessels, either destroyed by allied mining and aerial bombing or sunk by the withdrawing Germans in shallow and narrow transit points to prevent harbor traffic. Scuttling alongside by French crews had left large ships blocking access to many of the most important jetties.[24] Ironically, the most modern naval installations in France were those built by the German occupier to base U-boats on the Atlantic coast, but Rue Royale authorities could ill afford to maintain such a large number of facilities dispersed on the periphery of the country.

Nevertheless, the challenge did not dissuade French admirals from entertaining ambitious goals in the heady days of victory. Just as Lemonnier outlined a grand plan in the spring of 1945 to reconstitute a fleet and an *aéronavale* of the first rank, his staff championed a parallel effort to rejuvenate a worldwide network of naval bases and airfields to support the navy's presence across the breath of the colonial empire.[25] Proposed while the Provisional Government was still in power, the vision was certainly Gaullian in its ambition. It presumed an orderly return of territories that had slipped out of French control during the war (Lebanon and Indochina) as well as a long-term presence in dependencies where insurrections would soon erupt (Madagascar, North Africa). It acknowledged lessons of World War II and the dawn of the atomic age by putting forward Mers el-Kébir and Bizerte as France's main operational bases in the Mediterranean. Both locations were sited on rocky soil next to large mountains that offered much potential for the construction of vast subterranean facilities, providing France the ability to continue fighting if the Cold War went nuclear and the Soviets overwhelmed the *métropole*, as the Germans had done just five years earlier.[26] While Toulon would lose its primacy in the Mediterranean under this vision, Brest retained its central role as the main arsenal on the Atlantic coast, including the potential for the surrounding area to accommodate an underground complex of communications facilities and machine shops as well as fuel and ammunition storage.

Vice Admiral Thierry d'Argenlieu turned these ambitions into a draft policy on bases submitted for discussion at the pivotal session of the Superior Council of the Navy held on 11 July 1945.[27] However, the plan foundered upon the harsh economic realities then facing the Provisional Government. One naval estimate stated that the rejuvenation of bases alone would necessitate an investment of 100 billion FF, and a later report placed that figure at 220 billion but by July 1947 only 14 billion had been spent for work on naval bases.[28] The hard decision came at the session of the Superior Council of the Navy held on 9 July 1947.[29] Maintaining their focus on rebuilding the fleet and growing the Aéronavale, French admirals accepted to suspend most work on the navy's shore infrastructures for the time being, limiting new investments to Brest and Mers el-Kébir. Interest in these two ports showed the strategic primacy of the North Atlantic and the Western Mediterranean lines of communications for the Marine nationale. The abandonment of earlier ambitions regarding Dakar in the Southern Atlantic, Diego Suarez (Madagascar) in the Indian Ocean, and Cam Ranh in the Pacific was telling but most striking was the reversal on Bizerte.

Virtually no progress had taken place in overseas establishments since 1945, but an important part of those few resources that could be spared at the time had been directed to the Tunisian base.[30] Within two years, however, what many perceived as a critical outpost overlooking the eastern approaches to Algeria and southern France and capable of supporting the projection of forces to the Bosporus, the Suez Canal, and the Middle East became a potential liability. Given the dawn of the Cold War, it now sat exposed to airstrike from Central Europe, and an enemy could easily mine or blockade its narrow canal leading to the immense inland lake that had made it such an attractive anchorage in the first place. And as valuable as Bizerte's position overlooking the east–west traffic across the central Mediterranean appeared, the north–south line of communication between the *métropole* and Africa remained the primary axis of strategic importance to France. If a choice had to be made, French admirals remained committed to dominance over the Western Mediterranean, at the expense of the more developed Tunisian outpost, hence their recommendation to invest in Mers el-Kébir instead, at least until France could afford to augment its defense budget substantially.

The emergence of the Soviet threat in Europe resulted in increased defense budgets in the following years, but even then the proportion allocated to naval bases fell well short of the requirements expressed by Rue Royal planners. They sought 6 billion FF in 1949 but only received 3.16 billion for that purpose.[31] The conundrum continued into the early 1950s until reprieve appeared possible under the aegis of the NATO Infrastructure Programme, the follow-on to an initiative first discussed by the five nations that joined the Brussels Pact in 1948. In addition to building up ground forces to face down a potential offensive by the Soviet Union across Germany, signatories agreed to stand up integrated air defenses across Western Europe. The bulk of the work required for this pressing requirement—thirty new airfields, one combined headquarter complex, and thirty-four communications centers—would take place in France and the Netherlands, given their geographic position, but the two countries could not afford the £32 million necessary to complete this effort.[32] In 1949 the Western Union powers accepted to share these costs as they contributed to the common defense, a concept adopted by NATO when the Atlantic Treaty came into force that same year.

The NATO Western European allies took on this initial commitment—known as the "First Slice"—and adopted a second one the following year. In September 1951 the United States and Canada agreed to participate in the cost-sharing scheme as their air forces would also operate in Europe. This influx funded the Third Slice, but the 1952 Lisbon Summit resulted in dramatically increased infrastructure needs to take into account standing up Supreme Allied Commander Atlantic as well as the accession of Greece and Turkey. Initial estimates for the Fourth Slice reached a staggering £182 million, but the rapid stifling of ambitions that followed Lisbon led to a reviewed figure of £80 million in December 1952 (NATO continued the Western Union practice of accounting for infrastructure costs in British pounds until well into the 1960s).[33] That year leaders of the Atlantic Alliance also realized that infrastructure work required long-term planning and commitment and that common needs existed beyond the realm of air defense. The Fifth Slice approved in December 1953 became the first installment of a three-year program that included for the first time a naval allocation to build oil and ammunition storage facilities, maritime airfields, and "a chain of stations providing navigational aids in the Eastern Atlantic."[34]

The Marine nationale needed those funds badly. By then, Mers el-Kébir was the only French naval base where extensive work on new infrastructures continued, with the remaining funds allocated for limited improvements to existing facilities in Brest and Bizerte and nothing but basic maintenance in remaining locations at home and overseas. Even in 1954 Saigon, then the sole naval base located in an active theater of war, the commander planned to dedicate his meager infrastructure budget to river dredging instead of work on the base itself, while any ambition of building new facilities in Cam Ranh had been abandoned long ago.[35] Less than 10 percent of the naval budget went to infrastructure work in the early 1950s as Admiral Nomy and his staff continued to focus on rejuvenating the fleet and expanding the Aéronavale.[36] But reprieve on the bases front was forthcoming, at least in North Africa, as France's national interests and Alliance strategy soon merged. General Augustin-Léon Guillaume, then *résident général* (governor general) in Morocco, wrote in November 1953:

> The defense of the Western Europe peninsula . . . can only be achieved by controlling its maritime approaches in order to maintain secure access for the troops and material from overseas, especially from the gigantic American arsenal. Given the distances involved, transport fleets need maritime way stations. Nature has happily placed two such relay points which can shoulder the defense of Europe: Great Britain and French North Africa. These two flank guards, protected by their own maritime approaches, can indeed play the role of defensive bastions or offensive springboards in relation to the European theatre. . . . Such would be the value of North Africa for the Atlantic Alliance in another world war.[37]

Two years later, Admiral Pierre Barjot, while in command of the Mediterranean fleet, wrote:

> Tomorrow, to avoid a nuclear Pearl Harbor, our fleet must disperse, not remain concentrated in one port. Concentration in Toulon almost led to its capture from the land on 27 November 1942. Today, Mers el-Kébir as a Toulon replica, the roadsteads of Hyères [east of Toulon] and Sfax [south of Tunis], the Bizerte Lake, and the port of Bougie [200 kilometers east of Algiers] all offer possibilities for dispersion, as well as the potential for mobility and ubiquity essential to maintain control of the Western Mediterranean so vital to France and the free world.[38]

It followed that, just as quickly as Bizerte had lost its priority in the late 1940s, French and Allied admirals expressed renewed interest in that base in the mid-1950s. Despite the vulnerability of its lake canal, its location fitted well in the context of the nuclear threat and the Alliance's strategy of forward defense.[39] Tunisia should no longer end up on the front line within days of a Soviet advance into Western Europe and across Egypt as NATO committed to holding Italy and preventing an enemy thrust into the Levant. These assumptions turned Bizerte from an exposed defensive outpost to an offensive stronghold from where allied ships, submarines, and air bombers could sally forth to strike against the soft underbelly of a Soviet thrust into Western Europe. Admiral Barjot grandly described the Tunisian position as an "extraordinary combination of Pearl Harbor and Gibraltar."[40] As the Alliance's interest in the Mediterranean grew, NATO authorities queried Paris in 1953 about developing air and naval facilities across French North Africa, from Morocco to Tunisia. The Americans were particularly interested in transit airfields for nuclear bombers, installing early-warning systems, pre-positioning fuel and ammunition stockpiles, and supporting antisubmarine patrols in the region.

Discussions led to a momentous decision on 25 March 1954 when France authorized NATO to access "bases in the Maghreb, Bizerta and Sfax in particular, in recognition that such deployments were integral to wider alliance plans for European and Mediterranean defense."[41] And Allied requests for access to France's North African bases were not one-way demands, formulated as they were while negotiations over an addendum to the 1952 Fourth Slice and the upcoming Fifth Slice of the NATO Infrastructure Programme took place. These tranches, approved respectively in April and December 1953, included the first financial contributions to the rejuvenation of French naval bases in the *métropole* and North Africa with significant sums, at 19 billion FF and 6 billion FF each.[42] They provided an important boost to French ambitions regarding their bases even as ships and submarine construction, as well as aircraft acquisition, kicked into high gear, severely straining the navy's budget.

As table 8.1 shows, subsequent tranches also provided subsidies for the Marine nationale, including the eighth, ninth, and tenth slices approved together as a single-three-year plan in 1957, but these propitious circumstances did not last. The three-year infrastructure plan showed dramatically reduced funding with less than 1 billion FF per year. This reflected increasing doubts in allied capitals—particularly in Washington—as to the sagacity of directing more Alliance money to French projects in the Maghreb. One could argue that the overall needs of the Marine nationale had shrunk following the withdrawal from Indochina and the consolidation of some establishments in the *métropole*, presenting the potential to redirect the savings to other bases. However, their future ownership appeared at risk. Each of the agreements that led to independence in Morocco and Tunisia in 1956, as well as to the 1962 Evian Accords for Algeria, included clauses allowing France to maintain exclusive use of key military installations in these territories. And yet, follow-on confrontations with the local authorities and anticolonial pressure conveyed through the United Nations and other fora eventually led de Gaulle to abandon Port Lyautey and Casablanca in 1961, Bizerte in 1963, and Mers el-Kébir in 1968.[43]

By the fall of 1965, authorities at the Rue Royale had resolved themselves to a much-reduced base framework in the postcolonial era as laid out in a lengthy journal article by a serving flag officer.[44] Brest and Toulon remained the only two main bases of operations, while Cherbourg, Lorient, Dakar, and Diego Suarez were more akin to logistics and maintenance facilities. La Pallice, Fort-de-France, Nouméa, and Djibouti became mere *points d'appui* (points of support). Boulogne, Le Havre, Bordeaux, Marseille, Ajaccio, and Papeete would be known as *ports de relâche*—"ports of call," literally, but better

Table 8.1: NATO Infrastructure Program Allocations to the French Navy

Slices (Approval)	Projects	Allocations (billion FF)
Fourth Slice Addendum (April 1953)	Bizerte: underground ammunition magazines and fuel tanks, waterfront jetties	5.197
	Mers el-Kébir: underground ammunition magazines and fuel tanks, waterfront jetties	6.079
	Lartigues (near Oran): upgrade to NATO standards of existing Aéronavale base	3.183
	Nîmes–Garons (southern France): new Aéronavale base	2.118
	Nîmes–Garons (southern France): new Aéronavale base	2.118
	Cherbourg-Maupertus (near Cherbourg): new Aéronavale base	2.320
	Total	18.897
Fifth Slice (December 1953)	Bizerte: Fuel tanks	1.135
	Mers el-Kébir: Ammunition/fuel storage	1.625
	Oran: Electric generation station	0.572
	Brest: HQ and radio station, LORAN station	0.556
	Lann-Bihoue (near Lorient): upgrade to NATO standards, navigational aids	1.808
	Total	5.696
Sixth Slice (December 1954)	Bizerte: Fuel tanks	2.184
	Mers el-Kébir: Fuel tanks	2.280
	Algier: Radio station	0.171
	Casablanca: Radio station	0.105
	Total	4.740
Seventh Slice (1956)	Algiers: Radio station	1.167
Eighth Slice (April 1957)	Brest: Underground ammunition magazines	0.444
Ninth Slice (April 1957)	Mers el-Kébir: Headquarters improvements	0.360
	Oran: Tropospheric radio station	0.340
	Total	0.700
Tenth Slice (April 1957)	Lann-Bihoue (near Lorient): various upgrades	0.137
Total		31.781

translated as "auxiliary stations"—where the navy maintained just enough installations and supplies to sustain a limited number of vessels deployed on local operations. Despite this shrinking footprint and seemingly dwindling ambitions, this structure served France well for the remainder of the Cold War. The network allowed the fleet to maintain an adequate level of worldwide reach—admittedly not without some critical shortcomings, especially the lack of drydocks beyond the *métropole*—by optimizing those dependencies that remained attached to the Communauté française under the Fifth Republic. And French admirals again demonstrated a unique talent in leveraging allied assistance to subsidize projects that served both France and the Alliance while appropriating purely national funds for national projects, including a remarkable new initiative in the Pacific.

Despite its classification as mere *port de relâche*, the Tahitian facility of Papeete was in the midst of a huge expansion in view of its role in support of the Centre d'expérimentation du Pacifique (Pacific Experimentation Centre), which was then under construction on the Polynesian island of Moruroa and was destined to replace the nuclear testing facility in Algeria, site of the first detonation of a French atomic device on 13 February 1960.[45] The navy led the building of the Polynesian center. With the loss of Algeria, French admirals no longer pursued the security of the Mediterranean line of communications between France and North Africa as their overriding priority. De Gaulle assigned them a new task, deploying nuclear weapons at sea in support of the national strategy of "deterrence of the strong by the weak." Even more quickly than Nomy had to abandon the ambition of maintaining an elaborate network bases in the 1950s, his successor—Admiral Georges Cabanier, appointed on 1 July 1960—found himself forced to tackle the new vision of sea power championed by le Général.

Nuclear Deterrence, Nuclear Submarines

The rise of Admiral Cabanier to the top Marine nationale post marked both continuity and a break for the postwar navy. Like Lemonnier and Nomy, who each served lengthy tours as *chef de l'État-major général de la Marine*—seven and nine years, respectively, split by the very short tenures of Battet and Lambert—Cabanier would remain in place for eight years, overseeing the navy's fortunes as it joined the nuclear age into the 1960s. But his appointment broke with tradition for two reasons. He was the first submariner to move in the Rue Royale highest office since Admiral Georges Durand-Viel in 1931 (Rear Admiral Gabriel Auphan, also a submariner, served as head of the Vichy navy in 1941–42, but he was of little influence, serving as he did under Darlan).[46] And Cabanier was the first "true" Free French promoted to that post since the reunification of 1943. Battet had waited until the North African landings before joining the FNFL, while Lemonnier, Lambert, and Nomy rallied to Giraud.

Born in 1906, Cabanier entered the École navale in 1925 and transferred to the submarine service in 1932. A lieutenant in 1934, he quickly rose to command the submarine minelayer *Rubis* in 1938. Ordered to join a British flotilla operating out of Scotland in early 1940, Cabanier distinguished himself during successful minelaying operations in the North Sea and off the Norwegian coast prior to the armistice. The Royal Navy seized *Rubis* in July but soon returned it to Cabanier as he convinced the majority of his crew to join the Free French movement and resume operations at the side of the Allies, the first unit in the United Kingdom to do so, which earned high praise from de Gaulle.[47] Promoted to the rank of lieutenant commander in January 1941, he left *Rubis* to join the staff of Captain d'Argenlieu, Free French High Commissioner in the Pacific. After a brief stint at FNFL headquarters in London and a promotion to commander in 1943, he returned to the Pacific in 1944 to take command of the armed merchantman *Cap des Palmes*, then serving with the USN 3rd Fleet on convoy escort missions in the Solomon Islands.

A member of the French legation dispatched to San Francisco for the founding of the United Nations in 1945, Cabanier returned to France to take command of the École navale as a captain and transferred to the training cruiser *Jeanne d'Arc* in 1947. He went to Washington as naval attaché in 1949, became a rear admiral in 1951, and served on the French joint defense staff in 1953–54 before his dispatch to the Far East to command naval forces in southern Indochina until 1955. Back in France, Cabanier joined the personal staff of the minister of defense for one year, earning a promotion to vice admiral and taking command in late 1956 of the Toulon-based Groupe d'action anti-sous-marin (the ASW action group that had just returned from Suez).

As soon as he took power in June 1958, de Gaulle recalled Cabanier to Paris to work in his military cabinet and made him the commander of the navy when Nomy reached retirement age in 1960.[48] The archives and de Gaulle's personal recollections tell little as to why le Général selected that admiral for the post, but a review of these career milestones shows that Cabanier's background fit squarely within his agenda. Cabanier—a Free French of the first hour who remained an avowed Gaullist after the war, a proven sailor with a solid track record in staff appointments—had experience working with the Americans, and his submariner background would greatly assist future discussions with Washington. As relevant, perhaps, were his lack of attachment to Algeria and his limited experience with NATO.

By the summer of 1960 the estrangement between France and the Atlantic Alliance was already under way, and the unraveling had commenced well before the General's return to power. Worsening relations between French leaders and les Anglo-Saxons, especially the United States, after the exhilarating days of signing the North Atlantic Treaty in 1949, cannot be ascribed to any single event. Successive crises contributed to the rising tensions. Discord continued over priorities in provision of allied support to French rearmament and Eisenhower refused to engage militarily in Indochina, particularly during the Dien Bien Phu debacle. Debates over German rearmament, Washington's tacit support to decolonialization and its public criticism of France's approach in Algeria also played a role. These cumulative disagreements, capped by dramatic confrontation during the Suez crisis, led an increasing number of Fourth Republic leaders to doubt the political commitment of the United States to the French ally. As concerning, development of the Soviet atomic arsenal—in numbers and reach—caused many in the métropole to turn skeptical of the American military guarantee, resting as it did on nuclear deterrence.[49] Although simplistic, asking whether the United States would sacrifice New York for Paris provided potent symbolism for those advocating that France acquire atomic means of its own.

In that regard, the Gaullist myth is not quite correct in attributing all credit to the General for turning his country into a nuclear power. He could not have achieved that goal without the efforts undertaken during the years of the Fourth Republic. French interest in the atom's military applications began in the early 1950s, starting with the creation in December 1952 of the Army's Special Weapons Command under Colonel Charles Ailleret, "no more than a nuclear, biological, and chemical (NBC) protection command at the beginning, but soon to become a real 'nuclear think-tank'."[50] Earlier, in July, during parliamentary debates over a bill sponsoring an ambitious five-year plan for development of a civilian nuclear industry, parties from the Left tried to include an amendment preempting use of these facilities for military purpose in the future but the motion was defeated in the National Assembly.[51] The Cabinet then ordered the formation of a joint committee between the civilian-led Commissariat à l'énergie atomique (CEA, or Atomic Energy Commission) and the Ministry of Defense in October 1954. Two months later, Président du Conseil Pierre Mendès France took the fateful step of standing up a secret military division within the CEA, funded from the defense budget and headed by army general Jean Crépin.[52] Its immediate tasks were to study the requirements for building an atomic bomb and develop options for submarine nuclear propulsion.

The second goal was not entirely new. The 1952 five-year plan had already mandated the CEA to build two nuclear submarines, for scientific research rather than military application, but the project languished among competing priorities.[53] French admirals remained of two minds about the future of nuclear propulsion, certainly conscious of its potential but equally concerned with its great cost and the impact it could have on the rejuvenation of the surface fleet and the Aéronavale. The subject was first brought to the attention of the Conseil supérieur de la Marine in 1947, acknowledged but without follow-up action.[54] By the early 1950s a concerted effort was under way to grow the submarine arm, and debate arose whether future plans should focus on nuclear or conventional propulsion. Among others, Nomy and Lemonnier promoted the former while Pierre Barjot and Paul Ortoli (another Free French of the first hour, filling the post of inspector general of the navy in 1952–54) militated for the latter. The dissonance delayed a decision as the council remained a consensual body charged with providing unified views to the minister.[55] A compromise was eventually reached in 1955, endorsing the development of one nuclear-powered submarine for service in the navy—implying abandonment of the earlier CEA initiative of two submersibles for civilian research—while maintaining the current emphasis on the construction of diesel-electric platforms, the *Narval*-, *Aréthuse*-, *Daphné*-class mix already approved by the National Assembly.

Although the result of a compromise preceded by the fall of the Mendès France government in February 1955, naval authorities pursued the new plan aggressively. Leveraging the exploratory work of a CEA-navy liaison committee formed in April 1954, the Rue Royale quickly provided a detailed proposal, which was approved on 20 May 1955 by the government of Edgar Faure—who, by and large, continued the nuclear program launched by his predecessor.[56] On 24 June Cherbourg was selected as the building site, a budget of 16 billion FF authorized, and *ingénieur général de 1ère classe* (engineering vice admiral) Roger Brard took charge of the Groupe des bâtiments à propulsion atomique (Nuclear-Powered Vessels Group), the office established to lead the project, designated *projet Q-244*. However, Brard soon faced insurmountable technical challenges in this endeavor.

French engineers had explored two modes of nuclear propulsion, one fueled by enriched uranium and the other relying on natural uranium that required heavy water as a coolant (hence the 1952 ambition to build two submarines, one of each type). USS *Nautilus*, in service since January 1955, used the former in a small but highly efficient reactor. France, however, did not have the means to produce enriched uranium or access to U.S. sources as the Atomic Energy Act of 1946 (the McMahon Bill) ruled out sharing nuclear research and transfer of fissile material, even with close allies, for fear of proliferation or misuse.[57] As sources of natural uranium existed in France and heavy water could be obtained from Norway, the Brard team resigned themselves to fit *Q-244* with the much larger reactor that this mode necessitated. But significant engineering issues remained. The machinery just could not be made to fit in a hull of a practical and affordable size. In two years, the design evolved to a point where the submarine's planned tonnage nearly tripled from 2,500 tons to 6,500 tons, compared to the 4,000 tons of the *Nautilus*. The expected costs rose to equal those that would allow for the construction of one enrichment plant, which could provide the enriched uranium needed for a range of other military needs, making the single submarine project increasingly contentious outside navy circles. De Gaulle put the project on hold soon after coming to power in the summer of 1958.[58]

Not that le Général abandoned those nuclear ambitions. While still isolated in the political wilderness, he claimed his support for a French atomic bomb during a widely covered press conference in April 1954: "France needs a defense system which is of course proportioned to her resources and associated with those of her allies but also autonomous and balanced. France needs to be a nuclear power."[59] Two years later, on 2 April 1956, he received the visit of French air force colonel Pierre Gallois, from the NATO New Approach Group. SACEUR himself, General Lauris Norstad, USAF, tasked Gallois to brief, separately, then–prime minister Guy Mollet and de Gaulle on the work of the group charged with developing the Alliance's nuclear strategy.[60] But Gallois also used the opportunity to expose le Général to his own ideas about the atomic bomb in terms of France's national security, which he had been reflecting upon since the end of World War II. Gallois himself later stated that he first drew inspiration from an article published in 1945 by retired admiral Raoul Castex who referred to the *facteur égalisateur* (strategic equalizer): "Just like a strong nation, a weak one will have nuclear weapons, in fewer number perhaps, but numbers matter little given the great power of individual devices."[61]

This statement embodied what became known as France's nuclear strategy of *dissuasion du faible au fort*, the deterrence of the strong by the weak. The weaker power did not need a deterrent comparable to that of the stronger enemy. It only needed the capacity to inflict greater damage than the opponent was willing to endure in comparison to the gains the latter sought to obtain by force. France could not compete with the superpowers in absolute terms, but it could assemble an instrument of sufficient size to maintain a sort of asymmetric or proportional deterrence.[62] In a seminal 1960 treatise Gallois outlined the characteristics that would come to shape de Gaulle's *force de frappe* (strike force) in the years ahead:

> Nuclear bombs and their vectors—be they aircraft or missiles—must, first of all, escape annihilation from an enemy first strike that uses surprise and an inherent superiority in numbers. This force must then be able to penetrate the opponent's air defenses. It is necessary that such retaliatory strike can be launched nearly automatically in case of an attack. . . .

Lastly, the "quantity of destruction" that can be inflicted once the strike force reaches its targets must nullify the gains the aggressor is seeking to achieve through his offensive. Naturally, what counts is that the aggressor country reaches this conclusion before launching a first strike.[63]

One must not overestimate the influence of Gallois over de Gaulle.[64] Le Général did not call Gallois to his side when he came to power, and the strategist grew isolated from the military elites in the 1960s. His early influence turned stale compared to that of rising practitioners and theoreticians such as Ailleret and Colonel Pierre Buchalet (a later head of the CEA's military division) as well as army generals André Beaufre and Lucien Poirier.[65] These minds expanded on Gallois' vision to embrace the morality of the first and second strike options, in both the tactical and strategic realms. They inspired de Gaulle to refer to a *force tous azimuts*, an "all-round force." This concept signified that France's deterrent was not aimed at one specific enemy (i.e., the Soviet Union) but provided defense against any threat, which could include the United States, even if left unsaid.[66] But these developments had yet to come. Gallois was the first French writer to reach widely beyond military circles to discuss strategy in the atomic age. His musings did much to shape the political and public debate in the late 1950s as France became an active nuclear power, even as her navy continued struggling to master the power of the atom.

Projet Q-244 was floundering at the dawn of the Fifth Republic, but other elements of the secret Mendès France initiative had progressed remarkably fast, especially in the wake of the Suez crisis. A new protocol was signed on 30 November 1956 between the nuclear commission and the military to clarify respective responsibilities in building a first atomic bomb. Funding was approved for a plutonium extraction facility as well as a uranium enrichment plant. Dassault Aviation took on the design of the Mirage IV jet capable of delivering gravity bombs at supersonic speeds while longer-term studies in ballistic missile technology gained renewed attention. In addition to approving continued work on Q-244 in July 1957, the short-lived Maurice Bourgès-Maunoury government passed a second five-year nuclear program (doubling its budget) and approved in the summer of 1957 the selection of Reggane in Algeria as the atomic test site. Work around the Saharan oasis commenced in November, and Ailleret, now a general, was appointed in February 1958 to oversee the first series of tests. On 11 April, Président du Conseil Félix Gaillard (who had shepherded the first five-year plan through the National Assembly in 1952), ordered completion of all preparations to allow detonation of an atomic device in 1960 but stopped short of formally ordering the test.[67] De Gaulle then came to power two months later.

Although not the father of France's atomic bomb, de Gaulle decisively ventured where previous *présidents du Conseil* did not dare. As put succinctly by professor Bruno Tertrais, historian of the French nuclear program, de Gaulle made two fundamental determinations: "the decision to test, build, and sustain an *operational* deterrent; and the decision to have a fully *independent* deterrent, not only in terms of use, but also in terms of procurement, planning, and operations" [Emphasis in the original].[68] He put the first question to rest quickly once briefed on the extent of the secret work of the previous years. On 22 July 1958 he ordered a first atomic test to take place no later than March 1960 and on 22 September made public the existence of a military division within the Atomic Commission, establishing through prime ministerial decree the Direction des applications militaires (Directorate of Military Applications) under General Buchalet.[69]

De Gaulle then confirmed the requirement for the delivery of fifty Dassault Mirage IV two-seater bombers between 1963 and 1967 (another twelve configured for strategic reconnaissance were ordered in 1964).[70] Ironically, the Mirage IV decision also showed that de Gaulle may not have been determined to pursue independence at all cost yet. Engineers realized in 1958 that French industry had not yet achieved the maturity necessary to produce a jet engine capable of the high performance required of the supersonic plane, thus the decision to seek engines from the American firm Pratt & Whitney, to be built under license in France.[71] The United States appeared open to greater collaboration with some of its allies as shown by the government's willingness to endorse this transfer of jet engine technology, even knowing that the Mirage IV could eventually become an atomic-bomb delivery vehicle.

A greater precedent occurred on 2 July 1958, when Congress amended the McMahon Bill of 1946, which had already been modified in 1954 to facilitate the development of civilian nuclear industry. The new act allowed sharing information as well as transfer of fissile material and related equipment to other countries for military purposes.[72] This set the stage for signing the U.K.–U.S. Mutual Defense Agreement, which codified bilateral cooperation between the two powers, including the sale to Great Britain of one complete submarine propulsion plant and the uranium needed to fuel it for a period of ten years.[73] Eisenhower's determination to repair relations in the wake of Suez extended to France as Secretary of State John Foster Dulles met with de Gaulle in Paris on 5 July to offer a similar level of cooperation in the nuclear realm: "We would be prepared to see French forces fully trained in the use of [U.S. nuclear] weapons and French equipment adapted to deliver them. This would be done in the context of NATO and NATO strategy. It was also our intention to assist, if so desired, in the development of atomic propulsion for French submarines."[74]

Although he immediately made an issue of the matter of control over nuclear weapons stored on French soil, de Gaulle also affirmed his interest in renewed collaboration. He dispatched a team to the United States in February 1959 with an ambitious agenda: negotiate the immediate purchase of a nuclear-powered submarine using current U.S. technology, obtain enriched uranium to fuel a French prototype atomic propulsion reactor, and discuss additional nuclear cooperation, including visits to American test sites.[75] By then, however, the spirit of conciliation had already faded on both sides. Congress proved lukewarm to Dulles' offer of nuclear cooperation with France while the Eisenhower administration continued demurring over an earlier proposal by de Gaulle to form a tripartite directorate where the United States, Great Britain, and France would "put into effect strategic plans of action, notably with regard to the employment of nuclear weapons."[76]

And this came after years of Washington and London denying demands from France for a major allied command in the Mediterranean. Le Général grandly elected to withdraw the fleet from the NATO framework in the Mediterranean on 7 March 1959, dramatically constraining the ability of the French delegation then in America to extract nuclear concessions from Washington. They succeeded in securing a deal on 7 May but fell quite short of their original goal, especially when contrasted with the terms obtained by the British the previous year. The agreement only provided for the sale of 440 kilos of enriched uranium, the use of which was restricted to fueling a land-based prototype submarine propulsion plant for a period of ten years.[77] Such an ambivalent result marked the final break between de Gaulle and Eisenhower over nuclear cooperation. In a 25 May 1959 letter to the U.S. president where he announced that he would deny the Alliance the use of facilities in France to store atomic weapons, le Général declared bitterly: "Obviously the question would appear quite differently if you made it possible for us to take advantage of your own achievements. But America intends to keep her secrets vis-à-vis France. This compels us to discover them ourselves and a tremendous cost. . . . The consequences which might result from any unilateral action which you might undertake in this area . . . [lead us] to adopt, insofar as possible, certain measures on our own behalf as safeguards."[78]

The decision to detonate a first atomic bomb and to acquire Mirage IV strategic bombers would operationalize France's *force de frappe*. De Gaulle now wanted to ensure its independence. He outlined his vision in a widely publicized address on 3 November 1959: "The defense of France must be French. . . . It ensues that we must, obviously, develop in the coming years a force which can act on our behalf, a *force de frappe* capable of deployment at anytime and anywhere. At the heart of this force will be atomic armament. . . . And, since potential opponents will eventually be able to destroy France from anywhere in the world, our force must be capable of reaching anywhere in the world."[79]

To sustain this effort, de Gaulle abandoned the Fourth Republic's practice of voting the defense budget through annual tranches in favor of five-year *lois de programmation militaire* (military programming acts), the first of which covered the 1960–64 period. Appropriating 5.44 percent of the country's gross domestic product in 1960 alone (still a considerable figure for a western country by 1960s standards), the program placed the *force de frappe* at the center of the defense budget.[80] Introduced to Parliament in July 1960, the first plan proved highly controversial in both the Assemblée nationale and the Senate. Debates lasted through the fall with Communists and Socialists opposed to a French nuclear deterrent altogether while the Center-Right Mouvement républicain populaire militated in favor of developing such armament but within the NATO framework. Nevertheless, the final version passed on 8 December still largely reflected de Gaulle's priorities.[81]

The bill proved the death of *project Q-244* but also marked the dawn of a renewed research effort in a different direction for the Marine nationale.[82] Abandoning the natural uranium and heavy water combination for good, French authorities tackled, in two cautious stages, the challenge of developing an entirely new means of submarine propulsion using enriched uranium. First, a newly designed prototype would be built in a shore facility to conduct extensive testing. Only then would a second plant be approved for construction and installation in a submarine of the next generation. Success followed quickly. On 9 April 1962 a small test reactor achieved criticality, and in February 1963 the main components of the actual prototype reactor were assembled in place. This *prototype à terre* (onshore prototype) first achieved full power in August 1964 and then completed a continuous run from October to December that same year, the period equivalent to a round-the-world, seventy-day patrol.[83] France had a working and proven nuclear-propulsion plant in hand. Next was the actual submarine.

Q-244 had been designed as an attack submarine armed with conventional torpedoes. Some visionaries conceived of her as a stepping-stone toward the design of a future missile-carrying submersible, but many others believed that capability far too advanced for development by France alone.[84] The U.S. Navy commissioned its first SSBN to great success—USS *George Washington* on 30 December 1959—but the Soviet experience with the infamous *K-19* the following years also showed the challenges of operating such a complex platform.[85] By 1961 the French navy did not yet have a serviceable submarine nuclear-propulsion plant, an advanced navigation system for extended underwater cruising and accurate ballistic targeting, a working submarine-launched missile, or a nuclear warhead that could fit such a missile. Research and development work had commenced in each of these areas, but France was unlikely to assemble and operationalize all four elements in one deployable platform for another decade at least[86]—unless the Americans would provide a shortcut if de Gaulle accepted it as supporting his effort to restore France's grandeur rather than undermining it.

Newly installed president John Kennedy seized upon a concept introduced in the closing days of the Eisenhower administration. The proposal for the creation of a multilateral force—as much a political gesture as a military initiative—sought to give European partners a more active role in the Alliance's nuclear deterrent.[87] Mixed multinational NATO crews would sail in USN and European ships and submarines armed with American ballistic missiles. The nuclear warheads would remain under U.S. control, but European authorities could be part of the decision-making cycle prior to launch, and European sailors would participate in execution of nuclear strikes at the behest of NATO. The concept did not prove viable in the long run, but it gave rise to a more immediate idea, that of the United States providing nuclear-tipped ballistic missiles to equip British and French submarines.

Prime Minister Macmillan readily agreed to this proposal during a conference held with President Kennedy in the Bahamas in December 1962. The Americans agreed to supply new Polaris missiles, launch tubes, reentry bodies, and fire-control systems to equip five submarines embarking sixteen SLBMs each. Great Britain would design and operate the submarines, incorporating the previously transferred U.S. propulsion technology in the first vessel. British crews would operate them but as part of the proposed Multilateral Force, with SACEUR providing targeting plans and Supreme Allied Commander Atlantic exercising operational control while the submarines were on patrol, unless reassigned by the prime minister to independent tasks when "supreme national interests are at stake."[88]

Despite this clause, many denounced the agreement, underlining that Great Britain acquired a modern, viable, and credible nuclear deterrent but at unacceptable cost in terms of national sovereignty and military autonomy. Macmillan bravely couched it as continuance of the two countries' special relationship of interdependence rather than subservience. This interpretation meant little for de Gaulle, and American advisers were unsure how he would react when Kennedy cabled a letter from Nassau that included an offer to "consider a similar agreement with you, should you so desire."[89] De Gaulle summarily dismissed the offer when he met in Paris with U.S. Ambassador Charles E. Bohlen on 4 January 1963: "We are not favorable to the concept of integrated forces. We believe that our atomic force must be a national force. We want to keep our hands on our bombs. We cannot entrust them to others nor share their employment as the stakes are too high. The position of the American government with regard to its own nuclear weapons is identical to our own, which is perfectly natural."[90]

Then came the memorable press conference of 14 January 1963 when de Gaulle unleashed, as recalled by U.S. Undersecretary of State George Ball, "the 'thunderbolts' that struck at the heart of Kennedy's Grand Design for an Atlantic partnership."[91] He abruptly closed the door to Great Britain's application to the European Economic Community and celebrated a renewed spirit of reconciliation and cooperation with West Germany in a continental Europe growing independent of the Anglo-American dominion. As curtly, Le Général announced his refusal to join the Multilateral Force and professed his continued commitment to an independent *force de frappe*. It would be built in France, operated by the French military, and controlled from Paris under presidential authority. Within weeks, he confirmed the central role the Marine nationale would assume at the heart of France's nuclear deterrent. The urgency of assembling an effective sea-based component as part of a credible and redundant nuclear triad showed in the number of initiatives launched nearly simultaneously to achieve this goal.

In March 1963, even as the components of the onshore nuclear-propulsion prototype were still being assembled, instructions went out to Cherbourg to begin construction of two new submarines. *Projet Q-252* started from scratch and eventually led to the launch of SSBN *Le Redoutable* in March 1967.[92] *Projet Q-251*, more immediately, recycled elements of the failed Q-244 hull, which lay dormant in Cherbourg, to expedite the construction of a large conventional diesel-electric submarine commissioned for experimentation.[93] Launched in March 1964 and operational two years later, *Gymnote* provided the platform to test-launch the ballistic missiles then under development for arming *Le Redoutable*. For that purpose, construction of the Centre d'essais des Landes (south of La Rochelle on the Atlantic coast) had already been authorized in July 1962. The conversion of a civilian tanker into a telemetry vessel (*Henri Poincaré*) followed in 1964 as well as an agreement with Portugal in 1966 to install sensors in the Azores for tracking ballistic test missiles launched from the metropole.[94]

Meanwhile, Parliament approved in December 1964 de Gaulle's second *loi de programmation militaire* for the period 1965–70. It included funds for the completion of the first three SSBNs (*Le Redoutable*, *Le Terrible*, and *Le Foudroyant*); development of the M1 MSBS (SLBM missile) as well as completion of *Gymnote*, the Landes test range, and the Pacific Experimentation Center; the Île Longue complex; the Rosnay very low frequency transmitter and its backup stations; and shore training facilities in Brest.[95] The Marine nationale was going nuclear, whatever the cost to its conventional forces. The sea-based vectors would soon assume a central role in the Gaullist vision of a credible and independent strategic deterrent for France. Having launched this colossal effort, le Général proclaimed grandly in 1965 the fleet's rise to unprecedented prominence in the nation's defense: "The navy now finds itself, no doubt for the first time in history, at the apex of France's military power. And this will become a little truer every day in the future."[96]

CONCLUSION

B attleship *Richelieu* last put to sea on Sunday, 25 August 1968. By then, however, she was no longer a battleship, or named *Richelieu*, or capable of making way under her own power. The ship, a floating barrack immobilized in Brest since May 1956, was disarmed by authorities on 30 September 1967 and decommissioned on 16 January 1968, at which point her designation reverted to that of the original hull number, Q-432. From then on, her fate was sealed. A skeleton crew expeditiously went about landing all equipment worthy of refurbishing for use in other vessels and transferring ashore what little fuel remained on board, while powerful cranes removed the last of her massive 15-inch guns. Tugs then took her away from the naval base itself and anchored the vessel in nearby Roscanvel Bay as the admiralty launched the bidding process to dispose of the former flagship, won by an Italian firm that brought her to La Spezia for scrapping.[1] The end of her sister ship *Jean Bart* proved as anticlimactic. Her last operation was the ill-fated Suez expedition, where she was not even allowed to fire her main battery. Barely four years later she joined *Richelieu* in the role of floating barrack but in Toulon, where she remained throughout the 1960s. Decommissioned as Q-466 on 10 February 1970, former *Jean Bart* shared the fate of her predecessor in falling to the acetylene torches of ship breakers.[2]

In an ironic twist of fate, former *Richelieu* had spent her final months rusting away at anchor next to Île Longue, which formed the eastern shore of the bay of Roscanvel. Since August 1967 hundreds of workers and heavy machinery were busily turning the once quiet pastoral land into a modern fortress of the nuclear age, the future home of France's Force océanique stratégique.[3] De Gaulle had personally identified the site in 1965, a direct follow-up to the momentous decision announced at the press conference of 14 January 1963 to turn the country's budding deterrence force of Mirage IV bombers into a nuclear triad. This milestone provides a suitable juncture to draw conclusions on the merits and weaknesses, successes and failures, of France's quest to achieve an independent naval policy within a strategy of alliance through the decades that followed the humiliating armistice of June 1940. Such an assessment must start with a portrait of the French fleet and the Aéronovale when le Général made his dramatic announcement, starting with the ships at table C.1 below.

As for the Aéronavale, it had surpassed the long-sought objective of growing into a versatile body of twenty squadrons, as first envisioned in 1943. On 1 January 1963, there were only nineteen such formations, but all were fighting units equipped with increasingly modern aircraft while support missions were attributed to a retinue of additional auxiliary units.[4] Two squadrons were not operational in 1963 but only as a result of their ongoing transition to the subsonic jet fighter-bomber Étendard IV designed for carrier operations. French firm Dassault delivered ninety aircraft of that type between 1961 and 1965, and those of the first tranche had already joined another squadron embarked on aircraft carrier *Clémenceau*.[5] One squadron still flew the first-generation jet Aquilon (the British Sea Venom) and two others the even older propeller-driven Corsairs (flying out of Bizerte), but plans were already afoot for their conversion to the American supersonic air superiority fighter jet Vought F-8 Crusader starting in 1965.[6]

While the Crusader provided for air defense and the Étendards could carry strike missions against surface targets at sea and ashore, the fixed-wing propeller-driven BR 1050 Alizé handled antisubmarine warfare tasks. Designed and produced by Breguet Aviation, this versatile aircraft, equipped with various sensors and carrying torpedoes or depth charges in its primary role, could also mount rockets and bombs to strike at enemy ships, even taking on the early-warning task later in the next decade.[7] Three squadrons flew the

Table C.1: Main French Fleet, 14 January 1963
(does not include floating barracks, repair ships, submarine tenders, and small auxiliaries)

Numbers of Hulls per Category	In Service and Modern	In Service but Obsolete	Under Construction	Remarks
0 Battleships	0	0	0	*Richelieu* and *Jean Bart* in reserve as alongside training/barrack ships
2 Aircraft carriers	1	0	1	*Clémenceau* in service 22 November 1961 *Foch* to enter service 15 July 1963
1 Helicopter carrier	1	0	0	*Arromanches* also retains a limited capacity to launch/recover aircraft for training/experimentation in peacetime
1 Cruiser helicopter carrier	0	0	1	The future *Jeanne d'Arc* to enter service in 1964 as a training cruiser (peacetime) and helicopter carrier (wartime)
3 Cruisers	2	1	0	*De Grasse*, AA cruiser in service 1956 *Colbert*, AA cruiser in service 1959 *Jeanne d'Arc*, training cruiser until 1964
1 Frigate	0	0	1	*Suffren*, AA missile frigate laid in 1962, will enter service in 1967
18 Fleet destroyers	18	0	0	12 T-47 entered service 1955–57 5 T-53 entered service 1957–58 1 T-56 entered service 1962
23 Destroyer escorts	18	5	0	4 E-50 entered service 1955–56 11 E-52A entered service 1956–58 3 E-52B entered service 1960 5 U.S. Cannon-class DEs to be decommissioned in 1964
30 Sloops / coastal escorts	17	7	6	9 *Commandant Rivière*–class *avisos-escorteurs* (sloop-escorts), 3 entered service 1962 and 6 more under construction 3 *Le Fougueux*–class coastal escorts entered service 1954 11 *L'Adroit*-class coastal escorts entered service 1957–59 1 Italian sloop, obsolete but adequate for Communauté française missions 4 prewar *avisos-dragueurs* employed for training tasks in the *métropole* 2 prewar *avisos-dragueurs* employed for Communauté française patrolling

(continued)

Table C.1 (continued)

Numbers of Hulls per Category	In Service and Modern	In Service but Obsolete	Under Construction	Remarks
100 Minesweepers	94	6	0	15 U.S. ocean minesweepers transferred to France in 1954–57 30 U.S. coastal minesweepers transferred to France in 1953–54 34 coastal minesweepers built in France in 1952–57 15 British inshore minesweepers transferred to France in 1954–55 6 obsolete Royal Canadian Navy Bay-class used for Communauté française patrolling
19 Coastal Patrol Craft	12	6	1	2 German motor launches built in 1954 10 French motor launches built in Germany and France in 1956–59 6 U.S. submarine chasers, obsolete, soon to be decommissioned 1 *La Combattante* class, laid in 1961 to enter service in 1964
24 Submarines	10	4	10	6 *Narval* class entered service 1957–60 4 *Aréthuse* class in service 1958–60 *L'Andromède* and *L'Artémis* (laid in 1939, 1940; commissioned in 1953, 1954) used for training/experimentation until 1965–67 Former U-boats *Millé* and *Roland Morillot* employed for training/experimentation, decommissioned July 1963 and 1967 9 *Daphné* class under construction (7 to enter service 1964 and 2 in 1966; 2 more ordered in 1965 to enter service in 1969–70) Experimental submarine *Gymnote* to be launched in 1964, in service 1966
14 Large amphibious	11	2	1	6 modern landing craft utility, built in France, entered service in 1958–59 5 modern landing ship, tank, built in France, entered service in 1959–60 1 World War II landing ship, dock 1 World War II landing ship, tank 1 landing platform dock *Ouragan*, laid down in 1962, commissioned in 1965 Plus a large variety of smaller landing craft

Table C.1 *(continued)*

Numbers of Hulls per Category	In Service and Modern	In Service but Obsolete	Under Construction	Remarks
13 Replenishment vessels	6	4	3	2 modern naval tankers in service (*La Seine, La Saône*) 4 militarized civilian oilers (*Berry, La Charente, Isère, Verdon*) 4 obsolete oilers in service (*La Baïsse, Lac Chambon, Lac Tchad, Lac Tonle Sap*) 2 logistical support ships under construction (*Rhin* and *Rhône*, with three more to follow) 1 militarized oiler under construction (*Aber Wrac'h*)
Total	**190**	**35**	**24**	**249**
Tons	**297,130**	**57,050**	**78,930**	**433,110**

Alizé, and another three handled Sikorsky HSS-1 helicopters, rounding out French carrier aviation. Initially designed as antisubmarine warfare platforms, the Sikorskys also carried out utility missions to transport personnel and supplies—between ships at sea and in support of troops fighting ashore as they had done in Algeria—as well conduct search-and-rescue tasks and fly as plane guard during carrier operations, standing ready to recover air crews ejecting from their planes in case of mishaps.[8]

The focus on carrier-borne aircraft did not leave shore-based units wanting. Six squadrons flew the Lockheed P2 Neptune maritime patrol aircraft. Although originally designed during World War II and first flown operationally by the U.S. Navy in 1947, this American plane remained a platform of choice among Western navies well into the 1970s for the conduct of long-range antisubmarine warfare. France received thirty-one P2V-6 airframes in the early 1950s under the terms of the Mutual Defense Assistance Program and thirty-four more advanced P2V-7 later in the decade.[9] MDAP also provided for ten P5M-2 Marlins flown by another squadron out of Dakar. Although modern—a postwar design delivered to France in 1959—these were the last flying boats operated by the French navy, which promptly returned them to the United States in 1964 as more Neptunes joined the air fleet.[10] Many more obsolete aircraft were left in the Aéronavale, such as C-47 Dakota transports, TBM Avenger torpedo planes, and a few seaplanes. But all of them were either on their way out or employed in support or training roles, leaving the most modern airframes available to deploy on operations overseas and patrol the seaward approaches to the *métropole* from a robust network of bases.

For an observer unaware of the level of ambition entertained by French admirals in the later years of World War II and immediately after the hostilities, table C.1 and this snapshot of the Aéronavale may present an impressive portrait. By 1963 Nomy and Cabanier had largely succeeded in eliminating most of the U.S., British, German, and Italian wartime transfers as well as older prewar French constructions. And those still present were adequately employed for experimentation missions, training tasks, and routine patrolling across a newly pacified Communauté française, freeing up new builds for Alliance and national tasks in the complex setting of the Cold War. These assets provided Rue Royale planners with the ability to assemble a powerful *groupe d'intervention naval* for NATO commitments or in defense of purely French interests, part of the larger Force interarmées d'intervention immédiate (Immediate Intervention Joint Force) that the three services were instructed to stand up in 1962.[11] Whenever called upon to deploy on operations, its naval element would center on either aircraft carriers *Clémenceau* or *Foch*, supported by one of the AA cruisers (*De Grasse* or *Colbert*), and escorted by a retinue of modern and well-armed fleet destroyers, smaller escorts, and mine warfare elements.

This force could operate with an amphibious group and submarines for an overseas commitment while sufficient escorts and minesweepers remained available to discharge convoy escort and coastal defense duties in European waters and across the Communauté française. The new carriers allowed the French navy to enter the jet age, embarking a potent mix of assets for strike, air defense, and antisubmarine missions. Modern shore-based maritime patrol aircraft extended the surveillance and strike range of forces at sea against hostile ships and submarines. Even the old *Arromanches* came to symbolize a new era, her conversion to the helicopter carrier role providing the ability to make a powerful impact in the littoral by projecting and supporting a force of *fusiliers-marins* and commandos ashore as well as providing humanitarian assistance in response to natural disasters. The inclusion of a new category—replenishment vessels—also showed that Admiral Cabanier and his staff had seized upon the importance of logistics at sea, especially given the shrinking network of French bases around the world.

Additional acquisitions later in the 1960s eventually allowed the French fleet to conduct underway replenishment operations at high speed. Such complex evolutions needed to occur regularly, regardless of heavy weather and often under the threat of enemy attacks, as learned by American carrier task force commanders in the Pacific War, lessons that the Marine nationale neglected in the immediate postwar era. As well, not listed in the table are those various vessels that allowed the French navy to discharge another range of responsibilities in peacetime that were necessary to support operations in times of crisis or hostilities. These ships were mostly older, slower, and smaller than the fighting units boasted about by proud admirals, but they often embarked state-of-the-art equipment manned by an eclectic mix of naval and civilian specialists with unique and highly valuable skills. They provided the hydrographic surveying, diving support, weather forecasting and mobile repair services necessary for a navy aspiring to conduct autonomous operations around in the world.

The 1963 fleet even bears a favorable comparison with that of 1939, when the Marine nationale was at its most powerful since Napoleon III's naval buildup in the mid-nineteenth century. In terms of numbers and tonnage, Darlan's navy dwarfed that of Cabanier, with three hundred vessels displacing more than 745,000 tons, hence the deadly race between Churchill and Hitler as to who would control those ships and submarines after the fall of France. And yet, an important part of that tonnage was taken up by obsolete battleships and heavy cruisers. The focus on a confrontation with the Italians within the narrow span of the Mediterranean shaped newer builds in the interwar period. This fixation resulted in faster and more heavily armed units but without the autonomy, carrier aviation, and fleet train capabilities that became hallmarks of the war at sea during the conflict and dominated naval strategy in the atomic age. The French lagged behind *les Anglo-Saxons* in terms of radars, sonars, and electronic warfare in 1939 as well as in antiair and antisubmarine weapons and tactics, and only allied assistance prevented the gap from becoming much larger during the war years.

French admirals of the early Cold War succeeded in overcoming many of these shortcomings. They decried the lack of shipbuilding in the immediate postwar years, but this involuntary pause allowed them to reflect more extensively on the lessons of World War II. They had time to include in-depth studies on the impact of the atomic factor at sea. The burst of naval construction that started in the early 1950s produced vessels and aircraft of much greater quality than what could have been built in the mid-1940s. Completed along her prewar design, *Richelieu* was obsolete in 1945 and, had French authorities accepted to expedite the completion of cruiser *De Grasse* immediately after the war, the latter would have proven as ill-adapted to the new realities of the Cold War era. And yet, armed for long-range antiair defense ten years later, *De Grasse* joined a rejuvenated fleet that included modern platforms fitted with some of the most advanced technologies France, Great Britain, and the United States could produce in terms of engineering plants, weapons, and sensors.

As good as the matériel state of the fleet was, so were the surface sailors, submariners, naval aviators, *fusiliers-marins*, and commandos of the Marine nationale. Cabanier and his fellow senior officers had fought throughout the years of World War II, at least in the case of those who rallied to the Gaulle after the armistice. Even those who waited on the sidelines while loyal to Pétain spent the last two years of the conflict engaged in renewed convoy battles and large-scale amphibious operations with the Allies. They observed the effects of new tactics and learned the intricacies of the complex equipment transferred from the United States after the adoption of the Anfa Plan. Regardless of their conflicting wartime allegiances, officers and sailors of both camps united after the defeat of the Axis powers to fight successive insurgencies, developing unique skills in littoral and riverine warfare. They had missed the American experience of carrier warfare in the Pacific, but continued participation in large-scale NATO exercises in the 1950s exposed them to all aspects of war at sea in the nuclear age. Although a political and strategic blunder, the Suez experience provided an impetus for France's admirals to review doctrine and training for the conduct of joint operations in the littoral and power projection ashore in cooperation with the other services.

Recognized within the Alliance as effective staff planners ashore and aggressive warriors at sea, French naval officers also proved themselves as innovators in close cooperation with the country's defense industry. By the early 1960s the Marine nationale was ready to enter the missile age and develop the technologies that would influence the later years of the Cold War at sea. Battleship *Jean Bart* and cruiser *De Grasse* were considered for extensive renovations that would have seen their main gun armament replaced by batteries of antiship and antiair missiles, but these proposals proved too expensive.[12] Nevertheless, frigate *Suffren* and fast patrol boat *La Combattante*, both under construction in 1963, served as test beds for the validation of the antiaircraft missile Masurca (*marine surface contre-avions*) and, later, the development of the famed Exocet ship-killer.[13] Submarine *Gymnote* not only conducted the first firings of the M1 MSBS ballistic missile but also supported evaluation of other advanced submarine systems, including the first French attempts at inertial navigation.[14] Variable-depth sonars would soon be deployed at sea, and escorts would be fitted with a flight deck and hangar facilities to accommodate a helicopter capable of detecting and fighting submarines well before they could pose a threat to their mother ship or the convoys they escorted.[15]

However, in contrast to these qualitative developments, French admirals remained aware that quantity provided an edge of its own in naval warfare. In that fundamental aspect, they failed to achieve the goals established by Chief of Staff Nomy in 1952 and 1955. Table C.1 shows an impressive figure of 79,000 tons in new ships and submarines soon to join the fleet. But these numbers included the last of only two aircraft carriers (*Foch*), and cruiser *Jeanne d'Arc*, which would be a one-for-one replacement for her predecessor to be employed mainly as a training platform. The groundbreaking fast patrol craft *La Combattante* and submarine *Gymnote* were trial vessels rather than actual fighting units. The six Commandant Rivière sloop-escorts and the nine *Daphné*-class submarines were welcome additions, but they replaced older vessels soon to go out of commission as well as the four modern *Aréthuse*-class submersibles, which had proved a flawed concept. Admittedly, the first-of-class amphibious vessel *Ouragan* and three new replenishment ships brought badly needed capabilities to the fleet. Nevertheless, most worryingly for Cabanier, de Gaulle's first five-year defense plan for the period 1960–64 did not include a third aircraft carrier or a third AA cruiser, and the plan limited funding for ships to the refit of five existing escort vessels to embark the French Malafon ASW system and another two to assume the AA role with the fitting of RIM-24 Tartar surface-to-air missile.[16]

Nomy only succeeded in securing the first two of the annual 30,000-ton building tranches he deemed necessary to make his Plan bleu a reality by 1963. The day-to-day burden of the Algerian War and the commitment to develop the atomic bomb greatly limited the ability of all three services to acquire modern conventional armament systems in sufficient numbers. For Rue Royale planners, this reality meant that the fleet could not always dispatch a high-readiness *groupe d'intervention naval* without much warning—let alone two, one for NATO and one for national tasks. Given the vagaries of planned refits and training cycles, they could not guarantee that at least one aircraft carrier and one AA cruiser would be available to join a suitable retinue of escorts to deploy without notice, should a crisis arise in Europe or further afar in the world. And even were such a pair available to respond to a particular flare-up, Admiral Cabanier would be hard pressed to deploy a similar force somewhere else or ensure a continuous rotation of carriers and cruisers to maintain a single, self-sustaining force deployed for any more than one year.

In this light, the Marine nationale in 1963 could be judged harshly for a navy that aspired to make an important contribution to the defense of the *métropole* and the Alliance in Europe and to project France's influence overseas through worldwide reach. French admirals never quite resolved the inherent tensions that arose in the 1960s between the development of an effective expeditionary fleet and the launching of a credible seagoing nuclear deterrent. De Gaulle himself put the matter to rest by unflinchingly favoring the latter in the two *lois-programmes* promulgated during his presidency and abandoning the country's integration in NATO. This realignment of priorities shocked many in the navy, just as it did in the other services where senior army and air force officers also denounced the rise of the *force de frappe*.[17] For them, the development of nuclear weapons could only come at an unacceptable cost to the conventional military capabilities of the country. They also believed that leaving the Alliance's integrated military structures severed invaluable access to the doctrinal and technical know-how of the Anglo-Americans and the aggregated benefits of working and training with much larger fleets, air wings and armies in realistic scenarios.

And yet Cabanier presided over this transition without complaint, at least publicly. There would be no "revolt of the admirals" under de Gaulle, just as there had not been one during the years of the Fourth Republic, or during the Vichy years for that matter. In late 1958 Admiral Nomy elaborated a draft update to the Plan bleu de 1955 outlining the composition of the fleet for 1970 wherein he underlined the importance of the number three to maintain a single capacity available for deployment at sea, hence the demand for a minimum of three aircraft carriers, three AA cruisers, and so on. Referring to this plan in a September 1961 report addressed to the *ministre des Armées*, Cabanier admitted that prevailing budgetary constraints placed such ambitions beyond reach: "I remind you of the circumstances which hamper the achievement of the [1958] vision. Thus, my staff used another volume of forces—a volume which I have said in the past is a forced compromise, the least bad possible between needs based on a rational assessments of the missions assigned and the financial considerations outlined hereafter. This provides us with a minimum plan better suited to the current situation."[18]

Neither a third aircraft carrier nor a third AA cruiser would be built in France during Cabanier's tenure as he accepted, instead, the immediate requirement to fund construction of three SSBNs (the other three were eventually funded in the 1970s). Within two years, the decision to purchase Crusader jet fighters from the United States negated the option of building a third *Suffren*-class frigate.[19] Philippe Quérel completed his study of the Fourth Republic's naval policy with a chapter titled "L'expansion brisée" [Broken growth]; the very last sentence in Philippe Masson's magisterial history of France's navy decried the propensity of the French nation to turn its back on the sea; and, most recently, retired Admiral Rémi Monaque denounced the rise in influence of civil servants at the expanse of professional military advice in the formulation of naval policy in France.[20] Such ominous formulas give a rather negative connotation to Cabanier's reference to "a forced compromise, the least bad possible." Nevertheless, can these words not be used today—with the unfair advantage of hindsight—to describe as a success France's quest for an independent naval policy within a strategy of alliance after the 1940 Armistice?

From the forlorn Muselier in London to the newly rallied Michelier in North Africa, from Lemonnier once back in Paris to his Cold War successors, was there any way to succeed but by shaping the least bad compromises forced on them by dire national circumstances and exacting Allied requirements? The only admiral who dealt with French political authorities from a position of strength after June 1940 was Darlan. He controlled a powerful fleet, the only potent military force still available to the Vichy regime to exercise some form of leverage in its dealing with the Axis and the Allies. But even then the Forces de haute mer were already on life support, with the formulation of naval policy limited to the terms of the armistice, which only allowed for a few units to continue operations. Any thoughts of modernization or rejuvenation remained in stasis until France could find its place in a new European order led by a victorious Germany. Defeatism led to collaboration under Pétain, and the fleet commanders refused to rally to Darlan in Algiers in November 1942. Thereafter, officers and sailors could only seek honor through abnegation by scuttling their ships and submarines in Toulon, a bitter end to a controversial episode of rare supremacy by the navy over the military affairs of a diminished France.

Another admiral thought himself in a position of strength vis-à-vis his political leader, but de Gaulle proved Muselier wrong. The young brigadier and the retired "swashbuckler" grieved together in the wake of Operation Catapult and the catastrophe at Mers el-Kébir in July 1940. The commander of the nearly still-birthed Forces navales françaises libres then showed his strength in quickly setting about building up a small but effective force of ships and submarines in close—if often tense—collaboration with the British. Within weeks, vessels put to sea and started making a fighting contribution to the Allied effort while serving the political ends of "the leader of all Free Frenchmen, wherever they may be." Both were supremely dedicated to their cause but, whenever conflict arose between these two fiery personalities, de Gaulle easily gained the upper hand over the politically inept sailor. Muselier vastly overestimated his following within the ranks of the Free French navy and among the British. When he sought support from both in March 1942, forcing them to make a choice between de Gaulle and himself, he should not have been surprised that they backed le Général.

That Muselier lost his post over personal differences with de Gaulle was regrettable as the first FNFL commander left an impressive professional legacy behind. He promoted some ill-thought schemes in the summer of 1940 (crewing the obsolete, manpower-intensive battleship *Courbet* and seeking a direct agreement with the Royal Navy that would have made the FNFL a foreign naval legion). One cannot ascribe to him the promulgation of an actual naval policy or a strategy during this turmoil, beyond the ambition to crew as many ships and submarines as quickly as recruitment and training of new sailors would allow. And de Gaulle, not Muselier, negotiated the August 1940 accord with Prime Minister Churchill that secured active political support for his movement and instituted the collaborative framework that shaped Free French military forces in subsequent years. Nevertheless, Muselier must be recognized for the large role he played in the application of the agreement's clauses. He was involved in several precedents in terms of allied naval cooperation that defined new command and control practices as well as matters of logistics and maintenance, combined training, and coordinated operations. These procedures endured through the remainder of the conflict and returned during the Cold War when the Atlantic Alliance was resurrected to face down the Soviet threat.

In that light, Muselier's tour proved quite successful in leveraging these precedents to assemble a small but effective instrument necessary for de Gaulle to lay a credible foundation for his claim to legitimacy as national leader and military commander in the early stage of the war. By 1942 his fleet symbolized the first of many least bad compromises forced on French admirals by their Anglo-American partners and their own political masters in the following decades. Muselier did not select the vessels he wished to take back; he received those that the Admiralty was willing to part with. Bringing these units into service depended as much on the availability of British yards as the Free French capacity to recruit and train new sailors. Acquisition of modern Flower-class corvettes did not result from Muselier's lobbying effort but rather from the Royal Navy's wish to avoid dedicating scarce resources to repairing and modernizing obsolete French ships for which no spares and ammunition could be found in England.

The initial deal struck between Darlan and Major General Mark Clark, USA, immediately after the North African landing, and the open-ended commitment of Roosevelt to rearming Giraud's forces in early 1943 seemed to place Vice Admiral Félix Michelier on firmer footing. Particularly symbolic was the early refit of battleship *Richelieu* in the United States, of major significance to the French but considered of less relevance by the Americans in terms of a making an effective fighting contribution to the Alliance. However, both Michelier and his successor, André Lemonnier, soon faced increased reluctance by the U.S. Navy to accept French priorities for modernization work in American shipyards. While light cruisers *Montcalm*, *Gloire*, *Georges Leygues*, and *Émile Bertin* were all modernized in the United States in 1943, Admiral Ernest King steadily refused pleas from Lemonnier for heavier and older cruisers to access American shipyards for the same purpose in 1944. The U.S. Navy clearly wished for the French navy to focus on local escort and coastal defense duties in North and West Africa rather than lose themselves in grandiose visions of a rejuvenated blue-water navy.

Ironically, direct U.S. support to the Marine nationale reached a crest that year, supplemented by smaller-scale but continued deliveries of British material to the former FNFL group still based in the United Kingdom. From August 1943 to the following summer, the newly reunited Marine nationale dramatically grew in strength with the import of six U.S. Cannon-class destroyer escorts, six U.K. River-class frigates, four RN submarines (including one captured from the Italians), thirty-two U.S. patrol craft, and fifty U.S. submarine chasers as well as thirty minesweepers from the U.S. Navy and another ten from the Royal Navy. Numerous fighters and patrol aircraft also provided the basis for the renaissance of the Aéronautique. Meanwhile, both Washington and London continued to provide direct financial and logistical support to the French navy; kept their schools open to French sailors, aviators, and submariners; provided refit and repair services to French vessels already in service; and dedicated valuable resources to rehabilitating and often expanding shore infrastructures of the reunited Marine nationale, in the colonies first and then in the *métropole* itself after the Liberation. Deliveries of amphibious craft followed in 1945 as the British and the Americans facilitated the return of French military forces to Indochina.

President Truman continued the policy of his predecessor regarding the French navy. Provision of financial and material support as well as transfer of ships and aircraft were guided by allied wartime needs, not postwar ambitions on the part of the Rue Royale staff. The latter reluctantly accepted the prevailing approach but even before the end of the hostilities they were already making plans to shape a truly national naval policy that would provide France with a blue-water fleet worthy of a continental power with worldwide interests. However, the continued rejuvenation of the French fleet depended on political support in France. De Gaulle and then his Fourth Republic successors faced a complex array of conflicting demands and priorities in rebuilding civilian infrastructure in the *métropole*, resuming control over the territories of the Union française and appropriating resources between the three military services. Although no political authority dared asking "what good will a navy be to us now," the grandiose naval plans of 1945 were quickly set aside. Instead, the wartime transfer of *Dixmude*, the modernization of obsolete cruisers, and the acquisition of humble escorts and coastal defense vessels suddenly assumed their full meaning as another form of least bad forced compromise.

Dixmude—soon joined by *Arromanches* on loan from the British—provided an essential platform to maintain the basic skills and develop the new procedures necessary to shape the future Aéronavale. Older French ships refitted in British and American yards transported and supported the forces dispatched from Europe to the former colonies. *Fusiliers-marins* and commando troops still donning U.S. uniforms and carrying weapons provided by the United States fought nationalist insurgencies in Madagascar, Indochina, and Algeria, supported by wartime aircraft that proved better suited for that purpose than the first jets then under development in France. American- and British-built minesweepers made a pivotal contribution to clearing the coasts of France and North Africa, allowing safe access to the ports needed to receive the material needed to rebuild the country's infrastructures and export manufactured goods from rejuvenated industrial hubs. Small but new escort and coastal defense vessels transferred from North America and Great Britain played a key role in the *métropole* and across the Union française. They discharged important security duties and supported the training of the next generation of French officers and sailors who went on to crew and eventually command the Cold War ships, submarines, air squadrons, and *fusiliers-marins* regiments of the next two decades.

Transferred allied equipment and older French units modernized in British and North American shipyards during the hostilities provided the essential means for the French navy to bridge the gap in a peacetime world devoid of allies. France lacked the resources to rejuvenate its fleet independently during those years, but the gradual return to a strategy of alliance in 1947–48 provided French admirals with a new combination of threats and opportunities. The moment of greatest danger came in 1948–49, when defense minister Paul Ramadier sought to implement a new military policy facilitated by the return of the Atlantic Alliance. He championed a powerful *corps aéroterrestre* dedicated to the defense of the Rhine, leaving the security of the country's sea lines of communications to the Anglo-Americans. Ironically, pressure from the United States and the United Kingdom prevented this potential eclipse of French sea power as USN and RN admirals favored mission specialization among the Alliance's navies.

They needed the continental navies to look after their own coasts and local convoys. Ramadier's overly simplistic *défense du Rhin* quickly faded from view, and French admirals enthusiastically set about negotiating new terms for allied assistance, a prospect heightened by the start of Korean War in June 1950. The execution of this renewed aid program relied on World War II procedural and technical precedents, which laid the foundations for the highly efficient distribution of matériel, training, and financial support through the following decade. But these precedents also gave rise to bitter tensions similar to those that had often soured naval relations between France and the Anglo-American powers during the previous hostilities.

Allied assistance finally allowed Admiral Nomy to lead the fleet and the Aéronavale on a path of simultaneous qualitative and quantitative growth. Had the era of least bad forced compromises come to an end? Not quite. As in the days of World War II, the ambitions of French admirals vying to create a blue-water navy clashed with allied naval priorities. Rue Royale demands for the provision of fleet aircraft carriers and large, fast destroyers to form the nucleus of task groups capable of discharging the full range of carrier operations—shore and surface strike, air defense, ASW—repeatedly met with firm rebuffs. American insistence that France grows its forces at sea as well as the *corps aéroterrestre* in Germany certainly assisted Admiral Nomy in dealing with political authorities in France to shape a more balanced policy in the wake of Ramadier's doctrine of defense of the Rhine. However, it failed to support a narrative behind the rejuvenation of a larger, multipurpose naval force, U.S. and British admirals reiterating that France ought to focus its effort at sea on subordinate missions.

Pentagon planners accepted that the Marine nationale faced circumstances different than those of its continental neighbors, such as Belgium and Italy (and the Netherlands, once they let go of the Dutch East Indies in 1949). The French fleet divided its ships, submarines, and aircraft between two maritime fronts (the Atlantic and the Mediterranean) and maintained more extensive sea lines of communications to North and West Africa as well as Union française territories well beyond NATO's area of responsibility. U.S. military chiefs also adhered to the White House view that fighting in faraway Indochina was part of the larger containment of Communism. The provision of material assistance to the French navy made allowance for these specific needs. MDAP deliveries of smaller and slower escorts, coastal patrol craft, and minesweepers were supplemented by two light aircraft carriers and different types of aircraft that allowed for the conduct of antisubmarine operations in European waters but could easily be adapted to provide air support to troops ashore in theaters further afield. Additional military production subsidized production in French yards of large fleet destroyers of the T-47 and T-53 types. The loan of old British S-class submarines made a considerable contribution to the ASW readiness of the surface fleet and the growth of the next generation of French submariners, especially as the U.S. Navy repeatedly refused to transfer, loan, or sell modern submarines to France.

The debate over aircraft carriers and submarines was representative of another compromise forced on the French navy by the Allies. They provided the means needed by the Marine nationale to meet its Alliance commitments in the North Atlantic and the Mediterranean but nothing further, with the notable exception of Indochina, an experience not repeated in Algeria even though that territory was officially included in the NATO region until 1962. But it also showed Nomy's ability to make this compromise another "least bad one" as previous naval commanders had succeeded doing since 1940. Allied assistance filled genuine needs. Nomy and his colleagues welcomed direct transfers and subsidies provided to the navy and French shipbuilding industry. They did not allow disagreements with their Anglo-American counterparts to undermine that effort within the strategy of alliance pursued by Fourth Republic political leaders. Instead, they framed a naval policy that secured national resources—financial and material—for the production of those remaining means necessary for the fleet to resume its status as an effective blue-water force capable of autonomous operations in all three dimensions of the maritime domain, in European waters and around the world.

Nomy's draft Statut naval de 1952 and Plan bleu de 1955 achieved just that, including the provisions for annual building tranches of 30,000 tons. Nomy secured inclusion of the first two in the 1956 and 1957 defense budgets, thus allowing for the construction of two aircraft carriers designed and built in France. However, that he could not repeat this success in 1958 was ominous. The 30,000-ton figure rested in part on three key assumptions: allied assistance was set to continue, hostilities in Algeria would soon come to an end, and the quest for an atomic bomb did not involve the navy at this early stage. All three proved flawed just as de Gaulle returned to power.

The rearmament of West Germany, the Suez crisis, the increasing reluctance of the U.S. Congress to fund European armies and defense industries, and France's constant bickering about its roles and proper place within NATO formed a background of increasing strains that drove the Eisenhower administration to end direct aid to European allies by 1960. Although brought to power by a quasi-military coup in order to resolve the Algerian question, de Gaulle realized that a quick solution was nowhere in sight. If anything, he needed to increase the commitment of economic and military resources to the Algerian departments in order to achieve conditions that would allow for an acceptable peace. And, of most impact on the future development of the country's conventional forces, especially the navy, the leader of the Fifth Republic took two fateful decisions in quick succession: operationalize an independent *force de frappe* and grow the nuclear deterrent into a full triad.

Nomy spent his last two years in command of the Marine nationale accepting that the implementation of his 1952 and 1955 plans were delayed as a result of the increase in defense funding directed to Algeria and atomic research. The end of allied assistance compounded the issue, but he believed that peace in North Africa would provide an opportunity for his successor to resume course toward a balanced, aircraft carrier-centric expeditionary fleet by 1970. However, within a year of taking charge at the Rue Royale, Cabanier had already accepted another forced compromise—the "least bad" possible, perhaps, but a significant concession nevertheless—agreeing to a further delay in the construction of a third aircraft carrier. Two years later, de Gaulle's decision to pursue the construction of ballistic nuclear submarines in France irremediably crippled the naval staff's original vision. The third carrier project was set aside indefinitely. Acquisition of additional American aircraft showed the continued inability of French industry to provide for Aéronavale needs in the coming years, even forcing cancellation of a third AA cruiser in 1965. And yet the French president proclaimed that same year that the navy stood at "the apex of France's military power."

Such dissonance often results from the varied interpretations forced compromises can give rise to, especially as perceived by contemporary observers. On the one hand, the fractured history of the Marine nationale after the armistice—a navy at war with itself, its allies, and its government—can be derided as a succession of broken dreams, misplaced ambitions, betrayals by perfidious partners overseas and an ungrateful nation at home. None of the commanders, from Muselier to Cabanier, ever achieved the elaborate visions outlined through the years. On the other hand, hindsight shows their remarkable ability to shape the compromises forced on them by allied military leaders and national political figures through the fall and rise of French sea power during these years. Securing such "least bad" arrangements allowed successive ministers and admirals to rebuild the fleet and the Aéronavale with a rare singularity of purpose—an independent naval policy within a strategy of alliance—through the terrible ordeal of World War II and the arduous renaissance of the Cold War.

NOTES

INTRODUCTION

1. "Cuban Missile Crisis: Telegram From the Embassy in France to the Department of State," 22 October 1962, Yale Law School, The Avalon Project, http://avalon.law.yale.edu/20th_century/msc_cuba046.asp#1.

2. John F. Kennedy, "Address given by John F. Kennedy in Philadelphia, 4 July 1962," in *John F. Kennedy, Containing the public messages, speeches and statements of the president: January 1 to December 31, 1962* (Washington: U.S. Government Printing Office, 1963), 1018.

3. "Conférence de presse du 14 janvier 1963" [Press Conference 14 January 1963], Fondation Charles de Gaulle, http://fresques.ina.fr/de-gaulle/fiche-media/Gaulle00085/conference-de-presse-du-14-janvier-1963-sur-l-entree-de-la-grande-bretagne-dans-la-cee.html.

4. "Traité de l'Élysée (22 janvier 1963)" [Élysée Treaty (22 January 1963)], franco-allemand, http://www.france-allemagne.fr/Traite-de-l-Elysee-22-janvier-1963.

5. Eric J. Grove, *Vanguard to Trident: British Naval Policy since World II* (Annapolis, MD: Naval Institute Press, 1987), 235–39; and Andrew Priest, "In American Hands: Britain, the United States and the Polaris Nuclear Project 1962–1968," *Contemporary British History* 19, no. 3 (Autumn 2005): 353–76.

6. No single and universally accepted definition of the term "blue-water navy" exists, especially as technology evolved through the centuries. For the purpose of this text, and given the period in question, the term will refer to a navy that can discharge, independently of other nations, the full range of military missions in the three dimensions of the maritime realm—that is, in the air, on the surface, and below—off the country's shores in permanence and in regions overseas for extended periods of time. For an insight into the complexities of using particular

typologies or assigning ranking when discussing navies, see Eric Grove, *The Future of Sea Power* (London: Routledge, 1990), 236–40.

7. For the de Gaulle's own perspective, see his *Le salut, 1944–1946*, tome 3 de *Mémoires de guerre* (Paris: Plon, 1959), 179–80; and its English translation, *Salvation, 1944–1946*, trans. Richard Howard, vol. 3 of *War Memoirs* (London: Weidenfled and Nicholson, 1960), 178–79.

8. Rob Stuart, "Was the RCN Ever the Third Largest Navy?" *Canadian Naval Review* 5, no. 2 (Fall 2009): 8–9.

9. Quoted in Theodore Ropp, *The Development of a Modern Navy—French Naval Policy, 1871–1904*, ed. Stephen S. Roberts (Annapolis, MD: Naval Institute Press, 1987), 31.

10. *"Métropole"* will be used throughout this text in reference to "metropolitan France," understood to encompass the mainland in continental Europe and the island of Corsica but exclusive of the Algerian departments (although legally considered part of the French mainland until 1962) and all other overseas possessions.

11. Adm. Georges Cabanier, Chief of Staff of the French Navy, to *ministre des Armées* Pierre Messmer, "Révision du plan naval à long terme—Perspectives et implications d'un 2ᵉ plan quinquennal" [Review of the Naval Long-term Plan—Perspectives and Consequences of a 2nd Five-Year Plan], 5 September 1961, in Service historique de la Défense [Defense Historical Service], Vincennes, FR [hereafter, SHD], 3 BB 8 CEM 19.

12. This is especially genuine in French naval historiography when consulting studies such as Philippe Masson, *La Marine française et la guerre, 1939–1945* [The French navy and the War, 1939–1945], 2nd ed. (Paris: Tallandier, 2000); Philippe Quérel, *Vers une marine atomique: La marine française (1945–1958)* [Toward a Nuclear Navy: The French navy (1945–1958)] (Paris: LGDJ, 1997); and Philippe Strub, "La renaissance de la marine française sous la Quatrième République (1945–1956): La Quatrième République a-t-elle eu une ambition navale pour la France"? [Renewal of the French navy during the Fourth Republic (1945–1956): Did the Fourth Republic have a naval ambition?] (PhD thesis, Université Paris I, 2006). The more recent Alain Boulaire, *La marine française: De la Royale de Richelieu aux missions d'aujourd'hui* [The French navy: From Richelieu's *Royale* to the missions of today] (Quimper, FR: Éditions Palantines, 2011); and Étienne Taillemite, *Histoire ignorée de la Marine française* [Unknown history of the French navy], 3rd ed. (Paris: Perrin, 2010) also separate the later part of their respective studies into similar blocks.

13. Some examples: Jean Moulin, *Les porte-avions français* [French aircraft carriers] (Rennes, FR: Marines Éditions, 2008); John Jordan and Robert Dumas, *French Battleships: 1922–1956* (Annapolis, MD: Naval Institute Press, 2009); Bernard Estival, *La marine française dans la guerre d'Indochine* [The French navy in the Indochina war] (Rennes, FR: Marines Éditions, 2007); Bernard Estival, *La Marine française dans la guerre d'Algérie* [The French navy in the Algerian war]

(Rennes, FR: Marines Éditions, 2012); and Jean-Jacques Hucherot, *La marine française en Afrique subsaharienne de 1946 à 1960* [The French navy in sub-Saharan Africa from 1946 to 1960] (Paris: Institut catholique de Paris, 2001).

14. Both Ernest H. Jenkins, *A History of the French Navy: From Its Beginnings to the Present Day* (London: Macdonald and Jane's, 1973); and Philippe Masson, *De la vapeur à l'atome*, vol. 2 of *Histoire de la marine* [From steam to the atom, vol. 2 of History of the French navy] (Paris: Lavauzelle, 1992) are typical and valuable accounts shaped along the chronological approach. Two rare studies dedicated to naval policy under the Fourth Republic remain the works of French doctoral candidates, each more concerned with the budgetary process than the shaping of the strategy at the origins of such financial demands: Philippe Quérel, "La politique navale de la France sous la Quatrième République" [The naval policy of France under the Fourth Republic] (PhD thesis, Université de Reims, 1992) and the previously cited Strub, "La renaissance de la marine française."

15. Sean M. Maloney, *Securing Command of the Sea: NATO Naval Planning, 1948–1954* (Annapolis, MD: Naval Institute Press, 1995), 2.

16. For another representative work, see Joel J. Sokolsky, *Sea power in the Nuclear Age: The United States Navy and NATO, 1949–1980* (London: Routledge, 1991).

17. Although offering contrasting political perspectives, two sources provide complimentary operational histories of the competing French navies during the Second World War: Paul Auphan and Jacques Mordal, *La Marine française dans la Seconde Guerre mondiale* [The French navy and the Second World War], 2nd ed. (Paris: France-Empire, 1967); and Émile Chaline and Pierre Santarelli, *Historique des Forces Navales Françaises Libres* (2 tomes) [History of the Free French Naval Forces (2 vols.)] (Paris: Service historique de la marine, 1990 and 1992). Bernard Estival's previously referenced volumes on French naval operations in Indochina and Algeria are also valuable. For more recent treatments, see the last two chapters in Rémi Monaque's magisterial *Une histoire de la marine de guerre française* [A history of the French navy] (Paris: Perrin, 2016), 389–454; as well as Jean-Baptiste Bruneau and Thomas Vaisset, "Déchirements, déclassement et relèvement (1939–1945)" [Fractures, fall and rise (1939–1945)], *L'histoire d'une révolution: La Marine depuis 1870* [History of a revolution: The navy since 1870] Études marines no. 4 (March 2013): 68–81; and Philippe Vial and Patrick Boureille, "Guerres, modernisation et expansion (1945–1958)" [Wars, modernization and expansion (1945–1958)], *L'histoire d'une révolution: La Marine depuis 1870* [History of a Revolution: The Navy Since 1870] Études marines no. 4 (March 2013): 82–104.

18. For an excellent treatment of this particular subject, one can consult Bernard Cassagnou, *Les grandes mutations de la Marine marchande française (1945–1995)* [The great changes in the French merchant navy (1945–1995)], 2 vols. (Vincennes, FR: Comité pour l'histoire économique et financière de la France, 2003).

19. Richard Harding, *Modern Naval History: Debates and Prospects* (London: Blooms-bury, 2016), 1. The citation is from John Ehrman, *The Navy in the War of William III, 1689–1697: Its State and Direction* (Cambridge: Cambridge University Press, 1953), xxii.

CHAPTER 1. SETTING THE PRECEDENT

1. "Admiralty—Diary of Events—Wednesday, 3rd July, 1940," Admiralty, Cor-respondence and Papers, ADM 1/10321: French Warships at Oran and Alexandria on the Surrender of France 1940, The National Archives, Kew, UK (hereafter, TNA). Excellent book-length treatments of that dramatic episode can be found in Hervé Coutau-Bégarie and Claude Huan, *Mers el-Kébir (1940), la rupture franco-britannique* [Mers el-Kébir (1940), the Franco-British Rupture], (Paris: Economica, 1994); and David Brown, *The Road to Oran: Anglo-French Naval Relations, September 1939–July 1940* (London: Frank Cass, 2004).

2. "Commander-in-Chief, Mediterranean at Alexandria—Diary of Events—From Wednesday, 3rd July, 1940 and Thursday, 4th July, 1940," ADM 1/10321, TNA; and Attack on Richelieu, 1940, "Signals from the Admiralty to HMS *Hermes*," 7 and 11 July 1940, ADM 1/10835, TNA.

3. "Signals Exchanged Between Admiralty, C-in-C Mediterranean and Vice Admiral Force H," 30 June to 2 July 1940, ADM 1/10321, TNA; and "Force H—Diary of Events—From Wednesday, 3rd July, 1940," ADM 1/10321, TNA. For the battle's impact on the Vichy navy, see Odile Girardin-Thibeaud, *Les amiraux de Vichy* [Vichy's admirals] (Paris: Nouveau Monde, 2016), 187–202.

4. Charles de Gaulle, *L'Appel, 1940–1942*, tome 1 de *Mémoires de guerre* (Paris: Plon, 1954), 77–78; and Charles de Gaulle, *The Call to Honour, 1940–1942*, trans. Jonathan Griffin, vol. 1 of *War Memoirs* (London: Collins, 1955), 96–97; as well as Émile Muselier, *Marine et résistance* [Navy and resistance] (Paris: Flammarion, 1945), 71–72; and Émile Muselier, *De Gaulle contre le Gaullisme* [De Gaulle against Gaullism] (Paris: Éditions du Chêne, 1946), 20–21.

5. Éric Roussel, *Charles de Gaulle* (Paris: Gallimard, 2002), 152–53; see also Edward Spears, *Two Men Who Saved France: Petain and de Gaulle* (London: Eyre & Spottiswoode, 1966), 164–65.

6. Jonathan Fenby, *The General: Charles de Gaulle and the France He Saved* (London: Simon & Schuster, 2010), 141.

7. Philippe Masson, *Histoire de l'armée française de 1914 à nos jours* [History of the French Army from 1914 to today] (Paris: Perrin, 1999), 325–26 and 340–42.

8. Thierry d'Argenlieu, "Les origines des FNFL" [Origins of the FNFL], *Revue de la France libre* 29 (June 1950): 17.

9. De Gaulle, *Call to Honour*, 97. Original statement in French in de Gaulle, *L'Appel*, 78.

10. Spears, *Two Men Who Saved France*, 136–39; and Christine Levisse-Touzé, "Le Général de Gaulle et les débuts de la France libre" [General de Gaulle and the beginnings of Free France], *Revue historique des Armées* 219, no. 2 (June 2000): 66.

11. "Leader of Free Frenchmen—Recognition by British Govt. of Gen. de Gaulle," *Barrier Miner*, 29 June 1940, 1.

12. Roussel, *Charles de Gaulle*, 150.

13. François Charles-Roux, *Cinq mois tragiques aux Affaires* étrangères [Five tragic months at Foreign Affairs] (Paris: Plon, 1949), 158; and "France Breaks with Britain—'Unjustifiable' Oran Attack," *Daily Telegraph*, 6 July 1940, p. 1.

14. Mr. Dupuy (1941), Foreign Office (FO) 371/28234 and FO 371/28235, TNA; and Olivier Courteaux, *Canada between Vichy and Free France, 1940–1945* (Toronto, ON: Toronto University Press, 2013), 53–84.

15. Richard Griffiths, *Marshal Pétain* (London: Constable,1970), 248. For a recent, in-depth study, see Bénédicte Vergez-Chaignon, *Pétain* (Paris: Perrin, 2014).

16. Roussel, *Charles de Gaulle*, 160; and Daniel J. Mahoney, *De Gaulle: Statesmanship, Grandeur, and Modern Democracy*, 2nd ed. (New Brunswick, NJ: Transaction, 2000), 87–90.

17. Claude Huan, "Les négociations franco-britanniques de l'automne 1940" [The Franco-British negotiations of the fall of 1940], *Guerres mondiales et conflits contemporains* 176 (1994): 140–41; and Simon Berthon, *Allies at War: The Bitter Rivalry among Churchill, Roosevelt, and de Gaulle* (New York: Carroll & Graph, 2001), 31–32.

18. "Memorandum from Prime Minister Churchill to General Ismay," dated 12 July 1940, Cabinet Office, Special Secret Information Centre, CAB 121/541, France: French Fleet, TNA. For more statements on Churchill's role in these early months, see Spears, *Two Men Who Saved France*, 157–59; and Bernard Costagliola, *La Marine de Vichy: Blocus et collaboration* (Paris: Éditions Tallandier, 2009), 48–52.

19. Muselier commanded the Free French Air Force until a flying officer of suitable seniority rallied the movement in June 1941. De Gaulle, *L'Appel*, 76; de Gaulle, *Call to Honour*, 95; and Muselier, *Marine et résistance*, 27–28.

20. Girardin-Thibeaud, *Les amiraux de Vichy*, 14 and 184. The only biography of the admiral was published by his grandson, rich in details but to be approached cautiously given the family relationship. See Renaud Muselier, *L'amiral Muselier, 1882–1965: Le créateur de la croix de Lorraine* [Admiral Muselier, 1882–1965: Creator of the cross of Lorraine] (Paris: Perrin, 2000).

21. D'Argenlieu, "Les origines des FNFL," 17–20.

22. Hervé Coutau-Bégarie and Claude Huan, *Darlan* (Paris: Fayard, 1989), 32.

23. Claude Guy, *En écoutant de Gaulle: Journal 1946–1949* [Listening to de Gaulle: A journal 1946–1949] (Paris: Grasset, 1996), 182–83. See also Muselier, *L'amiral Muselier*, 107.

24. De Gaulle, *L'Appel*, 75; de Gaulle, *Call to Honour*, 93; Muselier, *Marine et résistance*, 32 and 51; and Émile Chaline, "Les Forces navales françaises libres" [The free French naval forces], *Espoir* no. 100 (January 1995), http://www.charles-de-gaulle .org/pages/l-homme/dossiers-thematiques/1940-1944-la-seconde-guerre -mondiale/forces-navales-francaises-libres/analyses/les-forces-navales-francaise -libre-fnfl.php.

25. Spears, *Two Men Who Saved France*, 158–59; and Anthony Heckstall-Smith, *The Fleet That Faced Both Ways* (London: Blond, 1963), 72.

26. Dorothy Shipley White, *Seeds of Discord: De Gaulle, Free France, & the Allies* (Syracuse, NY: Syracuse University Press, 1964), 215.

27. Spears, *Two Men Who Saved France*, 157–58; and Étienne Schlumberger and Alain Schlumberger, *Les combats et l'honneur des Forces navales françaises libres, 1940–1944* [The fighting and the honour of the Free French Naval Forces, 1940–1944] (Paris: Le cherche midi, 2007), 34–38.

28. "Armament Supplies for French Ships," 20 July 1940, Cabinet Office, Minister of Defence Secretariat, CAB 120/285, Re-commissioning of French Ships, TNA; and Coutau-Bégarie, *Mers el-Kébir*, 110.

29. "Note from the Prime Minister to the First Lord and the First Sea Lord," 5 July 1940, Cabinet Office, Minister of Defence Secretariat, CAB 120/541—*French Fleet*, TNA.

30. Muselier, *De Gaulle contre le Gaullisme*, 27–32 and 32–36; and Masson, *La Marine française et la guerre*, 195. Muselier may have been inspired in this initiative by the Polish–British naval agreement signed on 18 November 1939, but he does not refer to this particular document in his memoirs. Michael Alfred Peszke, "The British-Polish Agreement of August 1940: Its Antecedents, Significance, and Consequences," *Journal of Slavic Military Studies* 24, no. 4 (2011): 653.

31. Muselier, *De Gaulle contre le Gaullisme*, 42–43.

32. Muselier, *Marine et résistance*, 74–76; and Jacques Cornic, "Sous la Croix de Lorraine (under the Cross of Lorraine): The FNFL (*Forces Naval Françaises Libres*) 1940–1943 (Free French Naval Forces)," in *Warship International* 24, no. 1 (1987): 36 and 39.

33. Muselier, *Marine et résistance*, 77–78; and Chaline, "Les Forces navales françaises libres."

34. "Armament Supplies for French Ships," 9 August 1940, CAB 120/285, TNA.

35. Maguire, *Anglo-American Policy towards the Free French* (London: Macmillan, 1995), 6 and 12–13; and René Cassin, "Comment furent signés les accords Churchill-de Gaulle du 7 août 1940," in *Revue de la France Libre* 154 (January–February 1965), http://www.france-libre.net/accords-churchill-de-gaulle/.

36. "Minute from the Prime Minister to General Ismay," 26 July 1940, Cabinet Office, Minister of Defence Secretariat, CAB 120/539, General de Gaulle and Free French Forces, TNA.

37. "Accord du 7 août 1940 entre la France libre et le Royaume-Uni" [Agreement of 7 August 1940 between Free France and the United Kingdom], Digithèque MJP, last accessed 7 February 2015, http://mjp.univ-perp.fr/france/co1940fl2.htm#3.

38. Foreign Office (U.K.), *Command Paper 6220: Exchange of Letters Between the Prime Minister and General de Gaulle Concerning the Organisation, Employment and Conditions of Service of the French Volunteer Force, London 7 August 1940* (London: Her Majesty's Stationery Office, 1940).

39. Winston S. Churchill, *Their Finest Hour*, vol. 2 of *The Second World War* (Cambridge: Riverside Press, 1949), 508.

40. Cassin, "Comment furent signés les accords Churchill-de Gaulle."

41. De Gaulle, *Call to Honour*, 100–101. Original quote in French in de Gaulle, *L'Appel*, 81.

42. The agreement came after a similar entente was agreed to on 5 August with the Polish government in exile, but the scale of the Free French agreement dwarfed the other as precedent setting. Peszke, "The British-Polish Agreement of August 1940," 648–50 and 656–58.

43. "Anglo-French Conversations—Minutes of a Meeting Held at Alexandria," 2 June 1939, ADM, Correspondence and Papers, 1/9962, Anglo-French Co-operation in Mediterranean & Middle East 1939, TNA; and "Minutes of Anglo-French Conversations Held at Alexandria," 12 June 1939, ADM 1/9962, TNA.

44. The assignment of geographic areas of operation to French and British forces in the Mediterranean is best illustrated with a detailed map in Auphan and Mordal, *La Marine française*, 160–61. For an overall treatment of the 1939 Anglo-French naval talks, see George E. Melton, *From Versailles to Mers El-Kebir: The Promise of Anglo-French Naval Cooperation, 1919–40* (Annapolis, MD: Naval Institute Press, 2015), 113–33.

45. Auphan and Mordal, *La Marine française*, 156–57; and René-Émile Godfroy, *L'aventure de la Force X (Escadre française de la Méditerranée orientale) à Alexandrie (1940–1943)* [The adventure of Force X (French Eastern Mediterranean Fleet) in Alexandria (1940–1943)] (Paris: Plon, 1953), 3–5.

46. Godfroy, *L'aventure de la Force X*, 7–8. Cunningham confirmed this convivial spirit in his own memoirs, *A Sailor's Odyssey: The Autobiography of Admiral of the Fleet Viscount Cunningham of Hyndhope* (London: Hutchinson, 1951), 225.

47. Godfroy, *L'aventure de la Force X*, 57–78; Masson, *De la vapeur à l'atome*, 417–18; and Melton, *From Versailles to Mers El-Kebir*, 187–88.

48. Auphan and Mordal, *La Marine française*, 250–52; and Cornic, "Sous la Croix de Lorraine," 36.

49. Chaline, "Les Forces navales françaises libres"; and Masson, *La Marine française et la guerre*, 193.

50. Émile Chaline and P. Santarelli, "L'activité des F.N.F.L. du 18 juin 1940 au 3 août 1943" [Activity of the *FNFL* 18 June 1940 to 3 August 1943], *Revue historique de la*

Défence 176, no. 3 (September 1989): 72; and Jacques Cornic, "Ships for Crews," *Warship International* 22, no. 3 (1985), 252–53 and 257.

51. Cornic, "Ships for Crews," 252–53 and 257; and J. Lambert and A. Ross, *Allied Coastal Forces of World War II*, vol. 2 (London: Barnsley, 2019), 245.

52. French Western Africa (Afrique occidentale française) was a federation of eight colonial territories: Mauritania, Senegal, French Sudan (now Mali), French Guinea, Ivory Coast, Upper Volta (now Burkina Faso), Dahomey (now Benin), and Niger. The capital of the federation was Dakar.

53. Monaque, *Une histoire de la marine*, 415–17; and Costagliola, *La Marine de Vichy*, 64–66. For a full treatment, see Arthur J. Marder, *Operation Menace: The Dakar Expedition and the Dudley North Affair* (London: Oxford University Press, 1976).

54. Jordan and Dumas, *French Battleships*, 141–47.

55. De Gaulle, *L'Appel*, 108–10; de Gaulle, *The Call to Honour*, 133–35; Churchill, *Their Finest Hour*, 492–94; Godfroy, *L'aventure de la Force X*, 153–56; and Fenby, *The General*, 152–53.

56. The capital of the L'Afrique-équatoriale française was in Brazzaville, Congo. Chad, Cameroon, Congo, and Oubangui-Chari (today's Central African Republic) joined the Free French movement in quick succession on 26, 27, 28, and 29 August 1940. Maguire, *Anglo-American Policy towards the Free French*, 8; and Sylvain Cornil, "La France libre et l'Empire: le ralliement de l'Afrique" [Free France and the rallying of the empire], Fondation de la France libre, last modified 28 February 2009, http://www.france-libre.net/fl-empire-afrique/.

57. Schlumberger and Schlumberger, *Les combats et l'honneur*, 53–58; and Barthélémy Ntoma Mengome, *La bataille de Libreville—De Gaulle contre Pétain: 50 morts* [The battle of Libreville—De Gaulle against Pétain: 50 Killed] (Paris: L'Harmattan, 2013).

58. "General de Gaulle Honours Free French Navy 1941," British Pathé, 23 October 1941, https://www.britishpathe.com/video/general-de-gaulle-honours-free-french-navy; and "Free French Submarine," British Movietone, YouTube, 21 July 2015, https://www.youtube.com/watch?v=qbxovyWywto.

59. Chaline and Santarelli, "L'activité des F.N.F.L.," 70.

60. Monaque, *Une histoire de la marine*, 436–37.

61. Costagliola, *La Marine de Vichy*, 201. For a full treatment of Djibouti during those years, see Lukian Prijac, *Le blocus de Djibouti: Chronique d'une guerre décalée (1935–1943)* [The blockade of Djibouti: Chronicle of an asynchronous war (1935–1943)] (Paris: L'Harmattan, 2015).

62. D. Ignatieff, "Présence dans le Pacifique des navires de la France libre" [Presence in the Pacific of the Free French], *Bulletin de la Société d'Études historiques de la Nouvelle-Calédonie* 77 (2001): 33–43; and Thomas Vaisset, "Défendre et maintenir la France Libre aux antipodes" [To defend and keep Free France at the ends of the world], in *Les Français libres et le monde* [The Free French and the world] (Paris: Nouveau monde éditions, 2015), 75–88.

63. Berthon, *Allies at War*, 149–59; and Muselier, *De Gaulle contre le Gaullisme*, 299–316.

64. Yvan Combeau, "Le ralliement de La Réunion et de Madagascar à la France libre" [The rallying of La Réunion and Madagascar to Free France], *Les chemins de la mémoire* 231 (November 2012): 2–4; and Hervé Le Joubioux, "L'île de La Réunion dans la Seconde Guerre mondiale" [Réunion Island during the Second World War], *Revue historique des Armées* 263 (2011): 85–87.

65. Martin Thomas, "Imperial Backwater or Strategic Outpost? The British Takeover of Vichy Madagascar, 1942," *Historical Journal* 39, no. 4 (1996): 1058; and Louis-Gilles Pairault, "Le verrou de la mer Rouge: L'armée et la côte française des Somalie, 1884–1977" [Latch on the Red Sea: The army and French Somaliland, 1884–1977], *Institut de Stratégie Comparée*, last accessed 16 March 2020, http://www.institut-strategie.fr/RIHM_82_PAIRAULT2.html.

66. Masson, *Histoire de l'armée française*, 306–8; and *De la vapeur à l'atome*, 457–59.

67. Musée de l'Ordre de la Libération, "Le Groupe de chasse 'Île de France' (1941–1945)" [Fighter Group "Île de France" (1941–1945)], last accessed 4 November 2015, http://www.ordredelaliberation.fr/fr/compagnons/les-unites-militaires/le-groupe-de-chasse-_ile-de-france_-1941-1945.

68. Charles Edward La Haye, "L'aéronautique navale française libre" [Free French Naval Air], *Revue de la France libre* (18 June 1951), 25 May 2010, http://www.france-libre.net/aeronautique-navale-fl/.

69. Musée de l'Ordre de la Libération, "Le 1er Régiment de fusilier-marins" [The 1st Regiment of Naval Troops], last accessed 2 November 2015, http://www.ordredelaliberation.fr/fr/compagnons/les-unites-militaires/le-1er-regiment-de-fusiliers-marins.

70. Office national des anciens combattants, "Le 1er Bataillon de Fusiliers Marins Commandos" [1st Battalion of Naval Commandos], last accessed 13 November 2013, http://www.onac-vg.fr/files/uploads/le-1er-bataillon-de-fusiliers-marins-commandos.pdf.

71. Sources vary in stating the date of the sinking, alternating between 6 October and 7 November 1940. Auphan et Mordal, *La Marine française*, 252; Musée de la Résistance en ligne, "*Le patrouilleur* Poulmic" [Patrol Vessel *Poulmic*], last accessed 2 November 2015, http://museedelaresistanceenligne.org/media2880-Le-patrouilleur-iPoulmic-i.

72. Musée de la Résistance en ligne, "*Sous-marin* Narval" [Submarine *Narval*], last accessed 3 November 2015, http://museedelaresistanceenligne.org/media2879-Sous-marin-iNarval-i.

73. Auphan and Mordal, *La Marine française*, 251; and Monaque, *Une histoire de la marine*, 436.

74. Georges Robert, *La France aux Antilles de 1939 à 1943* [France in the Caribbean from 1939 to 1943] (Paris: Plon, 1950), 109–15; and F. A. Baptiste, "Le régime de Vichy à la Martinique (juin 1940 à juin 1943)" [The Vichy regime in Martinique

(June 1940 to June 1943)], *Revue d'histoire de la Deuxième Guerre mondiale* 28, no. III (July 1978): 12–13.

75. Spears, *Two Men Who Saved France*, 168; and Thomas, "Imperial Backwater or Strategic Outpost?," 1060.

76. Muselier, *De Gaulle contre le Gaullisme*, 26–27 and 64–71; Muselier, *L'amiral Muselier*, 117 and 124–25; and White, *Seeds of Discord*, 214 and 216.

77. De Gaulle, *Call to Honour*, 124; and de Gaulle, *L'Appel*, 101.

78. Muselier, *De Gaulle contre le Gaullisme*, 92–106; and Edmond Pognon, *De Gaulle et l'armée* [De Gaulle and the army] (Paris: Plon, 1976), 143.

79. Muselier, *Marine et résistance*, 100–101; Muselier, *L'amiral Muselier*, 106; and Pognon, *De Gaulle et l'armée*, 141.

80. De Gaulle, *L'Appel*, 119; de Gaulle, *Call to Honour*, 145; Muselier, *De Gaulle contre le Gaullisme*, 39–41; and Roussel, *Charles de Gaulle*, 196.

81. Muselier, *De Gaulle contre le Gaullisme*, 126–28; de Gaulle, *L'Appel*, 119; and de Gaulle, *Call to Honour*, 145.

82. Muselier, *De Gaulle contre le Gaullisme*, 226–36; de Gaulle, *L'Appel*, 219–21; de Gaulle, *Call to Honour*, 256–59; Pognon, *De Gaulle et l'armée*, 147–52; and Fenby, *The General*, 175–77.

83. Muselier, *De Gaulle contre le Gaullisme*, 38.

84. Pognon, *De Gaulle et l'armée*, 143. Muselier's growing esteem for the Westminster cabinet model is highlighted in Muselier, *L'amiral Muselier*, 123.

85. Muselier, *De Gaulle contre le Gaullisme*, 320–87; de Gaulle, *L'Appel*, 221–23; de Gaulle, *Call to Honour*, 259–61; Pognon, *De Gaulle et l'Armée*, 154–59; Roussel, *Charles de Gaulle*, 271–80; and White, *Seeds of Discord*, 328.

86. De Gaulle, *Call to Honour*, 258 and 261; and de Gaulle, *L'Appel*, 220–21 and 223.

87. Godfroy, *L'aventure de la Force X*, 135–37; Musée de l'Ordre de la Libération, "Philippe Auboyneau," last accessed 30 January 2020, https://www.ordredelaliberation .fr/fr/compagnons/philippe-auboyneau; and Étienne Taillemite, *Dictionnaire des marins français* [Dictionary of French sailors] (Paris: Tallandier, 2002), 18–19.

CHAPTER 2. LAYING THE FOUNDATIONS FOR REARMAMENT

1. Mark W. Clark, *Calculated Risk* (New York: Harper, 1950), 67–89; Charles Mast, *Histoire d'une rébellion—Alger, 8 novembre 1942* [History of a Rebellion—Algiers, 8 November 1942] (Paris: Plon, 1969), 97–114; and Robert Murphy, *Diplomat among Warriors* (Garden City, NY: Doubleday, 1964), 117–20. A witness account by Jacques Teissier, who lived in the house where the conference took place, appears in John H. Waller, *The Unseen War in Europe: Espionage and Conspiracy in the Second World War* (London: I. B. Tauris, 1996), 255–56.

2. Cable from General George C. Marshall to Lieutenant General Dwight D. Eisenhower, 17 October 1942, quoted by Marcel Vigneras in *Rearming the French*, United States Army in World War II series (Washington, DC: Center of Military History United States Army, 1989), 111.

3. Retransmission of a report from Major General Mark W. Clark to Lieutenant General Dwight D. Eisenhower in a cable from European Theater of Operations, United States Army (ETOUSA) to Adjutant General, War Department (AGWAR), 25 October 1942. Official Cables, 31 July–12 November 1942, Box 131, Principal File Series—Papers, Pre-Presidential, 1941–1952, Dwight D. Eisenhower Presidential Library, Abilene, KS (hereafter, DDEPL).

4. For overall surveys of the preparations for, execution of, and reactions to the North African landings, see No. 38: Invasion of North Africa (Operation TORCH) Nov. 1942–Feb. 1943, in Admiralty, Naval Staff History, ADM 234/359, The National Archives, Kew, UK (hereafter, TNA); Auphan and Mordal, *La Marine française*, 263–93; Masson, *La Marine française*, 356–78; Monaque, *Une histoire de la marine*, 422–28; and Christine Levisse-Touzé, *L'Afrique du Nord dans la guerre, 1939–1945* [North Africa during the War, 1939–1945] (Paris: Albin Michel, 1998), 233–61.

5. Mario Rossi, *Roosevelt and the French* (New York: Praeger, 1993), 93–94; and Canadian Forces College Information Resources Centre (hereafter CFC IRC), *Minutes of the Combined Chiefs of Staff Meetings, 1942–1945*, microfilms holdings, CFC IRC, Toronto, ON, Minutes of the 22nd CCS Meeting, 4 August 1942.

6. Charles de Gaulle, *L'unité, 1942–1944*, tome 2 of *Mémoires de guerre* [Unity, 1942–1944, vol. 2 of War memoirs] (Paris: Plon, 1956), 41–43; and Charles de Gaulle, *Unity, 1942–1944*, vol. 2 of *War Memoirs*, trans. Richard Howard (London: Weidenfled and Nicholson, 1959), 46–48. Churchill himself did not refer to the meeting in his memoirs but did go over the exchange of cables he had on this subject with President Roosevelt in *The Hinge of Faith*, vol. 4 of *The Second World War* (Cambridge: Riverside, 1950), 604–6. These cables can be found in full in Warren F. Kimball, ed., *Alliance Emerging, October 1933–November 1942*, vol. 1 of *Churchill and Roosevelt: The Complete Correspondence* (Princeton, NJ: Princeton Legacy Library, 1984), 660–61.

7. For a magisterial but concise analysis of Roosevelt's geopolitical thought through the interwar period to the fall of France, see Henry Kissinger, *Diplomacy* (New York: Simon & Schuster, 1994), 369–87. For Churchill's perspective, although he was out of power for much of that time, see B. J. C. McKercher, "The Limitations of the Politician-Strategist: Winston Churchill and the German Threat, 1933–1939," in *Churchill and the Strategic Dilemmas before the World Wars: Essays in Honor of Michael I. Handel*, ed. John H. Maurer, 88–120 (London: Frank Cass, 2003).

8. Steve Weiss, *Allies in Conflict: Anglo-American Strategic Negotiations, 1938–1944* (London: Macmillan, 1996), 15; and Kissinger, *Diplomacy*, 387.

9. Berthon, *Allies at War*, 87–88.

10. Yves Gras, "L'intrusion japonaise en Indochine (juin 1940–mars 1945)" [The Japanese Intrusion into Indochina (June 1940–March 1945)], *Revue historique des Armées* 153, no. 4 (1983): 88–90; Hesse d'Alzon, "La présence militaire française

en Indochine de 1940 à la capitulation japonaise" [French military presence in Indochina from 1940 to the Japanese surrender], in *Les armées françaises pendant la Seconde Guerre mondiale, 1939–1945* [The French armed forces during the Second World War, 1939–1945] (Paris: F.E.D.N.-I.H.C.C, 1986), 282–84; and Ikuhiko Hata, "The Army's Move into French Indochina," in *The Fateful Choice: Japan's Advance into Southeast Asia, 1939–1941*, ed. James W. Morley (New York: Columbia University Press, 1980), 155–208.

11. Jean Decoux, *À la barre de l'Indochine: Histoire de mon Gouvernement Général (1940–1945)* [At Indochina's helm: History of my general governship (1940–1945)] (Paris: Plon, 1950), 91–122; and Chizuru Namba, *Français et Japonais en Indochine, 1940–1945: Colonisation, propagande et rivalité culturelle* [French and Japanese in Indochina, 1940–1945: Colonization, propaganda and cultural rivalry] (Paris: Karthala, 2012), 29–30.

12. Costagliola, *La Marine de Vichy*, 288–93; and Steven T. Ross, ed., *U.S. War Plans: 1938–1945* (Boulder, CO: Lynne Rienner, 2002), 33–54.

13. Cable from Chargé d'affaires in France H. Freeman Matthews to the Secretary of State dated 26 October 1940, in Department of State, *Foreign Relations of the United States Diplomatic Papers, 1940*, vol. 2: *General and Europe* (hereafter, *FRUS 1940*) (Washington, DC: U.S. Government Printing Office, 1957), 395–97; Churchill, *Their Finest Hour*, 524–27; and Charles Williams, *Pétain: How the Hero of France Became a Convicted Traitor and Changed the Course of History* (New York: Palgrave Macmillan, 2005), 177–80.

14. William D. Leahy, *I Was There: The Personal Story of the Chief of Staff to Presidents Roosevelt and Truman Based on His Notes and Diaries Made at the Time* (New York: Whittlesey House, 1950), 6.

15. Geoffrey Till, "Adopting the Aircraft Carrier: The British, American, and Japanese Case Studies," in *Military Innovation in the Interwar Period*, ed. Williamson Murray and Allan R. Millett, 191–226 (Cambridge: Cambridge University Press, 1996); and Holger H. Herwig, "Innovation Ignored: The Submarine Problem—Germany, Britain, and the United States, 1919–1939," in *Military Innovation in the Interwar Period*, ed. Williamson Murray and Allan R. Millett, 227–64 (Cambridge: Cambridge University Press, 1996).

16. Quoted by Dwight D. Eisenhower in his wartime memoirs, *Crusade in Europe* (New York: Doubleday, 1948), 105.

17. Monaque, *Une histoire de la marine*, 415–16; and Arthur J. Marder, *Operation Menace: The Dakar Expedition and the Dudley North Affair* (London: Oxford University Press, 1976).

18. Two cables from Roosevelt to Churchill dated 13 and 18 November 1940, in Kimball, *Alliance Emerging*, 82–84.

19. Rossi, *Roosevelt and the French*, 67–68. Cordell Hull reports his own views in volume 2 of *The Memoirs of Cordell Hull: In Two Volumes* (New York: Macmillan, 1948), 961–62.

20. Varian Fry, "Justice for the Free French," *New Republic* 106, no. 23 (8 June 1942): 785–87; and Rossi, *Roosevelt and the French*, 63–66.

21. Memorandum of conversation by Acting Secretary of State Sumner Wells dated 8 July 1941, in *Foreign Relations of the United States Diplomatic Papers, 1941*, vol. 6: *The American Republics* (hereafter, *FRUS 1941*) (Washington, DC: Government Printing Office, 1963), 574.

22. Hull, *Memoirs*, 2:958–60; Leahy, *I Was There*, 31–32; and Costagliola, *La Marine de Vichy*, 189–96.

23. Levisse-Touzé, *L'Afrique du Nord dans la guerre*, 113–21.

24. Williams, *Pétain*, 202–3; and Julian Jackson, *France: The Dark Years, 1940–1944* (Oxford: Oxford University Press, 2001), 181–85.

25. De Gaulle, *L'Appel*, 183 and 192–93; and de Gaulle, *The Call to Honour*, 215 and 220; François Kersaudy, *De Gaulle et Roosevelt: Le duel au sommet* [De Gaulle and Roosevelt: Duel at the top] (Paris: Perrin, 2006), 95–96 and 116–17; and Rossi, *Roosevelt and the French*, 82–86.

26. Cited in James J. Dougherty, *The Politics of Wartime Aid: American Economic Assistance to France and French Northwest Africa, 1940–1946* (Westport, CT: Greenwood, 1978), 57.

27. Hull, *Memoirs*, 2:1042.

28. Dougherty, *The Politics of Wartime Aid*, 59.

29. Letter from Ambassador Leahy to President Roosevelt, 22 November 1941, reproduced in Leahy, *I Was There*, 59–60.

30. Aide-Mémoire from the United States Department to the British Embassy, 11 June 1942 in *Foreign Relations of the United States Diplomatic Papers, 1942: Europe* (hereafter, *FRUS 1942*) (Washington, DC: Government Printing Office, 1972), 523–24.

31. "Henri Giraud, 1879–1949," last accessed 22 December 2018, Chemins de la Mémoire, Ministère de la Défense, France, http://www.cheminsdememoire .gouv.fr/fr/henri-giraud.

32. For a narration of his escape during the Great War and that from Kœnigstein, see Henri Giraud, *Mes évasions* [My escapes] (Paris: Julliard, 1946), 13–72 and 73–130. See a briefer narrative in William B. Breuer, *Daring Missions of World War II* (New York: Wiley, 2001), 17–20.

33. For more fulsome treatments, see the contrasting assessments in the previously cited Coutau-Bégarie and Huan, *Darlan*; and Bernard Costagliola, *Darlan: La collaboration à tout prix* (Paris: CNRS Éditions, 2015).

34. Coutau-Bégarie and Huan, *Darlan*, 395–421 and 479–508; and Costagliola, *Darlan*, 217–34. For a more positive portrait, see George E. Melton, *Darlan: Admiral and Statesman of France 1881–1942* (Westport, CT: Praeger, 1998), 104–5, 110–14, and 152–55.

35. Heckstall-Smith, *The Fleet That Faced Both Ways*, 178. Admittedly, the actual numbers and the full extent of the influence exercised by these officers within the

Vichy regime was challenged more recently in Girardin-Thibeaud, *Les amiraux de Vichy*, 203–21 and 290–306.

36. Dispatch from Consul General in Algiers to the War Department (from Murphy for Leahy), dated 15 October 1942, *FRUS 1942*, 394; Leahy, *I Was There*, 33 and 74; Murphy, *Diplomat among Warriors*, 112–13 and 128–29; and Rossi, *Roosevelt and the French*, 91–92.

37. Melton, *Darlan*, 163–65; and Costagliola, *Darlan*, 235–36.

38. Coutau-Bégarie and Huan, *Darlan*, 575–78; and Costagliola, *Darlan*, 241.

39. Levisse-Touzé, *L'Afrique du Nord dans la guerre*, 248–49; and Monaque, *Une histoire de la marine*, 428.

40. Cable to CCS dated 13 November 1942. Box 131, DDEPL; and Costagliola, *Darlan*, 250–58.

41. De Gaulle, *L'unité*, 45–50; de Gaulle, *Unity*, 50–55; Mast, *Histoire d'une rébellion*, 379; and Anthoine Béthouart, *Cinq années d'espérance: Mémoires de guerre 1939–1945* [Five years of hope: War memories 1939–1945] (Paris: Plon, 1968), 174–76.

42. François Kersaudy, *De Gaulle et Churchill: La mésentente cordiale* [De Gaulle and Churchill: Cordial disagreement] (Paris: Perrin, 2001), 239.

43. Coutau-Bégarie et Huan, *Darlan*, 683 and 723–28; and Costagliola, *Darlan*, 266–68.

44. Kersaudy, *De Gaulle et Roosevelt*, 191. For a range of views from contemporary observers, see Eisenhower, *Crusade in Europe*, 129–30; Clark, *Calculated Risk*, 128–32; Murphy, *Diplomat among Warriors*, 140–43; Churchill, *The Hinge of Faith*, 643–44; de Gaulle, *L'unité*, 67–69; de Gaulle, *Unity*, 71–74; Mast, *Histoire d'une rébellion*, 415–19; Béthouart, *Cinq années d'espérance*, 178–80; Henri Giraud, *Un seul but: La victoire, Alger 1942–1944* [Only one goal: Victory, Algiers 1942–1944] (Paris: Julliard, 1949), 70–81; and André Beaufre, *Mémoires, 1920–1940–1945* (Paris: Presses de la Cité, 1965), 396–403.

45. On the formation of the Imperial Council, see a cable from Eisenhower to CCS dated 4 December 1942 in *Relations with the French Committee of National Liberation, Algiers*, vol. 1, CAB 121/398, TNA; and Coutau-Bégarie and Huan, *Darlan*, 653–55.

46. Cable from Eisenhower to the CCS dated 26 December 1942 in CAB 121/398, TNA. For a variety of views on the negotiations that took place that day, see Giraud, *Un seul but*, 79–80; Beaufre, *Mémoires*, 403–4; Mast, *Histoire d'une rébellion*, 418–19; Eisenhower, *Crusade in Europe*, 130; and Murphy, *Diplomat among Warriors*, 159.

47. Martin S. Alexander, *The Republic in Danger: General Maurice Gamelin and the Politics of French Defence, 1933–1940* (Cambridge: Cambridge University Press, 1992), 169–70; John McVickar Haight, "Les négociations françaises pour le fourniture d'avions américains, 1ère partie: Avant Munich" [French Negotiations to Acquire American Planes, Part 1: Before Munich], *Forces aériennes françaises*

198 (December 1963): 807–39; John McVickar Haight, *American Aid to France, 1938–1940* (New York: Atheneum, 1970), 23–47; and Gavin J. Bailey, *The Arsenal of Democracy: Aircraft Supply and the Anglo-American Alliance, 1938–1942* (Edinburgh: Edinburgh University Press, 2013), 46–48.

48. Robert, *La France aux Antilles*, 48 and 82–84; Haight, *American Aid to France, 1938–1940*, 253; and Charles W. Koburger, *Franco-American Naval Relations, 1940–1945* (Westport, CT: Praeger, 1994), 34.

49. Beaufre, *Mémoires*, 273–74 and 287–98; Murphy, *Diplomat among Warriors*, 85; Hull, *Memoirs*, 2:1039–40; and Mast, *Histoire d'une rébellion*, 103–5 and 469–78.

50. Mast, *Histoire d'une rébellion*, 477.

51. Cited in Vigneras, *Rearming the French*, 14.

52. The tonnage figure appears in Situation de la Flotte, Tonnage, de 1939 à 1950 [Fleet Status, Tonnage, from 1939 to 1950], report from the Direction centrale des constructions et armes navales [Central Directorate of Constructions and Naval Armaments] to the Minister of the Navy, "Situation de la Flotte de Toulon" [Status of the Toulon Fleet], 16 November 1944, 3 BB 2 SEC 114, Service historique de la Défense (SHD), Section Marine, Vincennes, France. The debate continues as to whether de Laborde and the fleet should have escaped Toulon earlier. For a variety of views, see Masson, *La Marine française*, 354–403; Monaque, *Une histoire de la marine*, 428–34; and Charles W. Koburger, *The Cyrano Fleet, France and Its Navy, 1940–1942* (New York: Praeger, 1989), 79–90.

53. Costagliola, *Pétain*, 250 and 260; and Girardin-Thibeaud, *Les amiraux de Vichy*, 313–19.

54. Gras, "L'intrusion japonaise en Indochine," 93; and Decoux, À la barre de l'Indochine, 150–56.

55. Coutau-Bégarie and Huan, *Darlan*, 639–50; Masson, *La Marine française*, 405–9; Melton, *Darlan*, 186–87 and 203; and Heckstall-Smith, *The Fleet That Faced Both Ways*, 208–11. On their reasoning to refuse switching their allegiance from Vichy to Algiers, see for Robert, *La France aux Antilles*, 223–28; and Godfroy, *L'aventure de la Force X*, 336–67.

56. Coutau-Bégarie and Huan, *Darlan*, 636–39; and Levisse-Touzé, *L'Afrique du Nord dans la guerre*, 274.

57. Jordan and Dumas, *French Battleships*, 150.

58. The agreement appears in full in *FRUS 1942*, 453–57.

59. *FRUS 1942*, 453.

60. "Agreement with General de Gaulle," 7 August 1940, CAB 121/411, TNA.

61. *FRUS 1942*, 455.

62. *Re-equipment and Employment of French Forces*, Vol. 1: *October 1942–December 1943*, Cable from British Admiralty to Flag Officer Commanding West Africa Station, 27 December 1942, CAB 121/401, TNA.

63. Admittedly these monotonous patrols proved rather fruitless, as the first intercept did not occur until 12 April 1943 when *Georges Leygues* sank the German raider *Portland* near the equator, but their symbolic value was undeniable. Auphan and Mordal, *La Marine française*, 433; and Martin Brice, *Axis Blockade Runners of World War II* (Annapolis, MD: Naval Institute Press, 1981), 124–25.

64. Koburger, *Franco-American Naval Relations*, 50.

65. Claude Huan, "La Marine française dans la guerre (1943)" [The French Navy during the war (1943)], *Revue historique des Armées* 188, no. 3 (September 1992): 116.

66. Huan, 116; and cable from Admiralty to RN Admiral Andrew Cunningham, Eisenhower's naval commander, 11 December 1942, CAB 121/398, TNA.

67. Frédérique Chapelay, "Le réarmement de la Marine par les Américains" [The rearmament of the Navy by the Americans], in *Les armées françaises pendant la Seconde Guerre mondiale, 1939–1945* [The French Armed Forces during the Second World War, 1939–1945] (Paris: F.E.D.N.-I.H.C.C, 1986), 348.

68. Cable, Cunningham to Admiralty, 19 November 1942, CAB 121/398, TNA.

69. Weiss, *Allies in Conflict*, 69.

70. The main venue for the talks was the Hôtel Anfa, which had previously hosted the officers of the German Armistice Commission. Berthon, *Allies at War*, 232.

71. David Stone, *War Summits: The Meetings That Shaped World War II and the Postwar World* (Washington, DC: Potomac, 2005), 70–77; and Department of State, *Foreign Relations of the United States: The Conferences at Washington, 1941–1942, and Casablanca, 1943* (hereafter, *FRUS Casablanca 1943*) (Washington, DC: U.S. Government Printing Office, 1968), 485–849.

72. Cited in Berthon, *Allies at War*, 234; and Kersaudy, *De Gaulle et Churchill*, 247.

73. Giraud, *Un seul but*, 84–85; and Beaufre, *Mémoires*, 408–10.

74. De Gaulle, *L'unité*, 74–76; de Gaulle, *Unity*, 78–80; Roussel, *Charles de Gaulle*, 339–44; and Fenby, *The General*, 194–96.

75. De Gaulle, *L'unité*, 85–86; de Gaulle, *Unity*, 90; Giraud, *Un seul but*, 109–10; Beaufre, *Mémoires*, 415; Churchill, *The Hinge of Fate*, 693; Murphy, *Diplomat among Warrior*, 175–76; Roussel, *Charles de Gaulle*, 347; and Fenby, *The General*, 200–201.

76. Cited in French in Beaufre, *Mémoires*, 416; and in English in a cable from British resident minister in Algiers Harold MacMillan to Foreign Secretary, 25 January 1943, CAB 121/398, TNA.

77. De Gaulle, *L'unité*, 83; de Gaulle *Unity*, 86; Giraud, *Un seul but*, 109–10; and Musée de l'Ordre de la Libération, "Georges Catroux," last accessed 18 March 2020, https://www.ordredelaliberation.fr/fr/compagnons/georges-catroux.

78. Cited in Berthon, *Allies at War*, 247.

79. Cited in Kersaudy, *De Gaulle et Roosevelt*, 219; and Berthon, *Allies at War*, 236.

80. Giraud, *Un seul but*, 96.

81. Cited in Vigneras, *Rearming the French*, 35.

82. Giraud, *Un seul but*, 353–54; and *FRUS Casablanca 1943*, 823–25.

CHAPTER 3. REARMING FOR WAR

1. Béthouart, *Cinq années d'espérance*, 192–93; and M. Cointet, *De Gaulle et Giraud: L'affrontement, 1942–1944* [De Gaulle and Giraud: The confrontation, 1942–1944] (Paris: Perrin, 2005), 317.

2. René Sarnet and Éric Le Vaillant, *Richelieu* (Rennes, FR: Marines Éditions, 1997), 170; and Julien Lombard, "Le *Richelieu* dans la tourmente (1939–1945)" [*Richelieu* into the storm (1939–1945)], *Guerres mondiales et conflits contemporains* 188 (December 1997): 71.

3. Jordan and Dumas, *French Battleships*, 182–90; Robert Dumas, *Le cuirassé Richelieu 1935–1968* [Battleship *Richelieu* 1935–1968] (Bourg-en-Bresse, FR: Marines Éditions, 1992), 50–51; and David Brown, "Le H.M.S. *Richelieu*," *Revue historique des Armées* 199 (June 1995): 117–18.

4. Vigneras, *Rearming the French*, 217.

5. Auphan and Mordal, *La marine française*, 434; and Koburger, *Franco-American Naval Relations*, 51.

6. Stone, *War Summits*, 43–49; Weiss, *Allies in Conflict*, 43–51; *Proceedings of the American-British Joint Chiefs of Staff Conference Held in Washington, DC on Twelve Occasion between December 24, 1941 and January 14, 1942*, CAB 99/17, TNA; and *FRUS Casablanca 1943*, 1–415.

7. Vigneras, *Rearming the French*, 10; and CFC IRC, Minutes of the 13th CCS Meeting, 24 March 1942.

8. Richard M. Leighton and Robert W. Coakley, *Global Logistics and Strategy: 1940–1943*, United States Army in World War II series (Washington, DC: U.S. Army Center of Military History, 1955), 271.

9. Vigneras, *Rearming the French*, 22.

10. Vigneras, 23. See also Leighton and Coakley, *Global Logistics and Strategy*, 271–75.

11. Leighton and Coakley, *Global Logistics and Strategy*, 512.

12. Eisenhower, *Crusade in Europe*, 118.

13. Leighton and Coakley, *Global Logistics and Strategy*, 468.

14. Cable from Eisenhower to CCS, 31 December 1942, Box 131, DDEPL.

15. Weiss, *Allies in Conflict*, 77–80.

16. Giraud, *Un seul but*, 95–96; and Beaufre, *Mémoires*, 390–91.

17. Béthouart, *Cinq années d'espérance*, 176–77; and Vigneras, *Rearming the French*, 26.

18. Béthouart, *Cinq années d'espérance*, 182; and cable from the British Joint Staff Mission (Washington) to the War Cabinet Offices (London), 22 December 1942, CAB 121/401, TNA.

19. Vigneras, *Rearming the French*, 27.

20. CFC IRC, Minutes of the 49th CCS Meeting, 20 November 1942.

21. Béthouart, *Cinq années d'espérance*, 337; and cable from Naval Commander Expeditionary Force to Admiralty, 25 December 1942, CAB 121/401, TNA.

22. Vigneras, *Rearming the French*, 25.

23. Chapelay, "Le réarmement de la Marine par les Américains," 350.

24. Béthouart, *Cinq années d'espérance*, 338–39; and Vigneras, *Rearming the French*, 31.

25. Cable from Joint Staff Mission to War Cabinet Offices, 6 February 1943, CAB 121/401, TNA.

26. Eisenhower cable to CCS, 20 November 1942, Box 131, DDEPL.

27. CCS cable to Eisenhower, 23 December 1942, CAB 121/401, TNA.

28. Eisenhower cable to CCS, 2 January 1943, CAB 121/401, TNA.

29. Eisenhower cable to CCS, 2 January 1943, CAB 121/401, TNA.

30. Eisenhower cable to CCS, 18 January 1943, CAB 121/401, TNA.

31. Admiralty cable to Cunningham, 1 January 1943, CAB 121/401, TNA.

32. French Warships Re-arming in Bermuda: Priority and Provision of RDF Equipment and Stores, cable from RN Commander-in-Chief Mediterranean Fleet to Senior British Naval Officer West Atlantic, 3 April 1943, ADM 1/13027, TNA.

33. Cable from CCS to Eisenhower, 22 January 1943, CAB 121/401, TNA.

34. Cable from Eisenhower to CCS, 26 January 1943, CAB 121/401, TNA.

35. Béthouart, *Cinq années d'espérance*, 191. Upon joining the navy in 1905, Fénard proved himself through a succession of tours at sea and in shore headquarters, taking command of the battleship *Dunkerque* in 1936. A rear admiral in 1939, he initially headed the Toulon defense sector. Promoted and transferred to Algiers after the armistice, he rose to take the post of secretary general to the general delegate to French Africa (General Weygand, then the civilian administrator Yves Châtel after November 1941). Loyal to Vichy, he still held that critical post at the time of Operation Torch and remained in place until his selection to lead the naval mission to the United States. Taillemite, *Dictionnaire des marins français*, 182–83; and Philippe Valode, *Le destin des hommes de Pétain de 1945 à nos jours* [The destiny of Pétain's men from 1945 to today] (Paris: Nouveau Monde, 2014), 214.

36. George W. Baer, *One Hundred Years of Sea Power: The U.S. Navy, 1890–1990* (Stanford, CA: Stanford University Press, 1994), 186–87.

37. Koburger, *Franco-American Naval Relations*, 77.

38. Cable from Eisenhower to the CCS, 1 March 1943, CAB 121/401, TNA.

39. Cable from British Joint Staff Mission to War Cabinet Offices, 3 April 1943, CAB 121/401, TNA.

40. Vigneras, *Rearming the French*, 219.

41. Cable from British Joint Staff Mission to War Cabinet Offices, 9 April 1943, letter from Admiralty Secretariat to War Cabinet Offices, 15 April 1945, and Cable from Air Ministry to British Joint Staff Mission, 15 April 1943, both CAB 121/401, TNA; as well as CFC IRC, Minutes of the 80th CCS Meeting, 17 April 1943.

42. Cable from Eisenhower to CCS, 3 May 1943, CAB 121/401, TNA.

43. Cable from British Admiralty Delegation Washington to Admiralty, 5 May 1943, CAB 121/401, TNA.

44. Cable from Cunningham to Admiralty, 29 December 1942, CAB 121/398, TNA.

45. Jean-Luc Barré, *Devenir de Gaulle, 1939–1943* [Becoming de Gaulle, 1939–1943] (Paris: Perrin, 2003), 229–30; and Charles de Gaulle, "Appellations 'France Libre' et 'France Combattante'" ("Free France" and "Fighting France" designations), *Journal Officiel de la France Combattante*, 28 August 1942.

46. Cointet, *De Gaulle et Giraud*, 301–8; and Kersaudy, *De Gaulle et Roosevelt*, 256–58. For a typical denunciation of Giraud's conservative ways in the American media at the time, see "The Problem of French Unity," *New Republic* 108, no. 12 (22 March 1943): 365–66.

47. For the Muselier episode in Algiers, see Muselier, *L'amiral Muselier*, 223–24; and Louis de Villefosse, *Souvenirs d'un marin de la France libre* [Memories of a Free France sailor] (Paris: Éditeurs français réunis, 1951), 253–77.

48. Auphan and Mordal, *La Marine française*, 445; and Girardin-Thibeaud, *Les amiraux de Vichy*, 318–35.

49. "La libération de la Corse, 9 septembre–4 octobre 1943" [Liberation of Corsica, 9 September–4 October 1943], *Chemins de la Mémoire*, last accessed 8 August 2016, http://www.cheminsdememoire.gouv.fr/fr/la-liberation-de-la-corse-9-septembre-4-octobre-1943-0.

50. Cointet, *De Gaulle et Giraud*, 440–60 and 495–98; de Gaulle, *L'unité, 1942–1944*, 141–40 and 167–69; de Gaulle, *Unity, 1942–1944*, 145–54 and 171–73; and Giraud, *Un seul but*, 260–64 and 281–312.

51. Cable from Churchill to Roosevelt, 10 November 1943, in Warren F. Kimball, ed., *Alliance Forged, October 1933–November 1942*, vol. 2 of *Churchill and Roosevelt: The Complete Correspondence* (Princeton, NJ: Princeton Legacy Library, 1984), 593.

52. Giraud, *Un seul but*, 315–32; and Cointet, *De Gaulle et Giraud*, 499–508.

53. Godfroy, *L'aventure de la Force X*, 333–465; Mast, *Histoire d'une rébellion*, 437–40; and Calvin W. Hines, "The Fleet Between: Anglo-American Diplomacy and Force X, 1940–43," in *Naval History: The Sixth Symposium of the U.S. Naval Academy*, ed. Daniel M. Masterson, 237–55 (Wilmington, DE: Scholarly Resources, 1987).

54. Godfroy, *L'aventure de la Force X*, 505; and Girardin-Thibeaud, *Les amiraux de Vichy*, 316–18.

55. Robert, *La France aux Antilles*, 139–223; Léo Elisabeth, "Vichy aux Antilles et en Guyane: 1940–1943" [Vichy in the Caribbean and Guyana], *Outre-mers* 91, no. 342 (1st Quarter 2004): 165–74; and Lawrence Douglas, "The Martinique Affair: The United States Navy and the French West Indies, 1940–1943," in *New Interpretations in Naval History: Selected Papers from the Ninth Naval History Symposium Held at the United States Naval Academy, 18–20 October 1989* (Annapolis, MD: Naval Institute Press, 1991), 132–36.

56. Monaque, *Une histoire de la marine*, 435; and Rodolphe Lamy, "Il y a 70 ans, le basculement de la Martinique" [70 years ago, the rallying of Martinique], *France-Antilles*, 22 June 2013, http://www.martinique.franceantilles.fr/actualite /culture/il-y-a-70-ans-le-basculement-de-la-martinique-209992.php.

57. Decoux, À la barre de *l'Indochine*, 148–350; d'Alzon, "La présence militaire française en Indochine," 281–90; Gras, "L'intrusion japonaise en Indochine," 93–102; and Paul Romé, *Les oubliés du bout du monde: Journal d'un marin d'Indochine de 1939 à 1946* [The forgotten at the other end of the world: Diary of an Indochina sailor from 1939 to 1946] (Paris: Éditions maritimes & d'outre-mer, 1983).

58. Hull, *Memoirs*, 2:1013–15; and Eri Hotta, *Japan 1941: Countdown to Infamy* (New York: Knopf, 2013), 130–48.

59. Masson, *Histoire de l'armée française*, 327.

60. Masson, 329; and "Communiqué officiel" [Official Press Release], *L'Écho d'Alger* 32, no. 12, 1 August 1943, http://gallica.bnf.fr/ark:/12148/bpt6k7587122x /f1.textePage.langES.

61. Auphan and Mordal, *La Marine française*, 445–46; and Huan, "La Marine française dans la guerre (1943)," 116–17.

62. Taillemite, *Dictionnaire des marins français*, 326–27; Monaque, *Une histoire de la marine*, 440; and "Parcours d'officiers dans la Royal: André Georges Lemon-nier (1896–1963)" [Officers journeys in *La Royale*: André Georges Lemonnier (1896–1963)], École navale, Espace Traditions, last accessed 20 August 2016, http://ecole.nav.traditions.free.fr/officiers_lemonnier.htm.

63. De Gaulle, *Unity, 1942–1944*, 251; and de Gaulle, *L'unité, 1942–1944*, 248.

64. Auphan and Mordal, *La Marine française*, 446; Masson, *La Marine française et la guerre*, 416; and Chaline, "Les Forces navales françaises libres."

65. For an introduction to d'Argenlieu, see Thomas Vaisset, "L'amiral d'Argenlieu, un croisé de la France libre" [Admiral d'Argenlieu, crusader of Free France], in *Les Chrétiens, la guerre et la paix* [Christians, war and peace] (Rennes, FR: Presses universitaires de Rennes, 2012), 193–208; and his more extensive *L'amiral d'Argenlieu: Le moine-soldat du gaullisme* [Admiral d'Argenlieu: Gaullism's monk-soldier] (Paris: Belin, 2017).

66. Cable from CCS to Eisenhower, 22 January 1943, CAB 121/401, TNA.

67. Auphan and Mordal, *La Marine française*, 434; as well as John Jordan and Jean Moulin, *French Cruisers, 1922–1956* (Barnsley, UK: Seaforth, 2013), 197.

68. Auphan and Mordal, *La Marine française*, 434; and M. J. Whitley, *Destroyers of World War Two: An International Encyclopedia* (Annapolis, MD: Naval Institute Press, 1988), 43–44.

69. "FR Archimède," Uboat.net, last accessed 21 August 2016, http://uboat.net/allies /warships/ship/6095.html; "FR Amazone," Uboat.net, last accessed 21 August 2016, http://uboat.net/allies/warships/ship/6124.html; "FR Le Glorieux," Uboat

.net, last accessed 21 August 2016, http://uboat.net/allies/warships/ship/6132. html; and Claude Huan, *Les Sous-marins français 1918–1945* [French submarines 1918–1945] (Rennes, FR: Marines Éditions, 2004), 152, 163, and 166.

70. Jordan and Moulin, *French Cruisers*, 197–98; and Masson, *La Marine française*, 418.

71. Jordan and Moulin, *French Cruisers*, 198; and Auphan and Mordal, *La Marine française*, 443.

72. Extensive correspondence can be found in "French Warships Re-arming in Bermuda: Priority and Provision of RDF Equipment and Stores," ADM 1/13027, TNA.

73. Cable from British Admiralty Delegation in Washington to Admiralty, 14 October 1943, ADM 1/13027, TNA; Letter from the French Committee of National Liberation (cosigned by Giraud and de Gaulle) to the British prime minister, the American president and the Soviet general secretary, 18 September 1943, CAB 121/401, TNA; and Huan, *Les sous-marins français*, 163–66.

74. Letter from the CCS to French Naval Mission in Washington, undated but likely drafted in late October 1943, CAB 121/401, TNA.

75. Huan, *Les sous-marins français*, 175–76; "FR Perlé," Uboat.net, last accessed 26 August 2016, http://uboat.net/allies/warships/ship/6114.html; "FR Le Centaure," Uboat.net, last accessed 26 August 2016, http://uboat.net/allies/warships/ship/6133. html; and "FR Casabianca," Uboat.net, last accessed 26 August 2016, http://uboat .net/allies/warships/ship/6139.html.

76. Huan, *Les sous-marins français*, 180; and "FR Antiope," Uboat.net, last accessed 26 August 2016, http://uboat.net/allies/warships/ship/6122.html.

77. Previously cited letter from the French Committee of National Liberation to the leaders of Great Britain, the United States and the Soviet Union, 18 September 1943, CAB 121/401, TNA.

78. As reported in a cable from the British Joint Staff Mission in Washington to the War Cabinet Office, 9 October 1943, CAB 121/401, TNA. See also Vigneras, *Rearming the French*, 220–21.

79. Jordan and Dumas, *French Battleships*, 162.

80. Jordan and Dumas; and Robert Dumas, *Le cuirassé Jean Bart 1939–1970* [Battleship *Jean Bart* 1939–1970] (Rennes, FR: Marine Éditions, 2001), 70–71.

81. Chapelay, "Le réarmement de la Marine par les Américains," 350–51; and Philippe Masson, "Le réarmement de la Marine française" [Rearmament of the French navy], *Revue historique des Armées* 3, no. 188 (September 1992): 113.

82. Koburger, *Franco-American Naval Relations*, 85.

83. CCS Directive 358 (Revised), Policies Regarding French Naval Vessels, 4 October 1943, CAB 121/401, TNA. CCS 358 had been promulgated in September but soon required slight amendments consolidated in CCS 358 (Revised).

84. Vigneras, *Rearming the French*, 222.

85. CCS Directive 358 (Revised), 2 and 3.

86. CCS Directive 358 (Revised), 2.

87. CCS Directive 358 (Revised), 2.

88. CCS Directive 358 (Revised), 4.

89. CCS Directive 358 (Revised), 3.

90. CCS Directive 358 (Revised), 5.

91. Letter from Admiral Fénard, French Naval Mission in Washington, to Admiral King, Commander-in-Chief US Fleet, 15 October 1943, CAB 121/401, TNA.

92. Vigneras, *Rearming the French*, 223.

93. Thomas B. Buell, *Master of Sea Power: A Biography of Fleet Admiral Ernest J. King*, 2nd ed. (Annapolis, MD: Naval Institute Press, 1995), 313. For more cynical views on the Anglo-American "generosity," see Chapelay, "Le réarmement de la Marine par les Américains," 351–53; and Masson, *De la vapeur à l'atome*, 488–89.

94. Vigneras, *Rearming the French*, 222; and CFC IRC, Minutes of the 147th CCS Meeting, 25 February 1944.

95. Lemonnier to Fénard, 11 January 1944, cited in Masson, "Le réarmement de la Marine française," 113.

CHAPTER 4. PLANNING FOR AN UNCERTAIN PEACE

1. *Richelieu*'s return was actually her second visit to France since 1940. The battleship had stopped briefly in Toulon in October 1944 on her way to a refit in Casablanca, between two deployments to the Indian Ocean. For an overview of *Richelieu*'s operations in 1943–46, see Jordan and Dumas, *French Battleships*, 190–201; and Dumas, *Le cuirassé* Richelieu, 50–54. Then-lieutenant Bernard Favin-Lévêque offers a firsthand account of *Richelieu*'s Far East campaigns in *Souvenirs de mer et d'ailleurs* [Recollections from the sea and other places] (Versailles, FR: Éditions des 7 vents, 1990), 113–20.

2. Jordan and Moulin, *French Cruisers*, 202–3; and Huan, "La Marine française dans la guerre (1943)," 118–19.

3. Auphan and Mordal, *La Marine française*, 451–52; and Whitley, *Destroyers of World War Two*, 43–44.

4. Huan, "La Marine française dans la guerre (1943)," 119–20; and Masson, *La Marine française*, 420–21.

5. Vigneras, *Rearming the French*, 225; and Barbara Brooks Tomblin, *With Utmost Spirit: Allied Naval Operations in the Mediterranean, 1942–1945* (Lexington: University Press of Kentucky, 2004), 379–83.

6. Jordan and Moulin, *French Cruisers*, 205–6; Tomblin, *With Utmost Spirit*, 401–28; and Masson, *Histoire de l'armée française*, 342–45.

7. Jordan and Moulin, *French Cruisers*, 206–9; and Pierre-Emmanuel Klingbeil, *Le front oublié des Alpes-Maritimes (15 août 1944–2 mai 1945)* [The forgotten front

of the *Alpes-Maritimes* (15 August 1944–2 May 1945)] (Nice, FR: Serre Éditeur, 2005), 199–205. For a contemporary account, see Hervé Jaouen, *Marin de guerre* [Wartime sailor] (Paris: Éditions du Pen Duick, 1984), 49–54.

8. Huan, *Les Sous-marins français*, 191–92.

9. Schlumberger and Schlumberger, *Les combats et l'honneur*, 122–26.

10. Huan, *Les sous-marins français*, 175–76; and Christian Lecalard, "Activités et disparition du sous-marin mouilleur de mines 'LA PERLE'" [Activities and disappearance of the submarine minelayer *La Perle*], *Amicale Rubis*, 14 January 2013, http://www.sectionrubis.fr/spip.php?article191.

11. Taillemite, *Histoire ignorée de la Marine française*, 585–87; and Claude Huan, "Les opérations des sous-marins français, Méditerranée 1944" [French submarine operations in the Mediterranean, 1944], *Revue historique des Armées* 156, no. 3 (October 1984): 57, 62.

12. Auphan and Mordal, *La Marine française*, 493–99; and Masson, *La Marine française*, 421.

13. Nick Van der Bijl, *No.10 (Inter-Allied) Commando 1942–45: Britain's Secret Commando* (Oxford: Osprey, 2006), 25–40; and Stéphane Simonnet, *Les 177 Français du Jour J* [The 177 frenchmen of D-day] (Paris: Tallandier, 2014).

14. Masson, *La Marine française*, 421.

15. Richard M. Leighton and Robert W. Coakley, *Global Logistics and Strategy: 1943–1945*. United States Army in World War II series (Washington, DC: U.S. Army Center of Military History, 1968), 372–74, 385–87, and 560–61; and Guy Hartcup, *Code Name Mulberry: The Planning, Building and Operation of the Normandy Harbours*, 2nd ed. (London: Pen & Sword Military, 2011).

16. Only one German garrison fell under French assault, that holding the Royan and Pointe de Grace complex, blocking the approaches to Bordeaux until its surrender on 30 April 1945. The other pockets were still in German hands on VE day. Stéphane Simonnet, *Les poches de l'Atlantique: Les batailles oubliées de la Libération, janvier 1944–mai 1945* [The Atlantic pockets: The forgotten battles of the liberation, January 1944–May 1945] (Paris: Tallandier, 2015).

17. Auphan and Mordal, *La Marine française*, 528–35; and Jaouen, *Marin de guerre*, 55–56.

18. The 4ᵉ Régiment de fusiliers-marins was formed to bring together all naval personnel who had served with the Forces françaises de l'intérieur (Free French Forces of the Interior). Jérôme Souverain, "Marine and F.F.I (1944–1945)" [The navy and the *FFI* (1944–1945)], *Revue historique des Armées* 199 (June 1995): 112–13.

19. Sources on all of these formations are too many to be listed here, but Auphan and Mordal provide an adequate summary of these operations on land sprinkled throughout part 4 (*Le Retour chez soi* [The return home]) of *La Marine française*, 493–561. For a full treatment, see George Fleury, *Fusiliers marins et commandos: Baroudeurs de la royale* [Naval infantry and commandos: The navy's daredevils] (Paris: Copernic, 1980).

20. The transfer to *Battler* followed the torpedoing of *Indomitable* on 16 July 1943, which did not sink the carrier but forced its evacuation to the United States for extensive repairs. The French aviators were dispersed among other British squadrons in November 1943. Jérôme Baroë, *Cent ans d'Aéronavale en France* [One hundred years of naval aviation in France] (Rennes, FR: Éditions Ouest-France, 2010), 34; and Jean Moulin, *Les porte-avions* Dixmude *& Arromanches* [Aircraft carriers *Dixmude* and *Arromanches*] (Nantes, FR: Marines Éditions, 1998), 40.

21. Baroë, *Cent ans d'Aéronavale*, 34; and Roger Vercken, *Histoire succincte de l'Aéronautique navale (1910–1998)* [A brief history of the naval aviation (1910–1998)] (Paris: ARDHAN, 1998), 75.

22. Baroë, *Cent ans d'Aéronavale*, 35; Vercken, *Histoire succincte de l'Aéronautique*, 77–84; and Chapelay, "Le réarmement de la Marine par les Américains," 352.

23. Auphan and Mordal, *La Marine française*, 555; Whitley, *Destroyers of World War Two*, 48; and John Jordan and Jean Moulin, *French Destroyers: Torpilleurs d'Escadre & Contre-Torpilleurs, 1922–1956* (Barnsley, U.K.: Seaforth, 2015), 265.

24. Auphan and Mordal, *La Marine française*, 590–91; and Koburger, *Franco-American Naval Relations*, 100.

25. Cornic, "Ships for Crews," 252–63.

26. Cornic, 252 and 254.

27. Koburger, *Franco-American Naval Relations*, 99. For a full listing, see his annex L at pages 144–45.

28. Alexandre Sheldon-Duplaix, "La Mission navale française à Washington et la renaissance de la Marine (3 janvier 1943–1er janvier 1946)" [The French naval mission to Washington and the rebirth of the navy (3 January 1943–1 January 1946)], *Relations internationales* 108 (Winter 2001): 518.

29. Jordan and Moulin, *French Cruisers*, 198–202; and Sheldon-Duplaix, "La Mission navale française à Washington," 518.

30. Alexandre Sheldon-Duplaix, *Histoire mondiale des porte-avions: Des origines à nos jours* [World history of the aircraft carriers: From the origins to today] (Paris: Éditions Techniques pour l'Automobile et l'Industrie, 2006), 79.

31. Robert J. Cressman, "Biter," Naval History and Heritage Command, last modified 6 February 2006, https://www.history.navy.mil/research/histories /ship-histories/danfs/b/biter-i.html; and Moulin, *Les porte-avions* Dixmude *& Arromanches*, 46–59.

32. Koburger, *Franco-American Naval Relations*, 90–91; and Sheldon-Duplaix, "La Mission navale française à Washington," 517–18.

33. Moulin, *Les porte-avions* Dixmude *& Arromanches*, 60–68.

34. Vigneras, *Rearming the French*, 225.

35. Vigneras, 225.

36. Forrest C. Pogue, *The Supreme Command*, United States Army in World War II: European Theater of Operations series (Washington, DC: U.S. Army Center

of Military History, 1954), 320. See also Leighton and Coakley, *Global Logistics and Strategy: 1943–1945*, 710.

37. Pogue, *Supreme Command*, 324; and Vigneras, *Rearming the French*, 381.

38. SHEAF instruction to SHAEF Mission (France), 22 December 1944, discussed in Pogue, *Supreme Command*, 339n15.

39. Vigneras, *Rearming the French*, 384–85.

40. Pogue, *Supreme Command*, 511–15; and Stephen E. Ambrose, *Eisenhower: Soldier and President* (London: Pocket Books, 1997), 213–20.

41. Vigneras, *Rearming the French*, 390; and Sheldon-Duplaix, "La Mission navale française à Washington," 523.

42. The agreement appears in full at the Library of Congress, "Principles Applying to Mutual Aid in the Prosecution of the War against Aggression—Preliminary Agreement between the United States of America and the Provisional Government of the French Republic," last accessed 20 October 2016, https://www.loc .gov/law/help/us-treaties/bevans/b-fr-ust000007-1075.pdf.

43. Dougherty, *The Politics of Wartime Aid*, 189–94.

44. Dougherty, 201.

45. Dougherty, 203.

46. Robert J. Cressman, "Lafayette (AP-53) 1941–1945," Naval History and Heritage Command, last modified 2 May 2007, https://www.history.navy.mil/research /histories/ship-histories/danfs/l/lafayette-ap-53.html.

47. Dougherty, *The Politics of Wartime Aid*, 208–10; and Gérard Bossuat, *Les aides américaines économiques et militaires à la France (1938–1960): Une nouvelle image des rapports de puissance* [American economic and military assistance to France (1938–1960): A new portrait of the power relationships] (Paris: Comité pour l'histoire économique et financière de la France, 2001), http://books.openedition .org/igpde/2023.

48. Stuart, "Was the RCN Ever the Third Largest Navy?," 8–9.

49. Monaque, *Une histoire de la marine*, 439; Auphan and Mordal, *La Marine française*, 594–600; and Girardin-Thibeaud, *Les amiraux de Vichy*, 339–64.

50. Philippe Masson, "La marine française en 1946" [The French navy in 1946], *Revue d'histoire de la Deuxième Guerre mondiale* 110 (April 1978): 81.

51. Letter from the French Committee of National Liberation (cosigned by Giraud and de Gaulle) to the British prime minister, the American president and the Soviet general secretary, 18 September 1943, CAB 121/401, TNA.

52. "Rapport au Ministre: Programme d'une flotte de transition" [Report to the Minister: Transition Fleet Programme], 6 November 1944, 3 BB 2 SEC 114, SHD.

53. "Rapport au Ministre: Statut naval d'après-guerre [Report to the Minister: Postwar Naval Statute]," 11 April 1945, 3 BB 2 SEC 114, SHD.

54. Quérel, *Vers une marine atomique*, 17.

55. Strub, "La renaissance de la marine française," 29.

56. Various Files, Conseil supérieur de la Marine [Superior Council of the Navy] 1945–1946, "Projet d'ordonnance du 28 juin 1945 fixant la composition de la flotte au cours des années 1945–1946" [Draft legislation determining the composition of the fleet for the years 1945–1946], 28 June 1945, 3 BB 8 CSM 1, SHD.

57. "Rapport au Ministre: Plan d'armement pour 1946" [Report to the Minister: 1946 Armament Plan], 17 September 1945, 3 BB 8 CSM 1, SHD.

58. René Courtin, "Réarmement ou reconstruction?" [Rearmament or reconstruction?] *Le Monde*, 18 August 1945, http://www.lemonde.fr/archives/article/1945/08/18/rearmement -ou-reconstruction_1860439_1819218.html?xtmc=rearmement _ou_reconstruction&xtcr=1.

59. Strub, "La renaissance de la marine française," 25.

60. De Gaulle, *Le salut, 1944–1946*, 235; and de Gaulle, *Salvation, 1944–1946*, 231.

61. De Gaulle, *Le salut, 1944–1946*, 7; and de Gaulle, *Salvation, 1944–1946*, 12.

62. "Décret du 4 août 1943 sur l'organisation du Haut Commandement" [Decree of 4 August 1943 on the organisation of high command], Digithèque MJP; and "Ordonnance du 4 avril 1944 concernant l'organisation de la défense nationale" [Order of 4 April 1944 Concerning the Organisation of National Defense], Le Comité français de la libération nationale, last accessed 11 January 2017, http:// mjp.univ-perp.fr/france/co1943cfln2.htm#HC; and Philippe Vial, "La genèse du poste de chef d'état-major des armées" [Genesis of the post of chief of staff of the armies], *Revue historique des Armées* 248 (2007): 32.

63. Vigneras, *Rearming the French*, 321.

64. Note from de Gaulle to Commissioner for War André Diethelm dated 16 October 1944, reproduced in full in de Gaulle, *Le salut, 1944–1946*, 333.

65. Jean Delmas, "De Gaulle, la défense nationale et les forces armées, projets et réalités (1944–janvier 1946)" [De Gaulle, national defense and the armed forces, ambitions and realities (1944–January 1946)], *Revue d'histoire de la Deuxième guerre mondiale* 110 (April 1978): 12–14.

66. Delmas, 15.

67. Minutes of the National Defense Committee, 13 September 1945, F/60/3009, Archives nationales, Pierrefitte-sur-Seine, France.

68. Minutes of the National Defense Committee, 4 December 1945, F/60/3009, Archives nationales.

69. Delmas, "De Gaulle, la défense nationale et les forces armées," 22.

70. Marcel Morabito, *Histoire constitutionnelle de la France de 1789 à nos jours* [Constitutional history of France from 1789 to today], 14th ed. (Paris: LGDJ, 2016), 391–93.

71. The debate continues today whether le Général was abandoning power for good at the time or expected instead that a popular uprising or even a military coup would result in his recall à la 1958. For the principal's views on this episode, see de Gaulle, *Le salut, 1944–1946*, 273–90; and de Gaulle, *Salvation, 1944–1946*,

267–84. For more objective assessments, see Roussel, *Charles de Gaulle*, 517–27; and Fenby, *The General*, 302–12.

CHAPTER 5. FACING OPPORTUNITIES, THREATS, AND UNCERTAINTIES

1. Moulin, *Les porte-avions* Dixmude & Arromanches, 68; and Baroë, *Cent ans d'Aéronavale*, 42.
2. The Aéronavale also dispatched four PBY-5A Catalina flying boats from Morocco to Cochinchina in the fall of 1945. Soon joined by four more, they would remain in theater until 1951 to perform reconnaissance and surveillance missions as well as transport tasks. Baroë, *Cent ans d'Aéronavale*, 42; and "Flottille 28F" [28 F Squadron], Marine nationale, last modified 8 October 2014, http://www.defense .gouv.fr/marine/operations/forces/aeronautique-navale/flottilles/flottille-28f.
3. Cited in Moulin, *Les porte-avions* Dixmude & Arromanches, 71.
4. Quérel, *Vers une marine atomique*, 20; Monaque, *Une histoire de la marine*, 440–41; and Taillemite, *Dictionnaire des marins français*, 392–93.
5. Strub, "La renaissance de la marine française" (PhD thesis), 32–33; and "Reconstitution des forces aéronavales" [Reconstitution of the Naval Air Forces], 27 June 1944, 3 BB 8 CSM 1, SHD.
6. Minutes of the Superior Council of the Navy held on 5 July 1945, 3 BB 8 CMS 1, SHD.
7. Philippe Quérel, "L'échec du *PA-28*, premier porte-avions française de l'après-guerre" [The failure of PA-28, the first postwar French aircraft carrier]. Institut de stratégie comparée, last accessed 23 November 2012, http://www.institut-strategie .fr/pub_m03_Querel.html; and Hervé Coutau-Bégarie, "Marine et innovation: La Marine française face au porte-avions après la Seconde Guerre mondiale" [Navy and innovation: The French navy and the aircraft carrier after the Second World War], *Guerre mondiale et conflits contemporains* 238 (2010): 122.
8. Minutes of the Superior Council of the Navy held on 21 September 1945, 3 BB 8 CMS 1, SHD.
9. Cited in Jordan and Dumas, *French Battleships*, 210.
10. Note from Commander Barjot to the Chief of the Naval General Staff, 10 September 1943, folder labeled *Achèvement du "Jean Bart"* [Completion of *Jean Bart*], 3 BB 8 CSM 1, SHD.
11. Minutes of the Superior Council of the Navy held on 2 October 1945, 3 BB 8 CMS 1, SHD.
12. Minutes of the Superior Council of the Navy held on 15 October 1945, 3 BB 8 CMS 1, SHD.
13. "The Franco-Soviet Treaty of Alliance and Mutual Aid," University of Hawaii eVols, https://evols.library.manoa.hawaii.edu/bitstream/10524/32777/1/17-Volume8 .pdf; de Gaulle, *Le salut, 1944–1946*, 54–79; de Gaulle, *Salvation, 1944–1946*, 58–82; and Georges-Henri Soutou, "General de Gaulle and the Soviet Union, 1943–5: Ideology or European Equilibrium," in *The Soviet Union and Europe in*

the Cold War, 1943–53, ed. Francesca Gori and Silvio Pons, 310–33 (London: Palgrave Macmillan, 1996).

14. John S. Hill, "American Efforts to Aid French Reconstruction between Lend-Lease and the Marshall Plan," *Journal of Modern History* 64 (September 1992): 520–22; and Gérard Bossuat, *Les aides américaines économiques et militaires à la France (1938–1960): Une nouvelle image des rapports de puissance* [American economic and military assistance to France (1938–1960): A new portrait of the power relationships] (Paris: Comité pour l'histoire économique et financière de la France, 2001), http://books.openedition.org/igpde/2023.

15. Moulin, *Les porte-avions* Dixmude & Arromanches, 63; and Coutau-Bégarie, "Marine et innovation," 123.

16. Moulin, *Les porte-avions* Dixmude & Arromanches, 44; and Quérel, *Vers une marine atomique,* 57–58.

17. Moulin, *Les porte-avions* Dixmude & Arromanches, 44; and Coutau-Bégarie, "Marine et innovation," 123.

18. Moulin, *Les porte-avions* Dixmude & Arromanches, 117–24; and Monaque, *Une histoire de la marine,* 445.

19. Anne Deighton, "Entente Neo-Coloniale: Ernest Bevin and the Proposals for an Anglo-French Third World Power, 1945–1949," in *Anglo-French Relations since the Late Eighteenth Century* (London: Routledge, 2008): 201–18; and Élisabeth du Réau, "Les origines et la portée du traité de Dunkerque vers une nouvelle 'entente cordiale'? (4 mars 1947)" [The origins and scope of the Treaty of Dunkirk toward a new 'entente cordiale'? (4 March 1947)] in *Matériaux pour l'histoire de notre temps* 18 (1990): 23–26.

20. Seafire Aircraft and Equipment for the French Naval Air Service, letter from Mr. J. G. Gibson (British Air Ministry) to Mr. D. F. C. Blunt (British Treasury), 10 November 1945, ADM 1/17529, TNA.

21. Quérel, *Vers une marine atomique,* 58.

22. "Condamnations de bâtiments faites depuis la Libération" [Paying off of Vessels since the Liberation], 10 December 1946, 3 BB 2 SEC 114, SHD.

23. Séances de la Commission de la Défense nationales 1944–1946 [Sessions of the National Defense Commission 1944–1946], statement by Minister Michelet, 13 February 1946, C//15275, Archives nationales.

24. Report from the Secrétariat d'état à la Marine to the General National Defense Staff, "Bilan de la Marine française au 1er janvier 1948" [State of the French Navy on 1 January 1948], 3 BB 2 SEC 114, SHD.

25. Statement by Commander Barthélémy at National Defense Commission on 20 February 1946, C//15275, Archives nationales. The quote is from Jordan and Dumas, *French Battleships,* 211.

26. Strub, "La renaissance de la marine française" (PhD thesis), 62; and Masson, "La marine française en 1946," 85.

27. Department of State, *Foreign Relations of the United States: Diplomatic Papers, The Conference of Berlin (The Potsdam Conference), 1945*, vol. 2, "Protocol of the Proceedings of the Berlin Conference (dated 1 August 1945)" (Washington, DC: U.S. Government Printing Office, 1959), https://history.state.org/historicaldocuments/frus1961-63v13/d273.

28. Quérel, *Vers une marine atomique*, 27; Claude Huan and Jean Moulin, *Les sous-marins français 1945–2000* [French submarines 1945–2000] (Rennes, FR: Marines Éditions, 2004), 9–11; and Olivier Huwart, *Sous-marins français:1944–1954, la décennie du renouveau* [French submarines: 1944–1954, the decade of renewal] (Rennes, FR: Marines Éditions, 2003), 70–97.

29. Quérel, *Vers une marine atomique*, 29; and Strub, *La renaissance de la marine française*, 90.

30. Report from the *Secrétariat d'état à la Marine* to the Minister of National Defense, "Bilan de la Marine française au 1er octobre 1950" [State of the French Navy, 1 October 1950], 3 BB 2 SEC 114, SHD.

31. Séances de l'Assemblée national constituante décembre 1945–avril 1946 [Sessions of the National Constituent Assembly December 1945–April 1946], minutes of the session held on 28 December 1945, C//15304, Archives nationales.

32. Cassagnou, *Les grandes mutations*, 37–61.

33. Quérel, *Vers une marine atomique*, 35–36; and Frédéric Marquié, "La reconversion des Chantiers et Arsenaux de la Marine (1946–1953)" [The reconversion of the navy's shipyards and dockyards (1946–1953)], *Revue historique des armées* 220, no 3 (September 2000): 112–27.

34. Quérel, *Vers une marine atomique*, 37; Marquié, "La reconversion des Chantiers et Arsenaux de la Marine," 124–26; and Charles Tillon, *On chantait rouge* [We were singing red] (Paris: Robert Laffont, 1977), 438–47.

35. Marquié, "La reconversion des Chantiers et Arsenaux de la Marine," 118–19.

36. Report from the Conseil supérieur de la Marine to the Ministère des Forces armées, "Renouvellement de la Flotte française" [Renewal of the French Fleet], 26 November 1947, 3 BB 2 SEC 114, SHD; and Quérel, *Vers une marine atomique*, 72.

37. Jaques Frémeaux, "L'union française: le rêve d'une France unie?" in *Culture impériale: Les colonies au coeur de la République, 1931–1961*, ed. Pascal Blanchard and Sandrine Lemaire, 163–73 (Paris: Éditions Autrement, 2004).

38. President of the Council of French Ministers Decree 47–1957 dated 9 October 1947, *Journal officiel de la République française—Débats parlementaires* [Official Journal of the French Republic—Parliamentary Debates; hereafter, *Journal officiel*] (10 October 1947), 10078, Archives de l'Assemblée nationale, Paris, France.

39. Quérel, "L'échec du *PA-28*."

40. Coutau-Bégarie, "Marine et innovation," 123.

41. Statement of Pierre Meunier, Chair of the Finance Committee, to the National Assembly on 6 August 1947, *Journal officiel* 90 (7 August 1947), 3970.

42. Report from the Conseil supérieur de la Marine to Ministère des Forces armées, "Renouvellement de la Flotte française" [Renewal of the French Fleet], 26 November 1947, 3 BB 2 SEC 114, SHD.

43. Various Records of the Conseil supérieur de la Marine [Superior Council of the Navy] 1947–1948, minutes of the Superior Council of the Navy session held on 24 March 1948, 3 BB 8 CMS 3, SHD.

44. Report from the Chief of the Naval General Staff to the Minister for the Navy, "Programme naval" [Naval Programme], 9 April 1948, 3 BB 2 SEC 114, SHD; and Note from the Minister for the Navy to the Chief of the Naval General Staff, 13 May 1948, 3 BB 8 CSM 2, SHD.

45. As reported to the National Defense Commission quoting a statement by Minister for the Armed Forces Teitgen. Séances de la Commission de la Défense nationales 1946–1948 [Sessions of the National Defense Commission 1946–1948], minutes of the session held on 9 June 1948, C//15339, Archives nationales.

46. "La Marine sur le Rhin" [The Navy on the Rhine], Marine nationale, last modified 28 June 2010, http://www.defense.gouv.fr/marine/manifestations/la-marine-sur-le-rhin; and Georges Prud'homme, Roland Oberlé, and Alain Kleimberg, *Les Forces Maritimes du Rhin* [The Rhine Maritime Forces] (Strasbourg, FR: Carré Blanc, 2007).

47. Alistair Horne, *A Savage War of Peace: Algeria, 1954–1962*, 2nd ed. (New York: New York Review Books, 2006), 23–28; and Jean-Louis Planche, *Sétif 1945: Histoire d'un massacre annoncé* [Sétif 1945: History of an expected massacre] (Paris: Perrin, 2006).

48. Jordan and Moulin, *French Cruisers*, 213; and "Bombardement de la région de Sétif par la marine" [Bombardment of the Sétif Area by the Navy], Algéroisement . . . Vôtre, last accessed 10 April 2017, http://algeroisementvotre.free.fr/site0301/mai1945/mai45101.html.

49. Anthony Clayton, *The Wars of French Decolonization* (London: Routledge, 1994), 79–87; and Hubert Granier, *Histoire des marins français: A Madagascar (1947–1948) et en Indochine (1946–1954)* [A history of the French sailors: In Madagascar (1947–1948) and Indochina (1946–1954)] (Rennes, FR: Marines Éditions, 2010), 208–12.

50. Strub, *La renaissance de la marine française*, 48 and 64; and Monaque, *Une histoire de la marine*, 442–43.

51. Moulin, *Les porte-avions* Dixmude *&* Arromanches, 72–74.

52. Moulin, 134–36.

53. Jaouen, *Marin de guerre*, 61–65; and Victor Croizat, *Vietnam River Warfare 1945–1975* (London: Blandford, 1986), 36–71.

54. Jaouen, *Marin de guerre*, 79–91; and Louis Durteste, "La marine dans la guerre d'Indochine: Une adaption retrouvée" [The Navy in the Indochina war: Adaption

found again] in *L'Armée française dans la guerre d'Indochine (1946–1954): Adaptation ou inadaptation?* [The French Army in the Indochina war (1946–1954): Adaptation or maladjustment?] (Paris: Complexe, 2000): 299–300.

55. Du Réau, "Les origines et la portée du traité de Dunkerque," 23–26; and Sean Greenwood, *The Alternative Alliance: Anglo-French Relations before the Coming of NATO, 1944–1948* (London: Minerva, 1996), 253–82.

56. Greenwood, *The Alternative Alliance*, 283.

57. North Atlantic Treaty Organization, *Brussels Treaty: Treaty of Economic, Social and Cultural Collaboration and Collective Self-Defence, 17 March 1948*, last modified 1 October 2009, http://www.nato.int/cps/en/natohq/official_texts_17072.htm; and Lawrence S. Kaplan, *NATO 1948: The Birth of the Transatlantic Alliance* (Plymouth, UK: Rowman & Littlefield, 2007), 59–62.

58. NATO, *The Brussels Treaty*, Article VII.

59. NATO, Article IV.

60. Kaplan, *NATO 1948*, 149–53; and Maloney, *Securing Command of the Sea*, 67–68.

61. On Jaujard, see Taillemite, *Dictionnaire des marins française*, 255.

62. Lord Ismay, *NATO: The First Five Years, 1949–1954* (Utrecht, Netherlands: Bosch, 1954), 9.

63. Lawrence S. Kaplan, *A Community of Interests: NATO and the Military Assistance Program (1948–1951)* (Washington, DC: Office of the Secretary of Defense Historical Publication, 1980), 20–22; and National Security Council Report (NCS 9/3), "The Position of the United States with Respect to Support for Western Union and Other Related Free Countries," 28 June 948, in Department of State, *Foreign Relations of the United States Diplomatic Papers, 1948*, vol. 3, *Western Europe* (hereafter, *FRUS 1948*) (Washington, DC: U.S. Government Printing Office, 1948), 140–41.

64. Harry S. Truman, "The Truman Doctrine, delivered 12 March 1947 before a Joint Session of Congress," American Rhetoric, Top 100 Speeches, last modified 8 March 2017, http://www.americanrhetoric.com/speeches/harrystrumantrumandoctrine.html.

65. Trevor Salmon and William Nicoll, ed., *Building European Union: A Documentary History and Analysis* (Manchester, U.K.: Manchester University Press, 1997), 28–30.

66. "Minutes of the Second Meeting of the United States–United Kingdom–Canada Security Conversations, Held at Washington, March 23, 1948," in *FRUS 1948*, 65.

67. "Senate Resolution 239 (Vandenberg Resolution), June 11, 1948," in *FRUS 1948*, 136.

68. NSC 9/3, in *FRUS 1948*, 141.

69. Kaplan, *A Community of Interests*, 20–21.

70. Georgette Elgey, *Histoire de la IVᵉ République: La République des Illusions, 1945–1951* [History of the Fourth Republic: The Republic of Illusions, 1945–1951], 2nd ed.

(Paris: Fayard, 1993), 488–500; and Frank Giles, *The Locust Years: The Story of the Fourth French Republic, 1946–1958* (London: Secker & Warburg, 1991), 104–9.

71. Letter from the Minister of National Defense to the Secretaries of State and Chiefs of Staff of the Armed Forces (War, Navy, Air), 16 September 1948, 3 BB 2 SEC 114, SHD.

72. Aline Fonvieille-Vojtovic, *Paul Ramadier (1888–1961)* (Paris: Publications de la Sorbonne, 1993), 383–86; Maurice Vaïsse, "Ramadier et les problèmes de défense nationale (1947–1949)" [Ramadier and the national defense problems (1947–1949)], In *Paul Ramadier, la République et le socialisme* [Paul Ramadier, the Republic and Socialism] (Brussels: Complexe, 1990), 281–83; and Élisabeth du Réau, "Paul Ramadier et les prémisses du pacte atlantique," in *Paul Ramadier, la République et le socialisme* [Paul Ramadier, the Republic and Socialism] (Brussels: Complexe, 1990), 292–302.

73. Letter from the Minister of National Defense to the Secretaries of State and Chiefs of Staff of the Armed Forces (War, Navy, Air), 16 September 1948, 3 BB 2 SEC 114, SHD.

74. Letter from the Secretary of State for the Navy to the Minister of National Defense, 27 September 1948, 3 BB 2 SEC 114, SHD.

75. Sally Rohan, *The Western European Union: International Politics between Alliance and Integration* (New York: Routledge, 2014), 22–23; and *Summary Records and Documents from the First Meeting of the Defence Ministers of Western Union (Paris, 27 and 28 September 1948)*, CVCE.eu, last accessed 20 March 2020, https://www.cvce .eu/en/obj/summary_records_and_documents_from_the_first_meeting_of_the _defence_ministers_of_western_union_paris_27_and_28_september_1948-en -94248092-cc19-4e48-a416-2f5851f5f1cd.html.

76. Kaplan, *A Community of Interests*, 23.

77. Dupraz to Ramadier, 27 September 1948, 3 BB 2 SEC 114, SHD.

78. Baroë, *Cent ans d'Aéronavale*, 38–39.

79. *Journal officiel*, 22 June 1949, 3532–38.

80. Various Records of the *Conseil supérieur de la Marine* [Superior Council of the Navy] 1947–1948, minutes of the Superior Council of the Navy held on 26 November 1947, 3 BB 8 CSM 3, SHD.

81. Jordan and Moulin, *French Cruisers*, 213–22.

82. "Note de présentation d'un projet de statut naval" [Briefing Note on a Draft Naval Law], 30 July 1949, 3 BB 2 SEC 114, SHD.

83. "Mémorandum sur la politique navale française" [Memorandum on French Naval Policy], 25 February 1949, 3 BB 2 SEC 114, SHD.

84. Philippe Vial, "De la nécessité de l'aide, des inconvénients de la dépendance: Le réarmement de la Marine sous la IVᵉ République" [Of the need for assistance and the drawbacks of dependency: The navy's rearmament under the Fourth Republic], *Revue historique des Armées* 215 (June 1999): 22.

CHAPTER 6. RETURNING TO A STRATEGY OF ALLIANCE

1. Jean Moulin, *Destroyers d'Escorte en France, 1944–1972* [Destroyer escorts in France, 1944–1972] (Nantes, FR: Marines Éditions, 2004), 96 and 101.

2. Moulin, 132–44; and Whitley, *Destroyers of World War Two*, 300–302.

3. Moulin, *Destroyers d'Escorte*, 94–96 and 99–101.

4. Maurice Vaïsse, "L'échec d'une Europe franco-britannique, ou comment le pacte de Bruxelles fut créé et délaissé" [The Failure of Franco-British Europe, or How the Brussels Pact Was Created and Abandoned] in *Histoire des débuts de la construction européenne (9 mars 1948–mai 1950)* [History of the beginnings of the construction of Europe (9 March–May 1950)] (Brussels: Bruylant, 1986), 369–89; and Pierre Guillen, "France and the Defence of Western Europe: from the Brussels Pact (March 1948) to the Pleven Plan (October 1950)," in *The Western Security Community, 1948–1950: Common Problems and Conflicting National Interests during the Foundation Phase of the North Atlantic Alliance* (Oxford: Berg, 1994), 125–30.

5. Cable from Secretary of State Marshall to the Embassy in France for relay to French foreign minister Georges Bidault, 12 March 1948, *FRUS 1948*, 50.

6. Minutes of the meeting held on 3 December 1948, Various Records of the *Conseil supérieur de la Marine* [Superior Council of the Navy] 1947–48, 3 BB 8 CSM 3, SHD.

7. Chester J. Pach, *Arming the Free World: The Origins of the United States Military Assistance Program, 1945–1950* (Chapel Hill: University of North Carolina Press, 1991), 130.

8. Pach, 131.

9. Kaplan, *A Community of Interests*, 44.

10. Charles C. Cogan, "From the Fall of France to the Force de Frappe: The Remaking of French Military Power, 1940–62," in *The Fog of Peace and War Planning: Military and Strategic Planning under the Fog of Uncertainty* (London: Routledge, 2006), 237. The text of the Mutual Defense Assistance Act of 1949 can be found in full in annex D of Kaplan, *A Community of Interests*, 214–22.

11. Kaplan, *A Community of Interests*, 51–52; and Steven L. Rearden, *The Formative Years 1947–1950*, vol. 1 of *History of the Office of the Secretary of Defense* (Washington, DC: Historical Office, Office of the Secretary of Defense, 1984), 504–6.

12. Cogan, "From the Fall of France to the *Force de Frappe*," 236–37; and Andrew M. Johnston, "The Construction of NATO's Medium Term Defence Plan and the Diplomacy of Conventional Strategy, 1949–1950," *Diplomacy & Statecraft* 12, no. 2 (June 2001): 94.

13. Rearden, *The Formative Years*, 482.

14. Maloney, *Securing Command of the Sea*, 88.

15. Rearden, *The Formative Years*, 482; Johnston, "The Construction of NATO's Medium Term Defence Plan," 94; and Department of State, *Foreign Relations of*

the United States, 1951, vol. 4, part 1: *Europe: Political and Economic Developments* (hereafter, *FRUS 1951*) (Washington, DC: U.S. Government Printing Office, 1985), 771.

16. Moulin, *Les porte-avions* Dixmude & Arromanches, 77–78; and Cogan, "From the Fall of France to the *Force de Frappe*," 237.

17. Kaplan, *A Community of Interests*, 54; and Bossuat, *Les aides américaines économiques et militaires*.

18. Masson, *Histoire de l'armée française*, 381; and Vaïsse, "Ramadier et les problèmes de défense nationale," 281.

19. Masson, *Histoire de l'armée française*, 376–77; Vial, "La genèse du poste de chef d'état-major des armées," 34; and Cogan, "From the Fall of France to the *Force de Frappe*," 231–32.

20. Kaplan, *A Community of Interests*, 56–57.

21. Quérel, *Vers une marine atomique*, 180; and Vial, "De la nécessité de l'aide," 25.

22. Vial, "De la nécessité de l'aide," 25; Strub, "La renaissance de la Marine française" (PhD thesis), 162; and Letter from US Ambassador to France to France Minister for Foreign Affairs, 31 May 1950, including the secret annex "Fiscal Year 1950 MDA Program—France," Foreign Service Posts of the Department of State, France, Paris Embassy: Mutual Defense Assistance Program (MDAP) Subject Files, 1949–1953, RG 84 Box 2, National Archives and Records Administration, College Park, MD (hereafter, NARA).

23. Philippe Strub, "La renaissance de la Marine française sous la Quatrième République, 1945–1956" [Renewal of the French navy under the Fourth Republic, 1945–1956)], *Bulletin de l'Institut Pierre Renouvin* 1, no. 25 (2007): 201.

24. Quérel, *Vers une marine atomique*, 20; and Taillemite, *Dictionnaire des marins français*, 32.

25. Strub, "La renaissance de la Marine française" (PhD thesis), 199; and Étienne Taillemite, *Dictionnaire des marins français*, 295–96.

26. Strub, "La renaissance de la Marine française" (PhD thesis), 205; and Jules Moch, *Une si longue vie* [Such a long life] (Paris: Robert Laffont, 1976), 403–4.

27. Taillemite, *Dictionnaire des marins français*, 393; and Taillemite, *Les hommes qui ont fait la Marine française* [The men who forged the French navy] (Paris: Perrin, 2008), 383.

28. Bernard B. Fall, *Street without Joy: The French Debacle in Indochina*, 3rd ed. (Mechanicsburg, PA: Stackpole, 2005), 33.

29. Masson, *Histoire de l'armée française*, 396–97; and Fredrik Logevall, *Embers of War: The Fall of an Empire and the Making of America's Vietnam* (New York: Random, 2012), 238–50.

30. Moulin, *Les porte-avions* Dixmude & Arromanches, 139–40.

31. "Special Message to the Congress Reporting on the Situation in Korea," 19 July 1950, Harry S. Truman Library & Museum, https://www.trumanlibrary.gov /library/public-papers/193/special-message-congress-reporting-situation-korea.

32. "A Report to the National Security Council—NSC 68," Executive Secretariat on United States Objectives and Programs for National Security, 14 April 1950, Harry S. Truman Library & Museum, https://www.trumanlibrary.gov/library /research-files/report-national-security-council-nsc-68.

33. Kaplan, *A Community of Interests*, 104–5.

34. Kaplan, 108.

35. Strub, "La renaissance de la Marine française" (PhD thesis), 167–68; and U.S. Ambassador to France to the Secretary of State, "Review of Political Developments during the Months of June, July and August 1950," 1 September 1950, in Department of State, *Foreign Relations of the United States, 1950*, vol. 3: *Western Europe* (hereafter, *FRUS 1950*) (Washington, DC: U.S. Government Printing Office, 1977), 1383–87.

36. Statement by Minister of National Defense Moch at the session held on 6 December 1950, *Séances de la Commission de la Défense* nationales 1950–1951 [Sessions of the National Defense Commission 1950–1951], C//15341, Archives nationales.

37. Telegram, US ambassador to France to the Secretary of State, 16 September 1950, *FRUS 1950*, 1388.

38. Logevall, *Embers of War*, 257; and Telegram from Department of State to American Embassy in Paris, 4 July 1950, RG 84 Box 1, NARA.

39. Telegram from American Embassy in Paris to Department of State, 11 May 1950, RG 84 Box 1, NARA.

40. USIS News Release, 6 July 1950, "MDAP Shipments to Indochina Announced," RG 84 Box 1, NARA. See also Logevall, *Embers of War*, 256.

41. NATO, *Report from the Military Committee to the North Atlantic Defense Committee on North Atlantic Treaty Organization Medium Term Plan* (dated 28 March 1950), last accessed 12 July 2017, http://www.nato.int/docu/stratdoc/eng/a500328d.pdf.

42. Maurice Vaïsse, *Les relations internationales depuis 1945* [International relations since 1945] 14th ed. (Paris: Armand Collin, 2015), 22–27; and Hermann-Josef Rupieper, "The United States and the Founding of the Federal Republic, 1948–1949," in *The United States and Germany in the Era of the Cold War, 1945–1968: A Handbook*, vol. 1, ed. Detlef Junker, 85–89 (Cambridge: Cambridge University Press, 2004).

43. *FRUS 1950*, 1388–95; Masson, *Histoire de l'armée française*, 384; and Dean Acheson, *Present at the Creation: My Years at the State Department* (New York: Norton, 1969), 441–45.

44. Kaplan, *A Community of Interest*, 121; and Masson, *Histoire de l'armée française*, 383–84.

45. *FRUS 1950*, 1396–434 provides a full record of these talks.

46. *FRUS 1950*, 1398 and 1405; and Quérel, *Vers une marine atomique*, 185.

47. *FRUS 1950*, 1405.

48. *FRUS 1950*, 1398.

49. Strub, "La renaissance de la Marine française" (PhD thesis), 203.

50. Cogan, "From the Fall of France to the *Force de Frappe*," 237.

51. Baer, *One Hundred Years of Sea Power*, 322; and David Miller, *The Cold War: A Military History* (New York: St. Martin's, 1998), 219–22.

52. Moulin, *Destroyers d'Escorte en France*, 115.

53. M.D.A.P. Orientation Meeting—January 11th & 12th 1950, RG 84 Box 2, NARA.

54. Curt Cardwell, *NSC 68 and the Political Economy of the Cold War* (New York: Cambridge University Press, 2011), 217.

55. M.D.A.P. Orientation Meeting (document not paginated), RG 84 Box 2, NARA; and Cardwell, *NSC 68*, 242.

56. "Plan de développement des Forces Armées—Marine" [Development Plan for the Armed Forces—Navy], 24 August 1950, 3 BB 2 SEC 114, SHD.

57. "Constructions navales à entreprendre entre 1950 et 1954 (Plan de cinq ans)" [Naval Shipbuilding to Be Undertaken Between 1950 and 1954 (Five-Year Plan)], 16 October 1950, 3 BB 2 SEC 114, SHD.

58. Jordan and Dumas, *French Battleships*, 211; and Dumas, *Le cuirassé Jean Bart*, 37–43.

59. Minutes of the Superior Council of the Navy meeting 11 October 1950, 3 BB 8 CSM 4, SHD.

60. Strub, "La renaissance de la Marine française" (PhD thesis), 202; Vercken, *Histoire succincte de l'Aéronautique*, 94.

61. Strub, "La renaissance de la Marine française" (PhD thesis), 180; and Kaplan, *A Community of Interests*, 155.

62. Strub, "La renaissance de la Marine française" (PhD thesis), 203–4; and Statement by Minister of National Defense Moch at the session of the Commission de la défense nationale held on 6 December 1950, C//15341, Archives nationales.

63. Statement by Secretary of State for the Navy Monteil at the session of the Commission de la défense nationale held on 6 December 1950, C//15341, Archives nationales.

64. Statement by Minister of National Defense Moch at the session of the Commission de la défense nationale held on 6 December 1950, C//15341, Archives nationales.

65. Masson, *Histoire de l'armée française*, 397–98; Logevall, *Embers of War*, 261–78; and Fall, *Street without Joy*, 37–44.

CHAPTER 7. BUILDING A BLUE-WATER FLEET

1. Ambrose, *Eisenhower*, 436–51; and Isaac Alteras, "Eisenhower and the Sinai Campaign of 1956: The First Major Crisis in US-Israeli Relations," in *The 1956 War: Collusion and Rivalry in the Middle East*, 2nd ed. (London: Routledge, 2013): 25–46.

2. Baer, *One Hundred Years of Sea Power*, 361–62; and William B. Garrett, "The U.S. Navy's Role in the 1956 Suez Crisis," *Naval War College Review* 22, no. 7 (March 1970): 66–78.

3. Grove, *From Vanguard to Trident*, 191–92; and Philippe Vial, "La Marine et l'opération de Suez" [The Navy and the Suez Operation], in *La France et l'opération de Suez* [France and the Suez Operation] (Paris: ADDIM, 1997), 181–226.

4. Alexandre Sheldon-Duplaix, *Histoire mondiale des porte-avions*, 100–101 and 107–16; Hervé Coutau-Bégarie, "Marine et innovation," 120–21 and 126; Baer, *One Hundred Years of Sea Power*, 335–39; and Grove, *From Vanguard to Trident*, 10–12 and 55–57.

5. Moulin, *Les porte-avions* Dixmude & Arromanches, 141; and Vercken, *Histoire succincte de l'Aéronautique*, 84.

6. Strub, "La renaissance de la marine française" (PhD thesis), 203; Vercken, *Histoire succincte de l'Aéronautique*, 116; and Jean Moulin, *Les porte-avions* La Fayette & Bois-Belleau [Aircraft carriers *La Fayette* and *Bois-Belleau*] (Nantes, FR: Marines Éditions, 2000), 49.

7. Moulin, *Les porte-avions* La Fayette & Bois-Belleau, 28–29; and "Langley II (CVL-27)," Naval History and Heritage Command, last modified 28 July 2015, https://www.history.navy.mil/research/histories/ship-histories/danfs/l /langley-cvl-27-ii.html.

8. Masson, *Histoire de l'armée française*, 406; and Vercken, *Histoire succincte de l'Aéronautique*, 107–11.

9. Moulin, *Les porte-avions* Dixmude & Arromanches, 77–85.

10. Aide-memoire from the United States Embassy in Paris to the French Ministry of National Defense, 4 February 1951, RG 84 Box 5, NARA.

11. Letter from Kahn to Deputy Special Assistant for MDAP France, 30 March 1951, RG 84 Box 5, NARA.

12. Huan and Moulin, *Les sous-marins français*, 14.

13. Huwart, *Sous-marins français: 1944–1954*, 77–80 and 177–80.

14. "Situation de la Flotte sous-marine. Besoins en sous-marins. Proposition de programme" [Situation of the Submarine Fleet. Needs for submarines. Proposal for a Programme], 19 September 1952, 3 BB 8 CSM 4, SHD.

15. Huwart, *Sous-marins français: 1944–1954*, 174–77; and Folder labeled "*CSM—Projet sous-marin E 48*" [CSM—Submarine Project E 48], 3 BB 8 CSM 4, SHD.

16. Huan and Moulin, *Les sous-marins français*, 15; and Quérel, *Vers une marine atomique*, 247.

17. Minutes of the Superior Council of the Navy meeting 15 May 1948, 3 BB 8 CSM 3, SHD.

18. Minutes of the Superior Council of the Navy meeting 15 May 1952, 3 BB 8 CSM 4, SHD.

19. Minutes of the Superior Council of the Navy meeting 2 October 1954, 3 BB 8 CSM 5, SHD; and "Les sous-marins à haute performance de 800 tonnes du type *Daphné*" [The *Daphné*-class high-performance submarines of 800 tons], Netmarine.net, last accessed 15 August 2017, www.netmarine.net/bat/smarins /junon/typedaphne/index1.htm.

20. Huan and Moulin, *Les sous-marins français*, 17.

21. Public Law 165, Mutual Security Act of 1951, 10 October 1951, https://www.gpo .gov/fdsys/pkg/STATUTE-65/pdf/STATUTE-65-Pg373.pdf.

22. Kaplan, *A Community of Interests*, 158–62; and Bossuat, *Les aides américaines*.

23. Bossuat, *Les aides américaine*. The text of the accord can be found in Department of State, *Foreign Relations of the United States, 1952–1954*, vol. 6: *Western Europe and Canada*, part 2 (hereafter, *FRUS Western Europe and Canada 1952–1954*) (Washington, DC: U.S. Government Printing Office, 1986), 1171–74.

24. U.S. Department of Defense, *United States—Vietnam Relations, 1945–1967: A Study Prepared by the Department of Defense* ("The Pentagon Papers"), vol. 1, chap. 4, "U.S. and France in Indochina, 1950–1956" (Boston: Beacon, 1971), https:// www.mtholyoke.edu/acad/intrel/pentagon/pent9.htm.

25. Monaque, *Histoire de la marine de guerre*, 443.

26. Ismay, *NATO*, 47–48; NATO, *North Atlantic Council Ninth Meeting Final Communiqué—Lisbon, 20–25 February 1952*, https://www.nato.int/docu/comm/49-95 /c520225a.htm; and John S. Duffield, *Power Rules: The Evolution of NATO's Conventional Force Posture* (Stanford, CA: Stanford University Press, 1995), 56–74.

27. Cogan, "From the Fall of France to the Force de Frappe," 238; and Ingo Trauschweizer, "Adapt and Survive: NATO and the Cold War," in *Grand Strategy and Military Alliances* (Cambridge: Cambridge University Press, 2016), 173.

28. Admiral Nomy, *Programme naval* [Naval Programme], 12 July 1952, 3 BB 8 CSM 5, SHD.

29. Quérel, *Vers une marine atomique*, 200–201.

30. Séances de la Commission des Finances 1950–1960 [Sessions of the Finance Commission 1950–1960], minutes of the session held on 4 March 1949, 20060132- 10, Archives nationales.

31. Edmond Delage, "Bilan naval" [Naval assessment], *Le Monde* (2 September 1949): 3.

32. Baer, *One Hundred Years of Sea Power*, 322–26; Antony Preston, "The Korean War's Naval Lessons: Influence on Naval Policy and Tactics," *DefenseMediaNetwork*, May 30, 2014, https://www.defensemedianetwork.com/stories/the-korean-wars -naval-lessons/2/; Charles W. Koburger, *The French Navy in Indochina: Riverine and Coastal Forces, 1945–54* (New York: Praeger, 1991), 91–108; and Durteste, "La marine dans la guerre d'Indochine," 303–6.

33. Sheldon-Duplaix, *Histoire mondiale des porte-avions*, 108–11; and Thomas C. Hone, Norman Friedman, and Mark D. Mandeles, "The Development of the Angled-Deck Aircraft Carrier," *Naval War College Review* 64, no. 2 (Spring 2011): 69–72.

34. Bruce Cunningham, "History of the Douglas A3D Skywarrior, Part 2: Early Production Testing," *American Aviation Historical Society* 51, no. 4 (Winter 2006): 272–88.

35. Robert J. Kowalski and Tommy H. Thomason, *Grumman S2F/SF-2 Tracker*, Part 1: *Development, Testing, Variants and Foreign Users* (Simi Valley, CA: Ginter, 2016).

36. David K. Stumpf, *Regulus: America's First Nuclear Submarine Missile* (Paducah, KY: Turner, 1996), 84.

37. Lawrence Sondhouse, *Navies in Modern World Histories* (London: Reaktion, 2004), 237–39.

38. "Soviet Navy Has 300 Submarines, 4 Times Nazis' in '39, Kimball Says," *New York Times*, 2 October 1952, http://www.nytimes.com/1952/10/02/archives/soviet-navy-has-300-submarines-4-times-nazis-in-39-kimball-says.html.

39. Dean C. Allard, "Strategic Views of the US Navy and NATO on the Northern Flank, 1917–1991," *Northern Mariner/Le marin du nord* 11, no. 1 (January 2001): 13; and Geoffrey Till, "Holding the Bridge in Troubled Times: The Cold War and the Navies of Europe," *Journal of Strategic Studies* 28, no. 2 (April 2005): 317.

40. *Journal officiel de la République française*, 11 juin 1952, p. 2810, Archives de l'Assemblée nationale, Paris, France.

41. Quérel, *Vers une marine atomique*, 141–45; Assemblée nationale, "Le Gouvernement provisoire et la Quatrième République (1944–1958)" [The Provisional Government and the Fourth Republic (1944–1958)], http://www2.assemblee-nationale.fr/decouvrir-l-assemblee/histoire/histoire-de-l-assemblee-nationale/le-gouvernement-provisoire-et-la-quatrieme-republique-1944-1958#node_2228; and Assemblée nationale, "Les commissions de l'Assemblée nationale" [The Commissions of the National Assembly], Secrétariat général de l'Assemblée nationale, *Connaissance de l'Assemblée* no. 12, last modified January 2000, http://www.assemblee-nationale.fr/connaissance/collection/12.asp.

42. Masson, *De la vapeur à l'atome*, 208–14; and Frédéric Saffroy, *Le bouclier de Neptune: La politique de défense des bases françaises en Méditerranée (1912–1931)* [Neptune's shield: Mediterranean bases defense policy (1912–1931)] (Rennes, FR: Presses universitaires de Rennes, 2015).

43. Masson discusses the draft statute in *De la vapeur à l'atome*, 323–30, and underlines the parallels between the 1924 and 1952 draft statutes at page 505. See also Taillemite, *Dictionnaire des marins français*, 479–80 (for Salaün) and 345–55 (for Leygues).

44. Bossuat, *Les aides américaines*.

45. Cable from the U.S. ambassador in France to the State Department, 8 May 1952, *FRUS Western Europe and Canada 1952–1954*, 1203–5.

46. Bossuat, *Les aides américaines*.

47. Baroë, *Cent ans d'Aéronavale*, 45; and Vercken, *Histoire succincte de l'Aéronautique*, 89.

48. Letter from Marshall Alphonse Juin to *Secrétaire d'État à la Marine* Jacques Gavini, 15 July 1952, 3 BB 8 CSM 5, SHD.

49. Briefing note from Vice-Admiral Henri Nomy to *Secrétaire d'État à la Marine* Jacques Gavini, 12 July 1952, 3 BB 8 CSM 5, SHD.

50. Minutes of the CSM session that took place on 15–16 July 1952, 19 July 1952, 3 BB 8 CSM 5, SHD.

51. Strub, "La renaissance de la Marine française" (PhD thesis), 235; and Quérel, *Vers une marine atomique*, 216.

52. *Journal officiel de la République française—Débats parlementaires*, 27 janvier 1953, p. 439, Archives de l'Assemblée nationale, Paris, France.

53. Jordan and Moulin, *French Cruisers*, 226.

54. Strub, "La renaissance de la marine française" (PhD thesis), 228; and STCAN Briefing Note 611/440 "Programme d'un porte-avions" [Aircraft Carrier Programme], dated 10 April 1953, 3 BB 8 CSM 5, SHD.

55. Response from the Naval General Staff to a query from the National Defense Commission of the National Assembly, 4 November 1953, 3 BB 8 CSM 5, SHD.

56. Vial, "De la nécessité de l'aide," 28.

57. Response from the Naval General Staff to a query from the National Assembly National Defense Commission, 4 November 1953, 3 BB 8 CSM 5, SHD; Strub, "La renaissance de la marine française" (PhD thesis), 244; and Quérel, *Vers une marine atomique*, 115.

58. Strub, "La renaissance de la marine française" (PhD thesis), 247.

59. Moulin, *Les porte-avions* La Fayette *&* Bois-Belleau, 105.

60. Ambrose, *Eisenhower*, 369–71; and Logevall, *Embers of War*, 338–44.

61. Moulin, *Les porte-avions* La Fayette *&* Bois-Belleau, 89–107; and Timothy L. Francis, *Belleau Wood (CV-24) I 1943–1960*, Naval History and Heritage Command, last modified 24 February 2006, https://www.history.navy.mil/research /histories/ship-histories/danfs/b/belleau-wood-cv-24-i.html.

62. Moulin, *Les porte-avions* La Fayette *&* Bois-Belleau, 63–64 and 65–67. *La Fayette*'s deployment to Indochina violated the terms of her loan to France but the Eisenhower administration elected to disregard this issue.

63. Minutes of the CSM session held on 25 March 1953, 3 BB 8 CSM 5, SHD.

64. *Journal officiel de la République française—Débats parlementaires*, 16 March 1953, 900.

65. Minutes of the CSM session held on 2 October 1954, 3 BB 8 CSM 5, SHD.

66. Dumas, *Le cuirassé* Jean Bart, 73; Jordan and Moulin, *French Cruisers*, 226; and John Jordan, "Surcouf—The French Postwar Destroyers, Part 1," *Warship* 9, no. 35 (1985): 153.

67. Jean Moulin, "Les escorteurs rapides, tomes 1 & 2" [Fast escorts, parts 1 & 2], *Marines—Guerre & Commerce* 42–43 (March–April 1996).

68. Huan and Moulin, *Les sous-marins français 1945–2000*, 102–5.

69. *Journal officiel de la République française—Débats parlementaires*, 17 March 1954, p. 901–2.

70. Various Records of the Conseil supérieur de la Marine [Superior Council of the Navy] 1955, "Directive pour le programme naval" [Naval Programme Directive], dated 14 March 1955, 3 BB 8 CSM 7, SHD.

71. Masson, *De la vapeur à l'atome*, 525; and Philippe Vial and Jean-Benoît Cerino, "La Marine et le nouveau monde: L'enseignement de l'École de guerre navale face aux bouleversements du second après-guerre (1945–1956)" [The navy and the new world: Teachings at the Naval War College and the turmoil of the second postwar era (1945–1956)]. *Revue historique des Armées* 202 (March 1996): 106–22.

72. "La situation de la Marine en 1957–58 vis-à-vis de ses missions" [Status of the Navy and Its Missions in 1957–58], 13 October 1955, 3 BB 8 CSM 7, SHD.

CHAPTER 8. GOING NUCLEAR

1. Huan and Moulin, *Les sous-marins français*, 72; and Jean-Marie Mathey and Alexandre Sheldon-Duplaix, *Histoire des sous-marins des origines à nos jours* [History of submarines from the origins to today] (Paris: Éditions E-T-A-I, 2002), 88–89.

2. On the SSBN as a strategic concept, see Lisle A. Rose, *A Violent Peace, 1946–2006*, vol. 3 of *Power at Sea* (Columbia: University of Missouri Press, 2007), 48–63; and Philippe Masson, *La puissance maritime et navale au XXe siècle* [Maritime and naval power in the twentieth century] (Paris: Perrin, 2002), 324–27.

3. Yves Cariou, *FOST: Force océanique stratégique* [FOST: Oceanic strategic force] (Rennes, FR: Marines Éditions, 2013), 24–31; and Bernard Jacquet, "La base opérationnelle de l'Ile Longue, à quoi ça sert? Comment ça marche?" [The Île Longue operational base: What is its purpose? How does it work?], 29 December 2010, http://www.defense.gouv.fr/marine/dossiers/l-ile-longue /la-base-operationnelle-de-l-ile-longue.

4. Claude Carlier, "La genèse du système d'arme stratégique piloté Mirage IV (1956–1964)" [Genesis of the piloted strategic weapon system Mirage IV (1956–1964)], in *Armement et Ve République, fin des années 1950–fin des années 1960* [Armament and the Fifth Republic, late 1950s–late 1960s] (Paris: CNRS Éditions, 2002), 215; and Jean Cabrière, "Le programme Mirage IV" [The Mirage IV program], *Institut de Stratégie Comparée*, last accessed 15 December 2017, http://www.institut-strategie.fr/ihcc_nucı_Cabriere.html.

5. Masson, *Histoire de l'armée française*, 453; and CapCom Espace, "Histoire de missiles . . . Le 1er GMS du plateau d'Albion—La réalisation du 1er GMS" [A story of missiles . . . The 1st SMG of the Albion Plateau—Standing up the 1st SMG], last accessed 16 December 2017, https://www.capcomespace.net/dossiers /espace_europeen/albion/albion_operationel.htm.

6. Jean Guisnel and Bruno Tertrais, *Le Président et la bombe: Jupiter à l'Élysée* [The president and the bomb: Jupiter at the *Élysée*] (Paris: Odile Jacob, 2016), 241–45; and Shaun R. Gregory, *Nuclear Command and Control in NATO: Nuclear Weapons*

Operations and the Strategy of Flexible Response (London: Palgrave Macmillan, 1996), 131–33.

7. Gregory, *Nuclear Command and Control in NATO*, 135; and Ministère des armées, "Les forces sous-marines et la force océanique stratégique" [The submarine forces and the strategic oceanic force], 28 January 2020, https://www.defense.gouv.fr/english/marine/operations/forces/forces-sous-marines/les-forces-sous-marines-et-la-force-oceanique-strategique.

8. On the submarine's first patrol, see Cariou, *FOST*, 22–23; and Vincent Groizeleau, "*Le Redoutable*, histoire d'une aventure technique, humaine et stratégique" [*Le Redoutable*, History of a Technical, Human and Strategic Adventure], *Mer et Marine*, 27 March 2017, https://www.meretmarine.com/fr/content/le-redoutable-histoire-dune-aventure-technique-humaine-et-strategique-0. The latter includes lengthy reminiscences from the submarine's first commanding officer.

9. Cariou, *FOST*, 15–21; and Jean Touffait, "La construction du *Redoutable*" [The building of *Le Redoutable*], in *Armement et Ve République, fin des années 1950–fin des années 1960* [Armament and the Fifth Republic, late 1950s–late 1960s] (Paris: CNRS Éditions, 2002), 337–46.

10. Patrick Boureille, "Le fait nucléaire à travers l'évolution du budget de la Marine (1959–1970)" [The nuclear factor through the evolution of the navy's budget (1959–1970)], in *Armement et Ve République, fin des années 1950–fin des années 1960* [Armament and the Fifth Republic, late 1950s–late 1960s] (Paris: CNRS Éditions, 2002), 51–61.

11. Estival, *La marine française dans la guerre d'Indochine*, 166, 173, and 199–200.

12. For a contemporary perspective on the vulnerability problem of military bases on land during the early Cold War period, see the April 1954 RAND Study R-266 by Albert Wohlstetter, Fred Hoffman, R. J. Lutz, and S. Rowen, *Selection and Use of Strategic Air Bases*, RAND R-266 (1 April 1954). https://www.rand.org/pubs/reports/R0266.html.

13. Georgette Elgey sheds much light on these events in the last two volumes of her *Histoire de la IVe République: La République des Tourmentes, 1954–1959, tome 3: La fin* [History of the Fourth Republic: The republic of torments, 1954–1959, vol. 3: The end] (Paris: Fayard, 2008); and *tome 4: De Gaulle à Matignon* [vol. 4: De Gaulle at Matignon] (Paris: Fayard, 2012). For shorter but valuable accounts, see Giles, *The Locust Years*, 297–365; Roussel, *Charles de Gaulle*, 578–628; and Fenby, *The General*, 376–414.

14. Masson, *De la vapeur à l'atome*, 531; and Patrick Boureille, "La Marine et la guerre d'Algérie: Périodisation et typologies des actions" [The navy and the Algerian War: Periodization and categorization], in *Militaires et guérilla dans la guerre d'Algérie* [Military and guerilla in the Algerian War] (Paris: Éditions Complexes, 2001), 102.

15. Patrick Boureille, "La Marine et le putsch d'Algérie" [The navy and the Algerian Putsch], *Revue d'histoire maritime* 14 (2011): 186–95.

16. Pierre Castagnos, *Charles de Gaulle face à la mer* [Charles de Gaulle facing the sea] (Paris: Alantica, 2004), 347; and Sofia Papastamkou, "De la crise au Liban au mémorandum du 17 septembre 1958: La politique étrangère de la France entre deux républiques et une guerre" [From the Lebanon crisis to the 17 September 1958 memorandum: The foreign policy of France between two republics and a war], *Matériaux pour l'histoire de notre temps* 3, no. 99 (2010): 79.

17. Dwight D. Eisenhower, "Special Message to the Congress on the Situation in the Middle East January 5, 1957," American Presidency Project, www.presidency .ucsb.edu/ws/index.php?pid=11007&st=&st1; and Peter L. Hahn, "Securing the Middle East: The Eisenhower Doctrine of 1957," *Presidential Studies Quarterly* 36, no. 1 (March 2006): 38–47.

18. Castagnos, *Charles de Gaulle face à la mer*, 348.

19. Norman Polmar and K. J. Moore, *Cold War Submarines: The Design and Construction of U.S. and Soviet Submarines, 1945–2001* (Dulles, VA: Brassey's, 2004), 58–60; and William R. Anderson with Don Keith, *The Ice Diaries: The Untold Story of the Cold War's Most Daring Mission* (Nashville: Thomas Nelson, 2008).

20. Miloud Barkaoui, "Managing the Colonial *Status Quo*: Eisenhower's Cold War and the Algerian War of Independence," *Journal of North African Studies* 17, no. 1 (2012): 125–41; and Ali Tablit, "The United States and the Algerian War," *Kadhaya Tarikhia* 5 (March 2017): 1–25.

21. Dwight D. Eisenhower, "Letter to Secretary Dulles Regarding Transfer of the Affairs of the Foreign Operations Administration to the Department of State, 15 April 1955," American Presidency Project, http://www.presidency.ucsb.edu /ws/index.php?pid=10454; and "USAID History," United States Agency for International Development, last modified 8 December 2010, https://web.archive .org/web/20111009131110/http://www.usaid.gov/about_usaid/usaidhist.html.

22. Andrew David and Michael Holm, "The Kennedy Administration and the Battle over Foreign Aid: The Untold Story of the Clay Committee," *Diplomacy & Statecraft* 27, no. 1 (2016): 66–67; and "USAID History."

23. Benoît Rossignol and Roland Le Borgne, "Reconstruction, restructuration et modernisation des bases navales (1944–1949)" [Reconstruction, restructuration and modernization of naval bases (1944–1949)], *Revue historique des Armées* 220, no. 3 (September 2000): 99–102.

24. "Note pour le ministre. Objet: politique générale des bases" [Note to the Minister. Subject: Bases General Policy], May 1945 (exact date not specified), 3 BB 8 CSM 1, SHD.

25. Strub, "La renaissance de la marine française" (PhD thesis), 262.

26. For contemporary views, see Barjot, *Vers la Marine de l'âge atomique* [Toward the navy of the atomic age] (Paris: Amiot Dupont, 1955), 185–88; as well as

Raoul Castex, "Aperçus sur la bombe atomique" [Overview of the atomic bomb], *Revue de Défense nationale* 10 (October 1945): 31–39; and "L'Afrique et la stratégie française" [Africa and French strategy], *Revue de Défense nationale* (May 1952): 523–34.

27. Minutes of the Superior Council of the Navy session held on 11 July 1945, 3 BB 8 CMS 1, SHD.

28. "Élaboration du Statut naval" [Formulation of the naval statute], 30 May 1945, 3 BB 8 CSM 1, SHD; and "Politique générale des bases" [Bases general policy], 25 June 1947, CSM 2, SHD.

29. Minutes of the Superior Council of the Navy session held on 9 July 1947, 3 BB 8 CMS 2, SHD.

30. Philippe Vial, "Un impossible renouveau: bases et arsenaux d'outre-mer, 1945–1975" [An impossible renewal: Overseas bases and dockyards], in *Les bases et les arsenaux français d'outre-mer, du Second Empire à nos jours* [Overseas bases and dockyards, from the Second Empire to today] (Panazol, FR: Charles-Lavauzelle, 2002), 238.

31. Vial, 239.

32. Ismay, *NATO*, 114; and NATO, Comité de l'Infrastructure Committee, *50 Years of Infrastructure: NATO Security Investment Programme Is the Sharing of Roles, Risks, Responsibilities, Costs and Benefits*, last accessed 3 February 2018, https://www.nato.int/structur/infrastruc/50-years.pdf, 16 and 23.

33. Ismay, *NATO*, 115–16; NATO, *50 Years of Infrastructure*, 23–24.

34. Ismay, *NATO*, 124.

35. Séances de la Commission de la Défense nationales 1953–1954 [Sessions of the National Defense Commission 1953–1954], minutes of the National Assembly National Defense Commission held on 3 March 1954, C//15601, Archives nationales.

36. Strub, "La renaissance de la marine française" (PhD thesis), 185; and Quérel, *Vers une marine atomique*, 151.

37. Augustin-Léon Guillaume, "L'importance stratégique de l'Afrique du Nord" [The strategic importance of North Africa], *Revue de défense nationale* 108 (November 1953): 423–24.

38. Barjot, *Vers la Marine de l'âge atomique*, 198.

39. Vial, "Un impossible renouveau," 253; and Philippe Quérel, "La Marine entre l'O.T.A.N. et l'Union française au début des années 1950" [The navy between NATO and French Union at the beginning of the 1950s], *Revue historique des Armées* 201 (December 1995): 51–52.

40. Pierre Barjot, "Bizerte, port anti-atomique et nouveau Gibraltar de la Méditerranée centrale" [Bizerte, anti-atomic harbor and the new Gibraltar of the central Mediterranean]. *Revue de défense nationale* (August–September 1952): 147.

41. Martin Thomas, "France's North African Crisis, 1945–1955: Cold War and Colonial Imperatives," *History* 92, no. 2 (April 2007): 231–32.

42. Ismay, *NATO*, 116–18; and Vial, "De la nécessité de l'aide," 30.

43. Vial, "Un impossible renouveau," 268–70; Damien Cordier-Féron, "La base navale stratégique de Bizerte (1943–1963)" [The strategic naval base of Bizerte (1943–1963)], *Guerres mondiales et conflits contemporains* 213 (2004): 58–59; and Isabelle Laporte, "Mers el-Kébir après Mers el-Kébir (1940–1945)" [Mers el-Kébir after Mers el-Kébir (1940–1945)], *Revue historique des Armées* 223, no 2 (June 2001): 323–31.

44. Yves de Bazelaire, "La Marine et ses bases (en deux parties)" [The navy and its bases (in two parts)], *Revue de défense nationale* 240–41 (November–December 1965): 1672–82 and 1865–77.

45. "Le centre d'expérimentation du Pacifique (1963–1974)" [The Pacific experimentation center (1963–1974)], ECPAD Agences d'images de la Défense, last accessed 14 February 2018, http://archives.ecpad.fr/wp-content/uploads/2013/08/2013 _CEP_Dossier.pdf; and Charles Ailleret, *L'aventure atomique française: Souvenirs et réflexions* [The French atomic adventure: Reminiscences and reflections] (Paris: Grasset, 1968), 226–38.

46. Girardin-Thibeaud, *Les amiraux de Vichy*, 217–21; and Jean-Baptiste Bruneau, "La Marine, cité terrestre du contre-amiral Auphan" [The navy, land city of Rear-Admiral Auphan] *Revue d'Histoire Maritime* 16 (2013): 51–64.

47. Georges Cabanier related his experience in the submarine *Rubis* in *Croisières périlleuses* [Perilous cruises] (Paris: Presses de la Cité, 1969).

48. Taillemite, *Dictionnaire des marins français*, 81; and "Georges Cabanier," Musée de l'Ordre de la Libération, France, last accessed 16 February 2018, https://www .ordredelaliberation.fr/fr/les-compagnons/163/georges-cabanier.

49. Bernard Brodie, *Strategy in the Missile Age* (Princeton, NJ: Princeton University Press, 1959), 173–222 and 264–304; and Albert Wohlstetter, *The Delicate Balance of Terror*, RAND Paper P-1472 (1958), https://doi.org/10.7249/P1472.

50. Bruno Tertrais, "*Destruction assurée*: The Origins and Development of French Nuclear Strategy, 1945–1981," in *Getting Mad: Nuclear Mutual Assured Destruction, Its Origins and Practice* (Carlisle, PA: Strategic Studies Institute, 2004), 53. For these early days, see Ailleret, *L'aventure atomique française*, 79–123.

51. Guisnel and Tertrais, *Le Président et la bombe*, 22–23; and Dominique Mongin, "Genèse de l'armement nucléaire français" [Genesis of French Nuclear Armament], *Revue historique des armées* 262 (2011): 3.

52. Ailleret, *L'aventure atomique française*, 143; and Guisnel and Tertrais, *Le Président et la bombe*, 24.

53. Maurice Vaïsse, "Le Q-244, le premier sous-marin atomique français" [Q-244, the first French atomic submarine], *Revue historique des armées* 3 (September 1990): 36.

54. November 1947 briefing note (actual date unspecified), 3 BB8 CSM 2, SHD.

55. Vaïsse, "Le Q-244," 37; and Cariou, *FOST*, 12.

56. Minutes of the sessions held on 21 and 30 March 1955, 3 BB 8 CEM 13, SHD; and Maurice Vaïsse, "La filière sans issue: Histoire du premier sous-marin atomique

français" [The problem with no solution: History of the first French atomic submarine], *Relations internationales* 59 (Fall 1989): 336–37.

57. Gabrielle Hecht, *The Radiance of France: Nuclear Power and National Identity after World War II* (Cambridge, MA: MIT Press, 1998), 60–62.

58. Cariou, *FOST,* 12; and Vaïsse, "Le Q-244," 41–46.

59. Cited in Dominique Mongin in *La Direction des applications militaires au cœur de la dissuasion nucléaire française: De l'ère des pionniers au programme simulation* [The military applications directorate at the heart of French nuclear deterrence: From the pioneers era to the simulation program] (Paris: CEA DAM, 2016), 19.

60. Saki Dockrill, *Eisenhower's New-Look National Security Policy, 1953–61* (London: Macmillan, 1996), 98–99.

61. Castex, "Aperçus sur la bombe atomique," 34. Gallois first referred to Castex's influence in "L'affaire de Berlin ou la peur de la bombe" [The Berlin affair or the fear of the bomb], *La Nef* 27 (April 1959): 28.

62. Philip H. Gordon, *A Certain Idea of France: French Security Policy and the Gaullist Legacy* (Princeton, NJ: Princeton University Press, 1993), 57–59; and François Géré, "P.M. Gallois, stratège et pédagogue de la dissuasion nucléaire" [P.M. Gallois, nuclear deterrence strategist and teacher], *La revue géopolitique,* 4 February 2017, https://www.diploweb.com/P-M-Gallois-stratege-et-pedagogue-de -la-dissuasion-nucleaire.html.

63. Pierre Marie Gallois, *Stratégie de l'âge nucléaire* [Strategy in the nuclear age], 2nd ed. (Paris: François-Xavier de Guibert, 2009), 151–52.

64. Géré, "P.M. Gallois"; and Gordon, *A Certain Idea of France,* 58.

65. André Beaufre, *Dissuasion et stratégie* [Deterrence and strategy] (Paris: Armand Collin, 1964); and Lucien Poirier, *Des stratégies nucléaires* [Of nuclear strategies] (Paris: Hachette, 1977).

66. Charles Ailleret, "Défense 'dirigée' ou défense 'tous azimuts'" ["Directed Defense" or "All-round Defense"], *Défense nationale* 23 (December 1967): 1923–32.

67. Mongin, *La Direction des applications militaires,* 36–39; and Claude Chartier, "La genèse de l'armement atomique français: L'oeuvre de la Quatrième République" [The genesis of French atomic weapons during the Fourth Republic], *Historiens et Géographes* 99, no. 397 (March 2007): 293–95.

68. Tertrais, *"Destruction assurée,"* 55.

69. Ailleret, *L'aventure atomique française,* 301; and Marcel Duval, "Les décisions concernant l'armement nucléaire: Pourquoi, comment, quand?" [Decisions Concerning Nuclear Weapons: Why, How, When?], in *Armement et Ve République, fin des années 1950–fin des années 1960* [Armament and the Fifth Republic, late 1950s–late 1960s] (Paris: CNRS Éditions, 2002), 297.

70. Carlier, "La genèse du système d'arme stratégique piloté," 201; and Cabrière, "Le programme Mirage IV."

71. Cabrière, "Le programme Mirage IV"; and Jean Forestier, "Le Mirage IV, arme de précocité" [The Mirage IV, a precocious weapon], in *Armement et Ve République, fin des années 1950–fin des années 1960* [Armament and the Fifth Republic, late 1950s–late 1960s] (Paris: CNRS Éditions, 2002), 198.

72. Public Law 85-479, "An Act to Amend the Atomic Energy Act of 1954 as Amended," Approved 2 July 1958, U.S. Government Printing Office, https://uscode.house.gov/statutes/pl/85/479.pdf.

73. "Agreement between the Government of the United Kingdom of Great Britain and Northern Ireland and the Government of the United States of America for Co-operation on the Uses of Atomic Energy for Mutual Defence Purposes (3 July 1958)," Foreign and Commonwealth Office (United Kingdom), http://treaties.fco.gov.uk/docs/pdf/1958/ts0041.pdf.

74. "Memorandum of Conversation: The Secretary's Talk with General de Gaulle in Paris, July 5, 1958," in *Foreign Relations of the United States, 1958–1960*, vol. 7, part 1: *Western European Integration and Security; Canada* (hereafter, *FRUS Western Europe 1958–1960*) (Washington, DC: U.S. Government Printing Office, 1993), 56.

75. Vaïsse, "La filière sans issue," 343; and Duval, "Les décisions concernant l'armement nucléaire," 300–301.

76. "Letter from President de Gaulle to President Eisenhower (17 September 1958)," in *FRUS Western Europe 1958–1960*, 81–83.

77. Vaïsse, "Le Q-244, le premier sous-marin atomique français," 45–46; and "Editorial Note (Author Unknown)," in *FRUS Western Europe 1958–1960*, 212.

78. "Letter from President de Gaulle to Eisenhower (25 May 1959)," in *FRUS Western Europe 1958–1960*, 230.

79. Digithèque MJP, "Charles de Gaulle—Allocution à l'École militaire, 3 novembre 1959" [Charles de Gaulle—Address to the *École militaire*, 3 November 1959], http://mjp.univ-perp.fr/text/degaulle03111959.htm.

80. Patrice Buffotot, "Les lois de programmation militaire en France: un demi-siècle de programmation" [Military programming acts in France: Half a century of programming], *Revues électroniques de l'Université de Nice* 4 (15 July 2016), last accessed 2 March 2018, http://revel.unice.fr/psei/index.html?id=1060.

81. "Loi de programme no. 60-1305 du 8 décembre 1960 relative à certains équipements militaires" [Program Law no. 60-1305 of 8 December 1960 for some military equipment], *Journal officiel de la République française* (10 December 1960): 11076, Archives de l'Assemblée nationales.

82. Statement by ministre des Armées Pierre Guillaumat to the National Defense Commission, 30 October 1959, 20060132-6, Archives nationales; andStatement by Admiral Cabanier to the National Defense Commission, 3 October 1960, 3 BB 8 CEM 19, SHD.

83. Jacques Chevallier, "La genèse de la propulsion nucléaire en France" [The genesis of nuclear propulsion in France], presentation at the 1899/1999, un siècle de construction sous-marine, held on 25 and 26 October 1999, Cherbourg, France. www.sous-mama.org/la-genese-de-la-propulsion-nucleaire-en-france-blog-254 .html, 286–89; and André Gempp, "La mise en place et le développement des sous-marins nucléaires" [Design and development of nuclear submarines], *Institut de Stratégie comparée*, last accessed 3 March 2018, http://www.institut-strategie .fr/ihcc_nuc1_Gempp.html.

84. Fiches sur les études de la Marine [Briefing note on navy studies], 1 June 1956, 3 BB 8 CEM 17, SHD.

85. Mathey and Sheldon-Duplaix, *Histoire des sous-marins*, 84–87; and David Miller, *The Illustrated Directory of Submarines of the World* (St. Paul, MN: MBI, 2002), 402–10.

86. "Étude relative aux hypothèses d'armement nucléaire stratégique" [Study of strategic nuclear armament hypothesis], 10 November 1961, submitted for the Chiefs of Staff Committee session held on 13 November 1961, 3 BB 8 CEM 20, SHD.

87. Colette Barbier, "La Force multilatérale dans le débat atomique française" [The multilateral force in the French atomic debate], *Revue d'histoire diplomatique* 107, no. 1 (1993): 55–89; and Evgeny Kustnetsov, "Le projet de Force multilatérale de l'OTAN" [The NATO Multilateral Force Project], European University Institute, 2004, https://www.cvce.eu/content/publication /1999/1/1/937a5818-7fea-47da-944e-11114da4e0a3/publishable_fr.pdf.

88. John F. Kennedy, "Joint Statement Following Discussions with Prime Minister Macmillan: The Nassau Agreement December 21, 1962," American Presidency Project, http://www.presidency.ucsb.edu/ws/index.php?pid=9063.

89. Letter from Kennedy to de Gaulle, dated 20 December 1962, cited in Sebastian Reyn, *Atlantis Lost: The American Experience with De Gaulle, 1958–1969* (Amsterdam: Amsterdam University Press, 2010), 153.

90. De Gaulle statement cited in Roussel, *Charles de Gaulle*, 740.

91. Quoted in Reyn, *Atlantis Lost*, 159.

92. Cariou, *FOST*, 15; and Touffait, "La construction du *Redoutable*," 337.

93. Huan and Moulin, *Les sous-marins français*, 26–27; and Cariou, *FOST*, 39–40.

94. Cariou, *FOST*, 35–38; and CapCom Espace, "Histoire de missiles . . ."

95. Christian Schmidt and Guy Vidal, "Le contexte économique et financier des deux premières lois de programme militaire" [Economic and financial context of the first two military program laws], in *Armement et Vᵉ République, fin des années 1950–fin des années 1960* [Armament and the Fifth Republic, late 1950s–late 1960s] (Paris: CNRS Éditions, 2002), 43–46.

96. President de Gaulle's address to the *École navale* class and staff, 15 February 1965, cited in Charles de Gaulle, *Discours et messages*, tome 4: *Pour l'effort (Août*

62–Decembre 65) [Addresses and speeches, vol. 4: For the effort (August 1962–December 1965)] (Paris: Plon, 1970), 345.

CONCLUSION

1. Jordan and Dumas, *French Battleships*, 208; and Dumas, *Le cuirassé Richelieu*, 60.

2. Dumas, *Le cuirassé Jean Bart*, 76.

3. Cariou, *FOST*, 24–28; and Geneviève Emon Naudin, "L'Île Longue: quelle histoire!" [Île Longue: What a history!], Marine nationale, 29 December 2010, http://www.defense.gouv.fr/marine/dossiers/l-ile-longue/l-ile-longue-quelle-histoire.

4. Vercken, *Histoire succincte de l'Aéronautique*, 102–5; Moulin, *Les porte-avions* Dixmude & Arromanches, 230–58; and Moulin, *Les porte-avions* La Fayette & Bois-Belleau, 197–209.

5. "Etendard," Dassault Aviation, last accessed 19 April 2018, https://www.dassault-aviation.com/fr/passion/avions/dassault-militaires/etendard/.

6. Eric Stijger, "Aéronavale Crusaders," *Air International* 45, no. 4 (October 1993): 192–96.

7. "Breguet Br.1050 Alizé," AviationsMilitaires.net, last accessed 19 April 2018, https://www.aviationsmilitaires.net/v2/base/view/Model/267.html; and Greg Goebel, "The Breguet Alize & Fairey Gannet," *AirVectors*, 1 October 2017, http://www.airvectors.net/avalize.html.

8. "Sikorsky S.58 (H34 ou HSS)," Netmarine, last accessed 19 April 2018, http://netmarine.net/aero/aeronefs/hss/index.htm.

9. "P2V-6/-7 (P-2H) Neptune," French Fleet Air Arm, last accessed 20 April 2018, www.ffaa.net/aircraft/neptune/neptune_fr.htm.

10. "Martin P5M-2 Marlin," Aéronavale & Porte-avions, last modified 2 May 2012, http://aeronavale-porteavions.com/viewtopic.php?t=2103.

11. Minutes of the *Comité des Chefs d'état-major* meeting held on 29 March 1962, 3 BB 8 CEM 21, SHD.

12. Dumas, *Le cuirassé Jean Bart*, 54–56; and Jordan and Moulin, *French Cruisers*, 158 and 227.

13. "Frégate *Suffren*," Netmarine.net, last accessed 22 April 2018, http://www.netmarine.net/bat/fregates/suffren/index.htm; and "Patrouilleur *La Combattante*," Netmarine.net, last accessed 22 April 2018, http://netmarine.net/f/bat/combatan/.

14. Statement by Minister Messmer to the National Defense and Armed Forces Commission, 15 February 1962, 20060132-8, Archives nationales.

15. Vercken, *Histoire succincte de l'Aéronautique*, 96–98; and Baroë, *Cent ans d'Aéronavale*, 47–58.

16. Minutes of the meeting of the *Conseil supérieur de la Marine*, 14 September 1960, 3 BB 8 CMS 13, SHD; and "Missile porte-torpille Malafon" [Torpedo-carrying missile Malafon], Netmarine.net, last accessed 22 April 2018, http://www.netmarine.net/f/armes/malafon/index.htm.

17. Masson, *Histoire de l'armée française*, 454–55; and Michel L. Martin, *Warriors to Managers: The French Military Establishment since 1945* (Chapel Hill, NC: University of North Carolina Press, 1981), 39–52.

18. "Révision du plan naval à long terme," 5 September 1961, 3 BB 8 CEM 19, SHD.

19. Taillemite, *Histoire ignorée de la Marine française*; and Minutes of the session held on 23 November 1959, 3 BB 8 CMS 12, SHD.

20. Quérel, *Vers une marine atomique*, 335–90; Masson, *De la vapeur à l'atome*, 546; and Monaque, *Histoire de la marine de guerre*, 481.

BIBLIOGRAPHY

PRIMARY SOURCES

Archival Material

Archives nationales, Pierrefitte-sur-Seine, France

   Dossiers des séances du Comité de défense nationale [Files of the sessions of the National Defence Committee]: Boxes F/60/3009 to 3023

   Séances de la Commission de la Défense nationale et des Forces armées [Sessions of the National Defence and Armed Forces Commission]: Boxes 20060132-6 to 20060132-8

   Séances de la Commission des Finances [Sessions of the Finance Commission]: Box 20060132-10

   Séances de la Commission de la Défense nationale [Sessions of the National Defense Commission]: Boxes C//15265, C//15275, C//15339 to 15341, C//15600 to 15602, C//15753, C//17096

   Séances de l'Assemblée national constituante [Sessions of the National Constituent Assembly]: Box C//15304

Archives de l'Assemblée nationale, Paris, France

   Journal officiel de la République française—Débats parlementaires de la 4ème *République et Constituantes* [Official Journal of the French Republic—Parliamentary Debates of the Fourth Republic and the Constitutional Assemblies] (1945–58)

Dwight D. Eisenhower Presidential Library, Abilene, Kansas, United States (DDEPL)

   Columbia University Oral History Project: Oral History Interview with Amory Houghton, 27 August 1968.

   Gruenther, Alfred M. Papers, 1941–83, Box 1: NATO Series.

Norstad, Lauris. Papers, 1930–87, Country Series, 1955–62: Boxes 47, 48, 87, 90.
Principal File Series. Diaries, 1935–38, 1942, 1948–53, 1966, 1968, 1969 (one box).
———. Papers, Pre-Presidential, 1941–52: Boxes 130, 131.
———. Papers as President, 1953–61: Boxes 11 and 12.
Harry S. Truman Library & Museum, Independence, Missouri, United States
    "A Report to the National Security Council—NSC 68," Executive Secretariat on United States Objectives and Programs for National Security. 14 April 1950. https://www.trumanlibrary.gov/library/research-files/report -national-security-council-nsc-68.
    "Special Message to the Congress Reporting on the Situation in Korea," 19 July 1950. https://www.trumanlibrary.gov/library/public-papers/193/special -message-congress-reporting-situation-korea.
The National Archives (TNA), Kew, United Kingdom
    Admiralty. Correspondence and Papers: DM 1/9786, 9962, 10321, 10835, 13027, 14959, 17529, 18109, 18173, 18497.
    ———. Record Office: ADM 116/5343.
    ———. Naval Staff History: ADM 234/359.
    ———. Office of the First Sea Lord: ADM 205/4, 11.
    Cabinet Office. Minister of Defence Secretariat: CAB 120/285, 539, 540, 541.
    ———. Special Secret Information Centre: CAB 121/365, 398 to 411, 541.
    Cabinet Papers. Proceedings of the American-British Joint Chiefs of Staff: CAB 99/17.
    Foreign Office. Political Departments: FO 371/24332, 24338, 24345, 24382, 24383, 28212, 28234, 28235.
    Prime Minister's Office. Operational Correspondence and Papers: PREM 3/179/4.
    War Cabinet and Cabinet Office. CAB 119/153.
National Archives and Records Administration (NARA), College Park, Maryland, United States
    Foreign Service Posts of the Department of State. France, Paris Embassy: Mutual Defense Assistance Program (MDAP). Subject Files, 1949–53: RG 84 Boxes 1–14.
Service historique de la Défense (SHD), Section Marine, Vincennes, France
    1 BB 2 Container 172: Résumé des activités de la Marine française du 1er au 30 septembre 1939 [Summary of the Activities of the French navy 1–30 September 1939]
    3 BB 2 EG 57: Various Records of the Direction centrale des constructions et armes navales [Central Directorate of Constructions and Naval Armaments]
    3 BB 2 SEC 114: Situation de la Flotte, Tonnage, De 1939 à 1950 [Fleet Status, Tonnage, from 1939 to 1950]

3 BB 8 CEM 4–22: Various Records of the Comité des Chefs d'état-major [Chiefs of Staff Committee] 1950–62

3 BB 8 CSM 1–13: Various Records of the Conseil supérieur de la Marine [Superior Council of the Navy] 1945–60

Published Works

Acheson, Dean. *Present at the Creation: My Years at the State Department*. New York: Norton, 1969.

"Agreement between the Government of the United Kingdom of Great Britain and Northern Ireland and the Government of the United States of America for Co-operation on the Uses of Atomic Energy for Mutual Defence Purposes (3 July 1958)." Foreign and Commonwealth Office (United Kingdom). http://treaties.fco .gov.uk/docs/pdf/1958/ts0041.pdf.

Ailleret, Charles. "Défense 'dirigée' ou défense 'tous azimuts'" ["Directed" defense or "all-round" Defense]. *Défense nationale* 23 (December 1967): 1923–32.

———. *L'aventure atomique française: Souvenirs et réflexions* [The French atomic adventure: Reminiscences and reflections]. Paris: Grasset, 1968.

Anderson, William R., with Don Keith. *The Ice Diaries: The Untold Story of the Cold War's Most Daring Mission*. Nashville: Thomas Nelson, 2008.

Argenlieu, Thierry d'. "Les origines des FNFL" [Origins of the FNFL]. *Revue de la France Libre* 29 (June 1950): 17–20.

Assemblée nationale (France). "Le Gouvernement provisoire et la Quatrième République (1944–1958)" [The Provisional Government and the Fourth Republic (1944–1958)]. http://www2.assemblee-nationale.fr/decouvrir-l-assemblee/histoire /histoire-de-l-assemblee-nationale/le-gouvernement-provisoire-et-la-quatrieme-republique-1944-1958#node_2228.

———. "Les commissions de l'Assemblée nationale" [The commissions of the National Assembly]. Secrétariat général de l'Assemblée nationale. *Connaissance de l'Assemblée* no. 12. Last modified January 2000. http://www.assembleenationale .fr/connaissance/collection/12.asp.

Barjot, Pierre. "Bizerte, port anti-atomique et nouveau Gibraltar de la Méditerranée centrale" [Bizerte, anti-atomic harbour and the new Gibraltar of the Central Mediterranean]. *Revue de défense nationale*, August–September 1952, 144–60.

———. *Vers la marine de l'âge atomique* [Toward the navy of the atomic age]. Paris: Amiot Dupont, 1955.

Bazelaire, Yves de. "La Marine et ses bases (en deux parties)" [The navy and its bases (in two parts)]. *Revue de défense nationale* 240–41 (November–December 1965): 1672–82 and 1865–77.

Beaufre, André. *Dissuasion et stratégie* [Deterrence and strategy]. Paris: Armand Collin, 1964.

————. *Mémoires, 1920–1940–1945.* Paris: Presses de la Cité, 1965.

Béthouart, Anthoine. *Cinq années d'espérance: Mémoires de guerre 1939–1945* [Five years of hope: War memories 1939–1945]. Paris: Plon, 1968.

Brodie, Bernard. *Strategy in the Missile Age.* Princeton, NJ: Princeton University Press, 1959.

Cabanier, Georges. *Croisières périlleuses* [Perilous cruises]. Paris: Presses de la Cité, 1969.

Canadian Forces College Information Resources Centre (CFC IRC). *Minutes of the Combined Chiefs of Staff Meetings, 1942–1945.* Microfilm holdings, CFC IRC, Toronto, ON.

Cassin, René. "Comment furent signés les accords Churchill-de Gaulle du 7 août 1940" [How the Churchill-de Gaulle accords of 7 August 1940 were negotiated]. *Revue de la France Libre* 154 (January–February 1965). http://www.france-libre .net/accords-churchill-de-gaulle/.

Castex, Raoul. "Aperçus sur la bombe atomique" [Overview of the atomic bomb]. *Revue de Défense nationale* 10 (October 1945): 31–39.

Chaline, Émile. "Les Forces navales françaises libres" [The free French naval forces]. *Espoir* 100 (January 1995). http://www.charles-de-gaulle.org/pages/l-homme /dossiers-thematiques/1940-1944-la-seconde-guerre-mondiale/forces-navales -francaises-libres/analyses/les-forces-navales-francaise-libre-fnfl.php.

Chaline, Émile, and P. Santarelli. "L'activité des F.N.F.L. du 18 juin 1940 au 3 août 1943" [Activities of the F.N.F.L. from 18 June 1940 to 3 August 1943]. *Revue historique de la Défence* 176, no. 3 (September 1989): 67–80.

"Charles de Gaulle—Allocution à l'École militaire, 3 novembre 1959" [Charles de Gaulle—Address to the *École* militaire, 3 November 1959]. Digithèque MJP. http://mjp.univ-perp.fr/text/degaulle03111959.htm.

Charles-Roux, François. *Cinq mois tragiques aux Affaires étrangères* [Five tragic months at Foreign Affairs]. Paris: Plon, 1949.

Chevallier, Jacques. "La genèse de la propulsion nucléaire en France" [The genesis of nuclear propulsion in France]. Presentation at the "1899/1999, un siècle de construction sous-marine," held on 25 and 26 October 1999, Cherbourg, France. www.sous-mama.org/la-genese-de-la-propulsion-nucleaire-en-france-blog-254 .html.

Churchill, Winston S. *The Hinge of Faith.* Vol. 4 of *The Second World War* Cambridge: Riverside, 1950.

————. *The Second World War.* 6 vols. Cambridge: Riverside, 1948–53.

————. *Their Finest Hour.* Vol. 2 of *The Second World War.* Cambridge: Riverside Press, 1949.

Clark, Mark W. *Calculated Risk.* New York: Harper, 1950.

"Communiqué officiel" [Official Press Release]. *L'Écho d'Alger* 32, no. 12 (1 August 1943). http://gallica.bnf.fr/ark:/12148/bpt6k7587122x/f1.textePage.langES.

"Conférence de presse du 14 janvier 1963" [Press conference 14 January 1963]. Fondation Charles de Gaulle. http://fresques.ina.fr/de-gaulle/fiche-media/Gaulle00085/conference-de-presse-du-14-janvier-1963-sur-l-entree-de-la-grande-bretagne-dans-la-cee.html.

Cressman, Robert J. "Biter." Naval History and Heritage Command. 6 February 2006. https://www.history.navy.mil/research/histories/ship-histories/danfs/b/biter-i.html.

———. "Lafayette (AP-53) 1941–1945." Naval History and Heritage Command. 2 May 2007. https://www.history.navy.mil/research/histories/ship-histories/danfs/l/lafayette-ap-53.html.

"Cuban Missile Crisis: Telegram from the Embassy in France to the Department of State." 22 October 1962. Yale Law School, The Avalon Project. http://avalon.law.yale.edu/20th_century/msc_cuba046.asp#1.

Cunningham, Andrew B. *A Sailor's Odyssey: The Autobiography of Admiral of the Fleet Viscount Cunningham of Hyndhope.* London: Hutchinson, 195.

Cunningham, Bruce. "History of the Douglas A3D Skywarrior, Part 2: Early Production Testing." *American Aviation Historical Society* 51, no. 4 (Winter 2006): 272–88.

De Gaulle, Charles. "Appellations 'France Libre' et 'France Combattante'" ["Free France" and "Fighting France" Designations]. *Journal officiel de la France combattante,* 28 August 1942. http://archive.wikiwix.com/cache/?url=http%3A%2F%2Fwww.france-libre.net%2Ftemoignages-documents%2Fdocuments%2Fappellations-fl-fc.phpb.

———. *The Call to Honour, 1940–1942,* trans. Jonathan Griffin. Vol. 1 of *War Memoirs* London: Collins, 1955.

———. *L'Appel, 1940–1942.* Tome 1 de *Mémoires de guerre.* Paris: Plon, 1954.

———. *Le salut, 1944–1946.* Tome 3 de *Mémoires de guerre.* Paris: Plon, 1959.

———. *L'unité, 1942–1944.* Tome 2 de *Mémoires de guerre* [Unity, 1942–1944. Vol. 2 of War memoirs]. Paris: Plon, 1956.

———. *Salvation, 1944–1946,* trans. Richard Howard. Vol. 3 of *War Memoirs.* London: Weidenfled and Nicholson, 1960.

———. *Unity, 1942–1944,* trans. Richard Howard. Vol. 2 of *War Memoirs.* London: Weidenfled and Nicholson, 1959.

De Villefosse, Louis. *Souvenirs d'un marin de la France libre* [Memories of a free France sailor]. Paris: Éditeurs français réunis, 1951.

Decoux, Jean. À la barre de *l'Indochine: Histoire de mon gouvernement général (1940–1945)* [At Indochina's helm: History of my general governship (1940–1945)]. Paris: Plon, 1950.

Department of State. *Foreign Relations of the United States: The Conferences at Washington, 1941–1942, and Casablanca, 1943* [FRUS Casablanca 1943]. Washington, DC: U.S. Government Printing Office, 1968.

―――. *Foreign Relations of the United States, 1950.* Vol. 3: *Western Europe* [*FRUS 1950*]. Washington, DC: U.S. Government Printing Office, 1977.

―――. *Foreign Relations of the United States, 1951.* Vol. 4, part 1: *Europe: Political and Economic Developments* [*FRUS 1951*]. Washington, DC: U.S. Government Printing Office, 1985.

―――. *Foreign Relations of the United States, 1952–1954.* Vol. 6: *Western Europe and Canada,* part 2 [*FRUS Western Europe and Canada 1952–1954*]. Washington, DC: U.S. Government Printing Office, 1986.

―――. *Foreign Relations of the United States, 1958–1960,* vol. 7, part 1: *Western European Integration and Security; Canada* [*FRUS Western Europe 1958–1960*]. Washington, DC: U.S. Government Printing Office, 1993.

―――. *Foreign Relations of the United States: Diplomatic Papers, The Conference of Berlin (The Potsdam Conference), 1945.* Vol. 2, "Protocol of the Proceedings of the Berlin Conference (dated 1 August 1945)." Washington, DC: Government Printing Office, 1959. https://history.state.gov/historicaldocuments/frus1961-63v13/d273.

―――. *Foreign Relations of the United States: Diplomatic Papers, 1940.* Vol. 2: *General and Europe* [*FRUS 1940*]. Washington, DC: U.S. Government Printing Office, 1957.

―――. *Foreign Relations of the United States: Diplomatic Papers, 1941.* Vol. 6: *The American Republics* [*FRUS 1941*]. Washington, DC: U.S. Government Printing Office, 1963.

―――. *Foreign Relations of the United States: Diplomatic Papers, 1942: Europe* [*FRUS 1942*]. Washington, DC: Government Printing Office, 1972.

―――. *Foreign Relations of the United States Diplomatic Papers, 1948.* Vol. 3, *Western Europe* [*FRUS 1948*]. Washington, DC: U.S. Government Printing Office, 1948.

Eisenhower, Dwight D. *Crusade in Europe.* New York: Doubleday, 1948.

―――. "Letter to Secretary Dulles Regarding Transfer of the Affairs of the Foreign Operations Administration to the Department of State, 15 April 1955." American Presidency Project. http://www.presidency.ucsb.edu/ws/index.php?pid=10454.

―――. "Special Message to the Congress on the Situation in the Middle East January 5, 1957." American Presidency Project. www.presidency.ucsb.edu/ws/index.php?pid=11007&st=&st1=.

Fall, Bernard B. *Street without Joy: The French Debacle in Indochina.* 3rd ed. Mechanicsburg, PA: Stackpole, 2005.

Favin-Lévêque, Bernard. *Souvenirs de mer et d'ailleurs* [Recollections from the sea and other places]. Versailles, FR: Éditions des 7 vents, 1990.

"Flottille 28F" [28 F Squadron]. Marine nationale. Last modified 8 October 2014. https://www.defense.gouv.fr/marine/operations/forces/aeronautique-navale/flottilles/flottille-28f.

Foreign Office (U.K.). *Command Paper 6220: Exchange of Letters between the Prime Minister and General de Gaulle Concerning the Organisation, Employment and Conditions of Service of the French Volunteer Force, London 7 August 1940.* London: Her Majesty's Stationery Office, 1940.

Forestier, Jean. "Le Mirage IV, arme de précocité" [The Mirage IV, a precocious weapon]. In *Armement et Ve République, fin des années 1950–fin des années 1960* [Armament and the Fifth Republic, late 1950s–late 1960s]. Paris: CNRS Éditions, 2002.

Francis, Timothy L. *Belleau Wood (CV-24) I 1943–1960*. Naval History and Heritage Command. Last modified 24 February 2006. https://www.history.navy.mil /research/histories/ship-histories/danfs/b/belleau-wood-cv-24-i.html.

"The Franco-Soviet Treaty of Alliance and Mutual Aid." University of Hawaii eVols. Last accessed 17 February 2017. https://evols.library.manoa.hawaii.edu /bitstream/10524/32777/1/17-Volume8.pdf.

Fry, Varian. "Justice for the Free French." *New Republic* 106, no. 23 (8 June 1942): 785–87.

Gallois, Pierre Marie. "L'affaire de Berlin ou la peur de la bombe" [The Berlin affair or the fear of the bomb]. *La Nef* 27 (April 1959): 28.

———. *Stratégie de l'âge nucléaire* [Strategy in the nuclear age]. 2nd ed. Paris: François-Xavier de Guibert, 2009.

Gempp, André. "La mise en place et le développement des sous-marins nucléaires" [Design and development of nuclear submarines]. *Institut de Stratégie comparée*. Last accessed 3 March 2018. http://www.institut-strategie.fr/ihcc_nuc1_Gempp .html.

Giraud, Henri. *Mes évasions* [My escapes]. Paris: Julliard, 1946.

———. *Un seul but: La victoire, Alger 1942–1944* [Only one goal: Victory, Algiers 1942–1944]. Paris: Julliard, 1949.

Godfroy, René-Émile. *L'aventure de la Force X (Escadre française de la Méditerranée orientale) à Alexandrie (1940–1943)* [The adventure of Force X (French Eastern Mediterranean Fleet) in Alexandria (1940–1943)]. Paris: Plon, 1953.

Groizeleau, Vincent. "*Le Redoutable*, histoire d'une aventure technique, humaine et stratégique" [*Le Redoutable*, history of a technical, human and strategic adventure]. *Mer et Marine*. 27 March 2017. https://www.meretmarine.com/fr/content /le-redoutable-histoire-dune-aventure-technique-humaine-et-strategique-0.

Guillaume, Augustin-Léon. "L'importance stratégique de l'Afrique du Nord" [The strategic importance of North Africa]. *Revue de Défense nationale* 108 (November 1953): 423–30.

Guy, Claude. *En écoutant de Gaulle: Journal 1946–1949* [Listening to de Gaulle: A journal 1946–1949]. Paris: Grasset, 1996.

Hahn, Peter L. "Securing the Middle East: The Eisenhower Doctrine of 1957." *Presidential Studies Quarterly* 36, no. 1 (March 2006): 38–47.

Hull, Cordell, and Andrew Berding. *The Memoirs of Cordell Hull: In Two Volumes*. New York: Macmillan, 1948.

Ismay, Lord. *NATO: The First Five Years, 1949–1954*. Utrecht, Netherlands: Bosch, 1954.

Jacquet, Bernard. "La base opérationnelle de l'Ile Longue, à quoi ça sert? Comment ça marche?" [The Île Longue operational base: What is its purpose? How does it work?]. Marine nationale. 29 December 2010. https://www.defense.gouv.fr /english/marine/dossiers/l-ile-longue/la-base-operationnelle-de-l-ile-longue.

Jaouen, Hervé. *Marin de guerre* [Wartime sailor]. Paris: Éditions du Pen Duick, 1984.

Kennedy, John F. "Address given by John F. Kennedy in Philadelphia, 4 July 1962." In *John F. Kennedy, Containing the Public Messages, Speeches and Statements of the President: January 1 to December 31, 1962.* Washington, DC: U.S. Government Printing Office, 1963.

————. "Joint Statement Following Discussions with Prime Minister Macmillan: The Nassau Agreement December 21, 1962." American Presidency Project. http:// www.presidency.ucsb.edu/ws/index.php?pid=9063.

Kimball, Warren F., ed. *Alliance Emerging, October 1933–November 1942.* Vol. 1 of *Churchill and Roosevelt: The Complete Correspondence.* Princeton, NJ: Princeton Legacy Library, 1984.

————, ed. *Alliance Forged, October 1933–November 1942.* Vol. 2 of *Churchill and Roosevelt: The Complete Correspondence.* Princeton, NJ: Princeton Legacy Library, 1984.

————, ed. *Churchill and Roosevelt: The Complete Correspondence.* 2 vols. Princeton, NJ: Princeton Legacy Library, 1984.

La Haye, Charles Edward. "L'aéronautique navale française libre" [Free French Naval Air]. *Revue de la France libre.* 18 June 1951. http://www.france-libre.net /aeronautique-navale-fl/.

"La libération de la Corse, 9 septembre–4 octobre 1943" [Liberation of Corsica, 9 September–4 October 1943]. *Chemins de la Mémoire.* Last accessed 8 August 2016. http://www.cheminsdememoire.gouv.fr/fr/la-liberation-de-la -corse-9-septembre-4-octobre-1943-0.

"La Marine sur le Rhin" [The navy on the Rhine]. Marine nationale. Last modified 28 June 2010. http://www.defense.gouv.fr/marine/manifestations /la-marine-sur-le-rhin.

"Langley II (CVL-27)." Naval History and Heritage Command. Last modified 28 July 2015. https://www.history.navy.mil/research/histories/ship-histories/danfs/l /langley-cvl-27-ii.html.

Leahy, William D. *I Was There: The Personal Story of the Chief of Staff to Presidents Roosevelt and Truman Based on His Notes and Diaries Made at the Time.* New York: Whittlesey House, 1950.

Leighton, Richard M., and Robert W. Coakley. *Global Logistics and Strategy.* 2 vols., United States Army in World War II series. Washington, DC: U.S. Army Center of Military History, 1955 and 1968.

"Loi de programme no. 60-1305 du 8 décembre 1960 relative à certains équipments militaires" [Programme law no. 60-1305 of 8 December 1960 for some military equipment]. *Journal officiel de la République française* (10 December 1960): 11076.

Mast, Charles. *Histoire d'une rébellion: Alger, 8 novembre 1942* [History of a rebellion: Algiers, 8 November 1942]. Paris: Plon, 1969.

Moch, Jules. *Une si longue vie* [Such a long life]. Paris: Robert Laffont, 1976.

Mongin, Dominique. *La Direction des applications militaires au cœur de la dissuasion nucléaire française: De l'ère des pionniers au programme simulation* [The military applications directorate at the heart of French nuclear deterrence: From the pioneers era to the simulation program]. Paris: CEA Direction des applications militaires, 2016.

Murphy, Robert. *Diplomat among Warriors.* Garden City, NY: Doubleday, 1964.

Muselier, Émile. *De Gaulle contre le Gaullisme* [De Gaulle against Gaullism]. Paris: Éditions du Chêne, 1946.

———. *Marine et résistance* [Navy and resistance]. Paris: Flammarion, 1945.

Naudin, Geneviève Emon. "L'Île Longue: Quelle histoire!" [Île Longue: What a history!]. 29 December 2010. Marine nationale, https://www.defense.gouv.fr/marine/dossiers/l-ile-longue/l-ile-longue-quelle-histoire.

North Atlantic Treaty Organization (NATO). *Brussels Treaty: Treaty of Economic, Social and Cultural Collaboration and Collective Self-Defence, 17 March 1948.* Last modified 1 October 2009. http://www.nato.int/cps/en/natohq/official_texts_17072.htm.

———. *North Atlantic Council Ninth Meeting Final Communiqué: Lisbon, 20–25 February 1952.* https://www.nato.int/docu/comm/49-95/c520225a.htm.

———. *Report from the Military Committee to the North Atlantic Defense Committee on North Atlantic Treaty Organization Medium Term Plan.* 28 March 1950. http://www.nato.int/docu/stratdoc/eng/a500328d.pdf.

North Atlantic Treaty Organization (NATO), Comité de l'Infrastructure Committee. *50 Years of Infrastructure (1951–2001): NATO Security Investment Programme is the Sharing of Roles, Risks, Responsibilities, Costs and Benefits.* Last accessed 3 February 2018. https://www.nato.int/structur/infrastruc/50-years.pdf.

Pogue, Forrest C. *The Supreme Command.* United States Army in World War II: European Theater of Operations series. Washington, DC: U.S. Army Center of Military History, 1954.

Poirier, Lucien. *Des stratégies nucléaires* [Of nuclear strategies]. Paris: Hachette, 1977.

Principles Applying to Mutual Aid in the Prosecution of the War against Aggression: Preliminary Agreement between the United States of America and the Provisional Government of the French Republic. 28 February 1945. Library of Congress. https://www.loc.gov/law/help/us-treaties/bevans/b-fr-ust000007-1075.pdf.

"The Problem of French Unity." *New Republic* 108, no. 12 (22 March 1943): 365–66.

Rearden, Steven L. *The Formative Years 1947–1950.* Vol. 1 of *History of the Office of the Secretary of Defense.* Washington, DC: Historical Office, Office of the Secretary of Defense, 1984.

Robert, Georges. *La France aux Antilles de 1939 à 1943* [France in the Caribbean from 1939 to 1943]. Paris: Plon, 1950.

Romé, Paul. *Les oubliés du bout du monde: Journal d'un marin d'Indochine de 1939 à 1946* [The forgotten at the other end of the world: Diary of an Indochina sailor from 1939 to 1946]. Paris: Éditions maritimes & d'outre-mer, 1983.

Ross, Steven T., ed. *U.S. War Plans: 1938–1945*. Boulder, CO: Lynne Rienner, 2002.

Salmon, Trevor, and William Nicoll, ed. *Building European Union: A Documentary History and Analysis*. Manchester, U.K.: Manchester University Press, 1997.

Schlumberger, Étienne, and Alain Schlumberger. *Les combats et l'honneur des Forces navales françaises libres, 1940–1944* [The fighting and the honor of the free French naval forces, 1940–1944]. Paris: Le cherche midi, 2007.

Spears, Edward. *Two Men Who Saved France: Pétain and de Gaulle*. London: Eyre & Spottiswoode, 1966.

Tillon, Charles. *On chantait rouge* [We were singing red]. Paris: Robert Laffont, 1977.

Truman, Harry S. "The Truman Doctrine," delivered 12 March 1947 before a Joint Session of Congress. American Rhetoric, Top 100 Speeches. Last modified 8 March 2017. http://www.americanrhetoric.com/speeches/harrystrumantrumandoctrine.html.

U.S. Department of Defense. *United States—Vietnam Relations, 1945–1967: A Study Prepared by the Department of Defense* ("The Pentagon Papers"). Vol. 1, chap. 4, "U.S. and France in Indochina, 1950–1956." Boston: Beacon, 1971. https://www.mtholyoke.edu/acad/intrel/pentagon/pent9.htm.

Vigneras, Marcel. *Rearming the French*. United States Army in World War II series. Washington, DC: U.S. Army Center of Military History, 1957.

Wohlstetter, Albert. *The Delicate Balance of Terror*. RAND P-1472 (1958). https://doi.org/10.7249/P1472.

Wohlstetter, Albert, Fred Hoffman, R. J. Lutz, and S. Rowen. *Selection and Use of Strategic Air Bases*. RAND R-266 (1 April 1954). https://www.rand.org/pubs/reports/R0266.html.

SECONDARY SOURCES

Alexander, Martin S. *The Republic in Danger: General Maurice Gamelin and the Politics of French Defence, 1933–1940*. Cambridge: Cambridge University Press, 1992.

Allard, Dean C. "Strategic Views of the US Navy and NATO on the Northern Flank, 1917–1991." *Northern Mariner / Le marin du nord* 11, no. 1 (January 2001): 11–24.

Alteras, Isaac. "Eisenhower and the Sinai Campaign of 1956: The First Major Crisis in US–Israeli Relations." In *The 1956 War: Collusion and Rivalry in the Middle East*. 2nd ed. London: Routledge, 2013.

Alzon, Claude Hesse d'. "La présence militaire française en Indochine de 1940 à la capitulation japonaise" [French military presence in Indochina from 1940 to the Japanese surrender]. In *Les armées françaises pendant la Seconde Guerre mondiale, 1939–1945* [The French armed forces during the Second World War, 1939–1945]. Paris: F.E.D.N.-I.H.C.C, 1986.

Ambrose, Stephen E. *Eisenhower: Soldier and President*. London: Pocket Books,1997.

Auphan, Gabriel, and Jacques Mordal. *La marine française dans la Seconde Guerre mondiale* [The French navy during the Second World War], 2nd ed. Paris: France-Empire, 1967.

Baer, George W. *One Hundred Years of Sea Power: The U.S. Navy, 1890–1990*. Stanford, CA: Stanford University Press, 1994.

Bailey, Gavin J. *The Arsenal of Democracy: Aircraft Supply and the Anglo-American Alliance,1938–1942*. Edinburgh: Edinburgh University Press, 2013.

Baptiste, F. A. "Le régime de Vichy à la Martinique (juin 1940 à juin 1943)" [The Vichy regime in Martinique (June 1940 to June 1943)]. *Revues d'histoire de la Deuxième guerre mondiale* 28, no. 111 (July 1978): 1–24.

Barbier, Colette. "La Force multilatérale dans le débat atomique française" [The multilateral force in the French atomic debate]. *Revue d'histoire diplomatique* 107, no. 1 (1993): 55–89.

Barkaoui, Miloud. "Managing the Colonial Status Quo: Eisenhower's Cold War and the Algerian War of Independence." *Journal of North African Studies* 17, no. 1 (2012): 125–41.

Baroë, Jérôme. *Cent ans d'Aéronavale en France* [One hundred years of naval aviation in France]. Rennes, FR: Éditions Ouest-France, 2010.

Barré, Jean-Luc. *Devenir de Gaulle, 1939–1943* [Becoming de Gaulle, 1939–1943]. Paris: Perrin, 2003.

Berthon, Simon. *Allies at War: The Bitter Rivalry among Churchill, Roosevelt, and de Gaulle*. New York: Carroll & Graph, 2001.

Bossuat, Gérard. *Les aides américaines économiques et militaires à la France (1938–1960): Une nouvelle image des rapports de puissance* [American economic and military assistance to France (1938–1960): A new portrait of the power relationships]. Paris: Comité pour l'histoire économique et financière de la France, 2001. http://books .openedition.org/igpde/2023.

Boulaire, Alain. *La marine française: De la Royale de Richelieu aux missions d'aujourd'hui* [The French navy: From Richelieu's Royale to the missions of today]. Quimper, FR: Éditions Palantines, 2011.

Boureille, Patrick. "La Marine et la guerre d'Algérie: Périodisation et typologies des actions" [The navy and the Algerian war: Periodization and categorization of actions]. In *Militaires et guérilla dans la guerre d'Algérie* [Military and guerilla in the Algerian war]. Paris: Éditions Complexes, 2001.

———. "La Marine et le putsch d'Algérie" [The navy and the Algerian putsch]. *Revue d'histoire maritime* 14 (2011): 183–98.

———. "Le fait nucléaire à travers l'évolution du budget de la Marine (1959–1970)" [The nuclear factor through the evolution of the navy's budget (1959–1970)]. In *Armement et Ve République, fin des années 1950–fin des années 1960* [Armament and the Fifth Republic, late 1950s–late 1960s]. Paris: CNRS Éditions, 2002.

Breuer, William B. *Daring Missions of World War II*. New York: Wiley, 2001.

Brice, Martin. *Axis Blockade Runners of World War II*. Annapolis, MD: Naval Institute Press, 1981.

Brown, David. "Le H.M.S. *Richelieu*." *Revue historique des Armées* 199 (June 1995): 117–30.

———. *The Road to Oran: Anglo-French Naval Relations, September 1939–July 1940*. London: Frank Cass, 2004.

Bruneau, Jean-Baptiste. "La Marine, cité terrestre du contre-amiral Auphan" [The navy, land city of Rear-Admiral Auphan]. *Revue d'Histoire Maritime* 16 (2013): 51–64.

Bruneau, Jean-Baptiste, and Thomas Vaisset. "Déchirements, déclassement et relèvement (1939–1945)" [Fractures, fall and rise (1939–1945)]. In *L'histoire d'une révolution: La Marine depuis 1870* [History of a revolution: The navy since 1870] Études marines no. 4 (March 2013): 68–81.

Buell, Thomas B. *Master of Sea Power: A Biography of Fleet Admiral Ernest J. King*. 2nd ed. Annapolis, MD: Naval Institute Press, 1995.

Buffotot, Patrice. "Les lois de programmation militaire en France: Un demi-siècle de programmation" [Military Programming Acts in France: Half-a-Century of Programming]. *Revues électroniques de l'Université de Nice* 4 (15 July 2016). http://revel.unice.fr/psei/index.html?id=1060.

Cabrière, Jean. "Le programme Mirage IV" [The Mirage IV Programme]. *Institut de Stratégie Comparée*. Last accessed 15 December 2017. http://www.institut-strategie.fr/ihcc_nuc1_Cabriere.html.

Canuel, Hugues. "From *Richelieu* to *Le Redoutable*: France's Quest for an Independent Naval Policy within a Strategy of Alliance, 1940–1963." PhD thesis, Royal Military College of Canada, 2018.

Cardwell, Curt. *NSC 68 and the Political Economy of the Cold War*. New York: Cambridge University Press, 2011.

Cariou, Yves. *FOST: Force océanique stratégique* [*FOST*: Oceanic Strategic Force]. Rennes, FR: Marines Éditions, 2013.

Carlier, Claude. "La genèse du système d'arme stratégique piloté Mirage IV (1956–1964)" [Genesis of the piloted strategic weapon system Mirage IV (1956–1964)]. In *Armement et Ve République, fin des années 1950–fin des années 1960* [Armament and the Fifth Republic, late 1950s–late 1960s]. Paris, FR: CNRS Éditions, 2002.

Cassagnou, Bernard. *Les grandes mutations de la Marine marchande française (1945–1995)* [The great changes in the French merchant navy (1945–1995)]. 2 vols. Vincennes, FR: Comité pour l'histoire économique et financière de la France, 2003.

Castagnos, Pierre. *Charles de Gaulle face à la mer* [Charles de Gaulle facing the sea]. Paris: Atlantica, 2004.

Chaline, Émile, and Pierre Santarelli. *Historique des Forces Navales Françaises Libres*, 2 tomes [History of the Free French naval forces, 2 vols.]. Paris, FR: Service historique de la marine, 1990 and 1992.

Chapelay, Frédérique. "Le réarmement de la Marine par les Américains" [The Rearmament of the navy by the Americans]. In *Les armées françaises pendant la Seconde Guerre mondiale, 1939–1945* [The French armed forces during the Second World War, 1939–1945]. Paris: F.E.D.N.-I.H.C.C, 1986.

Chartier, Claude. "La genèse de l'armement atomique français: L'oeuvre de la Quatrième République" [The genesis of French atomic weapons during the Fourth Republic]. *Historiens et Géographes* 99, no. 397 (March 2007): 289–95.

Clayton, Anthony. *The Wars of French Decolonization*. London: Routledge, 1994.

Cogan, Charles C. "From the Fall of France to the *Force de Frappe*: The Remaking of French Military Power, 1940-62." In *The Fog of Peace and War Planning: Military and Strategic Planning under the Fog of Uncertainty*. London: Routledge, 2006.

Cointet, Michèle. *De Gaulle et Giraud: L'affrontement, 1942–1944* [De Gaulle and Giraud: The confrontation, 1942–1944]. Paris: Perrin, 2005.

Combeau, Yvan. "Le ralliement de La Réunion et de Madagascar à la France libre" [The rallying of La Réunion and Madagascar to Free France]. *Les chemins de la mémoire* 231 (November 2012): 2–4.

Cordier-Féron, Damien. "La base navale stratégique de Bizerte (1943–1963)" [The strategic naval base of Bizerte (1943–1963)]. *Guerres mondiales et conflits contemporains* 54, no. 213 (2004): 39–62.

Cornic, Jacques. "Ships for Crews." *Warship International* 22, no. 3 (1985): 251–66.

———. "Sous la Croix de Lorraine (Under the Cross of Lorraine): The FNFL (Forces Naval Françaises Libres) 1940–1943 (Free French Naval Forces)." *Warship International* 24, no. 1 (1987): 34–43.

Cornil, Sylvain. "La France libre et l'Empire: Le ralliement de l'Afrique" [Free France and the rallying of the empire]. *Fondation de la France libre*. Last modified 28 February 2009. http://www.france-libre.net/fl-empire-afrique/.

Costagliola, Bernard. *Darlan: La collaboration à tout prix* [Darlan: Collaboration at any cost]. Paris: CNRS Éditions, 2015.

———. *La Marine de Vichy: Blocus et collaboration*. Paris: Éditions Tallandier, 2009.

Courteaux, Olivier. *Canada between Vichy and Free France, 1940–1945*. Toronto, ON: Toronto University Press, 2013.

Coutau-Bégarie, Hervé. "Marine et innovation: La Marine française face au porte-avions après la Seconde Guerre mondiale" [Navy and innovation: The French navy and the aircraft carrier after the Second World War]. *Guerre mondiale et conflits contemporains* 238 (2010): 117–27.

Coutau-Bégarie, Hervé, and Claude Huan. *Darlan*. Paris: Fayard, 1989.

———. *Mers el-Kébir (1940), la rupture franco-britannique* [Mers el-Kebir (1940), the Franco-British rupture]. Paris: Economica, 1994.

Croizat, Victor. *Vietnam River Warfare 1945–1975*. London: Blandford, 1986.

Cunningham, Bruce. "History of the Douglas A3D Skywarrior, Part 2: Early Production Testing." *American Aviation Historical Society* 51, no. 4 (Winter 2006): 272–88.

David, Andrew, and Michael Holm. "The Kennedy Administration and the Battle over Foreign Aid: The Untold Story of the Clay Committee." *Diplomacy & Statecraft* 27, no. 1 (2016): 65–92.

Deighton, Anne. "Entente Neo-Coloniale? Ernest Bevin and the Proposals for an Anglo-French Third World Power, 1945–1949." In *Anglo-French Relations since the Late Eighteenth Century*, ed. Glyn Stone and T. G. Otte, 201–18. London: Routledge, 2008).

Delmas, Jean. "De Gaulle, la défense nationale et les forces armées, projets et réalités (1944–janvier 1946)" [De Gaulle, national defense and the armed forces: Ambitions and realities (1944–January 1946)]. *Revue d'histoire de la Deuxième guerre mondiale* 110 (April 1978): 7–24.

Dockrill, Saki. *Eisenhower's New-Look National Security Policy, 1953–61.* London: Macmillan, 1996.

Dougherty, James J. *The Politics of Wartime Aid: American Economic Assistance to France and French Northwest Africa, 1940–1946.* Westport, CT: Greenwood, 1978.

Douglas, Lawrence. "The Martinique Affair: The United States Navy and the French West Indies, 1940–1943." In *New Interpretations in Naval History: Selected Papers from the Ninth Naval History Symposium Held at the United States Naval Academy, 18–20 October 1989.* Annapolis, MD: Naval Institute Press, 1991.

Du Réau, Élisabeth. "Paul Ramadier et les prémisses du pacte atlantique" [Paul Ramadier and the beginnings of the Atlantic pact]. In *Paul Ramadier, la République et le socialisme* [Paul Ramadier, the republic and socialism]. Brussels, BE: Complexe, 1990.

Duffield, John S. *Power Rules: The Evolution of NATO's Conventional Force Posture.* Stanford, CA: Stanford University Press, 1995.

Dumas, Robert. *Le cuirassé Jean Bart 1939–1970* [Battleship *Jean Bart* 1939–1970]. Rennes, FR: Marine Éditions, 1992.

———. *Le cuirassé Richelieu 1935–1968* [Battleship *Richelieu* 1935–1968]. Bourg-en-Bresse, FR: Marines Éditions, 1992.

Durteste, Louis. "La marine dans la guerre d'Indochine: Une adaption retrouvée" [The Navy in the Indochina War: Adaption Found Again]. In *L'Armée française dans la Guerre d'Indochine (1946–1954): Adaptation ou inadaptation?* [The French Army in the Indochina war (1946–1954): Adaptation or maladjustment?]. Paris: Complexe, 2000.

Duval, Marcel. "Les décisions concernant l'armement nucléaire: Pourquoi, comment, quand?" [Decisions concerning nuclear weapons: Why, how, when?]. In *Armement et Ve République, fin des années 1950–fin des années 1960* [Armament and the Fifth Republic, late 1950s–late 1960s]. Paris: CNRS Éditions, 2002.

Ehrman, John. *The Navy in the War of William III, 1689–1697: Its State and Direction.* Cambridge: Cambridge University Press, 1953.

Elgey, Georgette. *Histoire de la IVe République*, 6 tomes [History of the fourth republic, 6 Vols]. Paris: Fayard, 1993–2012.

Elisabeth, Léo. "Vichy aux Antilles et en Guyane: 1940–1943" [Vichy in the Caribbean and Guyana]. *Outre-mers* 91, no. 342 (1st Quarter 2004): 145–74.

Estival, Bernard. *La marine française dans la guerre d'Algérie* [The French navy in the Algerian war]. Rennes, FR: Marines Éditions, 2012.

———. *La marine française dans la guerre d'Indochine* [The French navy in the Indochina war]. Rennes, FR: Marines Éditions, 2007.

Fenby, Jonathan. *The General: Charles de Gaulle and the France He Saved*. London: Simon & Schuster, 2010.

Fleury, Georges. *Fusiliers marins et commandos: Baroudeurs de la royale* [Naval infantry and commandos: The navy's daredevils]. Paris: Copernic, 1980.

Fonvieille-Vojtovic, Aline. *Paul Ramadier (1888–1961)*. Paris: Publications de la Sorbonne, 1993.

Frémeaux, Jacques. "L'union française: le rêve d'une France unie?" In *Culture impériale 1931–1961*. Paris: Éditions Autrement, 2004.

Garrett, William B. "The U.S. Navy's Role in the 1956 Suez Crisis." *Naval War College Review* 22, no. 7 (March 1970): 66–78.

Géré, François. "P.M. Gallois, stratège et pédagogue de la dissuasion nucléaire" [P.M. Gallois, nuclear deterrence strategist and teacher]. *La revue géopolitique*, 4 February 2017. https://www.diploweb.com/P-M-Gallois-stratege-et-pedagogue -de-la-dissuasion-nucleaire.html.

Giles, Frank. *The Locust Years: The Story of the Fourth French Republic, 1946–1958*. London: Secker & Warburg, 1991.

Girardin-Thibeaud, Odile. *Les amiraux de Vichy* [Vichy's admirals]. Paris: Nouveau Monde, 2016.

Gordon, Philip H. *A Certain Idea of France: French Security Policy and the Gaullist Legacy*. Princeton, NJ: Princeton University Press, 1993.

Granier, Hubert. *Histoire des marins français: A Madagascar (1947–1948) et en Indochine (1946–1954)* [A history of the French sailors: In Madagascar (1947–1948) and Indochina (1946–1954)]. Rennes, FR: Marines Éditions, 2010.

Gras, Yves. "L'intrusion japonaise en Indochine (Juin 1940–Mars 1945)" [The Japanese intrusion in Indochina (June 1940–March 1945)]. *Revue historique des Armées* 153, no. 4 (1983): 86–102.

Greenwood, Sean. *The Alternative Alliance: Anglo-French Relations before the Coming of NATO, 1944–1948*. London: Minerva, 1996.

Gregory, Shaun R. *Nuclear Command and Control in NATO: Nuclear Weapons Operations and the Strategy of Flexible Response*. London: Palgrave Macmillan, 1996.

Griffiths, Richard. *Marshal Pétain*. London: Constable, 1970.

Grove, Eric J. *The Future of Sea Power*. London: Routledge, 1990.

———. *Vanguard to Trident: British Naval Policy since World II*. Annapolis, MD: Naval Institute Press, 1987.

Guillen, Pierre. "France and the Defence of Western Europe: From the Brussels Pact (March 1948) to the Pleven Plan (October 1950)." In *The Western Security Community, 1948–1950: Common Problems and Conflicting National Interests during the Foundation Phase of the North Atlantic Alliance.* Oxford: Berg, 1994.

Guisnel, Jean, and Bruno Tertrais. *Le Président et la bombe: Jupiter à l'Élysée* [The president and the bomb: Jupiter at the Élysée]. Paris: Odile Jacob, 2016.

Hahan, Peter L. "Securing the Middle East: The Eisenhower Doctrine of 1957." *Presidential Studies Quarterly* 36, no. 1 (March 2006): 38–47.

Haight, John McVickar. *American Aid to France, 1938–1940.* New York: Atheneum, 1970.

———. "Les négociations françaises pour la fourniture d'avions américains, 1ère partie: Avant Munich" [French negotiations to acquire American planes, part 1: Before Munich]. *Forces aériennes françaises* 198 (December 1963): 807–39.

Harding, Richard. *Modern Naval History: Debates and Prospects.* London: Bloomsbury, 2016.

Hartcup, Guy. *Code Name Mulberry: The Planning Building and Operation of the Normandy Harbours.* 2nd ed. London: Pen & Sword Military, 2011.

Hata, Ikuhiko. "The Army's Move into French Indochina." In *The Fateful Choice: Japan's Advance into Southeast Asia, 1939–1941,* ed. James W. Morley. New York: Columbia University Press, 1980.

Hecht, Gabrielle. *The Radiance of France: Nuclear Power and National Identity after World War II.* Cambridge, MA: MIT Press, 1998.

Heckstall-Smith, Anthony. *The Fleet That Faced Both Ways.* London: Blond, 1963.

Herwig, Holger H. "Innovation Ignored: The Submarine Problem—Germany, Britain, and the United States, 1919–1939." In *Military Innovation in the Interwar Period,* ed. Williamson Murray and Allan R. Millett, 227–64. Cambridge: Cambridge University Press, 1996.

Hill, John S. "American Efforts to Aid French Reconstruction between Lend-Lease and the Marshall Plan." *Journal of Modern History* 64 (September 1992): 500–524.

Hines, Calvin W. "The Fleet Between: Anglo-American Diplomacy and Force X, 1940–43." In *Naval History: The Sixth Symposium of the U.S. Naval Academy,* ed. Daniel M. Masterson, 237–55. Wilmington, DE: Scholarly Resources, 1987.

Hone, Thomas C., Norman Friedman, and Mark D. Mandeles. "The Development of the Angled-Deck Aircraft Carrier." *Naval War College Review* 64, no. 2 (Spring 2011): 63–78.

Horne, Alistair. *A Savage War of Peace: Algeria, 1954–1962.* 2nd ed. New York: New York Review of Books, 2006.

Hotta, Eri. *Japan 1941: Countdown to Infamy.* New York: Knopf, 2013.

Huan, Claude. "La Marine française dans la guerre (1943)" [The French navy during the war (1943)]. *Revue historique des Armées* 188, no. 3 (September 1992): 115–24.

————. "Les négociations franco-britanniques de l'automne 1940" [The Franco-British negotiations of the fall of 1940]. *Guerres mondiales et conflits contemporains* 176 (1994): 139–54.

————. "Les opérations des sous-marins français, Méditerranée 1944" [French submarine operations in the Mediterranean, 1944]. *Revue historique des Armées* 156, no. 3 (October 1984): 55–62.

————. *Les sous-marins français 1918–1945* [French submarines 1918–1945]. Rennes, FR: Marines Éditions, 2004.

Huan, Claude, and Jean Moulin. *Les sous-marins français 1945–2000* [French submarines 1945–2000]. Rennes, FR: Marines Éditions, 2004.

Hucherot, Jean-Jacques. *La marine française en Afrique subsaharienne de 1946 à 1960* [The French navy in sub-Saharan Africa from 1946 to 1960]. Paris: Institut catholique de Paris, 2001.

Huwart, Olivier. *Sous-marins français: 1944–1954, la décennie du renouveau* [French submarines: 1944–1954, the decade of renewal]. Rennes, FR: Marines Éditions, 2003.

Ignatieff, D. "Présence dans le Pacifique des navires de la France libre" [Presence in the Pacific of Free French ships]. *Bulletin de la Société d'Études historiques de la Nouvelle-Calédonie* 77 (2001): 33–54.

Jackson, Julian. *France: The Dark Years, 1940–1944*. Oxford: Oxford University Press, 2001.

Jenkins, Ernest H. *A History of the French Navy: From Its Beginning to the Present Day*. Annapolis, MD: Naval Institute Press, 1973.

Johnston, Andrew M. "The Construction of NATO's Medium Term Defence Plan and the Diplomacy of Conventional Strategy, 1949–1950." *Diplomacy & Statecraft* 12, no. 2 (June 2001): 79–124.

Jordan, John. "*Surcouf*—The French Postwar Destroyers, Parts 1 and 2." *Warship* 9, no. 35 (1985): 146–53; no. 36 (1985): 261–69.

Jordan, John, and Robert Dumas. *French Battleships: 1922–1956*. Annapolis, MD: Naval Institute Press, 2009.

Jordan, John, and Jean Moulin. *French Cruisers, 1922–1956*. Barnsley, UK: Seaforth, 2013.

————. *French Destroyers: Torpilleurs d'Escadre & Contre-Torpilleurs, 1922–1956*. Barnsley, UK: Seaforth, 2015.

Kaplan, Lawrence S. *A Community of Interests: NATO and the Military Assistance Program (1948–1951)*. Washington, DC: Office of the Secretary of Defense Historical Publication, 1980.

————. *NATO 1948: The Birth of the Transatlantic Alliance*. Plymouth, UK: Rowman & Littlefield, 2007.

Kersaudy, François. *De Gaulle et Churchill: La mésentente cordiale* [De Gaulle and Churchill: Cordial disagreement]. Paris: Perrin, 2001.

————. *De Gaulle et Roosevelt: Le duel au sommet* [De Gaulle and Roosevelt: Duel at the top]. Paris: Perrin, 2006.

Kissinger, Henry. *Diplomacy*. New York: Simon & Schuster, 1994.

Klingbeil, Pierre-Emmanuel. *Le front oublié des Alpes-Maritimes (15 août 1944–2 mai 1945)* [The forgotten front of the Alpes-Maritimes (15 August 1944–2 May 1945)]. Nice, FR: Serre Éditeur, 2005.

Koburger, Charles W. *The Cyrano Fleet, France and Its Navy, 1940–1942*. New York: Praeger, 1989.

————. *Franco-American Naval Relations, 1940–1945*. Wesport, CT: Praeger, 1994.

————. *The French Navy in Indochina: Riverine and Coastal Forces, 1945–54*. New York: Praeger, 1991.

Kowalski, Robert J., and Tommy H. Thomason. *Grumman S2F/SF-2 Tracker*, Part 1: *Development, Testing, Variants and Foreign Users*. Simi Valley, CA: Ginter, 2016.

Kustnetsov, Evgeny. "Le projet de Force multilatérale de l'OTAN" [The NATO Multilateral Force Project]. European University Institute. 2004. https://www .cvce.eu/content/publication/1999/1/1/937a5818-7fea-47da-944e-11114da4e0a3 /publishable_fr.pdf.

Lambert, J., and A. Ross. *Allied Coastal Forces of World War II*. Vol. 2. London: Barnsley, 2019.

Lamy, Rodolphe. "Il y a 70 ans, le basculement de la Martinique" [70 years ago, the rallying of Martinique]. *France-Antilles*, 22 June 2013. http://www.martinique .franceantilles.fr/actualite/culture/il-y-a-70-ans-le-basculement-de-la-martinique -209992.php.

Laporte, Isabelle. *La base française de Mers el-Kébir (1930–1968): De la genèse à l'évacuation* [The French Base of Mers el-Kebir (1930–1968): From Its Genesis to the Evacuation]. Paris: Université Paris I, 2000.

————. "Mers el-Kébir après Mers el-Kébir (1940–1945)" [Mers el-Kebir after Mers el-Kebir (1940–1945)]. *Revue historique des Armées* 223, no 2 (June 2001): 71–80.

Le Joubioux, Hervé. "L'île de La Réunion dans la Seconde Guerre mondiale" [Réunion Island during the Second World War]. *Revue historique des Armées* 263 (2011): 85–87.

Levisse-Touzé, Christine. *L'Afrique du Nord dans la guerre, 1939–1945* [North Africa during the war, 1939–1945]. Paris: Albin Michel, 1998.

————. "Le Général de Gaulle et les débuts de la France Libre" [General de Gaulle and the beginnings of Free France]. *Revue historique des armées* 219, no. 2 (June 2000): 63–70.

Logevall, Fredrik. *Embers of War: The Fall of an Empire and the Making of America's Vietnam*. New York: Random House, 2012.

Lombard, Julien. "Le *Richelieu* dans la tourmente (1939–1945)" [*Richelieu* into the storm (1939–1945)]. *Guerres mondiales et conflits contemporains* 188 (December 1997): 65–83.

Maguire, G. E. *Anglo-American Policy towards the Free French*. London: Macmillan, 1995.

Mahoney, Daniel J. *De Gaulle: Statesmanship, Grandeur, and Modern Democracy*. 2nd ed. New Brunswick, NJ: Transaction, 2000.

Maloney, Sean M. *Securing Command of the Sea: NATO Naval Planning, 1948–1954*. Annapolis, MD: Naval Institute Press, 1995.

Marder, Arthur J. *Operation Menace: The Dakar Expedition and the Dudley North Affair*. London: Oxford University Press, 1976.

Marquié, Frédéric. "La reconversion des Chantiers et Arsenaux de la Marine (1946–1953)" [The Reconversion of the Navy's Shipyards and Dockyards (1946–1953)]. *Revue historique des armées* 220, no. 3 (September 2000): 112–27.

Martin, Michel L. *Warriors to Managers: The French Military Establishment since 1945*. Chapel Hill: University of North Carolina Press, 1981.

Masson, Philippe. *De la vapeur à l'atome*. Tome 2 of *Histoire de la marine*. [From steam to the atom, Vol. 2 of History of the French navy]. Paris: Lavauzelle, 1992.

———. *Histoire de l'armée française de 1914 à nos jours* [History of the French Army from 1914 to today]. Paris: Librairie académique Perrin, 1999.

———. "La marine française en 1946" [The French navy in 1946]. *Revue d'histoire de la Deuxième guerre mondiale* 110 (April 1978): 79–86.

———. *La Marine française et la guerre, 1939–1945* [The French navy and the war, 1939–1945]. 2nd ed. Paris: Tallandier, 2000.

———. *La puissance maritime et navale au XXᵉ siècle* [Maritime and naval power in the twentieth century]. Paris: Perrin, 2002.

———. "Le réarmement de la Marine française" [Rearmament of the French navy]. *Revue historique des armées* 3, no. 188 (September 1992): 106–14.

Mathey, Jean-Marie, and Alexandre Sheldon-Duplaix. *Histoire des sous-marins des origines à nos jours* [History of submarines from the origins to today]. Paris: Éditions E-T-A-I, 2002.

McKercher, B. J. C. "The Limitations of the Politician-Strategist: Winston Churchill and the German Threat, 1933–1939." In *Churchill and the Strategic Dilemmas before the World Wars: Essays in Honor of Michael I. Handel*, ed. John H. Maurer, 88–120. London: Frank Cass, 2003.

Melton, George E. *Darlan: Admiral and Statesman of France 1881–1942*. Westport, CT: Praeger, 1998.

———. *From Versailles to Mers El-Kebir: The Promise of Anglo-French Naval Cooperation, 1919–40*. Annapolis, MD: Naval Institute Press, 2015.

Mengome, Barthélémy Ntoma. *La bataille de Libreville—De Gaulle contre Pétain: 50 morts* [The battle of Libreville—De Gaulle against Pétain: 50 killed]. Paris: L'Harmattan, 2013.

Miller, David. *The Cold War: A Military History*. New York: St. Martin's, 1998.

——. *The Illustrated Directory of Submarines of the World.* St. Paul, MN: MBI, 2002.

Monaque, Rémi. *Une histoire de la marine de guerre française* [A history of the French navy]. Paris: Perrin, 2016.

Mongin, Dominique. "Genèse de l'armement nucléaire français" [Genesis of French nuclear armament]. *Revue historique des armées* 262 (2011): 1–12.

——. *La Direction des applications militaires au cœur de la dissuasion nucléaire française: De l'ère des pionniers au programme simulation* [The military applications directorate at the heart of French nuclear deterrence: From the pioneers era to the simulation program]. Paris: CEA DAM, 2016.

Morabito, Marcel. *Histoire constitutionnelle de la France de 1789 à nos jours* [Constitutional history of France from 1789 to today], 14th ed. Paris: LGDJ, 2016.

Moulin, Jean. *Destroyers d'escorte en France, 1944–1972* [Destroyer escorts in France, 1944–1972]. Nantes, FR: Marines Éditions, 2004.

——. "Les escorteurs rapides, tomes 1 & 2" [Fast escorts, parts 1&2]. *Marines—Guerre & commerce* 42–43 (March–April 1996).

——. *Les porte-avions* Dixmude *& Arromanches* [Aircraft carriers *Dixmude* and *Arromanches*]. Nantes, FR: Marines Éditions, 1998.

——. *Les porte-avions français* [French aircraft carriers]. Rennes, FR: Marines Éditions, 2008.

——. *Les porte-avions* La Fayette *& Bois-Belleau* [Aircraft carriers *La Fayette* and *Bois-Belleau*]. Nantes, FR: Marines Éditions, 2000.

Muselier, Renaud. *L'amiral Muselier, 1882–1965: Le créateur de la croix de Lorraine* [Admiral Muselier, 1882–1965: Creator of the cross of Lorraine]. Paris: Perrin, 2000.

Namba, Chizuru. *Français et Japonais en Indochine, 1940–1945: Colonisation, propagande et rivalité culturelle* [French and Japanese in Indochina, 1940–1945: Colonization, propaganda and cultural rivalry]. Paris: Karthala, 2012.

Pach, Chester J. *Arming the Free World: The Origins of the United States Military Assistance Program, 1945–1950.* Chapel Hill: University of North Carolina Press, 1991.

Pairault, Louis-Gilles. "Le verrou de la mer Rouge: L'armée et la côte française des Somalie, 1884–1977" [Latch on the Red Sea: The army and French Somaliland, 1884–1977]. *Institut de Stratégie Comparée.* Last accessed 16 March 2020, http://www.institut-strategie.fr/RIHM_82_PAIRAULT2.html.

Papastamkou, Sofia. "De la crise au Liban au mémorandum du 17 septembre 1958: La politique étrangère de la France entre deux républiques et une guerre" [From the Lebanon crisis to the 17 September 1958 memorandum: The foreign policy of France between two republics and a war]. *Matériaux pour l'histoire de notre temps* 3, no. 99 (2010): 76–83.

Peszke, Michael Alfred. "The British-Polish Agreement of August 1940: Its Antecedents, Significance, and Consequences." *Journal of Slavic Military Studies* 24, no. 4 (2011): 648–58.

Planche, Jean-Louis. *Sétif 1945: Histoire d'un massacre annoncé* [Sétif 1945: History of an expected massacre]. Paris: Perrin, 2006.

Pognon, Edmond. *De Gaulle et l'armée* [De Gaulle and the army]. Paris: Plon, 1976.

Polmar, Norman, and K. J. Moore. *Cold War Submarines: The Design and Construction of U.S. and Soviet Submarines, 1945–2001.* Dulles, VA: Brassey's, 2004.

Priest, Andrew. "In American Hands: Britain, the United States and the Polaris Nuclear Project 1962–1968." *Contemporary British History* 19, no. 3 (Autumn 2005): 353–76.

Prijac, Lukian. *Le blocus de Djibouti: Chronique d'une guerre décalée (1935–1943)* [The blockade of Djibouti: Chronicle of an asynchronous war (1935–1943)]. Paris: L'Harmattan, 2015.

Prud'homme, Georges, Roland Oberlé, and Alain Kleimberg. *Les Forces maritimes du rhin* [The Rhine Maritime Forces]. Strasbourg: Carré Blanc, 2007.

Quérel, Philippe. "La Marine entre l'O.T.A.N. et l'Union française au début des années 1950" [The Navy between NATO and French union at the beginning of the 1950s]. *Revue historique des Armées* 201 (December 1995): 43–52.

———. "La politique navale de la France sous la Quatrième République" [The naval policy of France under the Fourth Republic]. PhD thesis, Université de Reims, 1992.

———. "L'échec du *PA-28*, premier porte-avions française de l'après-guerre" [The failure of *PA-28*, the first postwar French aircraft carrier]. *Institut de stratégie comparée.* Last accessed 23 November 2012. http://www.institut-strategie.fr /pub_mo3_Querel.html.

———. *Vers une marine atomique: la marine française (1945–1958)* [Toward a nuclear navy: The French navy (1945–1958)]. Paris: LGDJ, 1997.

Réau, Élisabeth du. "Les origines et la portée du traité de Dunkerque vers une nouvelle 'entente cordiale'? (4 mars 1947)" [The origins and the impact of the Treaty of Dunkirk toward a new *"entente cordiale"*? (4 March 1947)]. *Matériaux pour l'histoire de nos temps* 18 (1990): 23–26.

Reyn, Sebastian. *Atlantis Lost: The American Experience with De Gaulle, 1958–1969.* Amsterdam: Amsterdam University Press, 2010.

Rohan, Sally. *The Western European Union: International Politics between Alliance and Integration.* New York: Routledge, 2014.

Ropp, Theodore. *The Development of a Modern Navy: French Naval Policy, 1871–1904,* ed. by Stephen S. Roberts. Annapolis, MD: Naval Institute Press, 1987.

Rose, Lisle A. *A Violent Peace, 1946–2006.* Vol. 3 of *Power at Sea.* Columbia: University of Missouri Press, 2007.

Rossi, Mario. *Roosevelt and the French.* New York: Praeger, 1993.

Rossignol, Benoît, and Roland Le Borgne. "Reconstruction, restructuration et modernisation des bases navales (1944–1949)" [Reconstruction, restructuration and modernization of naval bases (1944–1949)]. *Revue historique des Armées* 220, no. 3 (September 2000): 98–111.

Roussel, Éric. *Charles de Gaulle*. Paris: Gallimard, 2002.

Rupieper, Hermann-Josef. "The United States and the Founding of the Federal Republic, 1948–1949." In *The United States and Germany in the Era of the Cold War, 1945–1968: A Handbook*, Vol. 1., ed. Detlef Junker, 85–89. Cambridge: Cambridge University Press, 2004.

Saffroy, Frédéric. *Le bouclier de Neptune: La politique de défense des bases françaises en Méditerranée (1912–1931)* [Neptune's shield: Mediterranean bases defense policy (1912–1931)]. Rennes, FR: Presses universitaires de Rennes, 2015.

Sarnet, René, and Éric Le Vaillant. *Richelieu*. Rennes, FR: Marines Éditions, 1997.

Schmidt, Christian, and Guy Vidal. "Le contexte économique et financier des deux premières lois de programme militaire" [Economic and Financial Context of the First Two Military Programme Laws]. In *Armement et Vᵉ République, fin des années 1950–fin des années 1960* [Armament and the Fifth Republic, late 1950s–late 1960s]. Paris: CNRS Éditions, 2002.

Sheldon-Duplaix, Alexandre. *Histoire mondiale des porte-avions: Des origines à nos jours* [World history of the aircraft carriers: From the origins to the present day]. Paris, FR: Éditions Techniques pour l'Automobile et l'Industrie, 2006.

———. "La Mission navale française à Washington et la renaissance de la Marine (3 janvier 1943–1 janvier 1946)" [The French naval mission to Washington and the rebirth of the navy (3 January 1943–1 January 1946)]. *Relations internationales* 108 (Winter 2001): 503–23.

Simonnet, Stéphane. *Les 177 Français du Jour J* [The 177 frenchmen of D-day]. Paris: Tallandier, 2014.

———. *Les poches de l'Atlantique: Les batailles oubliées de la Libération, janvier 1944 mai 1945* [The Atlantic pockets: The forgotten battles of the liberation, January 1944–May 1945]. Paris: Tallandier, 2015.

Sokolsky, Joel J. *Seapower in the Nuclear Age: The United States Navy and NATO, 1949–1980*. London: Routledge, 1991.

Sondhouse, Lawrence. *Navies in Modern World Histories*. London: Reaktion, 2004.

Soutou, Georges-Henri. "General de Gaulle and the Soviet Union, 1943–5: Ideology or European Equilibrium." In *The Soviet Union and Europe in the Cold War, 1943–53*, ed. Francesca Gori and Silvio Pons, 310–33. London: Palgrave Macmillan, 1996.

Souverain, Jérôme. "Marine et F.F.I (1944–1945)" [The navy and the FFI (1944–1945)]. *Revue historique des Armées* 199 (June 1995): 105–16.

Stijger, Eric. "Aéronavale Crusaders." *Air International* 45, no. 4 (October 1993): 192–96.

Stone, David. *War Summits: The Meetings That Shaped World War II and the Postwar World*. Washington, DC: Potomac, 2005.

Strub, Philippe. "La renaissance de la Marine française sous la Quatrième République, 1945–1956" [Renewal of the French navy under the Fourth Republic, 1945–1956)]. *Bulletin de l'Institut Pierre Renouvin* 1, no. 25 (2007): 197–206.

———. "La renaissance de la Marine française sous la Quatrième République (1945–1956): La Quatrième République a-t-elle eu une ambition navale pour la France?" [Renewal of the French navy under the Fourth Republic (1945–1956): Did the Fourth Republic have a naval ambition?]. PhD thesis, Université Paris I, 2006.

Stuart, Rob. "Was the RCN Ever the Third Largest Navy?" *Canadian Naval Review* 5, no. 2 (Fall 2009): 4–9.

Stumpf, David K. *Regulus: America's First Nuclear Submarine Missile.* Paducah, KY: Turner, 1996.

Tablit, Ali. "The United States and the Algerian War." *Kadhaya Tarikhia* 5 (March 2017): 1–25.

Taillemite, Étienne. *Dictionnaire des marins français* [Dictionary of French sailors]. Paris: Tallandier, 2002.

———. *Histoire ignorée de la Marine française* [Unknown history of the French navy]. 3rd ed. Paris: Perrin, 2010.

———. *Les hommes qui ont fait la Marine française* [The men who forged the French navy]. Paris: Perrin, 2008.

Tertrais, Bruno. "*Destruction assurée*: The Origins and Development of French Nuclear Strategy, 1945–1981." In *Getting Mad: Nuclear Mutual Assured Destruction, Its Origins and Practice*, ed. Henry D. Sokolski, 51–122. Carlisle Barracks, PA: Strategic Studies Institute, 2004.

Thomas, Martin. "France's North African Crisis, 1945–1955: Cold War and Colonial Imperatives." *History* 92, no. 2 (April 2007): 207–34.

———. "Imperial Backwater or Strategic Outpost? The British Takeover of Vichy Madagascar, 1942." *Historical Journal* 39, no. 4 (1996): 1049–74.

Till, Geoffrey. "Adopting the Aircraft Carrier: The British, American, and Japanese Case Studies." In *Military Innovation in the Interwar Period*, ed. Williamson Murray and Allan R. Millett, 191–226 (Cambridge: Cambridge University Press, 1996).

———. "Holding the Bridge in Troubled Times: The Cold War and the Navies of Europe." *Journal of Strategic Studies* 28, no. 2 (April 2005): 309–37.

Tomblin, Barbara Brooks. *With Utmost Spirit: Allied Naval Operations in the Mediterranean, 1942–1945.* Lexington: University Press of Kentucky, 2004.

Touffait, Jean. "La construction du *Redoutable*" [The building of *Le Redoutable*]. In *Armement et Vᵉ République, fin des années 1950–fin des années 1960* [Armament and the Fifth Republic, late 1950s–late 1960s] Paris: CNRS Éditions, 2002.

Trauschweizer, Ingo. "Adapt and Survive: NATO and the Cold War." In *Grand Strategy and Military Alliances*. Cambridge: Cambridge University Press, 2016.

Vaïsse, Maurice. "La filière sans issue: Histoire du premier sous-marin atomique français" [The file without a solution: History of the first French atomic submarine], *Relations internationales* 59 (Fall 1989): 331–46.

———. "Le Q-244, le premier sous-marin atomique français" [Q-244, the first French atomic submarine]. *Revue historique des armées* 3 (September 1990): 35–46.

————. "L'échec d'une Europe franco-britannique, ou comment le pacte de Bruxelles fut créé et délaissé" [The Failure of Franco-British Europe, or How the Brussels Pact Was Created and Abandoned]. In *Histoire des débuts de la construction européenne (9 mars 1948–mai 1950)* [History of the beginnings of the construction of Europe (9 March–May 1950)]. Brussels: Bruylant, 1986.

————. *Les relations internationales depuis 1945* [International relations since 1945]. 14th ed. Paris: Armand Collin, 2015.

————. "Ramadier et les problèmes de défense nationale (1947–1949)" [Ramadier and the national defense problems (1947–1949)]. In *Paul Ramadier: La République et le socialisme* [Paul Ramadier: The republic and socialism], ed. Serge Berstein. Brussels: Complexe,1990.

Vaisset, Thomas. "Défendre et maintenir la France Libre aux antipodes" [To defend and keep Free France at the ends of the world]. In *Les Français libres et le monde* [The Free French and the world]. Paris: Nouveau monde éditions, 2015.

————. "L'amiral d'Argenlieu, un croisé de la France libre" [Admiral d'Argenlieu, crusader of Free France]. In *Les Chrétiens, la guerre et la paix* [Christians, war and peace]. Rennes, FR: Presses universitaires de Rennes, 2012.

————. *L'amiral d'Argenlieu: Le moine-soldat du gaullisme* [Admiral d'Argenlieu: Gaullism's monk-soldier]. Paris: Belin, 2017.

Valode, Philippe. *Le destin des hommes de Pétain de 1945 à nos jours* [The destiny of Pétain's men from 1945 to today]. Paris: Nouveau Monde, 2014.

Van der Bijl, Nick. *No. 10 (Inter-Allied) Commando 1942–45: Britain's Secret Commando.* Oxford: Osprey, 2006.

Venier, Pascal. "Défense impériale et politique des points d'appui de la flotte (1898–1905)" [Imperial defense and fleet support points policy (1898–1905)]. In *Les bases et les arsenaux français d'outre-mer, du Second Empire à nos jours* [Overseas bases and dockyards, from the second empire to today]. Panazol, FR: Charles-Lavauzelle, 2002.

Vercken, Roger. *Histoire succincte de l'Aéronautique navale (1910–1998)* [A brief history of naval aviation (1910–1998)]. Paris: ARDHAN, 1998.

Vergez-Chaignon, Bénédicte. *Pétain.* Paris: Perrin, 2014.

Vial, Philippe. "De la nécessité de l'aide, des inconvénients de la dépendance: Le réarmement de la Marine sous la IVe République" [Of the need for assistance and the drawbacks of dependency: The navy's rearmament under the Fourth Republic]. *Revue historique des Armées* 215 (June 1999): 17–36.

————. "La genèse du poste de chef d'état-major des armées" [Genesis of the post of chief of staff of the armies]. *Revue historique des Armées* 248 (2007): 29–41.

————. "La Marine et l'opération de Suez" [The navy and the Suez operation]. In *La France et l'opération de Suez* [France and the Suez operation]. Paris: ADDIM, 1997.

————. "L'aide américaine au réarmement français (1948–1956)" [American support to French rearmament (1948–1956)]. In *La France et l'OTAN (1949–1996)* [France and NATO (1949–1996)]. Brussels: Complexe, 1996.

————. "Un impossible renouveau: bases et arsenaux d'outre-mer, 1945–1975" [An impossible renewal: Overseas bases and dockyards]. In *Les bases et les arsenaux français d'outre-mer, du Second Empire à nos jours* [Overseas bases and dockyards, from the second empire to today]. Panazol, FR: Charles-Lavauzelle, 2002.

Vial, Philippe, and Patrick Boureille. "Guerres, modernisation et expansion (1945–1958)" [Wars, modernization and expansion (1945–1958)]. In *L'histoire d'une révolution: La Marine depuis 1870* [History of a revolution: The navy since 1870]. Études marines no. 4 (March 2013): 82–104.

Vial, Philippe, and Jean-Benoît Cerino, "La Marine et le nouveau monde: L'enseignement de l'École de guerre navale face aux bouleversements du second après-guerre (1945–1956)" [The navy and the new world: Teachings at the naval war college and the turmoil of the second postwar era (1945–1956)]. *Revue historique des Armées* 202 (March 1996): 106–22.

Waller, John H. *The Unseen War in Europe: Espionage and Conspiracy in the Second World War*. London: I. B. Tauris, 1996.

Weiss, Steve. *Allies in Conflict: Anglo-American Strategic Negotiations, 1938–1944*. London: MacMillan, 1996.

White, Dorothy Shipley. *Seeds of Discord: De Gaulle, Free France, & the Allies*. Syracuse, NY: Syracuse University Press, 1964.

Whitley, M. J. *Destroyers of World War Two: An International Encyclopedia*. Annapolis, MD: Naval Institute Press, 1988.

Williams, Charles. *Pétain: How the Hero of France Became a Convicted Traitor and Changed the Course of History*. New York: Palgrave Macmillan, 2005.

INDEX

Page numbers followed by *t* indicate a table.

ABOUT THE AUTHOR

Hugues Canuel is a defense attaché in Japan. He earned a PhD in war studies from the Royal Military College of Canada. Following command at sea, he served with the NATO Training Mission—Afghanistan. He focuses his research on Cold War history and East Asian contemporary affairs.

The Naval Institute Press is the book-publishing arm of the U.S. Naval Institute, a private, nonprofit, membership society for sea service professionals and others who share an interest in naval and maritime affairs. Established in 1873 at the U.S. Naval Academy in Annapolis, Maryland, where its offices remain today, the Naval Institute has members worldwide.

Members of the Naval Institute support the education programs of the society and receive the influential monthly magazine *Proceedings* or the colorful bimonthly magazine *Naval History* and discounts on fine nautical prints and on ship and aircraft photos. They also have access to the transcripts of the Institute's Oral History Program and get discounted admission to any of the Institute-sponsored seminars offered around the country.

The Naval Institute's book-publishing program, begun in 1898 with basic guides to naval practices, has broadened its scope to include books of more general interest. Now the Naval Institute Press publishes about seventy titles each year, ranging from how-to books on boating and navigation to battle histories, biographies, ship and aircraft guides, and novels. Institute members receive significant discounts on the Press' more than eight hundred books in print.

Full-time students are eligible for special half-price membership rates. Life memberships are also available.

For a free catalog describing Naval Institute Press books currently available, and for further information about joining the U.S. Naval Institute, please write to:

Member Services
U.S. Naval Institute
291 Wood Road
Annapolis, MD 21402-5034
Telephone: (800) 233-8764
Fax: (410) 571-1703
Web address: www.usni.org